Development Communication and Information Economics in the New Millennium

Development Communication and Information Economics in the New Millennium

Dr. Ashok Purohit

RANDOM

RANDOM PUBLICATIONS

NEW DELHI (INDIA)

Development Communication and Information Economics in the New Millennium

ISBN 978-93-5111-969-2

Published in 2016 in India by

RANDOM PUBLICATIONS

4376-A/4B, Gali Murari Lal, Ansari Road
New Delhi-110 002
Phone : +9111-43580356, 011-23289044, 011-43142548
e-mail: sales@randompublications.com,
info@randompublications.com, randomexports@gmail.com

Reprinted 2026

Type Setting by : Friends Media, Delhi-110089

Preface

The book Development Communication and Information Economics in the New Millennium attempts formulation of new paradigms of development communication for the new millennium.

Development communication refers to the use of communication to facilitate social development. Development communication engages stakeholders and policy makers, establishes conducive environments, assesses risks and opportunities and promotes information exchanges to bring about positive social change via sustainable development. Development communication techniques include information dissemination and education, behavior change, social marketing, social mobilization, media advocacy, communication for social change and community participation.

Development is primarily the activation of a country's human and material resources in order to increase the production of goods and services, thereby leading to the general progress and welfare of its people. The role of communication in socio-economic and cultural development at national and international levels has been recognised over the past two decades. The key role of development communication is to help people change their behaviour.

Development journalism does not mean any particular institution. It means the whole communication process.It means new attitudes on the part of the government, the Press, radio and TV. Development issues could consist of these major policy decisions made by a nation that directly or indirectly affect the life of its people. Development issues could range from the government's decision to subsidise the price of fertilizer to its planned products, from the bargain for fair prices for its primary products, from the developed countries. These issues basically call for a detailed mosaic of development information intelligently pieced together from a variety of sources that will provide an articulate opinion to both the people and the government.

The book is therefore, a must reading for persons in media, communication, information technology, development planning, economics, sociology and a host of related disciplines.

– ***Author***

Contents

1

The Communication Process

Whenever we ask workshop participants how they would define communication, we hear responses such as"transmitting ideas,""talking and listening," or"sending messages using words and movements." Each person has some notion of what it means to communicate with another and knows how it feels when communication attempts are successful or unsuccessful, yet they have not thought deeply about the communication process itself. People seem to assume that communication works or it does not work, more as a matter of fate than as a process that can be changed or improved. Because communication itself is so complex, we could list multiple elaborate and highly technical definitions of it. For our purposes, however, a simple phrase is an appropriate starting point. As we view it, communication is the symbolic process of sharing meanings. Because this definition is almost deceptively simple, each of these key words needs to be developed.

SYMBOLIC

By saying that communication is symbolic, we mean that symbols are used to transmit messages. Symbols are representations of a person, event, place, or object. Words, or verbal expressions, are the most commonly understood symbols, but symbolic actions also include the whole range of non-verbal behaviours: facial expressions, vocal tone, eye contact, gestures, movement, body posture, appearance, context, and spatial distance. In addition, objects and ideas can be used as symbols. For example, friends often exchange gifts, food, or e-mails as symbols of connectedness. You have learned to use verbal and non-verbal symbols both as a message creator and as a message interpreter. As a speaker (or sender), you create messages by selecting the most appropriate symbols from a range of options in order to reach your intended receivers most effectively.

As a listener (or receiver), you attempt to interpret the symbols others convey to you. Although exchanging appropriate symbols appears rather simple and straight-forward, we are constantly amazed at the communication breakdowns that occur as symbols are misinterpreted. Effective communicators are those who are able to select the most appropriate symbols or messages for specific other persons and who are able to interpret the intended message symbols of other speakers. As a child you learned to encode one type of message to ask your father for money and another to request a loan from your best friend. You learned to interpret your brother's gestures indicating if he is feeling sad, worried, or exhausted. You have learned who will be enraged if you roll your eyes at them, and who will decode your non-verbal cue as humorous. For effective communication to occur, the speaker and listener must share the same meanings for the symbolic messages they exchange.

Process

Relational communication involves a process, a dynamic and continuous process. Each relationship develops its own communication history, a history that cannot be rewritten. Someone once said,"It's unfortunate you only get one chance to make a first impression." A relationship's communication pattern begins at the first moment of contact- at a party, in a classroom, in a meeting. The relationship may start in any number of ways: a question, a glance, an introduction, or a smile. Once contact is made, the relationship begins to develop its history, which is constructed and reflected by its communication patterns. A relationship's ongoing development may be interrupted by physical or psychological distance; relational partners may move in and out of each others' lives over many years, but the history of the relationship continues from that first meeting. Sometimes people say they wish to wipe out a time period of their relationship or forget a painful argument that occurred. Individuals may choose to emphasize or deemphasize certain communication events throughout their relationship history, but they can never go back to"how things used to be," or delete a piece of that history. Although some models of the communication process portray it as a circular process, our preferred model for understanding this process comes from the thinking of Frank Dance,whoproposed a helical representation. Imagine the form of a helix, in which the continuousness of the process is represented by the infinity sign. This model depicts the ever-widening scope of the relationships as participants continuously re-encounter each other, a process that continues indefinitely.

Whereas a circular model suggests that communication returns to the same place, the helical model implies the ever-changing, progressive, and evolving nature of relational interactions. The helix representation provides support for the concept that"you can't put a relationship into reverse and erase a difficult period of time."We have stopped counting the times workshop participants say,"If only things could go back to the way they were two years ago," or,"I want to wipe out the last six months of our marriage." In reality each encounter has inalterably added to their relationship, and this history cannot be denied. People in relationships cannot wipe out a huge hurtful fight, long periods of verbal aggression or silence, or, in romantic situations, the affair.Yet most friends, partners or colleagues can learn to manage their history in effective ways: through emphasizing positives, talking through the conflicts, and behaving in ways that affirm their ties. A conflictual father and son cannot pretend they never hurt one another with words or fists; friends cannot erase sarcastic comments. All they can do is work through the issues that currently keep them from dealing with each other in constructive or caring ways, and attempt to change their present communication patterns as they continue in their relational process. People can always choose to change, to do things differently. Such choices represent one of the most exciting parts of the relational development process.

Sharing

Even though the words speaker and listener are commonly used in communication terminology, communi-cation is not a process of trading messages. It does not resemble a poor tennis match in which one Player A hits the ball and then just stands there until the Player B hits the return. Symbolic messages do not travel from Person One to Person Two and back to Person One again in some turn-taking ritual. Rather, at its most basic level, communication requires mutual and continuous involvement, sometimes referred to as the transactional nature of communication.

This mutual influence process is similar to a skilled tennis match in which both players are always in motion based on what they anticipate the other will do. Similarly, in communication encounters both parties remain actively involved in the process.

For example, even though Michael may appear more talkative, Vanessa conveys non-verbally that she is bored or pleased or annoyed, thus influencing Michael's choice of future message symbols. Both are actively and continuously involved in every moment of the interactions; thus, the mutual influence process that characterizes interpersonal interaction.

As relationships develop over time, the transactional process becomes more complex. Your perception of another person and that individual's perception of you combine to form a context for your interactions. If you see Person X as warm and supportive, you will relate to him or her in an open manner. Person X is then likely to see you as open and friendly and relate to you with increasing warmth or support. Thus, your perceptions of each other affect each interaction as well as the overall perception of the relationship. The situation can also be reversed, creating a negative context. If you see another person as judgemental or sarcastic, this may lead you to interact in a defensive or combative manner.

You may be caught up in a type of negative spiral. Each communication exchange occurs within the context of a mutually constructed relationship. If the definition of a relationship remains relatively unchanged, for example boss and employee, romantic partners, and parent and child, the nature of the communication process becomes fixed. Each new encounter reinforces the good or the bad. A boss who constantly relates to staff members as incompetent may stifle their attempts to be innovative.

A parent who treats children as responsible persons fosters their ability to handle new situations. This process is captured in the statement"Over time we create an image of another person and relate to the image we create." Individuals construct a reality of themselves and of others through their interactions, and relate to those realities they constructed. The attempt to understand and adapt to another represents a communication challenge.

Meanings

Although verbal and non-verbal symbols permit us to transmit thoughts and feelings, the symbols must be mutually understood for the meanings to be truly shared. Common meanings make it possible for us to communicate. Since there is no absolute standard for all symbols, we are constantly trying to connect with people, even our family members, who do not share exactly the same meanings for the symbols that we use.

Therefore it is important to remember the expression "Words don't mean; people do." Each person's background, including physiological state, family and cultural background, and unique experiences, influences how he or she perceives the world and attaches meanings to symbols.

The experience of being nearsighted, athletic, extraverted, dyslexic, artistic, or shy affects how you perceive the world and relate to others. Your family of origin (the family or families in which you were raised) served as your first communication classroom, teaching you how to interpret messages and how to use communication to manage key relational issues such as intimacy and conflict. In addition, your cultural background, socioeconomic level, and educational experiences influence your perceptions. Based on your culture, you may interpret big hugs, multiple-course meals, and shouting voices as symbols of caring.

If you grew up in a lower-middle-class neighbourhood, you will have different meanings for money and security than someone who grew up in an affluent community. Finally, your own unique circumstances influence how you assign meanings. A painful custody battle affects how you discuss divorce.

Early school experiences influence how you participate in college classes. Living abroad affects how willing you are to interact with people of different cultures. Fortunately, most people report many similar experiences, but no two people develop the same set of meanings.

Each is a unique entity with particular meanings for certain symbols. Ninety dollars may represent a large purchase to one person, but her partner assumes that only purchases above $500 are large. A nickname may seem funny to you and insulting to your friend. Screaming may be viewed as an acceptable or terrible way to resolve conflicts. Breakdowns in communication often occur because of missed meanings. Only with knowledge and empathy can you walk in someone else's shoes, experience the world from a different perspective, and create messages that reflect that point of view.

Frequently, focus is placed on the words rather than on the entire range of verbal and non-verbal symbols that are constantly being used to create and interpret the meanings of messages. Therefore, at any point in time each person involved in communication is contributing to the process-and experiencing the transactional nature of the communication process. Effective communication requires the psychological presence of both parties-attention and connectedness are indicators that both parties are focused on the encounter. We find the following simple exercise very useful for demonstrating how individuals may differ in translating the meaning of everyday terms. Imagine yourself saying these phrases to a particular person. Think about exactly what you would hope that other person would do if you said these words to him or her. I need more respect from you. I feel there is a lack of trust in our relationship. Each of the italicized words receives many different responses.

Depending on the person responding, more respect may be indicated by:

- Listening to me,
- Asking for my opinion,
- Following my advice.

Trust may be indicated by:

- Keeping what I say confidential,
- Telling me your real feelings,
- Telling me when a painful event happens.

These are only examples of the many meanings that people have for the two common terms respect and trust. Shared meanings are critical because they help to create the context for a relationship in which participants learn to predict how the other will react to particular verbal and non-verbal messages.

INTERPERSONAL COMMUNICATION

Not all communication should be considered inter-personal communication. Frequently, you are engaged in impersonal interactions. When you ask for directions, pay for a purchase, or call for a doctor's appointment, you are not automatically involved in interpersonal communication. If you ask a teacher for clarification, discuss a project with a boss, or plan a family reunion with a distant cousin, you may be involved in necessary, functional interactions but you do not share a strong, significant relationship.

Interpersonal communication occurs when two or more people engage in voluntary, ongoing, interdependent interactions that involve meaningful interpretation of their verbal and non-verbal behaviours. In short, this implies a perception of the relationship as positive, reflecting a choice to continue to relate to each other over time in order to deepen the relationship and make it increasingly unique. There may be exceptions to this description, such as when you interact involuntarily with particular teachers or managers for a long period of time, learn how to communicate effectively with them, and eventually develop a voluntary interpersonal relationship.

In the case of involuntary but required relationships, it is likely that the person with the less power is adapting to the person with greater power, setting up a one-up/one-down interaction pattern. Such relationships tend to remain impersonal, although, on occasion, these persons develop a friendship. Relationships move from impersonal to increasingly personal as closeness develops. Therefore, you need to think about relationships on a continuum from impersonal to interpersonal, understanding that a particular relationship may move forward and backward at different times.

Patterns

In ongoing relationships, communication becomes patterned and predictable. As you relate with another person, you begin to create increasingly predictable interaction patterns. The more intense and personal the relationship becomes, the more unique the relational patterns. Relational patterns involve verbal and non-verbal communication acts that are:

- Recurring
- Relationship defining.

Over time, while people in a relationship develop their own ways of interacting, they evoke certain responses from each other and play off them. For example, you may know that you and Tony will joke around when you see each other, whereas you and Alberto will talk about poker. You may share your romantic problems with Sarah but never with Gail, who you know equally well. Observing an ongoing significant relationship, you may see a remarkably complex pattern, similar to a dance, emerge. For example:

- X makes a statement; Y answers with a complaint.
- X responds with a kidding remark; Y counters with sarcasm.
- X retorts angrily; Y suggests talking is useless.

One or the other stomps away. In his book Couplehood, Paul Reiser describes numerous examples of everyday patterns between partners. Like all businesses, couples engage in endless meetings to discuss areas of management concern and division of labour. "You know, we really should call the post office and tell them to hold our mail while we're away."

"We? You mean me, don't you?"

"No, I mean we. I didn't say'you.' I said'we.' You or me."

"Oh, really? Are you going to ever call the post office?"

A moment to think."No.""

Then you mean'me,' don't you?"

"Yeah."

As in many other areas of life, relationships become predictable; these patterns tend to create or constitute the relationship.

FUNCTIONAL AND NURTURING COMMUNICATION

In many relationships, the bulk of everyday communi-cation tends to be functional rather than nurturing. Functional communication involves managing day-to-day necessities and exchanging impersonal information such as getting plans coordinated, meals fixed, schedules arranged, and group projects finished-all the details that keep life running smoothly.

We estimate that 90 per cent of the communication that goes on between friends or colleagues, parents and children, and even spouses or partners tends to be functional communi-cation. If the only communication between closely connected persons is functional, that relationship is severely limited. If the necessary and desirable functional interactions are not accompanied by communication that is more personal, distance will characterise their ties, limiting their relationship. Nurturing communication occurs when participants send messages that are caretaking of the relationship-messages that indicate that the other person and the relationship are valued.

Such nurturing communicationmayinclude a hug, a special birthday celebration, a thinking-of-you phone call or IM, a deep conversation about feelings, or a direct personal statement such as"I'm glad we're friends." Nurturing communication involves emotional closeness and carries the"I care about you" messages. People who nurture each other confirm the other's existence-" You are there; I recognise you; I care about you."

Through our work with partners and families, we have developed an informal guideline that states the following: If there is 10 per cent nurturing communication going on in any relationship, that relationship is healthy.

When 10 per cent of the behaviours in a relationship are nurturing, we believe the people involved will feel cared for and valued. In our experience, when individuals in relationships come for counseling, functional messages account for about 95 per cent of their communication and the remaining 5 per cent is negative, often openly hostile.

Nurturing messages disappeared from their relational life. Nurturing takes different forms in different relationships, but no matter what the form of expression, everyone needs to experience it.

Coworkers, friends, and family members can all be involved in levels of nurturing communication.

Individuals who have been nurtured are likely to be good nurturers; those who have not been nurtured can learn to nurture others, but often this takes conscious effort and hard work. Nurturing communication serves as the lifeblood of any relationship. Without it, the relationship remains static and functional; with it, the relationship renews itself through continual growth.

Relational Culture

Persons in strong, highly developed interpersonal relationships eventually create their own relational culture. Relational culture describes a jointly constructed worldview, a personally developed set of understandings that affect the attitudes, actions, and identities of the relational partners. Over time many partners or best friends adapt to each other until they experience an evolving, unique set of meanings that are reflected in their relational culture. These private meanings, conveyed verbally and non-verbally, separate the partnership from other relationships; nicknames, joint storytelling, inside jokes, and code words contribute to the creation of a"world built for two." We find Julia Wood's description captures the essence of a relational culture:"processes, structures and practices that create, express and sustain personal relationships and the identities of partners". Communication patterns serve as the basis for relational cultures as they are constructed, maintained, or changed through communication. A strong relational culture is the hallmark of an intense, intimate interpersonal relationship. In a world of many stresses and changes, we need our relationships to sustain us and nourish us as human beings. Communication is central to the process of constructing meaningful and fulfilling relational support. The ability to build and nurture such relationships is a critical life skill, one to be learned and valued.

REASONS FOR COMMUNICATING

If we were to ask a small group of businesspeople to list reasons for needing to communicate with their customers, we might anticipate responses such as these: to sell a product or idea, to inform about some feature of a product or of the business itself, to build better customer relations, to stimulate interest in a product or issue. As diverse as these reasons may appear, communication specialists recognize two broad categories in which people engage in communications: to inform and to persuade. Even though we will attempt to deal with these as two separate categories, the distinction between them often will become cloudy and ill defined. Nonetheless, in order to provide a convenient point to begin this discussion, we will assume this two-point classification. To understand the distinction between communications that inform and those that persuade, recognize that we become familiar with a novel issue in two stages: knowledge acquisition and attitude formation.

KNOWLEDGE

In the first step, a receiver obtains knowledge about a topic. This knowledge may be complete, in which case all information about the subject is successfully acquired by the receiver. It is more likely, however, that information the receiver obtains will be incomplete in some details. This may be a result of insufficient information supplied to the receiver (the message is not complete), inadequate attention of the receiver to the message (the receiver selectively disregards information), or a combination of both.

Apart from incomplete information, a more troublesome condition exists from the communicator's viewpoint: A receiver's knowledge base may contain incorrect information or information that is, in some way, distorted. Here, as in the previous category, the trouble may lie in the message or the receiver.

Each can affect the accuracy of knowledge in one of two ways. First, information in the knowledge base (sent by the source) may omit relevant details from story accounts, presenting only one side of an issue.

For example, in a congressional newsletter, we may learn that our representative voted to reduce federal taxes, suggesting we have great reason to celebrate. But we are not told this action will require an increase in state and local taxes. Compensation for reductions in federal revenue sharing (necessitated by the tax cut) will force tax hikes in other areas. We have learned only the good news—none of the bad—and so have not been given the entire story.

A second form of information distortion may simply be an inaccuracy of some sort—a lie, a factual error, or a faulty representation or interpretation. In addition, inaccurate information may be a product of distortion or exaggeration or a characterization of details that are out of their correct proportion. For instance, the old "fish story" often has an accurate foundation—someone really did net a fish—only in the telling of the story, the fish may have acquired new and impressive dimensions. The public communicator struggles to modify such distortions because they contain an element of truth particularly resistant to correction. Fundamentally they are correct; factually they are distorted and inaccurate.

In these cases, messages bear information that may be distorted or wrong. The message source may err or intentionally deceive the audience and so present faulty information. If receivers are naive and have no basis on which to refute the inaccuracy, they may accept it as fact, thus contaminating their knowledge base. But the source of inaccurate knowledge often may be the receiver him- or herself, who, through processes of selective perception outlined earlier, may deliberately or unwittingly distort information that becomes part of this knowledge base. We like to believe that what we know is accurate and true, and often, in order to maintain that conviction, modify incoming information to conform to our preconceptions.

If we strongly support one team in a football game, we may "see" many fouls by the other team that go unrecognized by referees. We may recognize bad manners only by the other candidate in a political debate. We may hear nothing but sweet music in our own children's recitals. Our knowledge base, what we understand to be true, is constructed not only by input from outside messages, which may or may not be accurate, but from our own perceptions born of what we already hold to be true. It takes a skillful public communicator to change the knowledge base of receivers who are committed to a position and believe that what they know is accurate.

Attitudes

Knowledge is the precondition for attitude formation, a second feature of receiver response to an issue or event. Once we know about something, we tend to form attitudes about it. They may be subtle, ill-formed, and weak attitudes, but nonetheless they represent our inclinations, dispositions, and evaluative feelings towards a subject.

Understand several features of attitude formation: First, attitudes need not be articulated to exist. We do not need to state or even to recognize consciously our attitudes about a product or person before we act on them. We often buy one product instead of another not because we have explicated our feelings about the relative advantages of each, but because of some faint likes or dislikes that subtly bring us to make a selection. We may vote for a candidate because of some vague, ill-formed impression rather than for well developed and rational reasons.

Second, attitudes often are formed with incomplete information. Most of us have neither the need nor the desire to construct our attitudes from complete information that guarantees objectivity and rigour. Occasionally, for important decisions that have serious implications, we may become more analytical and thorough. But even in these instances, we terminate our investigation once we are comfortable with an evolving attitude. From this point forth, through the processes of selective exposure and selective perception, we seek out and interpret information that confirms the attitude. In this sense, we often deprive ourselves of valid and significant information that would otherwise contribute to an objective and rational process of attitude formation. Few of us are so temperate as to keep a completely open mind, particularly on matters about which we hold strong convictions.

The third feature of attitude formation derives from the previous discussion: Attitude formation is not often a conscious process that we approach in a logical, orderly manner. At times we may prepare to make a major decision by consciously seeking and evaluating information from many sources that contribute to a sound, well-reasoned judgement.

But most of our attitudes, particularly those about less-pressing issues, are shaped over time through slow, ongoing processes that often take place beyond our recognition. There is an important lesson in this for public communicators. While we may develop an uncontrollable enthusiasm for our product, we can rarely expect public audiences to share our excitement—either about the product or about the messages dealing with our product. Attitude formation often occurs subliminally and incrementally. People do not always seek information on which to base an attitude. Often such information must be imposed on them. A casual exposure to a message, a glimpse at the product on a store shelf, a passing conversation—all contribute to developing attitudes.

While we have argued that attitude formation is often a slow, passive activity, at times people approach matters with surprising enthusiasm. When people perceive something to be important or to have some recognizable utility, they become more active in the information-seeking process and develop more acute sensitivities to messages dealing with the issue. People in the market for a new automobile or appliance, or who are planning a vacation, often develop an interest in the array of possibilities and seek out information that will enable them to make an informed choice.

This characteristic response to issues of perceived significance suggests a technique through which the public communicator may make an impact on listless audiences. First, elevate the perceived importance of an issue. Show the audience how this matter relates directly to them. Cultivate within the audience a perception of personal relevance and concern for the topic. Then, proceed to deal with the substantive issues. For example, the large federal deficit has long escaped the concern of average Americans. In order to generate support for budgetary reform, a political candidate first must demonstrate how the deficit impacts, or will impact, on the average voter. Only then can the candidate get on with the job of convincing people about what should be done about the problem. We will take a closer look at this issue in the following section. This characteristic response to issues of perceived significance opens a wide range of opportunities through which the public communicator may make a substantial impact on intended audiences. Accordingly, the initial strategies of many communication campaigns may be to elevate the perceived importance of an issue and thus cultivate among audience members a need to become more active in the information-seeking process.

Elevating the Salience of an Issue

A recurring fantasy of many business communicators is to have customer audiences aggressively seek information about their products. Expectations, of course, are that with skillful management of the communication programme, enthusiasm for information will translate into demand for the product or service. Many businesses, however, face the formidable task of stimulating among potential audiences an initial interest in the product and in messages that advance that product. We will deal with this issue from several viewpoints throughout this book, but will begin with a discussion of agenda setting in order to place these matters into a larger context.

Agenda Setting

Our daily schedules are a mosaic of issues and events that demand our attention. Many of these are personal: a dreaded visit to the dentist, ways to occupy a houseful of visiting relatives, balancing our checkbooks.

A large number of issues, though, come from beyond our immediate personal domains. What is the Soviet policy towards arms control? How can we manage the acid rain problem? What teams will make it to the Super Bowl this year? Generally, for those matters beyond our personal experiences, the media serve as the primary sources of information. What we read, see, and hear through the mass media factor into the array of items on our daily agenda.

Agenda setting is really about the competition for our attention. At times a personal concern may become so compelling that we find little time or energy to deal with anything else. A single world event of major proportion may diminish the significance of all other events, intruding even on our personal lives.

The assassination of a president, explosion of a space shuttle, and core meltdown at a nuclear power station are so important and so preoccupy the agendas of population members that by comparison all other matters shrink.

Except for circumstances where one or two events may dominate the agenda, we typically establish, among all the issues with which we must deal, an informal ordering according to their perceived importance. Then we apportion our energies in dealing with them. Increasingly, the media are playing an important role in this process, not only by revealing topics that may be included in agendas, but by suggesting a weighting for the topics. Thus, they propose a rank order of importance. Considerable evidence substantiates that the media agenda serves as a model for individual agendas and, by extension, public agendas. Front page, top of the news, lead item stories become leads on the public agenda.

Personal items factor prominently into the overall agendas of an individual, and a history of personal tastes and interests is important in how one perceives the relevance and importance of ongoing events. There is not, however, a one-to-one correspondence between the media and personal agendas. The media serve rather as cuing agents. They suggest the relative importance of issues and events occurring outside the individual's scope of observation. Depending on individual characteristics and personal concerns, a person's agenda will usually reflect priorities suggested by the media.

For public communicators to influence desired audience members, therefore, they must compete for placement on personal agendas by establishing the importance of a product or service. The ultimate goal is to get on the agenda and therefore be worthy of the individual's consideration.

Towards this end, one strategy is to demonstrate the importance of a product, candidate, or issue at the personal level, thus exhibiting its significance among the things with which the individual must deal in his or her personal life. For instance, a communication campaign for microcomputers may attempt to demonstrate that such equipment will help a businessperson to do more work in less time, thus freeing him or her to spend more time with friends and family. The campaign implies that consideration of the microcomputer belongs on the personal agenda.

Depending on the nature of the product or service, the communicator may find it useful to link information in the campaign with issues beyond those of immediate personal utility. Demonstrating that a political candidate will help build the image of a community may have no direct usefulness to an individual, but it may be important in a larger sense of community pride. People do have concerns and interests that exceed their personal worlds.

Getting on their agendas may be accomplished by demonstrating the importance of an issue among all issues competing for their attention, even those without direct personal implications.

The notion of agenda setting helps us to conceptualize how people view issues worthy of their concern and, moreover, how they establish a priority among those items. From the public communicator's viewpoint, it provides a usable description of a process instrumental in developing strategies to inform or persuade. People enter on their agendas things they feel are important or useful. In order to be considered by an audience, then, a product or service must be portrayed as having some significance.

DEFINING COMMUNICATION

The root of the word "communication" in Latin is *communicare*, which means to share, or to make common. Communication is defined as the process of understanding and sharing meaning.

At the center of our study of communication is the relationship that involves interaction between participants. This definition serves us well with its emphasis on the process, which we'll examine in depth across this text, of coming to understand and share another's point of view effectively.

The first key word in this definition is process. A process is a dynamic activity that is hard to describe because it changes. Imagine you are alone in your kitchen thinking. Someone you know (say, your mother) enters the kitchen and you talk briefly. What has changed? Now, imagine that your mother is joined by someone else, someone you haven't met before—and this stranger listens intently as you speak, almost as if you were giving a speech. What has changed? Your perspective might change, and you might watch your words more closely. The feedback or response from your mother and the stranger (who are, in essence, your audience) may cause you to re-evaluate what you are saying. When we interact, all these factors—and many more—influence the process of communication.

The second key word is understanding: "To understand is to perceive, to interpret, and to relate our perception and interpretation to what we already know."

If a friend tells you a story about falling off a bike, what image comes to mind? Now your friend points out the window and you see a motorcycle lying on the ground. Understanding the words and the concepts or objects they refer to is an important part of the communication process.

Next comes the word sharing. Sharing means doing something together with one or more people. You may share a joint activity, as when you share in compiling a report; or you may benefit jointly from a resource, as when you and several coworkers share a pizza. In communication, sharing occurs when you convey thoughts, feelings, ideas, or insights to others. You can also share with yourself (a process called intrapersonal communication) when you bring ideas to consciousness, ponder how you feel about something, or figure out the solution to a problem and have a classic "Aha!" moment when something becomes clear.

Finally, meaning is what we share through communication. The word "bike" represents both a bicycle and a short name for a motorcycle. By looking at the context the word is used in and by asking questions, we can discover the shared meaning of the word and understand the message.

EIGHT ESSENTIAL COMPONENTS OF COMMUNICATION

In order to better understand the communication process, we can break it down into a series of eight essential components:

- Source
- Message
- Channel
- Receiver
- Feedback
- Environment
- Context
- Interference

Each of these eight components serves an integral function in the overall process. Let's explore them one by one.

Source

The source imagines, creates, and sends the message. In a public speaking situation, the source is the person giving the speech. He or she conveys the message by sharing new information with the audience. The speaker also conveys a message through his or her tone of voice, body language, and choice of clothing. The speaker begins by first determining the message—what to say and how to say it. The second step involves encoding the message by choosing just the right order or the perfect words to convey the intended meaning. The third step is to present or send the information to the receiver or audience. Finally, by watching for the audience's reaction, the source perceives how well they received the message and responds with clarification or supporting information.

Message

"The message is the stimulus or meaning produced by the source for the receiver or audience." When you plan to give a speech or write a report, your message may seem to be only the words you choose that will convey your meaning. But that is just the beginning. The words are brought together with grammar and organisation. You may choose to save your most important point for last. The message also consists of the way you say it—in a speech, with your tone of voice, your body language, and your appearance—and in a report, with your writing style, punctuation, and the headings and formatting you choose. In addition, part of the message may be the environment or context you present it in and the noise that might make your message hard to hear or see.

Imagine, for example, that you are addressing a large audience of sales reps and are aware there is a World Series game tonight. Your audience might have a hard time settling down, but you may choose to open with, "I understand there is an important game tonight." In this way, by expressing verbally something that most people in your audience are aware of and interested in, you might grasp and focus their attention.

Channel

"The channel is the way in which a message or messages travel between source and receiver." For example, think of your television. How many channels do you have on your television? Each channel takes up some space, even in a digital world, in the cable or in the signal that brings the message of each channel to your home. Television combines an audio signal you hear with a visual signal you see. Together they convey the message to the receiver or audience. Turn off the volume on your television. Can you still understand what is happening? Many times you can, because the body language conveys part of the message of the show. Now turn up the volume but turn around so that you cannot see the television. You can still hear the dialogue and follow the story line. Similarly, when you speak or write, you are using a channel to convey your message. Spoken channels include face-to-face conversations, speeches, telephone conversations and voice mail messages, radio, public address systems, and voice over Internet protocol (VoIP). Written channels include letters, memorandums, purchase orders, invoices, newspaper and magazine articles, blogs, e-mail, text messages, tweets, and so forth.

Receiver

"The receiver receives the message from the source, analyzing and interpreting the message in ways both intended and unintended by the source." To better understand this component, think of a receiver on a football team. The quarterback throws the football (message) to a receiver, who must see and interpret where to catch the ball. The quarterback may intend for the receiver to "catch" his message in one way, but the receiver may see things differently and miss the football (the intended meaning) altogether.

As a receiver you listen, see, touch, smell, and/or taste to receive a message. Your audience "sizes you up," much as you might check them out long before you take the stage or open your mouth. The non-verbal responses of your listeners can serve as clues on how to adjust your opening. By imagining yourself in their place, you anticipate what you would look for if you were them. Just as a quarterback plans where the receiver will be in order to place the ball correctly, you too can recognize the interaction between source and receiver in a business communication context. All of this happens at the same time, illustrating why and how communication is always changing.

Feedback

When you respond to the source, intentionally or unintentionally, you are giving feedback. Feedback is composed of messages the receiver sends back to the source. Verbal or non-verbal, all these feedback signals allow the source to see how well, how accurately (or how poorly and inaccurately) the message was received. Feedback also provides an opportunity for the receiver or audience to ask for clarification, to agree or disagree, or to indicate that the source could make the message more interesting. As the amount of feedback increases, the accuracy of communication also increases.

For example, suppose you are a sales manager participating in a conference call with four sales reps. As the source, you want to tell the reps to take advantage of the fact that it is World Series season to close sales on baseball-related sports gear. You state your message, but you hear no replies from your listeners. You might assume that this means they understood and agreed with you, but later in the month you might be disappointed to find that very few sales were made. If you followed up your message with a request for feedback ("Does this make sense? Do any of you have any questions?") you might have an opportunity to clarify your message, and to find out whether any of the sales reps believed your suggestion would not work with their customers.

Environment

"The environment is the atmosphere, physical and psychological, where you send and receive messages." The environment can include the tables, chairs, lighting, and sound equipment that are in the room. The room itself is an example of the environment. The environment can also include factors like formal dress, that may indicate whether a discussion is open and caring or more professional and formal.

People may be more likely to have an intimate conversation when they are physically close to each other, and less likely when they can only see each other from across the room. In that case, they may text each other, itself an intimate form of communication. The choice to text is influenced by the environment. As a speaker, your environment will impact and play a role in your speech. It's always a good idea to go check out where you'll be speaking before the day of the actual presentation.

Context

"The context of the communication interaction involves the setting, scene, and expectations of the individuals involved." A professional communication context may involve business suits (environmental cues) that directly or indirectly influence expectations of language and behaviour among the participants.

A presentation or discussion does not take place as an isolated event. When you came to class, you came from somewhere. So did the person seated next to you, as did the instructor. The degree to which the environment is formal or informal depends on the contextual expectations for communication held by the participants. The person sitting next to you may be used to informal communication with instructors, but this particular instructor may be used to verbal and non-verbal displays of respect in the academic environment. You may be used to formal interactions with instructors as well, and find your classmate's question of "Hey Teacher, do we have homework today?" as rude and inconsiderate when they see it as normal. The non-verbal response from the instructor will certainly give you a clue about how they perceive the interaction, both the word choices and how they were said.

Context is all about what people expect from each other, and we often create those expectations out of environmental cues. Traditional gatherings like weddings or quinceañeras are often formal events. There is a time for quiet social greetings, a time for silence as the bride walks down the aisle, or the father may have the first dance with his daughter as she is transformed from a girl to womanhood in the eyes of her community. In either celebration there may come a time for rambunctious celebration and dancing. You may be called upon to give a toast, and the wedding or quinceañera context will influence your presentation, timing, and effectiveness.

Interference

Interference, also called noise, can come from any source. "Interference is anything that blocks or changes the source's intended meaning of the message." For example, if you drove a car to work or school, chances are you were surrounded by noise. Car horns, billboards, or perhaps the radio in your car interrupted your thoughts, or your conversation with a passenger.

Psychological noise is what happens when your thoughts occupy your attention while you are hearing, or reading, a message. Imagine that it is 4:45 p.m. and your boss, who is at a meeting in another city, e-mails you asking for last month's sales figures, an analysis of current sales projections, and the sales figures from the same month for the past five years. You may open the e-mail, start to read, and think, "Great—no problem—I have those figures and that analysis right here in my computer." You fire off a reply with last month's sales figures and the current projections attached.

Then, at five o'clock, you turn off your computer and go home. The next morning, your boss calls on the phone to tell you he was inconvenienced because you neglected to include the sales figures from the previous years. What was the problem? Interference: by thinking about how you wanted to respond to your boss's message, you prevented yourself from reading attentively enough to understand the whole message.

Interference can come from other sources, too. Perhaps you are hungry, and your attention to your current situation interferes with your ability to listen. Maybe the office is hot and stuffy. If you were a member of an audience listening to an executive speech, how could this impact your ability to listen and participate?

Noise interferes with normal encoding and decoding of the message carried by the channel between source and receiver. Not all noise is bad, but noise interferes with the communication process. For example, your cell phone ringtone may be a welcome noise to you, but it may interrupt the communication process in class and bother your classmates.

TWO MODELS OF COMMUNICATION

Researchers have observed that when communication takes place, the source and the receiver may send messages at the same time, often overlapping. You, as the speaker, will often play both roles, as source and receiver.

You'll focus on the communication and the reception of your messages to the audience. The audience will respond in the form of feedback that will give you important clues. While there are many models of communication, here we will focus on two that offer perspectives and lessons for business communicators.

Rather than looking at the source sending a message and someone receiving it as two distinct acts, researchers often view communication as a transactionalprocess, with actions often happening at the same time. The distinction between source and receiver is blurred in conversational turn-taking, for example, where both participants play both roles simultaneously.

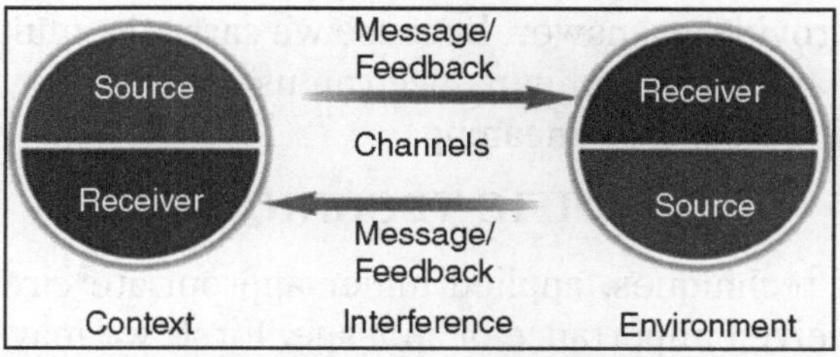

Fig. Transactional Model of Communication

Researchers have also examined the idea that we all construct our own interpretations of the message. As the State Department quote at the beginning of this chapter indicates, what I said and what you heard may be different. In the constructivist model, we focus on the negotiated meaning, or common ground, when trying to describe communication. ,

Imagine that you are visiting Atlanta, Georgia, and go to a restaurant for dinner. When asked if you want a "Coke," you may reply, "sure." The waiter may then ask you again, "what kind?" and you may reply, "Coke is fine."

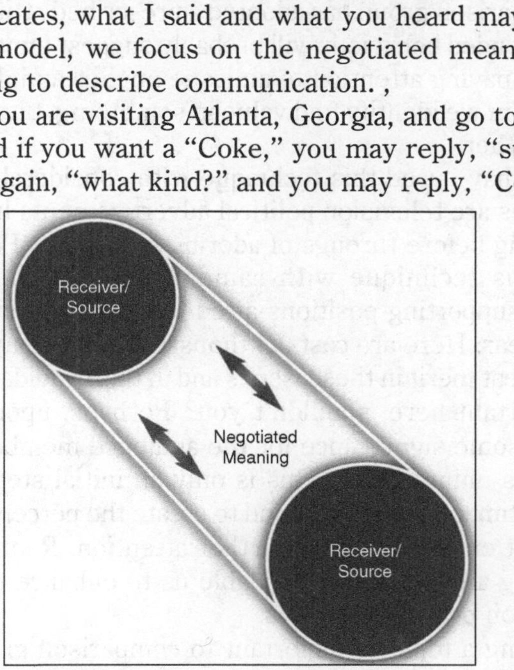

Fig. Constructivist Model of Communication.

The waiter then may ask a third time, "what kind of soft drink would you like?" The misunderstanding in this example is that in Atlanta, the home of the Coca-Cola Company, most soft drinks are generically referred to as "Coke." When you order a soft drink, you need to specify what type, even if you wish to order a beverage that is not a cola or not even made by the Coca-Cola Company.

To someone from other regions of the United States, the words "pop," "soda pop," or "soda" may be the familiar way to refer to a soft drink; not necessarily the brand "Coke." In this example, both you and the waiter understand the word "Coke," but you each understand it to mean something different. In order to communicate, you must each realize what the term means to the other person, and establish common ground, in order to fully understand the request and provide an answer. Because we carry the multiple meanings of words, gestures, and ideas within us, we can use a dictionary to guide us, but we will still need to negotiate meaning.

SPECIFIC TECHNIQUES

A variety of techniques, applied under appropriate circumstances, may enhance the perceived importance of an issue. First, we may portray an issue to be important to others and, through inference or direct claims, assert a logic that will compel target audience members to acknowledge personal importance. People evaluate themselves by observing others. Recognition that an individual's comparison group has adopted a prescribed attitude or has engaged in some recommended behaviour will probably suggest importance. Simply that other people are paying attention to an issue implies an inherent significance. If those with whom we identify find value in something, then we, too, may wish to examine it further.

Advertisers have used this technique with considerable success. Among the best examples are television political advertisements in which a candidate is shown speaking before throngs of adoring onlookers. Political conventions capitalize on this technique with camera shots of clamoring thousands enthusiastically supporting positions aired from the podium. The message in these cases is clear: Here are casts of thousands—made up of people just like you—who see great merit in these issues and in this candidate. If they recognize something important here, shouldn't you? Perhaps, upon inspection, these issues will hold some significance for the audience member, but at this point that conclusion is unimportant. This is only an initial step in the strategy to establish the legitimacy of the issue and to create the perception that something here is important enough to merit further attention. Remember at this point we are employing a tactic that will enable us to enhance the importance of a topic, to place it on personal agendas.

Characterizing a topic as important to comparison groups is only one of several approaches to establishing the significance of an issue. Another widely used tactic involves the linkage between something we wish to promote and something already important to audience members. We then equate our issue with one already installed on individual agendas. Successful use of this technique can establish the prominence of an issue within a short time. Consider a recent example in which medical research confirmed the role of calcium in preventing osteoporosis.

News of this discovery spread quickly. Because of its importance to public health, it has achieved a prominent place on personal agendas. Little was required to "promote" the significance of this information, given its inherent value to this health-conscious society. The lesson in this example, however, is found during the months that followed the revelation. Advertisers sought to demonstrate a linkage between the calcium content of their products and the now-recognized dietary importance of calcium. Vitamin companies, milk and cheese producers, and manufacturers of prepared foods that use high-calcium ingredients made bold claims in their advertisements.

They touted the health benefits of their products. In print and broadcast media, advertisements stated the virtues of calcium, then tied a specific product to the issue. Implications of such strategies are evident. While audiences may not have thought much about grated cheese before, if they think calcium intake is important—and we now all know it certainly must be-then they must also think cheese is important. The association between the product and the larger issue is evident.

A third design often used to establish a sense of the importance of an issue is a two-stage process involving first the creation of the perception of a need (where none already exists) and then identification of the product or service that can gratify this need. One might argue that audience members will see the logic of paying attention to something once they have been impressed with the need it is designed to satisfy. Through this approach, one creates a need where it had not existed before. People who, for their entire lives, have gotten along without a product or service must be convinced that they cannot now live without it. Although such an approach is often difficult, time consuming, and subject to problems, it does have a reasonable history of success.

An example is found in the burgeoning microcomputer industry that discovered an important first step in its marketing strategy: to convince small business owners they needed a microcomputer to maintain their competitive edge. Since the beginning of time, though, businesses have been run, many of them very successfully, without computers.

The industry, consequently, had to create the perception of a need for computers before it could mass market its innovation. Because of successful development of this perception, acceptance by a few early adopters, affordable prices, and other support marketing schemes, computers have in a short time—fewer than six or seven years—become as commonplace in offices as typewriters. With such a revolutionary innovation, one that had so few precursors that could have prepared an audience, it was essential that potential adopters become stimulated to recognize a need.

There are, of course, a wide range of needs that may serve the purposes stated in this discussion. The computer example describes a professional need to improve efficiency and remain competitive. But there are personal needs, too, that may be examined. For instance, consider the need to be informed about a topic (which perhaps may serve even deeper needs, such as the needs for self-esteem and the respect of others). Promoters of news magazines, adult education courses, and self-instruction computer software often suggest the need for a person to be knowledgeable about a given issue. Audience members may never have considered purchasing such a product until they were convinced of their need to be informed about issues or events.

Successful use of this technique stimulates audiences to recognize their need for information, then proposes a specific product as an answer to that need. Professional and personal needs are among many that have been used in recent campaigns. Scores of others include those based on stimulation of social, physical, and psychological categories of needs.

Need stimulation generally includes the early phases of product promotion, but alone cannot sustain public attention in a product or service. Assuming audiences recognize a genuine need for a product or service (and do not ultimately conclude there is no real need where one was suggested), other communication and promotional activities must be employed to continue audience interest and attention. Although need stimulation techniques may continue as part of an ongoing strategy, they are most effective in the early stages of a campaign to elevate on public agendas the merits of an issue.

All the techniques discussed in this section focus on that critical portion of the communication process where perceptions are elevated sufficiently to render an issue worthy of audience consideration—in other words, to enter the issue onto the audience agenda. Paraphrasing previous writings on agenda setting, this phase of the communication process is designed to suggest not what audiences should think, but what they should think about. Messages in this phase do not attempt to inform or to motivate as much as they attempt to suggest the issue is worthy of a person's attention.

Only after the relative importance of an issue has been recognized by audiences and has drawn their attention can the communicator begin to instruct and to persuade.

THE IMPORTANCE OF COMMUNICATION

Although the Internet may be portrayed as a communication technology unique to the 1990s, this depiction is somewhat misleading. The Internet's origins are in fact traceable to the 1960s development of the military-funded communication network, ARPANET, with the Internet officially making its debut as a civilian tool for communication in 1983.

However, widespread public awareness of the Internet's existence did not occur within the United States until the early 1990s when it was privatized and online services such as America Online (AOL) were developed to serve the general public. Hence, there is a tendency to think of it as a turn-of-the-twenty-first-century phenomenon.

Prior to the 1990s, early public access to the Internet was limited mostly to government agencies, universities, and computer-related organizations, such as hardware and software developers. Initially, users experienced the Internet in the form of text-based communication applications such as e-mail and navigation systems such as Telnet. In 1992, the World Wide Web (WWW) became publicly available in the United States and began to diffuse widely in 1993 with the release of the iconbased web browser Mosaic, which made web navigation more "user friendly" and visually appealing. Subsequently, use of the Web helped to popularize the Internet in general. As use of the Internet has shifted from a small community of researchers and government employees to a worldwide community, researchers recognize the Internet as an important area in need of study. The widespread diffusion and adoption of the Internet in the United States and abroad provides scholars with numerous research opportunities. Because the Internet functions as a channel for communication, this is especially true for the field of communication. However, as with any innovation, it can be difficult at first to know how to approach the investigation of an innovation's contribution to and effects on the society into which it is introduced.

With regard to the Internet, communication researchers, as well as others, must grapple with numerous decisions, such as determining how applicable existing theories and methods of enquiry are to this newest communication technology.

While the arguments for why and how to study the Internet vary, a common theme to arise within our discipline concerns the unique opportunity that today's communication scholars have to witness and record, first hand, the introduction of a major communication technology.

Scholarly journals are one forum where communication researchers record the results of their research for the benefit of current and future generations of scholars. Published articles inform other researchers of the types of approaches being used to study a wide variety of topics, including the Internet.

A number of disciplines are conducting Internet research as is evident when searching electronic databases. For example, a simple keyword search conducted in December 1999 in the Social Sciences Abstracts database on the term "Internet" yielded a return of 969 articles published across a diversity of disciplines, most notably in the areas of business, demographics, law, and policy studies.

Each discipline, including communication, typically contains a core set of journals considered to be "leaders" among all others in terms of their coverage of subject matter, length of publication, and quality of published articles. The question asked in this study concerns how leading journals in the field represent Internet-based research conducted by communication scholars, because an important goal of scholarly journals is to document a field's evolution over time.

This study examines the content, frequency, and pattern of published Internet-based research articles-studies that focus on some aspect of the Internet-in leading communication journals for the purpose of assessing how these journals are keeping pace with the Internet's influence on the communication process. It also considers how these journals represent our response to these changes to other disciplines in the social sciences.

THE IMPORTANCE OF COMMUNICATION SCHOLARS RESEARCHING THE INTERNET

Within the discipline, a handful of articles has addressed the importance of communication scholars studying the Internet. The reasons for study as well as the ways in which the Internet should be studied are varied. For example, in 1996, the Journal of Communication devoted the majority of its winter issue to "The Net."

Within this issue, in a dialogue between Newhagen and Rafaeli, Rafeali pointed out that the development of the Internet, in part, is rooted in academe and, as such, "this alone behooves our involvement" in its study. Beyond this statement Rafeali suggested that researchers focus on what he called the "five defining qualities of communication" on the Internet which, although somewhat abstract, included "multimedia, hypertextuality, packet switching, synchronicity, and interactivity."

Newhagen argued that communication researchers must take a more active role in understanding the Internet by first understanding computer architecture, an area often left to engineers. A bridge must be constructed between the worlds of communication and engineering so that communication researchers no longer find themselves in the position "where the engineers roll out a new technology, and we hold up numbers from 1 to 10, rating it."

Concerning the benefits of studying virtual reality, Biocca stated, "Communication researchers rarely have had the chance to observe the introduction, diffusion, and sociocultural presence of what may become the next dominant communication medium." However, he cautioned against viewing new communication technologies as a revolutionary by stating that many "new" technologies build upon, and borrow from, existing ones.

As such, researchers are likely to start out using existing theories and methods to study a new technology. He suggested focusing on questions such as the shape the medium is taking, and how the medium shapes and is shaped by the user-areas well suited to communication research. In a 1993 article, writing more broadly about humancomputer interface design, Biocca, as Newhagen was to do later in 1996, called for communication scholars to be more proactive in researching computer-mediated communication (CMC) by taking part in the design and development of new communication technologies.

Although, both of Biocca's articles were written just prior to the Internet's widespread public diffusion, his ideas, as if in anticipation of its introduction, are very applicable to the Internet and have been echoed in the later writing of Newhagen and Rafaeli. Other communication scholars assuming the importance of studying the Internet have suggested additional approaches to its study.

December argued for the need to define specific units of analysis for Internet research that would act as guideposts for researchers, helping to facilitate cross study comparisons.

These four units were defined as media space, media class, media object, and media instance. He also proposed a definition of Internet-based computer-mediated communication as that which involves information exchange that takes place on the global, cooperative collection of networks using the TCP/IP protocol suite and the client-server model for data communication. Messages may undergo a range of time and distribution manipulations and encode a variety of media types. The resulting information content exchanged can involve a wide range of symbols people use for communication.

As such, he argued that the Internet is not a single medium but is instead made up of several media. Additionally, he cautioned that researchers studying on-line services such as Prodigy or America OnLine (AOL) should be aware that they were not actually conducting Internet-based research because these access providers offer proprietary services not available on the Internet.

While this caveat is technically correct, it is perhaps overly restrictive. In addition to offering proprietary services to its users, on-line vendors such as AOL also function as Internet Service Providers (ISPs), allowing for communications to be exchanged via the global network.

In contrast to December, Morris and Ogan viewed the Internet as a single flexible mass medium capable of the synchronous and asynchronous transmission of text, audio, and video communication.They argued that the Internet provides the opportunity for communication researchers to rethink rather than abandon traditional views on mass media and to adopt a more flexible perspective on communication models.

Additionally, they suggested that researchers study the Internet using a variety of existing frameworks, such as network analysis, and theories, such as social presence. In summary, these scholars essentially argue that communication in relation to other disciplines should be a leader, if not the leader, in researching the Internet because it is a communication phenomenon.

Communication scholars need to be proactive and creative in their research designs in order to reach this goal. To do this, they must possess a thorough understanding of how the technology works by taking an active role in the design and evaluation of future Internet applications.

RATIONALE

Knowledge of the extent to which Internet-related topics have been addressed and what methods of enquiry have been applied can assist communication researchers in placing their work within a broader range of studies. This information also identifies over- and under-emphasized topics and methods.

Lastly, knowledge of the degree to which the Internet is represented within a discipline can provide researchers with a sense of the area's development and relative importance to the field as a whole. It is not uncommon for communication researchers to analyse articles within an individual journal or a range of journals in order to assess the status of the discipline as a whole with respect to a particular issue.

Examples of these studies include analyzing the frequency with which qualitative research is published, investigating the content and quality of published content analyses, and assessing the status of published mass communication articles by women across eight journals. Continuing this type of enquiry, this study examines the publication history of Internet research among five leading journals in the field.

JOURNAL SELECTION CRITERIA

While acknowledging the presence of newer electronic Internet and new technology-specific publications such as Internet Research and Journal of Computer-Mediated Communication, this study purposely focuses on mainstream, established communication journals. The reasons for this emphasis are threefold.

First, and most obvious, the Internet is a channel for communication and as such it falls within the realm for study by communication researchers and, in turn, publication in our leading, established communication journals. Second, established journals-those in existence for a period of decades-have the distinct advantage of having built both a reputation and a following over time.

These journals are widely read within the discipline, contributing to scholars' perceptions of and currency with changes in the field. A third reason, closely related to the second, is that established journals can be viewed as historical records that document the field's evolution. Ideally, these journals reflect trends in the development of a discipline and the segments of society with which it deals as accurately as possible for the benefit of current and future scholars.

Selection of the five journals examined in this study employed two criteria: previous research identifying leading journals in the field and the reputation of Social Sciences Abstracts as a valid resource for communication research. In a content analysis of women's published research in mass communication, Dupagne, Potter, and Cooper identified eight leading communication journals, defined according to high circulation counts and low acceptance rates.

The journals identified in their study included: Communication Monographs, Communication Research, Critical Studies in Mass Communication, Human Communication Research, Journal of Broadcasting and Electronic Media, Journal of Communication, Journalism Quarterly, and Quarterly Journal of Speech.

These journals functioned as a starting point for this study; however, application of the second criterion, communication research indexed in Social Sciences Abstracts, resulted in the omission of four titles from the original list.

The decision to further limit the journals examined was based on a twofold rationale. First, electronic databases are increasingly used by scholars to conduct literature searches because of their ease of use and convenience in comparison to print indexes. Within the vast realm of electronic indexes available for searching, Social Sciences Abstracts is a widely used leading index published by the highly reputable indexing service, H. W. Wilson Company.

Second, subject-specific indexes, such as Social Sciences Abstracts, are typically more useful to and more likely to be used by scholars than general indexes, such as Expanded Academic Index, because they cover indexed journals in more detail, are more likely to index all articles in a journal rather than a chosen few, and they provide longer, more detailed abstracts.

By restricting the focus to leading communication journals indexed in Social Sciences Abstracts, this study attempts to take into consideration a broader view concerning how scholars in other disciplines might perceive the role of our discipline in the area of Internet research based on the presence of communication journal articles contained in the index. With the application of this second criterion, the final list of journals examined in this study include: Communication Research, Human Communication Research, Journal of Broadcasting and Electronic Media, Journal of Communication, and Journalism and Mass Communication Quarterly. Measures. This study uses December's definition of Internet-based communication but with a slightly more liberal view on what constituted Internet-based communication.

An article was considered Internetbased if it focused on computer-mediated communication technologies requiring access to an ISP, including services such as AOL or Prodigy, or closely simulated an Internet-based communication environment (*e.g.*, intranets, e-mail exchange between AOL members).

This definition broadly included the Internet in general, intranets, World Wide Web (WWW), e-mail, mailing lists, bulletin boards, newsgroups, chat, virtual reality games such as multi-user domains (MUDs), and video/audio/text computer conferencing. From the interfaces specified above, it can be seen that in most instances Internet access was necessary for communication to occur.

As with any area of research, certain information is useful in providing scholars with an overall sense of an area's progress or current status. For the purpose of this study, the concept of current status is operationalized into nine measures-author name, authorship, author rank, affiliation, topic, interface, method, total number of Internet-based articles per issue, and total number of research articles per issue.

Identification of an area's primary researchers provides scholars with a sense of which perspectives may be dominant in an area of study. While quantity of publication by an author does not necessarily equate with quality of research, it can provide scholars, especially those new to an area, with a starting point in the literature. The same can be said for the order of authorship on an article.

Distinguishing between primary and secondary authors can indicate, but not necessarily guarantee, which researchers are initiating studies, taking primary responsibility for the studies, and acting as primary contacts or "experts" in an area. Knowledge of which universities or organizations are conducting research in a particular area is beneficial for those interested in matters such as networking, educational, and employment opportunities.

The rank (*e.g.*, faculty, staff, student) of an author provides information on the diversity or homogeneity of the contributors to an area of research. This study attempts to answer two basic questions. First, what is the frequency and pattern, if any, of published Internet-based research articles in five of the leading communication journals?

Second, what do the contents of these articles reveal about the status of Internet research within and outside of the communication discipline?

UNIT OF ANALYSIS

The unit of analysis for this study was the scholarly communication research article that focused on Internet-based communication. This included "research in brief" articles but excluded editorials, rejoinders, and book reviews.

Coders primarily read titles and abstracts to determine if an article fit this study's definition of Internetbased research. In instances where article titles and abstracts did not provide sufficient information, coders skimmed the articles for details.

POPULATION DATA

All research articles were examined in four major communication journals between the years 1994-1999. Because frequency of publication over time was one question asked by this study, population data were used instead of sample data in an effort to obtain a more accurate depiction of publishing trends across time by these journals.

The four journals selected for the main study included Communication Research, Human Communication Research, Journal of Broadcasting and Electronic Media, and Journal of Communication. A fifth journal, Journalism fa Mass Communication Quarterly, was selected for a pilot study to test the codebook. To identify leading communication journals publishing Internet-related articles, a basic keyword search was conducted using the term "Internet" in the Social Sciences Abstracts electronic database; four journals were consistently referenced in the search results and thus selected for closer examination. One limitation of this selection process concerns the exclusion of some communication journal titles from the Social Sciences Abstracts index. However, this limitation was considered acceptable given the broader focus of the study discussed earlier.

Despite this limitation, the five journals selected for this study are examples of the mainstream publication outlets available through most of the field's major associations: the Association for Education in Journalism and Mass Communication, Broadcast Education Association, and International Communication Association.

The starting year for the study, 1994, was selected because, based on the Social Sciences Abstracts search results, in general, Internet publications did not begin to increase until that point in time. The first recorded Internet article in the database occurred in 1992; one article was referenced in 1993. However, in each year thereafter, the number of articles increased steadily. This pattern is consistent with the growing popularity of the Internet with the general public in the United States. The communication journals selected for study during this time frame contained a total of 961 research articles (323 from the pilot study and 638 from the main study). Each article was examined to determine if it met the definition of Internet-based research. Those articles that qualified were then coded.

OPERATIONAL DEFINITIONS

To answer the questions proposed in this study, nine measures were recorded for each Internet-based research article: author name, authorship, author rank, affiliation, topic, interface, method, total number of Internet-based articles per issue, and total number of research articles per issue. For each article the last name and initials of all authors were recorded.

Authorship was coded as primary (first author) or secondary (all additional authors). The rank of each author was coded as faculty, student, staff (university affiliated, non-faculty/non-student employees), government employee, business employee, or other. Author affiliation was recorded as the name of the university or organization with which the author was identified at the time of publication.

Rather than attempt to anticipate the range in subject matter, article topic was recorded as open text by each coder and then later grouped into six broad categories: access, adoption/diffusion, policy, research/theory, social interaction, and other. Interface, the application used to communicate via a computer, was divided into eight categories: World Wide Web, e-mail, mailing lists/newsgroups/bulletin boards, chat rooms, virtual reality game sites (*e.g.*, MUDs, MOOs), video/audio/text-based conferencing, Internet in general (no specific interface identified), and other (coders recorded the specific interface).

Method of enquiry was coded as policy study, critique/essay (non-policy studies), interview/case study, content analysis (qualitative and quantitative), experiment, survey, other (coders recorded the specific method) and combination for multiple methods used within a single study (each method was recorded and then weighted).

Lastly, for each journal issue, coders recorded the total number of Internet-based articles and overall total number of research articles.

CODING PROCEDURES

The author and another communication researcher acted as coders. The codebook was created by the author and reviewed for clarity by the second coder. A pilot test to check for intercoder reliability was conducted on all issues of Journalism and Mass Communication Quarterly, 1994-1999, resulting in a 100 per cent overlap of 323 articles.

Discrepancies in coding were discussed, and slight modifications for the purpose of clarification were made to the codebook before proceeding to the four journals selected for the main study.

Reliabilities for the number of Internet-based research articles and total number of articles for the pilot test were at the acceptable levels allowing for the inclusion of these articles in the study, under separate reporting. Intercoder reliability for the main study was calculated using a 20 per cent overlap. Issues for the reliability check were selected using a stratified random sample. The total overlap between the coders contained 128 articles.

INTERCODER RELIABILITY

For the main study, the level of agreement concerning which articles qualified as Internet-based research was 98.4 per cent. Percentages of agreement and Scott's pi corrections for chance (where applicable) were as follows for the measures: author name, 97.9 per cent; authorship, 97.9 per cent.96; author rank, 97.9 per cent.97; affiliation, 97.9 per cent; topic, 94.3 per cent; interface, 96.9 per cent.96; method, 97.7 per cent.97; and total number of research articles per issue, 96.9 per cent.

For the pilot study, percentage of agreement for Internet-based research articles was 84.6 per cent and 99.7 per cent for total number of articles per issue. Frequency analyses are reported for each measure. With the exception of overall trends in publishing, all other measures report data collected from the four journals in the main study.

This is because intercoder reliability for the pilot study was only reached on the two measures: Internet-based articles per issue and total articles per issue.

TRENDS IN PUBLISHING

Of the 961 research articles analysed, 37 (3.9 per cent) were Internet-based. Among the four journals in the main study, 4.1 per cent (26 of 638 articles) were Internet-based. Trends in the publication of Internet-based articles across the five journals revealed no distinct pattern of increase, decrease, or stabilization during the six-year time period. This finding was also the case within each of the five journals.

Overall, the Journal of Communication (32 per cent) published Internet research articles the most frequently followed by Journalism and Mass Communication Quarterly (30 per cent), Journal of Broadcasting and Electronic Media (24 per cent), Human Communication Research (8 per cent), and Communication Research (6 per cent).

The percentage of published Internet-based research articles varied widely by year; however, a trend line reflecting a moving average suggests that the number of articles has increased over time.

TOPIC, INTERFACE, AND METHOD

Social interaction (31 per cent) was the topic most often researched. This was followed by research/theory (23 per cent); other (15 per cent), which included the topics of competition among local news web sites, digital art on the WWW, TV audience feedback via e-mail, and portrayals of the Internet in magazines; access (12 per cent) and adoption/diffusion (12 per cent); and policy issues (7 per cent).

The interface studied most often was the Internet in general (42 per cent) followed by mailing lists/newsgroups/bulletin boards (19 per cent), WWW (15 per cent), e-mail (12 per cent), and chat rooms (4 per cent), video/audio/text conferencing (4 per cent), and other (4 per cent) which included an Internet-based interactive health programme. The two most frequently used methods of enquiry were content analysis (27 per cent) and critique/essay (27 per cent).

These were followed by experiment (11 per cent) and survey (11 per cent), and, lastly, policy study (8 per cent), interview/case study (8 per cent), and combination (8 per cent), which included groupings such as network analysis and content analysis, and surveys and content analysis. The results of this study present a somewhat vague picture as to where this newest area of study is positioned within the selected journals.

In part, this is due to the low number of Internet articles available for examination and thus discussion. The results also indicate that scholars searching the Social Sciences Abstracts would find a scarcity of Internet-related research in our leading journals. It may be that the infrequent and uneven publication of Internet research in the journals examined is simply a typical reflection of any field's initial attempts to come to terms with a new area of study.

This finding suggests that Internet research is an area within the field that is clearly open for study. Within the four journals analysed, only two authors stood out in total number of publications potentially providing greater opportunity for other scholars to become better known through their research in comparison to more established areas in communication.

Not surprisingly, faculty are the dominant group publishing Internet research articles, but, again, because of the newness of the area student authors may have more opportunities to publish than in more established areas. While certain universities are represented more than others, it remains to be seen which programmes will eventually come to the fore regarding Internet-based communication research.

In the areas of topic, interface, and methods, similar opportunities for growth exist. However, as speculated by Biocca and Morris and Ogan, thus far, communication researchers primarily are using traditional methods to study the Internet (*e.g.*, content analysis, essays/critiques) with a few studies employing network analysis, as suggested by Morris and Ogan.

Additionally, research has tended to focus largely on the Internet in general, leaving specific interfaces such as mailing lists and e-mail in need of attention. Topics also seem to follow widely used categories (*e.g.*, adoption/diffusion, social interaction) in communication research. This trend may be useful for making comparisons across different types of media; however, it also risks overlooking effects that may be unique to the Internet.

The low number of Internet-based research articles (3.9 per cent) and the sporadic publication of the articles within the five communication journals examined may be attributed to several factors. To begin with, the Internet, despite nearly a three-decade history, is still a relatively new area of study. Although the World Wide Web, which helped make the Internet popular, became publicly available in 1992, it was not until 1995 that awareness of the Internet by the media and the general public began to increase.

With this increased awareness among the populace, researchers are realizing the importance of researching the Internet, but this can be a slow process. In 1995, Dennis Davis, the editor of Journal of Broadcasting and Electronic Media, wrote in his annual summary, "One of my editorial priorities is to increase the number of articles dealing with new technologies.

To do this, the number of submissions will need to be increased. This past year 10 submissions (4.9 per cent) dealt with new industries or new technologies. Three times as many manuscripts dealt with existing industries (30 papers, 14.8 per cent). I would like to see a more even balance between submissions dealing with old and new industries."

To its credit, the Journal of Communication published a symposium on "The Net" in its 1996 winter issue. Factoring in the timeframe necessary for the review, decision, and printing process, the calls to action contained within this issue may partially explain the noticeable increase in the publication of articles during 1998. The drop off in 1999 may be a reflection of this cycle as well, or possibly a reflection of changes in editors' interests. Still, it seems clear that some of these journals are demonstrating a desire to publish Internet-based research articles; however, as Davis indicates, perhaps few studies are being submitted.

Alternatively, it may be that a number of studies are being submitted; however, because of the relative newness of Internet-based research some of these studies may lack the theoretical grounding often desired in published works by our leading journals. A review of the literature reveals that communication researchers are attempting to unveil the parallels and distinctions between new and traditional technology theories and methodologies, but the research waters are still murky in this area.

Additionally, the emergence of new technology journals such as Internet Research and New Media and Society, may serve as alternative outlets for these studies, thus siphoning off submissions to the mainstream, established communication journals. As well, given the crossdisciplinary nature of the Internet (*e.g.*, computing, communication, human factors), depending on the topic, communication researchers may be submitting their works to journals in other fields.

If this is the case, then the communication journals examined might more actively solicit Internet research submissions in an attempt to better represent the amount and type of research being conducted in this area. While this author does not advocate the lowering of acceptance standards for research articles, communication journals could potentially foster increased publication of Internet research, following the lead of the Journal of Communication, by dedicating issues to symposia on the topic.

These symposia could be viewed as debuts of Internet research that, while possibly less theoretically rigorous, would be considered valuable contributors to the development of future, more theoretically based studies. The main point to be emphasized is that the communication research community is widely dispersed across numerous universities and organizations worldwide.

Scholarly journals function, in part, as a communication link between researchers. Communication scholars interested in studying the Internet benefit most by knowing who else is researching in the area and what results have been found. Leading journals play an important role in conveying this information, but only if that information is being published.

If it is the case, which remains to be seen, that Internet research is not being published because of a lack of strong theoretical foundations, then an important question needs to be addressed. Namely, how are scholars to build theory if they do not have access, which these journals can provide, to studies on which to build a foundation? The answer may lie in the emergence of topic-specific journals such as New Media and Society.

In 1996, Morris and Ogan, commenting on the Internet's growth (25 million at the time), asked, "Why, then, have communication researchers, historically concerned with exploring the effects of mass media, nearly ignored the Internet?" This is a question still in need of an answer, or possibly reformulation. We might also ask why our leading journals appear to be slow on the uptake.

Notably, Wartella and Reeves, in a 1985 study that examined historical trends in publishing about children and the media, observed "that the relationship between research activity and media popularity is not simultaneous." Their findings illustrated that research related to a communication technology (*e.g.*, film, radio, television) often lags behind the diffusion rate of the technology, a pattern confirmed in this study.

Nevertheless, Internet research appears to be an area of study with which communication researchers must become more comfortable and skilled at conducting. Unlike television, radio, or print media, the computer requires certain knowledge and skills to operate-and ultimately to study.

As Biocca and Newhagen and Rafaeli argue, communication scholars are being called upon to take a more active role in the understanding and design of new communication technologies. These challenges, as well as knowledge and skills requirements, may act as barriers for some researchers who are less technically oriented. This particular barrier may be offset over time as communication programmes develop tracks of study in new technologies on both the graduate and undergraduate levels that emphasize familiarity with and understanding of computer communication technologies.

Additionally, the Internet can simultaneously function as an interpersonal and mass channel for communication. This hybrid nature tends to blur the traditional lines used to distinguish different types of communication from one another. Is the Internet really a form of mass communication? Questions such as this one make it difficult for communication scholars to identify perspectives from which to study the Internet.

Finally, because Internet research is more or less in its infancy and as such lacks a strong history of research on which to build, communication researchers must be especially thoughtful about and creative in their approach to its study. They must also make the effort to network, outside of journal publications, with other Internet researchers to share research strategies and results. Certainly, not every communication researcher is interested in studying the Internet nor, given the numerous areas available for study within the field, should it be the focus of every communication scholar or the sole topic of our leading publications. However, in general, to overlook the Internet as an area for study is to be remiss as a discipline.

Before concluding, two limitations must be addressed regarding the narrow focus of the research. First, the conclusions drawn from this study are primarily limited to the five journals examined. It should be noted, though, that these journals have historically attempted to keep pace with changes in the discipline so that cautious speculations of a more general nature about the discipline's response to the Internet might be made. However, additional research examining a broader range of communication journals is necessary to confirm these speculations.

Second, the definition used to identify Internet-based research excluded articles examining computer-mediated communication more generally. Future studies may wish to examine this broader category of research as well. This study makes two primary contributions to the field. First, it informs communication scholars of the content and amount of published Internet research in leading journals that represent our research efforts both within and outside of the discipline. Second, it generates discussion concerning why the numbers are relatively low in light of earlier calls to action regarding the importance of studying the Internet. Both communication journals and communication scholars play important roles in determining where Internet research will be positioned within the discipline, as well as where the discipline will be placed relative to other fields investigating the technology.

Despite the small number of Internetbased articles published by five of our leading journals during the sixyear time period examined, communication scholars studying the Internet should be encouraged in that, overall, the number of articles published appears to be increasing. However, to more accurately reflect the Internet's importance as a research topic within the discipline, it is hoped that the findings in this study will encourage communication scholars to submit more of their Internet-based research to our leading journals while current and future editors of these journals will be encouraged to include more of these articles in their publications.

As a discipline we possess the potential be a leader in Internet research, and our core journals can, and should, reflect this potential not only to scholars within the field but also to the larger academic community.

2

Development of Local Communication and Interpersonal Communication

UNDERSTANDING THE LOCAL: SITUATED-NESS OF EFFORTS

In order to bring positive change via ICT use in community development, efforts need to be "grounded in local settings," a principle central to an information ecology that helps identify what information or a certain technology "means to the people who use it". Local relevance is related to the importance of context in understanding the nature of information and its meanings that are "unique to each case," and embedded in the set of relationships surrounding information exchange.

Adoption and implementation of technology are significantly related to its appropriation in varied settings that are determined by the extent of local control and adaptation that take place. Based on the past experience of community-based technology initiatives, local involvement and steering of policies to the needs of community users are important steps in the process to address broader issues of integration, identity, and power; they also prevent deepening of social exclusion of disadvantaged populations.

The Community Networking Initiative (CNI), a collabora-tion between the Graduate School of Information Science (GSLIS) at the University of Illinois at Urbana-Champaign (UIUC), Prairienet Community Network, and the Urban League, has the following goals:

- Analyzing local information needs and practices;
- Training and delivering computers to teens and adults;
- Providing technical assistance to community-based organizations;
- Enhancing Prairienet Community Network's information content and retrieval capabilities for low-income, African-American neighbourhoods.

An important strategy for community development in the CNI project involves the participation of people from within the local disadvantaged communities. This participation has been significant through the acknowledged recognition of local capacity and resources; the contextualized provision of information services to local expectations; and the enhanced contributions of local community members from minority and marginalized groups.

Various challenges were encountered with CNI. For example, while training different groups in the community, a major problem was "how to handle users of different skill levels". It was not possible to develop a "cookie-cut" solution to serve different needs of various participating groups, members of which included advanced adults, novice adults, advanced teens, novice teens, and others. In response to different contextual parameters (shaped by both social and technological factors) such as skill level, comfort with use of technology, social dynamics in each group, and delivery rate of information, a range of strategies were adopted. Strategies varied in terms of the duration of time, learning goals, training mechanisms, phase development trajectories, and broad and specific outcomes.

From these efforts in the application of training procedures and strategies to local populations, an important lesson was learned: the need for flexibility in process development and implementation. A situated understanding of technology recognizes multiple contexts of technology use in different settings. It helped develop a focus on the local context, on people's practices and applications, and on the systems of relations surrounding ICT use.

UNDERSTANDING THE LOCAL

Working with the community and letting its members decide what directions to choose are central for building capacity and engagement in participative democracy for making positive changes for a better quality of life. Empowerment endeavors can systematically support people, organizations, and communities achieve mastery over their own affairs.

These endeavors contribute to creating knowledge and developing culturally appropriate information resources that meet needs of actual users, for such resources are built by members of the community themselves. LIS faculty and students at UIUC are engaged in ongoing collective enquiry into the everyday lives of the community at the Puerto Rican Community Centre (PRCC) located in Chicago's Paseo Boricua neighbourhood. The goal is to incorporate localized knowledge and local narratives of community experiences in the online component of the Paseo Boricua Community Library (PBCL). Collaborative practices and equitable interactions with PRCC members are resulting in the development of Community Enquiry Labs (CIL) that include ICT use to "support community learning and action that addresses critical local problems in a democratic manner". CILs include online curriculum units, developed to address intersection of race, class, and technology-related issues that are incorporated into computer training classes for high school students at the Pedro Albizu Campos High School in Paseo Boricua. Training classes engage Latino youth to identify relevant concerns in the community, build culturally relevant community resources, and elicit their feedback about an online community information system that will form a part of the Paseo Boricua online community library.

MEASURING LOCAL CAPACITY: NEIGHBOURHOOD ASSET MAPPING

Understanding the extent and boundaries of an information ecology in the context of the community calls attention to the measurement of its existing skills and potentials. Community development efforts support community in ways that "assemble its assets and capacities into new combinations, new structures of opportunity, new sources of income and control, and new possibilities of production".

Community capacity is defined as the community's ability to identify, enhance, and mobilize its human promise, economic opportunities, social relationships, and ecological capital for the purpose of improved community stability. It provides a practical way to reach out to "marginalized" populations and target local neighbourhoods in order to enhance resident participation and build on existing ICT-related neighbourhood assets. LIS leadership in community development can be potent to help develop asset mapping as a community capacity measuring tool, as well as link service initiatives to the local community asset base.

Asset mapping is a "visual path displaying capacities and assets" in which" community members identify what is an asset and how it can benefit their community". It recognizes that all kinds of communities, including poor and disadvan-taged user groups, have assets that can be acknowledged within planning efforts.

Grounding strategies to existent geographic areas accommodates an integrative and comprehensive vision of community building. Several campus units at UIUC, such as the Department of Urban and Regional Planning, the Department of Landscape Architecture, the Department of Architecture, and GSLIS, are involved in service-learning activities in East St. Louis where faculty and students work with neighbourhood organizations to map community resources and "address the immediate and long-term needs of some of the city's most distressed communities".

Activities involved documentation and mapping of local community assets in order to build geographic information system (GIS) based databases for the visualization of community components and their relationships; to develop urban systems models to analyse census-based economic and environmental variables that impact community develop-ment; and to identify positive and negative factors that impact development of community technology centres across the city.

DIVERSITY AND EMPOWERMENT

Diversity is an important element of natural information ecology and an inherent feature in contemporary local on-site and online communities. As a Nations Bank official concluded at the end of the conference titled, Blueprint 2000: Accepting and working successfully within an increasingly diverse America is the nation's single largest challenge affecting community building.

If we are afraid of each other, full of hate for each other, or discriminate against one another, how can we expect to build communities that are livable? Within our increased diversity, we must work together to build a civil society. In order to promote such a civil society, it is important for there to be recognition and acceptance of a moral, social, legal, and intellectual equality in "our inherent differences". The participatory action research (PAR) framework gives an opportunity to actualize and operationalize the notion of equality in our practical work and personal lives by empowering all people who interact within settings that adopt the underlying PAR philosophy. PAR has been practiced under different names--action research, collaborative research, community-based research, amongst others.

There are common threads underlying PAR manifestations: a) democratization of the knowledge process in which the people who are usually considered "research subjects" become part of the research process as researchers analyzing their own experiences; and b) emphasis on social justice and social equity via action to change imbalances in distribution of resources, information, and power. Using PAR, participants draw intersections between social equity, economy, and ecology in ways that lead to empowerment of those traditionally "left out" in the process of resource-sharing and decision-making.

Empowerment in PAR comes from letting people on the margins themselves determine what meaningful intersections are and how they should address them in ways to improve their conditions. PAR is significant for community development in the use of ICT since it can be applied towards the process of knowledge creation, as well as in the context of taking action that brings about changes at different personal, social, political, economic, and cultural levels. Such initiatives will lead directly towards the empowerment of participants by helping them recognize their own worth as well as leading to their social recognition as creators of knowledge.

Additionally, PAR will provide an avenue for participants to take action that leads to an improvement in their own experienced situations. The LIS professions can play an important role in PAR processes by helping community development practitioners to reconfigure embedded relationships, practices, and values of people belonging to various segments in the community. One direct outcome of adopting a PAR approach by LIS professionals is the transference of power to make decisions during various stages of project implementation from external sources to the hands of the "insiders" in local communities. The Afya (Swahili for "health") project is an example in which the LIS faculty and students at UIUC are working with community activists to develop participative and democratic practices to bridge the social, economic, and political divides by targeting barriers that prevent access to health information and services experienced by African American women in the community.

Afya involved establishing partnerships with SisterNet, a local network of African American women committed to address their physical, emotional, intellectual, and spiritual health needs. LIS professionals worked towards building collaborations between local SisterNet women and community health care and information providers. Faculty and students at GSLIS helped to facilitate such collaborations, to advance participative techniques, and to develop online and offline resources that supported the work of community groups. SisterNet women shared their realities and experiences, played activist and leadership roles, and took action to bring changes in the community for improving their health-related situations.

Prairienet Community Network was an important partner in the Afya project and provided computer technology, training, and Web development services. Parkland College, the local community college, was a supporter of SisterNet through its Department of Adult and Continuing Education and provided access to computer hardware, software, and other resources. One major challenge in building community connections was the lack of a common vocabulary for communication between traditionally defined technological "experts" and disenfranchised users. Issues were greater than those related to language; barriers were more associated with established mindsets, existing institutional bureaucratic procedures and policies, and individual personality traits.

In such divergently disjoint situations, LIS professionals played significant roles to build bridges across social and technological gaps. Promoting Inclusiveness: Outreach in Planning and Policy Implementation Sustainable information ecology requires inclusiveness in the processes associated with its development, a fact that is also true for ICT use in community development projects. LIS professions can play active roles to promote outreach to local residents from minority and under-represented populations.

The goal is to develop successful user-centreed information services that are effective at the grassroots levels. Towards this vision, greater support in favour of disenfranchised groups is needed from civic and business associations, non-profit and voluntary organizations, public and private schools, community colleges and universities, health centres, and other local institutions. The underlying idea is to work "with" people rather than simply "for" them by integrating scientific knowledge, disciplined effort, and learned skills into a more contextualized interactive practice.

Zimmerman, et al. highlight the examination of grassroots community organizations for promoting empowerment of "marginalized" populations. Participation of local disenfranchised people in voluntary community organizations, for example, is empowering for "marginalized" individuals for it leads to higher competencies, confidence, sense of duty, and lower feelings of helplessness. In the Afya project, participation of SisterNet women insured that efforts were rooted in existing social institutions and activities of community African American women.

Locating computer-training labs in the local Urban League, Workforce Prep Centre, and within Prairienet Community Network's premises was significant in trying to integrate information access strategies within the daily social life of community members. Similarly, strategies such as developing SisterNet Resource Centres for making health-information resources available at local public spaces such as health salons, churches, libraries, and family centres are instrumental in this regard.

In order to incorporate libraries within the daily social experiences of African American women, the Afya project tried to develop public libraries as an important place for promoting collaborations between SisterNet women, health care and information providers, researchers, local organizations, and civic institutions, as well as other community stakeholders. Presenting participative strategies in public libraries, for promoting access to networked digital information for local Black women, was one such initiative. Similarly, the organization of the SisterNet Health Fair in a public library was another initiative that contributed in trust-building and knowledge exchange of relevant health-related social practices and availability of appropriate resources.

Future Directions Of Growth

"The modern public library in large measure represents the need of democracy for an enlightened electorate, and its history records its adaptation to changing social requirements". There is tremendous potential for future growth of the LIS professions as gateways of provision and access to the Information Age for all members in the community. In 1990, the American Library Association adopted the policy, "Library Services for the Poor," stating that libraries and LIS professionals should recognize their role "in enabling poor people to participate fully in a democratic society, by utilizing a wide variety of available resources and strategies".

There are strong critics of the LIS professions to achieve the goal of social equity for under-represented populations. Research by scholars like Chatman, Dervin, Bishop et al., and others has shown that libraries are the last places where minority and marginalized individuals seek information. In this context, community development practitioners need to realise the capabilities and capacities as well as some of the following challenges that the LIS professions face in community development efforts: a need for creativity and openness in outreach to disadvantaged community members; progressive strategies to develop increased involvement in local community initiatives; and greater flexibility and simplicity in policies and procedures. To strengthen their role in community development for social equity, LIS professions will have to loosen bureaucratic procedures, reconsider national and local limiting institutional practices, discard rigid administrative frameworks, and redefine policies of libraries and information systems based on incorporating representative community voices in planning and implement-ation deliberations.

Provision of greater proactive service to disenfranchised communities in different geographic areas to promote activities such as community development planning, assertive community asset mapping, and environmental scanning procedures are first steps in that direction. Other steps towards social equity are for LIS professionals to work together with community development practitioners and others and to bring change in broader policy issues via political action and legislation.

"Working our collaborative and citizen-based efforts into the formal, local political structure will not only create policy that reflects the values of citizens but will also hasten reform of local government from that of a purely representative form to a highly participatory and dynamic decision-making structure". The goal is to insure social equity for disadvantaged users by initiating whatever it may take, including political, cultural, and/or economic reforms.

In order for community development initiatives to be more meaningful to under-represented populations, it is important to recognize the intertwined relationships that occur in real-life situations between social equity, economy, and ecology. These factors emerge in settings as individual temperaments and personalities respond to social and cultural expectations and real-forces of politics, power, and economics come into play. Only when the complexities and the "messiness" of everyday life of the "marginalized" are acknowledged can there be actual changes in everyday operations and functioning for lay people.

For only then will community development reflect and represent reality in a more accurate manner; experiences that recognize the constant and multiple intersections between the information needs, daily practices, class and financial realities, and issues of social inequalities in the everyday lives of the disenfranchised.

The metaphor of information ecology as applied in the context of community provides a good mechanism for LIS professionals, community development practitioners, and others to draw connections between social equity, economy, and ecology, as well as to make ICT development and implementation more meaningful in the everyday lives of disadvantaged populations.

Future community development initiatives in LIS require creating constant awareness that even though tools may be technology-driven, the vision is yet to lean towards strengthening community in terms of "the common life of beings who are guided essentially from within, actively, spontaneously, and freely relating themselves to one another, weaving for themselves the complex web of social unity".

As information providers, LIS professionals can play an important role in this regard, not by finding piece-meal and isolated solutions to ICT use for social equity, but instead, by taking a holistic view that recognizes multiple perceptions and brings various elements of communities to work together for its sustainable development.

Some helpful steps include recognition of the capacity and strengths of local "marginalized" communities, implementation and use of ICT in relation to larger socioeconomic and sociopolitical experiences of under-represented populations, and provision of ICT functionalities that directly situate themselves in the context of everyday lives of disadvantaged users in terms of what is meaningful to them. Stronger ties between LIS professionals and community development practitioners can do wonders towards reaching this goal because both emerge from rich service-oriented traditions. The contemporary realities of ICT inequities and deepening divides in our communities demand greater efforts in collaboration between LIS professionals, community development practitioners, and others for building bridges to support social justice and promote sustainable community-wide development for all segments in society. Outdoor challenge education has become increasingly popular as a method of developing team cohesion.

Also referred to as adventure learning, experiential learning, and challenge programmes, such outdoor education involves having a group navigate a course of mental and physical challenge activities to improve its team relationships, group dynamics, cooperation, and communication. Such training typically provides a framework for group problem-solving exercises by requiring groups to develop a plan that enables all members to complete the exercise.

The physical elements of the course encourage participants to find strength from within and embrace the support they receive from their fellow team members. While educators often find outdoor activities impossible or impractical to implement, elements of the methods can be adapted for business communication courses and other disciplines in which team building and communication are emphasized. This chapter examines briefly the evolution, purpose, and components of outdoor challenge programmes and describes three indoor activities that incorporate some of the benefits found in such programmes.

Kurt Hahn is generally credited as the first person to use challenging outdoor experience as a medium for the development of the self and of groups.

Hahn was approached in 1941 by Lawrence Holt, the head of a large merchant shipping line, to address the problem of the poor survival rate of young sailors which Holt attributed to an inability to rely on their "inner resources."

Hahn developed a programme of physical experiences which were a medium for the sailors to mature and realise their full potential. While Hahn recognized its value, he never advocated adventure as an end in itself, but rather as a training vehicle through which youth would mature.

The key tenets of Hahn's concept may be summarized as an experience which:

- Takes place in the outdoors.
- Is structured to assist individuals to discover and realise their inner resources.
- Is designed to reflect the environment in which the participant is expected to operate.
- Is based on adventure activities which are inherently dangerous and deemed appropriate for meeting the first three objectives.

The establishment of the Outward Bound movement by Hahn popularized the challenge experience to a broad array of participants all over the world. Outward Bound is intended to be catalytic, to encourage change and to help each participant more fully achieve self-knowledge and understanding of others.

An Outward Bound trip, however, usually consists of a five-day wilderness challenge experience, so companies are turning to challenge courses, which are more convenient and shorter. Since the late 1970s, outdoor-based experiential training programmes have become increasingly popular; and surveys indicate that the trend continues.

Present-Day Outdoor Challenge Education

Entwined in the experiential learning process is a creative problem-solving process. The word "creative" differentiates the particular type of problem solving from an analytical or technical problem-solving process, in which equations or formulae may be used to reach a singular, "correct" solution. In creative problem-solving, a number of different solutions may be possible, but the solution sought is one that best fits the complex context of the problem. The "accuracy" or "correctness" of the solution is not the issue. Rather the issue is, "What can we do which will give us a very good chance of solving the problem?"

Challenge activities involve mental and physical challenges requiring strong individual and team skills. A facilitator may lead the group through the activities, stopping between them to discuss how the group worked together. During the debriefing, the group discusses how they decided to solve the problem, who took the lead, who held back, and how they can do better in the future. Even the most powerful training experience fades if it is not linked to the reality of the workplace.

For this reason, most reputable outdoor-training companies integrate the outdoor activities with classroom discussions, needs assessments, and extensive preparation and follow-up.

Outdoor training courses typically consist of "low elements" and "high elements." Low element activities rarely take place above eye level. Equipment can include props Or permanently installed "low ropes" courses. Some popular low element activities are summarized as follows:

- *The Web*: A group faces a spider web of rope strung between two trees. The challenge is to get the entire group through the web - without touching it and using each gap in the web only once. People have to let go and allow themselves to be hoisted into the air and put through the web.
- *The Beam*: Each group member must get over a six-foot-high beam between two trees without aids (other than help from the team). Once a participant is over the beam, he or she cannot help those who are not, except by "spotting" or watching them in case they lose their balance.
- *The Islands*: A shipwrecked group must travel from a large "island," which is sinking, to two successively smaller ones using only the ship's plank (a board). The plank, however, is not quite long enough to serve as a complete bridge between the islands. If participants touch the (pretend) shark-infested waters around the islands, they must start over.
- *Electric Fence*: Each member of the group must move from one side of the "electric" fence to the other, without touching the fence.
- *Tube Pass*: A bicycle inner tube must be passed around a circle of people who are holding hands, without either breaking the circle or letting the tube touch the ground.

High element activities often focus on a series of rope-based activities placed 4 to 40 feet above the ground, rock climbing, or rappelling. Course participants are held secure with harnesses and a system of ropes and pulleys. A climbing tower or wall may also be used. The goals may be to challenge a person to tackle his or her fears, learn to make decisions, and learn to lead a group. The purpose of the high element activities is to push people out of their comfort zones.

The advantages and disadvantages of outdoor experiential learning vary based on the type of programme selected. Some distinct benefits are associated with simply being outdoors and engaging in physical activity. One benefit is that physical risk forces participants to engage actively in the training. A person walking across a cable or falling from a table into the arms of teammates is likely to pay close attention to the experience. In typical indoor programmes, people are less likely to be forced to engage actively and participate because they tend to remain within their comfort zones. Another benefit to outdoor programmes is that participants often experience real feelings and emotions. They are not role-playing, and there is no place to hide from feeling the experience.

Many of the characteristics of outdoor training that contribute to the learning environment (especially in high-impact programmes) may also be those that create danger, emotional distress, and legal liability. In addition, the Americans with Disabilities Act (ADA) raises questions about equal access and fair treatment of employees based on abilities that are not relevant to their jobs. Outdoor activities that require people to touch each other also raise concerns.

For instance, the Spider Web exercise requires a team to lift its members one at a time and pass them through a "hole" in the "web." Some people absolutely love this activity, but others refuse to participate because of the amount of touching it requires. Some see this touching as an invasion of their privacy; the issue can be especially critical when programmes involve multicultural groups. A third concern with outdoor programmes is the outdoor setting itself. Rain, snow, and extremely hot and cold temperatures may not be conducive to the learning experience.

INTERPERSONAL COMMUNICATION

ONE-ON-ONE DESIGNS

In many business communication settings, interpersonal contacts will bring about the most tangible audience effects. Mass media messages can inform and, to a large extent, persuade audience members, but interpersonal communication will often serve to solidify attitudes and elicit behaviour. The use of interpersonal communication in specialized communication campaigns and explores reasons for its effectiveness. We also examine how mass media and interpersonal portions of a campaign should be joined to achieve an effective communication package.

Our love for the mass media has not dampened our passion for one-on-one, interpersonal communication. Distant third-party relationships, intrinsic to mass communication settings, have heightened our need to be treated as individuals. We appreciate the entertainment and information offered by the mass media, but we tire of being cast into large, anonymous audiences by programmers and advertisers who blend us into demographic blocks for generic treatment.

We prefer small shops to large department stores because the shopkeepers call us by name and cater to our personal needs; we know them and they know us. Letters addressed to us directly rather than to "occupant" usually attract our attention. A personal phone call or a visit from a political candidate has greater impact, not necessarily because of what the candidate says, but because he or she says it directly to us. Throughout this book we argue strongly for the use of mass media in public communication programmes. Their success has been well documented; indeed, we cannot communicate on any reasonable scale today without extensive media use. We describe a form of communication that supplements the mass media. We present a background discussion and examine details of interpersonal communication techniques to expand the repertoire of options available for specialized communi-cation campaigns. Some business communicators might find little application for such techniques. Other companies that have never considered such an approach to customer contact might find these methods an efficient and valuable means of reaching beyond mass media.

At the conceptual level, interpersonal techniques are no more than an extension of the targeting principles that have guided discussions of the mass media. Recall the scheme that placed media on a continuum ranging from those that serve broad, heterogeneous audiences at one end to those appealing to narrow, homogeneous audiences at the other. For the large mass media, such as network television, audiences are characterized by the blending of personal traits.

These audiences represent a cross section of the general population. For narrow media, we see select audiences identified by their parochialism and uniformity. Among these audiences, for instance, we may find sports fishermen with a special interest in surf casting or gourmet cooks with a flair for pastries. In addition to special interest divisions, we may also identify narrow audiences by demographic features, ideological commitment, group membership, and a variety of other characteristics. We recognize such groups by their commonalities.

Such identifying features are important. They serve as a basis for audience targeting or focusing communication activities towards ever more specific, distinctive, homogeneous clusters. Taken to its extreme, targeting converges with interpersonal, one-on-one communication.

Although definitions of interpersonal communication differ by author, most agree about what it involves. Wright describes interpersonal communication as "involving only a few people, often similar to one another in important respects, known to a communicator whose messages are addressed to them privately and are constructed and conveyed directly rather than through the complex formal organization of mass media". Rogers and Schoemaker see interpersonal communi-cation as involving a "faceto-face exchange between two or more individuals". Other writers offer similar descriptions that convey a relative intimacy between senders and receivers.

For our use of the term, people need not be face to face as Rogers and Schoemaker suggest, nor do they need to be similar, as Wright proposes. We hold that interpersonal communication, as applied to business communication, involves receiver-specific messages.

The source tailors his or her communication for each receiver, progressively modifying messages in an interactive fashion based on feedback information. Interpersonal communication can be face to face or it can be interposed by a medium that permits a two-way flow of information (for instance, a telephone or two-way radio).

Interactants need not know each other, although they must respond specifically to each other's messages.

POSITIVE FEATURES OF INTERPERSONAL CHANNELS

We examined three defence mechanisms that enable receivers to stave off the persuasive effects of a message. People can avoid or ignore a message and not have to deal with it at all (selective exposure). They can distort the meaning of a message so that it conforms to pre-existing beliefs; in other words, we can hear what we want to hear in a message (selective perception). Finally, people may recall only portions of a message, retaining what pleases them, discarding what annoys them (selective retention). Through any one or a combination of these processes, receivers become less vulnerable to persuasive messages. These mechanisms are in operation in both mass media and interpersonal communi-cation settings. Receivers are most likely to wield control, however, in a mass communication environment. They can control, interpret, and recall without challenge. Broadcast media can be shut off or ignored. Turn the page of a newspaper or magazine, and a message is out of sight and out of mind. Despite the bells and whistles advertisers use to attract and hold audiences, in the final analysis, the receiver is in charge.

Although a receiver continues to direct his or her own response to a message in the interpersonal communication setting, a variety of factors stands to weaken this control. We will discuss each of these in turn:

- Receiver involvement,
- Custom message design,
- Social features.

Receiver Involvement

In most interpersonal portions of special communication campaigns, receivers are self-selected. They participate in one-onone encounters with company representatives because they wish to, and they typically wish to because they recognize some ultimate benefit to themselves. They have chosen to become involved. As a result the receiver usually becomes an active participant in the communication event. He or she has sought information and is then brought into the process, serving not just as a spectator (as in mass media settings) but also as a player in the interchange of information.

Receivers find it difficult, under such conditions, to ignore information provided by the source. People are conditioned to listen to someone talking directly to them. They listen to be polite, but they listen, too, because they have sought out this information. They became involved when they took a step from the mass media to the interpersonal environment. They are part of the interaction so they are more likely to fulfill their listening role in the give-and-take of a conversation.

Seasoned salespeople know how important it is to get prospective customers to verbalize support for a product. This support reinforces people's commitment and helps solidify their decision to make a purchase. They become advocates of the product through their own words. When a receiver becomes involved in an interpersonal programme, it is more likely that he or she can be coaxed into such a position. The source can urge and cajole the receiver using techniques not possible in mass communication settings.

Involvement also implies effort justification. Earlier we said that when a person expends energy on a task, he or she imparts a significance to it. We justify our efforts. Energies spent on a project suggest the project is valuable.

We often see this in operation among students who claim they deserve a higher grade on an exam than they were given. Surely twenty hours of hard study deserved more than a C. (What about performance?) We believe our efforts are worth a great deal; we see a value in them that is manifest in various ways. In the case of interpersonal programmes, we come to value our involvement more highly because it costs us something. Recognition of this belief can be used by the message source to improve the persuasive potential of an interpersonal programme.

Custom Message Design

In the interpersonal setting, a source has a chance to shape a different message for each receiver. Feedback cues on all available levels (depending on physical features of the setting, for instance, face to face or a telephone conversation) enable the source to read the needs and wants of a receiver and adapt a message accordingly. Through give-and-take, the source can progress through a line of reasoning using necessary tactics to make the point with each receiver.

Feedback issues have entered many discussions throug-hout this book. Indeed, how could one examine specialized communication campaigns without frequent reference to feedback information? Feedback enables the source of a message to better meet the needs of the receiver. For the present discussion, we will investigate the role of feedback in the preparation of messages designed to overcome the receiver's selectivity processes.

Feedback in the interpersonal setting provides a running account of a receiver's reception of a message. Obvious cues such as direct questions show how well a receiver is processing the information. But subtle indicators also may provide information. For instance, a receiver's yawn, silence when comments are expected, or expressions of boredom suggest that selective exposure gates may be in operation. Rather than listening to the message, the receiver is mentally drifting and ignoring what you are saying. In a mass media setting, the communicator can do nothing about such gating.

In the interpersonal environment, though, a skillful communicator can employ a variety of tactics to bring the receiver back into the discussion. When the "drift" settles in, he or she can change the pitch and pace of the presentation, use humour to break the monotony, or restate the point using a different appeal. One of the strongest techniques to interrupt message blocking is to involve the receiver actively in the interaction. Ask questions and introduce rhetorical techniques that require an acknowledgment from the receiver. In face-to-face settings, the communicator can stimulate eye contact, use gestures, or show models and drawings to attract receivers into the discussion. The use of such techniques depends on the reception of the message, and the communicator determines the level of reception by monitoring the ongoing flow of feedback information. A perceptive person can detect disengagement by the receiver and, through a variety of techniques, overcome the selective exposure gates.

We know the selective perception process enables receivers to put their own meaning on a message and thereby distort the communicator's intent.

Although receivers may get away with this in the mass communication environment, a communicator can do much to ensure a correct interpretation in the interpersonal context. Feedback, again, is the key.

In the give-andtake of a conversation, we often reveal our understanding of a message by asking questions, restating points to determine the accuracy of our impressions, and expressing related thoughts.

Through such feedback the communicator can monitor a receiver's perception of a message. As soon as it becomes apparent that the meaning and the interpretation of a message are no longer the same, the communicator can reshape the message to drive home the point.

Even if the setting is not conducive to spontaneous receiver feedback, the communicator can monitor the interpretation of his or her message by asking questions. This involves the receiver in the communication process and takes advantage of feedback potentials in the interpersonal setting. Teachers use this approach all the time. "What do you think about this issue?" "Do you see how this process works?" Such questions help keep the receiver involved and focused on the topic, and they help the communicator bear on the receiver's understanding of that topic.

Since selective exposure and perception occur in the context of a communication event, the communicator can affect them directly. Selective retention, on the other hand, occurs after the communication event, and so control is more difficult. However, features of the interpersonal setting can improve the chances a receiver will retain information.

At the outset, remember that when the communicator improves the level of exposure to and perception of a message, he or she has advanced the likelihood that the receiver will retain the information. Obviously, if someone never gets the information or misunderstands what is said, he or she carries little away from the communication event.

Note also that receivers express an initial level of interest in a topic when they choose to engage in the interpersonal communication event. We might expect that such an interest would result in a higher retention of related information. We will give this point to interpersonal communication, even though it is a function of selection rather than of any feature in the interpersonal setting itself.

Specific features of the interpersonal communication environment improve the retention of information in several additional ways. First, when receivers become actively involved in the communication process, they are more likely to retain the information. Their active participation creates a stronger image and results in better recall. They are more likely to retain information from an event in which they have participated than one that they have just observed.

The communicator also can motivate a receiver to retain information. First, he or she can encourage the receiver to link information with everyday events, thereby creating an association between the new information and familiar experiences. One electric utility company used this technique with success when it encouraged customers to shift power consumption to less costly evening and early morning hours. In the interpersonal portion of the campaign, for example, company representatives suggested that every time the receiver took a shower or ran the dishwasher, he or she should think about what time it was. These behaviours then were linked to thoughts about "timeof-day (TOD) rates," which was the company's name for a new billing programme. In this example the receiver linked objectives of the programme with everyday behaviours, thus stimulating better retention of the information.

Another way of overcoming selective retention problems is to arrange with the receiver a specific time for a follow-up contact. Let the receiver know that the process is not over with the first meeting. In a designated number of days or weeks, the receiver can expect a phone call, letter, or visit to pursue items covered in the interpersonal setting. In this way, perceived need for the information is projected onto a future setting where the receiver can expect to draw on the information he or she has obtained during the initial meeting. Although we hardly expect people to prepare by studying the information, we can anticipate that they will retain at least an awareness of the issues discussed.

The final method of dealing with selective retention problems is an adaptation of the previous technique. In this case, we ask the receiver to accomplish some task within a specified time. We may ask him or her to complete a questionnaire, contact a representative, or inform us about a decision. We may encourage compliance by offering a premium or other inducement. Here, as in the previous approach, we provide the receiver with a reason to retain the information. He or she has engaged in an interpersonal encounter with someone who has requested something. It need not be much-just to fill out a postcard or make a call yet this simple behaviour compels retention of the information from the conversation.

We can use a variety of techniques to develop messages that overcome the natural defences receivers use to avoid the full impact of a communication. In the interpersonal setting, a communicator can examine the ongoing feedback and so assess the reception of a message. He or she can then employ strategies to draw in the receiver, to promote an accurate understanding of the issues, and to project a need for the information in the future. Inasmuch as any form of communication can deal with selective exposure, perception, and retention, designs available in interpersonal settings have the strongest possibility.

Social Features

Earlier we proposed that the receiver's involvement in the give-and-take of interpersonal communication contributed to the success of information exchange because it helped overcome selective blocks. We believe the receiver's involvement in social relationships, also part of the interpersonal communication setting, advances the same purpose. The bond established between two people in an interpersonal environment offers a major advantage over mass communication programmes for reasons we will examine.

Two aspects of the social features in interpersonal designs concern this discussion: personal attraction and personal responsibility. In the first case, we are referring to the simple notion that people enjoy other people, particularly if the other person is friendly, knowledgeable, and interested in the well-being of others.

Whether the other person is on a telephone, drafts a personal letter, or meets with us in person, it is the person-to-person contact that makes a difference in our reception to a message. We can walk out on a television programme. We can even walk out on a televised presidential address without concern for hurting anyone's feelings or breaching any social rules. On the other hand, it is difficult for many people to break off communication with another person. In telephone surveys when people are called by total strangers, it is not uncommon for a respondent to stay with an interview for fifteen to twenty minutes. If someone does not wish to participate in the survey or has other pressing matters at hand, he or she will generally provide an explanation for discontinuing the interview. Sometimes people even apologize because they do not wish to hurt the caller's feelings. It would be simpler to hang up the phone; and while some do, most do not without first explaining their reasons. As a comparison, some polling firms have attempted to automate the telephone surveying process. They have machines place the call and pose questions to a receiver who has a specified time in which to provide a response. In these approaches the portion of uncompleted interviews, as compared with human-administered surveys, is vastly larger. People will talk to people but not to a machine.

Bem's observation that people are the greatest influence on people is valid for reasons that are helpful in specialized communication programmes. People will usually listen to another person, at least for a while, and so this human delivered message has a much better chance of avoiding the selective gates that so often block mass media messages. Granted, they may allow only a few moments for the person to make the point, but for that time they will probably listen to the message. If the topic is relevant and the pitch is well crafted, then perhaps the receiver will stay with the entire message. Where the receiver selects himself or herself into the communication event, there is a strong chance the communicator will have his or her message heard.

If we like this person talking to us, we will probably look favorably on the message. If what he or she says is interesting and a logical argument is provided, we will likely listen to the message. Moreover, the developing relationship will allow us to feel comfortable about expressing our doubts and reservations or raising questions about the message. This social environment promotes the feedback so important in interpersonal settings. Misperceptions of the message are less likely where feedback abounds, and feedback is most likely when a good social relationship is established. This interpersonal contact is not desirable just because it is pleasant, but because it is productive. The communicator can engage the receiver's attention, then shape the message to make his or her point.

The social context of interpersonal communications is beneficial in staving off problems of selective retention. The receiver departs the communication event not only with content or subject cues, but also with social cues. In other words, the message and the messenger become linked. If the social encounter is pleasant, we can expect thoughts about the topic also to be viewed positively. Consequently, the relationship between the communicator and the receiver has a direct bearing on retention of the message.

An indirect effect of the relationship also occurs beyond the confines of the communication event. We can expect a higher response rate to follow through portions of the programme. As we discussed in the previous section, the communicator or the receiver initiates some action in the aftermath of the initial communication. People are more likely to complete and mail a questionnaire or to continue discussions when such action has been requested by a source with whom the receiver has established a social rapport. We do not want to let down someone we know and like, someone who may be disappointed if we ignore a simple request. Consequently, the selective retention matter—how long and how accurately someone keeps an active mental file on a communication—is enhanced by the social nature of interpersonal communication settings. We have described how social relationships are important in overcoming the barriers to successful communication. Consider yet another feature, known as the "focusing of responsibility." In order to describe the meaning of this term, it is helpful to understand first what is meant by the "diffusion of responsibility." Consider a situation in which a large number of people gathers in a single place—say, one thousand troops standing at attention on a drill field.

Suppose an officer addressing the troops asks for a volunteer to participate in some dangerous mission. We can expect a request of such a large group to yield a relatively low percentage of volunteers. As each soldier thinks about the appeal and weighs the advantages against the dangers of volunteering, he also is aware he is just one of a thousand being asked. Maybe someone else will raise his hand, and even if no one does, each soldier is just one of the many who hold back. There is safety in numbers. The responsibility to volunteer is diffused among all these soldiers and does not rest on the back of any one.

This diffusion of responsibility theory has been used to explain what appears to be apathy among people who view a crime committed in public. Latane and Darley explain that the costs of nonintervention are spread among all observers, so no one feels particularly responsible to aid the victim. Here, too, bystanders believe that perhaps someone else will lend a hand; and even if no one else does, the accountability is divided, so no one feels culpable. The responsibility and so ultimately the guilt for inaction are spread among many. While large numbers allow each person to find refuge in the crowd, small numbers or one-on-one encounters pinpoint the responsibility. If a sergeant asked each soldier individually to volunteer for the assignment, we would expect a much higher response rate. If only one passerby saw someone being assaulted, it is more likely that that person would intervene. The same idea of responsibility focusing applies to interpersonal communication settings.

We are less likely to daydream or discard a message if we are the sole receiver. We sense a responsibility to maintain our attention to a message in these communication events. If the communicator asks a question, who else can respond? No one else can share the burden. In a mass media environment, it is easy to ignore requests. Tens of thousands, perhaps millions of other people may respond to pleas for assistance or support. No single viewer is on the spot, and no single viewer feels the weight of responsibility.

INTERPERSONAL VERSUS MASS COMMUNICATION

Let us refine the notion of interpersonal communications for our particular application to specialized programmes by contrasting interpersonal with mass communication. We characterize these differences along several dimensions of utility for the programme designer.

These two forms of communication differ according to the following features:

- Feedback characteristics,
- Audience selection features, and
- Channels of communication.

FEEDBACK CHARACTERISTICS

Recall feedback (in its general meaning) is information obtained by the source from the receiver. It may be information acquired before the communication programme begins. In this case it is used to formulate strategy by providing details about receiver perceptions of the source, positions on the issues, and media usage patterns. Furthermore, feedback information obtained during a campaign helps the communicator adjust and modify programmes to accommodate changing audiences.

At best, mass audience feedback information reflects the statistical average of the studied population. We can examine groups and clusters, but we cannot focus on narrow audiences without losing statistical validity or engaging in elaborate research designs. Moreover, the information we obtain in large audience settings usually is structured and constrained. It is derived typically from survey questionnaires that offer preplanned (and usually sender-developed) questions and answers. Extemporaneous responses unique to individuals are rarely manageable, given the nature of survey research that imposes a high degree of uniformity on the data.

Since our ability to generalize sample data to the overall population is dependent in part on consistent responses, survey research procedures strive to cluster and collapse responses into uniform arrays. Simply put, except for anecdotal purposes, individual responses have no statistical validity and therefore are of little use in understanding an audience. All of this suggests that feedback obtained from mass audiences has restricted application: It is structured, non-specific, and limited in its capacity to describe small subgroups within the population. Beyond these drawbacks, feedback obtained in mass audience settings is nearly always delayed. It takes time to develop, administer, analyse, and deliver data from a large audience survey, despite major efforts in recent times to speed up the system. One political consulting outfit in Washington, D.C., has attempted to expedite the process by providing an overnight polling service. These, of course, are limited surveys with a small number of questions delivered by telephone to a limited voter sample. Furthermore, there is little possibility for subgroup study, given the small sample involved. Strides are being made to deliver mass audience survey information faster than previously possible, but even these efforts fail to overcome the inherent delays in mass audience feedback. Several technological innovations are being examined to gather feedback quickly. Test units in

Columbus, Ohio, and Rock Island, Illinois, have demonstrated the possibility for home television viewers to transmit their "votes" to a central computer for instant tabulation. At least in this limited setting, we may be able to poll certain segments of the audience and obtain results quickly. Even here, though, it is difficult to conceive of feedback information in the mass audience setting approaching the speed and quality of interpersonal feedback.

The short shelf life of data is one potentially serious problem with the delay of mass audience feedback information. During the time lapse between data collection and availability of information, conditions in the environment might change, rendering this information invalid. Take, for instance, a poll measuring public attitudes towards services provided by local governments. We know public attitudes on such issues shift daily according to headlines, public discussion, and other topics on the public agenda.

When we ask someone a question about government services may determine what that person's response will be. Our data gathered seven days earlier may not reflect public sentiment today. At most we can hope there have been no major events such as scandals in city hall or garbage workers' strikes that would affect large portions of the public, thus rendering useless any information gathered previously. Even without such major events impacting the population, we can anticipate some degree of change and therefore some inaccuracy as our data age. The older the data, the more skeptical we must become.

Feedback information available in an interpersonal exchange, however, is rich, specific, and rapid. Such characteristics enable the flow of interpersonal communication events to proceed with an ease and efficiency that cannot be replicated in a mass communication environment.

Interpersonal feedback information is rich because it can contain a wealth of information on a number of levels. In a typical conversation, for example, we obtain information from the other person first by listening to what that person has to say. We need only ask if we want to clarify an ambiguous point or to get more details. Typical conversations proceed through a series of repetitions that clarify, refine, and elaborate.

Besides the words exchanged, interactants learn information from each other through non-verbal cues. Vocal intonation reveals intensity of feeling and emotion that may be missed by the words alone. When asked how they are doing today, two people may respond that they are "fine." The first may have an upbeat tone and a lively bounce to his "fine," showing a positive state of mind.

The second person's "fine," however, with its unhappy, listless timbre, reveals a sour, despondent mood. Both have said the same word, but because the response tone differed in each case, the information obtained is not the same. The first person seems to be fine; the second appears to be troubled. In this case and in many instances, according to some non-verbal communication specialists, the tone used reveals more of the truth than the words themselves.

Feedback cues in interpersonal settings go beyond the words and vocal tone. We come to understand other people in conversations by observing their gesticulations (arm movements and gestures), facial expressions, posture, dress, and other physical features. They exhibit more than their words convey. A fist shaken in anger reveals an intense feeling that words may not express adequately. To some, folded arms suggest a person is blocking or wishes to protect something. We interpret differently someone's laughter, depending on whether it is a chortle, a giggle, or a guffaw.

As with verbal tone, such cues communicate information that is often more complete and representative of a person's frame of mind than are his or her words. When these cues are joined with verbal and tonal information, the richness of feedback available in an interpersonal setting becomes evident. Compared to the mass communication environment, we have a greater variety of levels from which to draw, and at each of these levels we often find cues more complete and detailed.

Specific Information

Feedback information in an interpersonal setting is specific to one individual. Recall in a previous discussion we noted that mass audience feedback is a statistical average of data provided by a large number of respondents. From this we are able to understand general sentiments and trends within a population, but cannot pinpoint any specific individual. Even small target groups within the general population often elude us because they cannot adequately be represented in fact-finding research. In personal conversations, though, we can obtain specific information. If the other person looks puzzled, or scratches his head, or expresses confusion or doubt, we know we must provide clarity or a new line of reasoning. The point is, we are able to provide a specific message because we have specific feedback information. Research and practical experience demonstrate that the success of our communications is directly related to the specificity of our messages.

Rapid Feedback

If, over a cup of coffee, you were to ask a friend whom she planned to vote for in an upcoming congressional election, you might have your answer within seconds. Assume you then asked why she intended to vote this way. Again, within seconds, you would have an answer. The feedback in such an interpersonal encounter is very fast. With such information at hand, you might then act immediately to confirm your friend's choice of candidates or challenge her decision with the hope of bringing her around to your viewpoint.

By contrast, the same questions about candidate preference are the stock and trade of many political polling firms that attempt to learn how people in the general public plan to vote in upcoming elections. For these outfits, however, there is considerable lag time between survey administration and information availability. Days may pass before information about voter preferences is accessible to campaign staffs for forming strategy. As we have discussed, not only does this protract the communication process, but also conditions and voter sentiments can change, thus making the facts outdated.

The rapid exchange of information common to interpersonal communications is one of its biggest advantages. The information can be used for an immediate response, thus sustaining the give-and-take features of interpersonal communication. It represents the individual's thinking at the moment; hence, it is fresh and uncontaminated by factors that occur over time.

In summary, despite the efforts of people in mass communication to improve the quality of feedback, it is doubtful that they can ever achieve the level of information we see in the interpersonal setting. The information in an interpersonal communication encounter is rich. There are a variety of cues that enhance and refine the communication's meaning. This information is specific to one individual and so allows individual treatment by communicators. Finally, the information (in most settings) is immediately available, allowing rapid assessment and response by others in the discussion.

Audience Selection

In mass communication settings, companies typically seek out the audience. In most of the recommended interpersonal designs, audiences seek out the companies. The distinction is significant for two reasons: (1) In the interpersonal context, audiences play an active role; and (2) they sort themselves into categories of interested information seekers. Businesses that employ interpersonal techniques find that in part because of these features, communication activities differ from those in the mass audience portions of their campaigns.

The receiver provides much of the energy getting information from the source to the receiver. In addition, largely because audiences are self-selected, a greater portion of the messages falls on receptive ears. A larger share of interested people exists in these audiences than in general mass audience groups. We will examine these two features of audience selection in more detail.

The Active Audience Role

In the mass communication setting, the burden of audience identification is on our shoulders. We gather survey data; then, we sort through them to identify target audiences. We match up audience needs and interests with appropriate messages, and we locate the media best suited to deliver these messages to target audiences. During all of this, audience members are passive players, perhaps choosing to examine our message, perhaps not, depending on distractions, our skill at stimulating attention, and the whim of the moment.

In the interpersonal designs we propose, audiences come to us for information and thereby shift at least a portion of the burden to their own shoulders. They identify themselves as prospects for information and place themselves in the path of our targeted messages. By taking this role, they eliminate a portion of our responsibility. Moreover, they commit themselves (however slight the commitment) to the communication transaction. They have expended an effort to call, write, or visit us, and accordingly have invested something of their own in the process. The time and energy involved in that phone call, or in filling out a postcard, or in driving to an exhibit represent a cost to the individuals that makes them more than passive onlookers.

The most important clues to an individual's inner states are found in his behaviour. When we want to know how a person feels, we look to see how he acts. Accordingly, my theory about the origins of an individual's self-knowledge predicts that he might also infer his own internal states by observing his own overt behaviour.

We believe, since we are thinking, rational people, that if we engage in some behaviour, it must be because we have sufficient reason to do so. We find an uncomfortable inconsistency between incompatible attitudes and behaviours. We believe our behaviours are underwritten by a set of consonant attitudes. To expect otherwise would cause doubt about our own rationality.

So it follows that if we can stimulate audience members to take an active role in the communication process by performing even some small behaviour, such as making a phone call or sending in a postcard, we may encourage formation of a positive attitude about the communication interaction. After all, they have invested something of themselves. There must be something valuable in the communication, or, as rational people, they would not have bothered to spend the time and effort. We see, then, that by engaging an audience in the interpersonal features of a communication campaign, we have begun to change the general nature of the receiver. The simple step of involving people in an active way may encourage development of attitudes that render message recipients more receptive to our arguments.

We should examine one additional feature of an active audience. As we describe recommended interpersonal programmes for business communication campaigns, the audience, through our promotion and encouragement, seeks us out for additional information. We then increase the level of information flow and ultimately establish a working interpersonal relationship.

At the point where receivers first request specific information and involve us in a one-on-one dialogue, they become the recipients of our offerings. They have requested something of us (even if it is only information designed to sell them something) and we have complied. To some, even limited degree, the recipients may feel a sense of obligation to us. After all, we have provided a booklet or letter, our time on the phone, or some premium based solely on their request. The scales of fair play may be tipped in our favour, and the recipients may feel they owe us something—even if only a bit more time or further consideration of our position. We are not suggesting the recipients perceive a great debt for our small accommodation. We propose only that they have formed an attitude that establishes a more desirable relationship between the communicator and the audience.

Note how this is different from, say, a direct mail campaign where the communicator sends out information and perhaps a premium. Receivers may read the material for a variety of reasons; they may even sense an obligation because of the free gift. But since the material was unsolicited, they do not feel the same level of responsibility to the source. The company has not responded to their request and provided information at their bidding. They are not responsible for the sender's efforts in this case, and therefore have little sense of indebtedness.

In summary, when audiences assume an active role in the communication process, several advantages accrue to the business source. First, when audiences come to the source for information, they save that source a good deal of energy. Those who become involved in interpersonal programmes infer from their behaviours an attitude about their own commitment to the process. Finally, by taking an active role, audiences develop some sense of indebtedness to a company that has responded to their requests. Even at the outset, interpersonal programmes enjoy several advantages over mass appeal portions of a communication campaign.

Audience Sorting

One of the biggest challenges faced in targeted audience campaigns is the identification of groups that will have a special interest in the topic at hand. Success of the targeted communication process is based in part on the capacity of a company to be effective at this task.

Once the company has found its audience and established initial mass media contact, it is up to the receivers to recognize their interest in an issue and take the next step in the communication process. Interpersonal audiences are self-selected. Those who choose to engage in interpersonal portions of a campaign do so because they see something relevant for themselves. They recognize a personal interest or merit in the topic that appeals especially to them.

Two advantages result from audience sorting. First, we expect those who have joined the interpersonal audience to have a reasonable level of interest in the topic. They should therefore require less persuading, thus allowing the company to devote more energy to information matters.

Interpersonal audiences also see that the issue relates to them personally. People who call hospital hot lines for help with particular medical or psychological difficulties do so because they are troubled by these problems.

They not only take an interest in the response, but know the answer relates to their own condition. Consequently, people running these hot lines need spend no time convincing callers that the proposed solutions apply to their ailment. People call precisely because they recognize this relevance.

This sorting process yields an audience ideal for the business communicator. Of the entire population, these receivers are most likely receptive to persuasion. They are interested, so they will listen. They see relevance, so they need little urging.

Physical Setting

In most of the interpersonal communication designs proposed, we attempt to maximize the face-to-face (or voice-to-voice) contact between the source and receiver. Interpersonal programmes that work closest with people work best. An increase in the number of physical barriers placed between the source and receiver decreases the impact of the communication.

Suppose we have fashioned our interpersonal communi-cation plan based on a correspondence course that uses the mail to carry messages between the source and receiver. This is an example of interpersonal communication. There is a one-on-one exchange of messages between the source and receiver, and each communication is tailored especially for the intended recipient. There are considerable physical barriers, however, that hamper the rapid, efficient information flow we have come to expect in interpersonal scenarios. Even on a good day, the mail will be too slow to permit a smooth, unbroken flow of messages. We are also limited in the kinds of information that can be transmitted. We lose rich detail because elements such as non-verbal facial and body cues and vocal intonations cannot be transmitted. The only special feature of interpersonal communication retained is the specificity and focus enjoyed when communi-cating with one rather than many receivers. Here, physical barriers have become obstacles that weaken the communi-cation process.

Many companies recognize that the mail is inefficient as the mainstay of an interpersonal programme; consequently, they have turned to the telephone and primarily the tollfree 800 numbers to provide customers with a convenient alternative. They employ the phone to establish initial contact, then follow through with mailings or personal visits. In other cases the phone is primary for all phases of the interpersonal programme.

In several respects, telephone programmes are a vast improvement over a mail-only design. First, phones require little effort by audience members and are convenient. People who will not take time to fill out and mail a postcard may find a moment to place a free call. They can make a phone call on impulse. Writing requires more effort. Hence, we may expect marginal audience members to be drawn into an interpersonal communication programme simply because the phone is easier than the mail. Phones also speed the exchange of information. No delay occurs between the delivery and receipt of a message, so one participant can react immediately to the comments of the other. Companies use phones to provide instant product information before and after a sale. Computer software companies maintain phone lines to explain new products and make immediate sales. Many also provide trouble lines to assist customers after the sale with technical information to get programmes up and running. Often, time and money are at stake for business software users; when customers need help, they need it right away.

Finally, the physical barriers imposed by telephones prohibit visual contact, but they do allow vocal cues. We hear not only what is said, but how it is said. We can often detect anger, excitement, anxiety, or pleasure by the way someone sounds. Sometimes in a telephone conversation, the most subtle cue—silence—can convey more information than words. For communications that require a visual component without special equipment, [1] the physical barriers of the telephone obviously render it useless. For other applications, though, telephones do not seriously impede the communi-cation flow.

Face-to-face communications are superior to all others. They permit the specific, directed message exchanges allowed by mail and telephone interactions, and, as in telephone conversations, they enable people to exchange information rapidly. Beyond this, however, they accommodate the full complement of non-verbal cues. Without any physical barriers to block, slow, or interfere with the exchange of information, face-to-face communications are superior. There may be other problems—logistics, cost, and resource commitment—but from the standpoint of persuasion, these interpersonal approaches offer the best communication environment.

CHANNELS

Mass media channels reach many receivers at one time, and interpersonal channels link the source to one receiver. It is easy to recognize the misappropriation of a channel. We would find it odd for Procter and Gamble to phone us (using a channel associated with interpersonal contact) with a thirtysecond discussion on the benefits of its floor wax. We expect to find such messages on television or radio. We also would find it strange if a senatorial candidate were to knock on the door of every home in the state to explain his or her position on pending legislation. Here, too, we expect to see such messages carried by one of the traditional mass media.

The use of public media for private messages also strikes us as strange. We laugh at the Romeo who asks his Juliet for her hand in marriage—in a newspaper classified ad. Many people feel awkward about televised discussions of sex by Dr. Ruth Westheimer. How can a topic so personal be aired in a medium so public? We feel acceptable channels exist for private communications, and these rarely include the public media. Distinctions between public and private channels reside in the capacity of a medium to designate its audience. If a medium enables us to reach only one person, we consider it to be an interpersonal channel. If it cannot single out just one person, we call it a public or mass audience channel. Commercial radio stations, for instance, may reach targeted audiences, but they cannot pinpoint one and only one listener. So they are not considered interpersonal channels. Ham radios and CBs, however, come very close to meeting the criteria of interpersonal media because people can use them to direct messages at individual operators. By the strictest definition, this is a hybrid category. Sometimes it can reach just one individual; at other times it may reach a large number of peripheral listeners. The telephone is the best telecommunication example of an interpersonal medium.

Feedback is one other characteristic that distinguishes public from private channels. In his early writings on comparisons between public and private communications, Deutschman noted that both could involve face-toface encounters. We can have a private (or interpersonal) face-to-face conversation over a cup of coffee or a public, face-to-face meeting at a political rally. Deutschman also observed that both could involve communications interposed by some medium. Our private conversation may be interposed by a telephone, and our public communication may be interposed by television, radio, or newspapers. The difference between the channels is their capacity to carry a two-way flow of information; in other words, how well they carry feedback.

Interpersonal channels provide for feedback. They allow the source to talk to the receiver, and they allow the receiver to talk back. Recall the importance of feedback in distinguishing mass from interpersonal communication. We provide better information when we know what the receivers want, and we may learn what they want if they can tell us. Faster, richer, more specific information is available in the interpersonal setting; mass audience feedback pales by comparison. In order to obtain such detail, we must have a channel that allows information to travel in both directions. In successful, interpersonal communication programmes, the communicator guarantees a two-way flow.

The trouble with mass communication is that movement of its feedback information is impeded. A channel that carries a sender's message cannot simultaneously carry a receiver's reply. This results in a unidirectional flow of information that is bound to be less responsive to audience needs than is a two-way system. When public communicators obtain feedback information, they must go outside their channel. They rely on public surveys, letters to the editor, phone calls, and other approaches. Distinctions, then, between interpersonal and mass audience channels are twofold: Interpersonal channels can pinpoint specific receivers; mass channels cannot. Interpersonal channels allow a bidirectional information flow; mass audience channels work in only one direction.

MASS MEDIA/INTERPERSONAL CONNECTIONS

Fortunately, in most communication campaigns, we do not have to choose between mass media and interpersonal programmes. The two can work together well in augmenting the impact of a programme. Each reinforces the effects of the other; one picks up where the other leaves off. In this section we will describe the relationship between mass media and interpersonal phases of a communication campaign and show how each contributes to the overall effectiveness of specialized communication activities.

In these discussions, we expect that companies becoming involved in specialized communications will want to reach a large number of people. They may wisely choose to divide the larger audience into smaller units for individual treatment, but their primary objective is to reach more than a handful of receivers. It is therefore given that the mass media will be involved in all programmes, even those that plan to reach people on a one-on-one basis.

Since we will assume one or some combination of media will be employed in all campaigns, we must view the use of interpersonal programmes in the context of the mass media scheme. With this in mind, let us make clear that adding an interpersonal feature to a communication campaign is not just like adding another car to a train. Do not view an interpersonal component as an addendum to a mass media programme, but as an integral feature of it. In a campaign that has an interpersonal component, mass media will be used differently than in cases where no interpersonal feature is planned. Our discussions here will be confined to the use of media that support an interpersonal component.

In this context the mass media serve two essential functions. First, they help familiarize the audience with basic concepts and issues involved in a campaign. They provide information that enables the audience to recognize how the service, product, or idea relates to them personally. They familiarize the audience and make people comfortable with the subject of the campaign. The second function of the media deals specifically with the interpersonal element: They inform people about what they should do to become involved in the interpersonal programme, and they persuade target audiences to take this step towards involvement. They may also incorporate more substantive persuasion elements dealing with issues, although major persuasive efforts will likely be reserved for the interpersonal programme.

INTRODUCING CONCEPTS

Whether a company is introducing an innovation that is unknown to an audience or presenting a familiar issue in a new wrapping, it is important to familiarize the audience with basic concepts. Audiences need access to fundamental information on which they can base decisions. We cannot expect people to invest personal energy in an interpersonal programme if they have no idea about the relevance and importance of the topic or product being promoted. Mass media are used as the primary means of acquainting audience members with these issues.

Take, for example, one of the many innovations in the computer industry. A company by the name of Cauzin Systems, Inc., has introduced a clever method of data storage for business computers. Unlike tape and floppy disks that store information on a magnetic medium, Cauzin's system uses a simple strip of paper with markings resembling three-dimensional dots that are read by a light beam. The company has a valuable product and obviously would like to market it to a specialized audience of business computer users.

In its initial advertising phases, the company bought space in major business computer magazines where it described the central features of its "Softstrip" technology. It provided the audience with basic information about how the product worked and suggested that businesses could use such an innovation in their operations.

They avoided technical discussions (which might have frightened their audience), and offered just enough information to help potential customers understand the concept of Softstrip technology and recognize its application to their activities. In this case, magazines provided the initial contact with primary target audience groups. They introduced the product name and described its basic functions. They also explained how the product might be used in business computer applications, showing the relevance of the product to potential customers. The Cauzin ads went one step further, however, by leading interested readers into the interpersonal phase of the communication programme through the magazine ads. We will discuss their techniques in the following section.

Interpersonal Link

In most interpersonal programmes, customers need to be invited into the programme, and the mass media are best used to extend the invitation. The media tell people something about the information available in an interpersonal programme, and they tell them how to go about obtaining this information.

The best techniques for drawing mass media audiences into interpersonal programmes involve a few simple principles. First, requirements of the receiver should be minimal and easy to fulfill. As long as someone is not obliged to invest much energy or spend much time, he or she is more likely to take that next step. This is why many companies have obtained toll-free 800 lines to accommodate customer requests for further involvement. Although a number of businesses still use postage-paid, returnable post cards, among many that rely heavily on interpersonal customer contact, the 800 lines have become an efficient alternative. It is easy to dial a few numbers, particularly for people who have grown comfortable with using the telephone for so many business and personal applications. Despite the technique eventually chosen, observe this basic rule: Keep the method of contact simple.

The second principle concerns the value of a reward. People will seek to become involved further in communi-cations with a company if they recognize a value in doing so. What do they get for their efforts? Some companies offer a nominal prize or gift for continuing the communication process, and for many audiences some tangible premium may be necessary. For your efforts, many computer software companies will send a free demonstration diskette that exhibits basic features of a programme without providing the full power of the product. Other companies send buttons, photos, or free samples of soap or perfume. We know of one company that even sends along samples of stained glass. Such premiums allow the potential customer to sample the wares before purchase, but they also serve as an inducement for the receiver to send in a bid for continuing the communication process.

Rewards need not be physical products. Often the dividend for investing one's energy will be the information itself. Receivers may not need more than the promise of becoming further involved in learning about a product, service, or idea. Based on what they see in the mass media, they may develop only a genuine interest in learning more—not the hope of acquiring some prize. The information itself is a prize. In this case, of course, the company must make the promise of information attractive. Receivers must be assured their efforts will result in something of use to them. Perhaps they will receive an attractive packet of information that will further describe a product or a telephone call from someone who will answer their questions and provide additional details. People rightly expect to get something for their efforts, and the mass media can best describe the reward.

The final technique of bringing people from a mass media environment to the interpersonal setting involves safety and respondent obligation. People have grown wary of becoming too involved too quickly. They may be willing to have a company mail information or even have a representative phone them, but when it comes to a personal visit, they may feel pressured and so shy away from making the initial reply. Whatever the company plans for a follow-up interpersonal contact, it should be certain not to imply a threat. Assure the receiver that he or she is not obligated to buy anything or do anything chosen not to do as a result of taking the next step.

With these features in mind—require little time, give fair rewards, and promise no hassle—the bid made in a mass media message will have a stronger chance of acceptance by potential customers. Such an approach requires minimum effort, promises a reasonable expectation of some return, and guarantees relative safety—three important characteristics of any business transaction. Although we have discussed designs in which a single type of follow-up interpersonal programme was implied, nothing limits companies from offering several of these programmes. A company may use the media to suggest a few ways to follow through, for instance, phoning the company, filling out a postcard, or visiting a shop or office. Each offers a different level of commitment by the receiver and a different intensity of interpersonal contact. By offering several such possibilities, the company can sort individuals into those who prefer to proceed slowly, minimizing initial involvement, and those who are ready for a more intensive interaction.

Such an approach has been well used in the magazine advertisements of Cauzin Systems, which we cited as an example earlier. Recall that this company markets a product that stores computer data on strips of ordinary typing paper and has chosen to promote this product to specialized audiences through targeted business computer magazines. It also has planned to reach customers with well-designed interpersonal components detailing the innovation.

Three interpersonal communication programme options were presented in the Cauzin ads. First, customers could write in for additional information. Recognizing that some people might be reluctant to write or might not wish to wait for a reply, Cauzin published an 800 number by which receivers could request the same information or talk directly with company representatives about the Softstrip product. In this second application, the company escalated the level of communication. For those ready to move more quickly with their decision or who had no need for the intermediate step of reading additional descriptions, the phone call offered more direct and immediate access to company representatives.

A clever inducement was used to urge receivers into the final interpersonal programme. A printed strip, about five and one-half inches long and five-eighth inch wide, appeared along the outside margin of the magazine page—it was a functional example of a Softstrip programme. Instructions beneath this oddlooking column of three-dimensional dots suggested the reader take the advertisement to the nearest computer store where the programme could be "read." The ad claimed that this strip, no bigger than three and one-half square inches, contained a large amount of interesting information. For a computer aficionado, the enticement was compelling. For the company, the potential payoff was substantial. Here was a fairly simple, high-reward, and relatively low-threat inducement to attract audience members willing to become involved more quickly. Of course, while customers were having their strips read, they should have been prepared for the sales pitch. Most people who would take the ad to a computer store probably would be willing to hear what the salesperson had to say. Those who were not might have opted for one of the less intense interpersonal programme alternatives—the postcard or the phone call. At the bottom line of this discussion lies the relationship between the mass media and interpersonal portions of a communication campaign. They work together, not in opposition. The mass media set up conditions of, announce the features of, and provide information about procedures necessary to take the step into interpersonal portions of the communication programme. In the following section, we will examine in more detail the association between these two forms of communication.

Programme Considerations

Think of the combined mass media/interpersonal communication programme as a series of steps that ratchet upward the level of involvement between message source and receiver. We begin with a general information forum and step up to more specific, refined, interpersonal transactions. In the early phases, a company seeks the audience through public channels. In the later phases, the receivers seek the company through private channels. We move from information to persuasion, from audience-passive to audience-active formats. At each level, as the receiver's involvement increases, the inherent strengths of interpersonal communications simultan-eously expand; the potential for successful persuasion becomes greater. Communicators must keep this perspective in view. The mass media involvement is a prelude to the interpersonal portions of the campaign.

The media serve as lures and bridges to interpersonal programmes. They function as lures by attracting receivers to the issues and providing sufficient information to stimulate an interest and perhaps a curiosity about the message. They act as bridges by furnishing details that enable receivers to pass from the general mass message environment to the specific interpersonal environment. They tell how the receiver may become involved further in the communication process.To use the mass media, follow several logical guidelines:

- Identify media that pinpoint desired audiences.
- Time delivery of the mass media message to coincide with the availability of interpersonal programmes.
- Determine product and programme features that hold the greatest lure for target audiences (strategy features).

3

Public Broadcasting

PUBLIC USE OF MEDIA

Media usage characteristics of American audiences reveal a population that is dependent on a heavy diet of information and entertainment. As the following statistics reveal, Americans spend more time engaged in media pastimes than they spend in any other activities except, perhaps, sleeping and working. Throughout their waking day, people in this culture are immersed in a crowded media environment.

TELEVISION

A television set in the average home was on for seven hours and ten minutes every day, representing the highest figure in this category ever recorded. With one exception in 1977 (when household viewing dropped eight minutes per day), daily set usage has increased every year—there never has been a recorded decrease.

Similarly, personal viewing statistics reveal a persistent racheting upward since commercial acceptance of the medium nearly four decades ago. Average daily viewing times in 1960 were estimated to be around two hours; twenty-five years later this figure increased to nearly four and onehalf hours. Following a substantial amount of daily viewing as youngsters (just over four hours per day), teenagers lower their overall viewing time as they become involved in school and social activities (about three hours and twenty minutes per day).

At around eighteen years of age, however, people resume a heavier viewing schedule that they maintain and even increase throughout the rest of their lives. Older audiences (over fifty-five years) are the heaviest viewers, spending, on average, more than five and one-half hours watching television every day.

Age is not the only characteristic by which television viewing can be delineated. A. C. Nielsen (1986) reports that females typically watch more television than males (5.19 to 4.4 daily viewing hours), and those in lowerincome brackets (under $19,999) watch more than those with higher incomes (over $40,000) (household average of 7.0 to 7.8 hours daily). Those with cable or

VCRs tend to spend more time watching television, perhaps because they have greater programming variety to stimulate their interest, perhaps they are inherently heavier viewers who have purchased auxiliary equipment to satisfy their greater appetites.

Whatever the reason, as programming variety increases, so, too, does television usage. Despite these differences evident within population subgroups, mainstream American audiences devote a considerable amount of time to television viewing. Although abundant evidence substantiates the importance of television, the time commitment alone shows that, for many, television viewing is not a casual activity to fill time, but the mainstay of their daily lives.

Radio. With such a large portion of the day committed to television viewing, one might expect there would be little time left to spend with alternative media. Generally, this is not so. According to the Radio Bureau of Advertising, the average American listens to more than three hours of radio every day. Although much listening may occur as a secondary activity, where radio serves as a background to higher-priority endeavors, radio programming stands as an important feature of the media diets of most people.

Even though nearly all stations routinely offer some form of news summary (thirty-eight radio stations employ all-news formats), it is entertainment and music not news and information that attracts radio audiences. Among the radio stations operating in 1985, 28 per cent aired country-and-western music, 24 per cent offered adult contemporary, 10 per cent carried top forty or rock, 9 per cent played middle-of-the-road music, and 7 per cent provided easy listening formats. About 2 per cent were news/talk or all news. The remaining stations had a variety of formats including religious, classical music, and foreign language programming.

This once-mass audience medium has, during the last forty years, expanded into varied programming formats. Radio has evolved into a channel that enables communicators to reach narrow segments of the population with specific and directed messages. Different formats appeal to different groups, and it is this natural audience selection that serves the process of targeted communication.

While the audience composition of the three major television networks differs little, constituent audiences of radio stations vary greatly. Within the radio station audience, however, there is often considerable uniformity. Radio audiences are specialized. They have a measurable similarity of demographic traits that provide public communicators with a natural forum for targeted communication strategies. Radio audiences may be smaller than those of television, but to the public communicator, the nature of an audience is often more important than its numbers.

With the possible exception of all-news formats, which draw more acute audience attention, radio typically is used as a background medium that provides company in an automobile, sets an atmosphere, or just breaks the silence. Few people sit in front of a radio with the unbroken attention they usually give television, so usage figures must be interpreted with such characteristics in mind. Advocates of the medium argue that this passive attention allows advertising messages to make a subliminal impact on listeners, to have subtle cognitive effects that may ultimately translate into attitudinal and behavioural modifications. Such effects remain to be demonstrated empirically. Nonetheless, despite arguments dealing with the potential impact of radio messages on listeners, exposure statistics remain: People spend more time listening to radio today than at any other time in the history of this medium. Radio continues to serve the communicator as an important point of contact with public audiences.

Newspapers

While radio and television have enjoyed considerable popularity in all demographic categories during the last four decades, for large segments of the population newspapers have lost considerable ground. Younger audiences, obviously the most important group for sustained newspaper vitality, have failed to adopt the readership patterns of older audiences. As recently as 1967, a readership survey found that among people aged fifty to fifty-nine, 78 per cent read a newspaper on a daily basis, while 64 per cent of those in the twenty- to twenty-nine-year-old group read papers every day.

By 1977, however, readership differences between the two groups had grown considerably. Although older respondents continued a strong pattern of newspaper readership (76 per cent) among the twenty- to twenty-nine-year-old group only 42 per cent reported reading a newspaper every day. These statistics and others recorded in recent years suggest newspaper usage is changing among younger audiences who, some in the industry fear, may carry such habits with them throughout their lives. If this is the case, newspapers face the considerable task of discovering ways to attract and retain young readers.

Reasons for the loss of young audiences are a matter of speculation. One immediate answer, not unanimously accepted by media researchers, is newspapers' competition with television. As people watch ever greater quantities of television, they have less time to spend reading a newspaper. This argument becomes even more focused in light of polls that have shown that for the last twenty years Americans have preferred to get their news from television rather than from newspapers. Without getting into a debate over the substance of television news, presentation style, and summary format, accessibility and ease of use have made television the news medium of choice for most Americans.

Others contend it is not so much the competition from television as it is the hectic and erratic life-styles that conflict with newspaper home delivery. Most newspapers rely on home delivery for the bulk of sales; therefore, when population employment patterns conflict with newspaper delivery schedules, overall readership is bound to decline. This argument holds that young people are most likely to engage in such employment patterns and life-styles, so young people are most likely to omit newspaper reading from their daily schedules. Publishers of *U.S.A. Today* gave such reasoning serious consideration.

As the second largest national newspaper, *U.S.A. Today* sells about one in five copies through newsstands and vending machines. Merits of this argument will be determined, in part, by statistics gathered over the next several years on whether better marketing and improved availability of newspapers through means other than home delivery increase newspaper readership among younger audiences.

Whether television or hectic life-styles account for diminished newspaper readership, particularly among younger audiences, it remains clear that uses of newspapers among American audiences involve a lot more than just news. Studies by numerous organizations, including the American Society of Newspaper Editors, have found that the largest number of readers turn to newspapers for advertisements, advice columns, comics, features, and entertainment. People read newspapers not to learn the news, about which they might have little interest and would rather get in a more enjoyable format on television, but to relax.

The role of newspapers in the American media diet is changing. It was once thought television would offer the headlines while newspapers would provide analysis and a more rigorous treatment of a story. Although this stratified approach to news presentation may appeal to certain segments of the population, it clearly is not appropriate for the largest. It assumes an active, news-seeking population that does not exist. In order to retain audiences today, many newspapers are not providing depth but short accounts, leaving details and thoughtful analyses to news magazines.

They are trimming news in favour of features, hard reporting for soft discussion. Newspapers have been able to retard the exodus of readers by following readership trends and providing material demanded by shifting audiences. Newspapers still continue to attract reasonably large audiences because of their willingness to provide what readers want, but readers are not much interested in the news.

Magazines

It would be incorrect to conclude from our discussion of newspapers that print media in general are suffering at the hands of broadcast media. There is little question that magazine formats have changed owing to the pressures of television, but the medium has not suffered. There are more than eleven thousand titles currently available in the United States, an increase of one thousand in the last five years alone. People read a variety of magazines and spend a good amount of time with the medium. Total circulation has increased steadily over the years. The MPA reports that 90 per cent of adults read a magazine during the average month, and they read an average of 7.82 different magazine copies during the month. They spend nearly one hour with each copy and typically go over each page 1.7 times. Magazines appear to be alive and well.

We will present a variety of statistics in this discussion, but first must offer one caveat. Our figures report general observations that summarize readership habits for the average reader for the average magazine. With more than eleven thousand titles, it is difficult to interpret such averages. There is incredible diversity among magazines and their audiences. In fact, it is this diversity that makes the medium so attractive to public communicators who recognize important differences among audiences and use magazines as a means of reaching individual groups. Readers of the *Columbia Journalism Review* will probably not be much like readers of *Dirt Rider*; *Harvard Business Review* readers will not resemble readers of *Seventeen*. There are great differences among magazines, and so it follows there are great differences in the characteristics of their audiences. Statistics reported here may imply a more unified audience than actually exists.

With this warning in mind, according to statistics gathered by the MPA, the average magazine reader has these traits: The person is married, is thirty-seven years old, and lives in a three-or-more-person household.

He or she has graduated from high school, has a fulltime job, and earns 15 per cent above the national average income. The heaviest readers look somewhat different. They are about the same age, but they are college educated and earn considerably above the national average income.

About 75 per cent retain their copies of magazines and refer to them at least one additional time before discarding them. The MPA reports that "magazine imperatives" (heavy magazine readers who are also light television viewers) are likely to be involved in public and social life, politics, and community activities. They are also likely to entertain more and attend spectator events outside the home. These traits and others, according to the MPA, suggest magazine readers are prime targets for advertisers.

As we have stated, such statistics may so generalize magazine audiences that they lose their meaning for any specific application. Audience details on individual magazines can be obtained from commercial sources and from publishers. The essential elements in this discussion of magazines and their audiences are these: Magazines remain popular with American audiences. Each magazine has a unique audience profile. People who read a particular magazine tend to be similar to others who read that magazine. Magazine formats are changing to accommodate the evolving needs of their audiences, and these needs have generally been towards specificity and narrowing of interest area.

DIRECT MAIL

Direct mail has become increasingly important as a means of audience contact. We discuss direct mail only briefly in this section, but will take a more detailed look, at how it can be used in a public communication campaign.

It is easy to obtain usage statistics on the mass media since there are only a relatively few outlets. Over the years industry watchers have gathered reliable and detailed information on how people use radio and television and even the eleven thousand magazines currently in publication. Direct mail statistics are more difficult to assemble. Every business, agency, and organization serves as its own outlet. While there may be hundreds or thousands of media channels, there are millions of direct mail channels, making it impossible to compile specific usage information. Direct mail usage is therefore based on assumptions and extrapolations, and even compilers of these statistics caution that there is a reasonable margin of error in the data.

Nonetheless, the DMA has attempted to track the use of direct mail based in part on U.S. Postal Service reports. Over the years there has been a steady increase in the mailing technique. Between 1982 and 1985, there was a 40 per cent increase in the total number of direct mail pieces. In 1985 the DMA reports there were more than 55 billion direct mailings within the United States and 16 million from the United States to overseas destinations.

From these figures it is evident that direct mail is becoming increasingly popular among U.S. companies and organizations. They are using direct mail to get their messages across to voters, consumers, and supporters. They are sending letters, brochures, fliers, coupons, and dozens of other forms to convince, cajole, inform, and stir people about issues of all sorts. Direct mail picks up where the mass media leave off. Direct mail provides targeted and personal contact with audiences. Computers, sophisticated mailing lists, and other technological advancements have made direct mail a convenient and affordable way to reach specific audience members. It enables communicators to shape their messages to meet individual needs.

An effective communication programme must account for all essential elements of the communication process. Occasionally, a seat-of-the-pants campaign brings about the intended education or persuasion of an audience, but such examples are few and far between. The mass communication process has become far too complex in recent times to allow campaigns based on a hunch to have much success. With the expanded array of available media options, exposure patterns of audiences have become more complicated and difficult to pinpoint by intuition.

The vast array of messages competing for attention diminishes the probability that audiences will recognize any one of them and that, by even a smaller chance, the message will have an intended effect on individuals. One observer estimates the average American is exposed to some sixteen hundred commercial messages per day but notices only eighty of them. Only twelve of these messages, Parker says, elicit any response at all from the recipient. In order to be among the fortunate few to win the notice of an audience, communicators must draw from a variety of techniques to improve their chances in the competitive information marketplace.

The complexity of media exposure patterns and competition for audience attention present obstacles that some public communicators are willing to concede when they conduct a seat-of-the-pants campaign. Most acknowledge the inadequacy of such an approach, however, when faced with current message production and placement charges. Production and distribution of messages are expensive. Radio spots may cost several hundreds to several thousands of dollars to produce. A thirty-second radio spot aired during drive time in an average city may cost as much as four hundred dollars or more. Television spot production has run as high as several hundred thousand dollars for a thirty-second network-quality advertisement, although the average is a little under $100,000. Smaller television stations may charge several hundred to several thousand dollars to air a thirty-second spot during prime time, and for the same time slot, networks typically charge between $150,000 and $200,000. Of course, for special programmes, network rates can be even more shocking.

USES OF RADIO

Early uses were maritime, for sending telegraphic messages using Morse code between ships and land. The earliest users included the Japanese Navy scouting the Russian fleet during the Battle of Tsushima in 1905. One of the most memorable uses of marine telegraphy was during the sinking of the RMS *Titanic* in 1912, including communications between operators on the sinking ship and nearby vessels, and communications to shore stations listing the survivors.

Radio was used to pass on orders and communications between armies and navies on both sides in World War I; Germany used radio communications for diplomatic messages once it discovered that its submarine cables had been tapped by the British. The United States passed on President Woodrow Wilson's Fourteen Points to Germany via radio during the war. Broadcasting began from San Jose, California in 1909, and became feasible in the 1920s, with the widespread introduction of radio receivers, particularly in Europe and the United States. Besides broadcasting, point-to-point broadcasting, including telephone messages and relays of radio programmes, became widespread in the 1920s and 1930s. Another use of radio in the pre-war years was the development of detection and locating of aircraft and ships by the use of radar. Today, radio takes many forms, including wireless networks and mobile communications of all types, as well as radio broadcasting. Before the advent of television, commercial radio broadcasts included not only news and music, but dramas, comedies, variety shows, and many other forms of entertainment. Radio was unique among methods of dramatic presentation in that it used only sound.

AUDIO

AM radio uses amplitude modulation, in which the amplitude of the transmitted signal is made proportional to the sound amplitude captured by the microphone, while the transmitted frequency remains unchanged. Transmissions are affected by static and interference because lightning and other sources of radio emissions on the same frequency add their amplitudes to the original transmitted amplitude. In the early part of the 20th century, American AM radio stations broadcast with powers as high as 500 kW, and some could be heard worldwide; these stations' transmitters were commandeered for military use by the US Government during World War II. Currently, the maximum broadcast power for a civilian AM radio station in the United States and Canada is 50 kW, and the majority of stations that emit signals this powerful were grandfathered in. In 1986 KTNN received the last granted 50,000 watt license. These 50 kW stations are generally called "clear channel" stations because within North America each of these stations has exclusive use of its broadcast frequency throughout part or all of the broadcast day.

FM broadcast radio sends music and voice with higher fidelity than AM radio. In frequency modulation, amplitude variation at the microphone causes the transmitter frequency to fluctuate. Because the audio signal modulates the frequency and not the amplitude, an FM signal is not subject to static and interference in the same way as AM signals. Due to its need for a wider bandwidth, FM is transmitted in the Very High Frequency radio spectrum. VHF radio waves act more like light, traveling in straight lines; hence the reception range is generally limited to about 50–100 miles. During unusual upper atmospheric conditions, FM signals are occasionally reflected back towards the Earth by the ionosphere, resulting in long distance FM reception. FM receivers are subject to the capture effect, which causes the radio to only receive the strongest signal when multiple signals appear on the same frequency. FM receivers are relatively immune to lightning and spark interference.

High power is useful in penetrating buildings, diffracting around hills, and refracting in the dense atmosphere near the horizon for some distance beyond the horizon. Consequently, 100,000 watt FM stations can regularly be heard up to 100 miles away, and farther if there are no competing signals. A few old, "grandfathered" stations do not conform to these power rules. WBCT-FM (93.7) in Grand Rapids, Michigan, USA, runs 320,000 watts ERP, and can increase to 500,000 watts ERP by the terms of its original license. Such a huge power level does not usually help to increase range as much as one might expect, because VHF frequencies travel in nearly straight lines over the horizon and off into space. Nevertheless, when there were fewer FM stations competing, this station could be heard near Bloomington, Illinois, USA, almost 300 miles away. FM subcarrier services are secondary signals transmitted in a "piggyback" fashion along with the main programme. Special receivers are required to utilize these services. Analog channels may contain alternative programming, such as reading services for the blind, background music or stereo sound signals. In some extremely crowded metropolitan areas, the sub-channel programme might be an alternate foreign language radio programme for various ethnic groups. Sub-carriers can also transmit digital data, such as station identification, the current song's name, web addresses, or stock quotes. In some countries, FM radios automatically re-tune themselves to the same channel in a different district by using sub-bands.

Aviation voice radios use VHF AM. AM is used so that multiple stations on the same channel can be received. Aircraft fly high enough that their transmitters can be received hundreds of miles away, even though they are using VHF.

Marine voice radios can use single sideband voice in the shortwave High Frequency radio spectrum for very long ranges or narrowband FM in the VHF spectrum for much shorter ranges. Narrowband FM sacrifices fidelity to make more channels available within the radio spectrum, by using a smaller range of radio frequencies, usually with five kHz of deviation, versus the 75 kHz used by commercial FM broadcasts, and 25 kHz used for TV sound.

Government, police, fire and commercial voice services also use narrowband FM on special frequencies. Early police radios used AM receivers to receive one-way dispatches. Civil and military HF voice services use shortwave radio to contact ships at sea, aircraft and isolated settlements. Most use single sideband voice, which uses less bandwidth than AM. On an AM radio SSB sounds like ducks quacking, or the adults in a Charlie Brown cartoon. Viewed as a graph of frequency versus power, an AM signal shows power where the frequencies of the voice add and subtract with the main radio frequency. SSB cuts the bandwidth in half by suppressing the carrier and one of the sidebands. This also makes the transmitter about three times more powerful, because it doesn't need to transmit the unused carrier and sideband.

TETRA, Terrestrial Trunked Radio is a digital cell phone system for military, police and ambulances. Commercial services such as XM, WorldSpace and Sirius offer encrypted digital Satellite radio.

TELEPHONY

Mobile phones transmit to a local cell site that ultimately connects to the public switched telephone network through an optic fibre or microwave radio and other network elements. When the mobile phone nears the edge of the cell site's radio coverage area, the central computer switches the phone to a new cell. Cell phones originally used FM, but now most use various digital modulation schemes. Recent developments in Sweden allow for the instant downloading of digital material from a radio broadcast to a mobile phone. Satellite phones use satellites rather than cell towers to communicate.

VIDEO

Television sends the picture as AM and the sound as AM or FM, with the sound carrier a fixed frequency away from the video carrier. Analog television also uses a vestigial sideband on the video carrier to reduce the bandwidth required.

Digital television uses 8VSB modulation in North America and COFDM modulation elsewhere in the world. A Reed–Solomon error correction code adds redundant correction codes and allows reliable reception during moderate data loss. Although many current and future codecs can be sent in the MPEG transport stream container format, as of 2006 most systems use a standard-definition format almost identical to DVD: MPEG-2 video in Anamorphic widescreen and MPEG layer 2 audio. High-definition television is possible simply by using a higher-resolution picture, but H.264/AVC is being considered as a replacement video codec in some regions for its improved compression. With the compression and improved modulation involved, a single "channel" can contain a high-definition programme and several standard-definition programmes.

Navigation

All satellite navigation systems use satellites with precision clocks. The satellite transmits its position, and the time of the transmission. The receiver listens to four satellites, and can figure its position as being on a line that is tangent to a spherical shell around each satellite, determined by the time-of-flight of the radio signals from the satellite. A computer in the receiver does the math.

Radio direction-finding is the oldest form of radio navigation. Before 1960 navigators used movable loop antennas to locate commercial AM stations near cities. In some cases they used marine radiolocation beacons, which share a range of frequencies just above AM radio with amateur radio operators. LORAN systems also used time-of-flight radio signals, but from radio stations on the ground. VOR, systems have an antenna array that transmits two signals simultaneously. A directional signal rotates like a lighthouse at a fixed rate. When the directional signal is facing north, an omnidirectional signal pulses. By measuring the difference in phase of these two signals, an aircraft can determine its bearing or radial from the station, thus establishing a line of position. An aircraft can get readings from two VORs and locate its position at the intersection of the two radials, known as a "fix." When the VOR station is collocated with DME, the aircraft can determine its bearing and range from the station, thus providing a fix from only one ground station. Such stations are called VOR/DMEs. The military operates a similar system of navaids, called TACANs, which are often built into VOR stations. Such stations are called VORTACs. Because TACANs include distance measuring equipment, VOR/DME and VORTAC stations are identical in navigation potential to civil aircraft.

Radar

Radar detects objects at a distance by bouncing radio waves off them. The delay caused by the echo measures the distance. The direction of the beam determines the direction of the reflection. The polarization and frequency of the return can sense the type of surface. Navigational radars scan a wide area two to four times per minute. They use very short waves that reflect from earth and stone. They are common on commercial ships and long-distance commercial aircraft.

General purpose radars generally use navigational radar frequencies, but modulate and polarize the pulse so the receiver can determine the type of surface of the reflector. The best general-purpose radars distinguish the rain of heavy storms, as well as land and vehicles. Some can superimpose sonar data and map data from GPS position.

Search radars scan a wide area with pulses of short radio waves. They usually scan the area two to four times a minute. Sometimes search radars use the Doppler effect to separate moving vehicles from clutter. Targeting radars use the same principle as search radar but scan a much smaller area far more often, usually several times a second or more. Weather radars resemble search radars, but use radio waves with circular polarization and a wavelength to reflect from water droplets. Some weather radar use the Doppler effect to measure wind speeds.

RADIO EDUCATION

According Butcher "radio has been used in education ever since it became available". Pennycuick, of the Centre for International Education at the University of Sussex, states a bit more specifically that interactive radio instruction is characterized by "highly coordinated" instructional materials and delivery strategies, and includes elements of active participation on the part of the students. He goes on to say that IRI "is effective, is cost-effective, and teachers are enthusiastic about it".

In support of this, the South African Institute for Distance Education stated that "radio remains the key media to which most rural people have access" and that educational radio initiatives in South Africa were "effective in providing topical programmes and reaching large numbers of learners rapidly". Going further, they state that "the impact of the radio programmes was greater when used with other text-based materials, such as posters and comics".

In fact, the Department for International Development stated quite clearly:

- Our view is that radio is, for the time being, the most cost effective ICT for enhancing the quality of education in the classroom. Radio remains the most widespread and accessible ICT in Africa. In some countries it has near universal penetration. The costs of producing educational material for radio are one tenth of the costs of producing material for television, which has much lower coverage and is more expensive to access.

In response to the educational needs of rural poor populations throughout the developing world, there are several large-scale operations conducting radio education projects. The Freeplay Foundation, the developers of the Lifeline Wind-up/Solar-Powered Radio, "is committed to ...ensuring sustained access to information and education via radio". According to the Freeplay Foundation's web site, "radio is the primary medium of communication in developing countries, where most people live below the poverty line..., therefore, is the lifeline of information." In support of its goals, the Freeplay Foundation has distributed radios in countries as diverse as Afghanistan, Indonesia and Zambia, among others.

As part of this process, the Freeplay Foundation "collaborates with in-country non-governmental organisations, government ministries, international organisations and broadcasters to ensure radio information and education reaches the widest possible rural populations." In order to do this, the foundation works with international and local broadcasters to assure that the content is appropriate. In addition, the foundation works with local populations to facilitate the creation of listening groups, distributing radios, and evaluating the impact of the programming. Another organization that is also working extensively with IRI is the International Education Systems division of the Educational Development Center, Inc. This programme "grew out of a concentrated focus on the use of technologies to expand access to basic education and improve its quality" and goes "beyond basic education in classrooms to design many radio-delivered education systems". Working in 25 developing countries, the IES is focused on improving the quality of teaching and learning and uses "traditional technologies such as radio to deliver interactive instruction where school systems have broken down or never existed, or to reach refugees, nomads and children who cannot afford to go to school".

Current Initiatives

There are numerous radio-education initiatives that have the education of primary-age children at their core occurring throughout the developing world.

The Sudan Radio Service

Serving adults at all levels throughout Sudan, this programme provides instruction concerning civic education, current events, health, general education, agriculture and animal husbandry, and culture, among other content areas. Programming is conducted primarily in Arabic, however it includes English and local languages such as Nuer and Dinka. Starting with 2 hours of daily programming in 2003, the current schedule includes 6 hours of daily programming, 3 hours in the morning and 3 in the evening.

Southern Sudan Interactive Radio Instruction

This project anticipates reaching over 100,000 children in grades 1 to 4 through daily half-hour radio programmes per grade. The lessons teach math, local language literacy, English, peace building, and life skills. The broadcasts are in English, with instructions for the local instructor to translate directions into the local language as may be necessary depending on the grade level and the subject matter.

In addition, SSIRI is developing an English language series for youth and adults consisting of 240 half-hour programmes ranging from beginning to advanced levels. In addition to teaching English, the programmes provide information on civic education, health, and numeracy. Finally, SSIRI has developed the first of several planned modules of radio programmes to support teacher training.

Zambia Quality Education Services Through Technology Project

This project "aims to improve the quality of basic education delivery systems". Serving rural, hard-to-reach students from grades 1 through 7, this programme teaches math, science, social studies, language, literacy, and Health. More than 1,100 hours of English-language radio content has been produced, and the radio instruction has reached "over 100,000 children in community schools and 120,000 in government schools." Also, this programme has piloted the use of iPods and cell phones in instructional settings.

Somali Interactive Radio Instruction Programme

Designed to reach students both in and out of the formal education system, this programme uses radio to reach students in grades 1 to 5 to teach Reading, Math and Life skills. Instruction is conducted in Somali, and has already reached nearly 120,000 students, and has a goal of reaching 400,000 students.

Somalia Distance Education Literacy Programme

As part of the BBC World Services Trust, this project used radio instruction to teach more than 10,000 Somalis basic literacy, numeracy, and life skills. Using teachers who were nominated by the community, this project allowed for substantial community involvement in determining when and where classes would be held. "Of the 10,908 people on Somdel, 9,000 passed their final exam. Of those, 70 per cent were women".

Farm Radio International

This organization works " in direct partnership with approximately 300 radio broadcasters in 39 African countries to fight poverty and food insecurity". Working mostly on the production end of the radio education continuum, this project researches and develops the scripts that are then used to produce content for delivery through the radio. With an emphasis on increasing food supplies in an ecologically sounds and environmentally sustainable fashion, this organization disseminates information about low cost, successful agricultural practices throughout Africa.

DATA (DIGITAL RADIO)

The oldest form of digital broadcast was spark gap telegraphy, used by pioneers such as Marconi. By pressing the key, the operator could send messages in Morse code by energizing a rotating commutating spark gap. The rotating commutator produced a tone in the receiver, where a simple spark gap would produce a hiss, indistinguishable from static. Spark-gap transmitters are now illegal, because their transmissions span several hundred megahertz. This is very wasteful of both radio frequencies and power.

The next advance was continuous wave telegraphy, or CW, in which a pure radio frequency, produced by a vacuum tube electronic oscillator was switched on and off by a key. A receiver with a local oscillator would "heterodyne" with the pure radio frequency, creating a whistle-like audio tone. CW uses less than 100 Hz of bandwidth. CW is still used, these days primarily by amateur radio operators. Strictly, on-off keying of a carrier should be known as "Interrupted Continuous Wave" or ICW or on-off keying.

Radioteletype equipment usually operates on short-wave and is much loved by the military because they create written information without a skilled operator. They send a bit as one of two tones using frequency-shift keying. Groups of five or seven bits become a character printed by a teleprinter. From about 1925 to 1975, radioteletype was how most commercial messages were sent to less developed countries. These are still used by the military and weather services.

Aircraft use a 1200 Baud radioteletype service over VHF to send their ID, altitude and position, and get gate and connecting-flight data. Microwave dishes on satellites, telephone exchanges and TV stations usually use quadrature amplitude modulation. QAM sends data by changing both the phase and the amplitude of the radio signal. Engineers like QAM because it packs the most bits into a radio signal when given an exclusive fixed narrowband frequency range. Usually the bits are sent in "frames" that repeat. A special bit pattern is used to locate the beginning of a frame.

Communication systems that limit themselves to a fixed narrowband frequency range are vulnerable to jamming. A variety of jamming-resistant spread spectrum techniques were initially developed for military use, most famously for Global Positioning System satellite transmissions. Commercial use of spread spectrum began in the 1980s. Bluetooth, most cell phones, and the 802.11b version of Wi-Fi each use various forms of spread spectrum.

Systems that need reliability, or that share their frequency with other services, may use "coded orthogonal frequency-division multiplexing" or COFDM. COFDM breaks a digital signal into as many as several hundred slower subchannels. The digital signal is often sent as QAM on the subchannels. Modern COFDM systems use a small computer to make and decode the signal with digital signal processing, which is more flexible and far less expensive than older systems that implemented separate electronic channels. COFDM resists fading and ghosting because the narrow-channel QAM signals can be sent slowly. An adaptive system, or one that sends error-correction codes can also resist interference, because most interference can affect only a few of the QAM channels. COFDM is used for Wi-Fi, some cell phones, Digital Radio Mondiale, Eureka 147, and many other local area network, digital TV and radio standards.

Heating

Radio-frequency energy generated for heating of objects is generally not intended to radiate outside of the generating equipment, to prevent interference with other radio signals. Microwave ovens use intense radio waves to heat food. Diathermy equipment is used in surgery for sealing of blood vessels. Induction furnaces are used for melting metal for casting, and induction hobs for cooking.

AMATEUR RADIO SERVICE

Amateur radio, also known as "ham radio", is a hobby in which enthusiasts are licensed to communicate on a number of bands in the radio frequency spectrum non-commercially and for their own enjoyment. They may also provide emergency and public service assistance. This has been very beneficial in emergencies, saving lives in many instances. Radio amateurs use a variety of modes, including nostalgic ones like Morse code and experimental ones like Low-Frequency Experimental Radio. Several forms of radio were pioneered by radio amateurs and later became commercially important, including FM, single-sideband, AM, digital packet radio and satellite repeaters. Some amateur frequencies may be disrupted by power-line internet service.

Unlicensed Radio Services

Unlicensed, government-authorized personal radio services such as Citizens' band radio in Australia, the USA, and Europe, and Family Radio Service and Multi-Use Radio Service in North America exist to provide simple, short range communication for individuals and small groups, without the overhead of licensing. Similar services exist in other parts of the world. These radio services involve the use of handheld units.

Free radio stations, sometimes called pirate radio or "clandestine" stations, are unauthorized, unlicensed, illegal broadcasting stations. These are often low power transmitters operated on sporadic schedules by hobbyists, community activists, or political and cultural dissidents. Some pirate stations operating offshore in parts of Europe and the United Kingdom more closely resembled legal stations, maintaining regular schedules, using high power, and selling commercial advertising time.

Radio Control

Radio remote controls use radio waves to transmit control data to a remote object as in some early forms of guided missile, some early TV remotes and a range of model boats, cars and airplanes. Large industrial remote-controlled equipment such as cranes and switching locomotives now usually use digital radio techniques to ensure safety and reliability. In Madison Square Garden, at the Electrical Exhibition of 1898, Nikola Tesla successfully demonstrated a radio-controlled boat. He was awarded U.S. patent No. 613,809 for a "Method of and Apparatus for Controlling Mechanism of Moving Vessels or Vehicles."

HISTORY

19th Century

The meaning and usage of the word "radio" has developed in parallel with developments within the field of communications and can be seen to have three distinct phases: electromagnetic waves and experimentation; wireless communication and technical development; and radio broadcasting and commercialization. Many individuals—inventors, engineers, developers, businessmen - contributed to produce the modern idea of radio and thus the origins and 'invention' are multiple and controversial. Early radio designs could not transmit sound or speech and were called the "wireless telegraph".

Development from a laboratory demonstration to a commercial entity spanned several decades and required the efforts of many practitioners. In 1878, David E. Hughes noticed that sparks could be heard in a telephone receiver when experimenting with his carbon microphone. He developed this carbon-based detector further and eventually could detect signals over a few hundred yards. He demonstrated his discovery to the Royal Society in 1880, but was told it was merely induction, and therefore abandoned further research.

Experiments, later patented, were undertaken by Thomas Edison and his employees of Menlo Park. Edison applied in 1885 to the U.S. Patent Office for his patent on an electrostatic coupling system between elevated terminals. The patent was granted as U.S. Patent 465,971 on December 29, 1891. The Marconi

Company would later purchase rights to the Edison patent to protect them legally from lawsuits.

In 1893, in St. Louis, Missouri, Nikola Tesla made devices for his experiments with electricity. Addressing the *Franklin Institute* in Philadelphia and the *National Electric Light Association*, he described and demonstrated the principles of his wireless work. The descriptions contained all the elements that were later incorporated into radio systems before the development of the vacuum tube. He initially experimented with magnetic receivers, unlike the coherers used by Guglielmo Marconi and other early experimenters.

A demonstration of wireless telegraphy took place in the lecture theater of the Oxford University Museum of Natural History on August 14, 1894, carried out by Professor Oliver Lodge and Alexander Muirhead. During the demonstration a radio signal was sent from the neighbouring Clarendon laboratory building, and received by apparatus in the lecture theater.

In 1895 Alexander Stepanovich Popov built his first radio receiver, which contained a coherer. Further refined as a lightning detector, it was presented to the Russian Physical and Chemical Society on May 7, 1895. A depiction of Popov's lightning detector was printed in the Journal of the Russian Physical and Chemical Society the same year. Popov's receiver was created on the improved basis of Lodge's receiver, and originally intended for reproduction of its experiments.

In 1895, Marconi built a wireless system capable of transmitting signals at long distances. In radio transmission technology, early public experimenters had made short distance broadcasts. Marconi achieved long range signalling due to a wireless transmitting apparatus and a radio receiver claimed by him. From Marconi's experiments, the phenomenon that transmission range is proportional to the square of antenna height is known as "Marconi's law". This formula represents a physical law that radio devices use. Marconi's experimental apparatus proved to be a complete, commercially successful radio transmission system. According to the *Proceedings of the United States Naval Institute* in 1899, the Marconi instruments had a " coherer, principle of which was discovered some twenty years ago, the only electrical instrument or device contained in the apparatus that is at all new". In 1896, Marconi was awarded British patent 12039, *Improvements in transmitting electrical impulses and signals and in apparatus there-for*, for radio. In 1897, he established a radio station on the Isle of Wight, England. Marconi opened his "wireless" factory in Hall Street, Chelmsford, England in 1898, employing around 50 people. Shortly after the 1900s, Marconi held the patent rights for radio.

20th Century

The next advancement was the vacuum tube detector, invented by Westinghouse engineers. On Christmas Eve, 1906, Reginald Fessenden used a synchronous rotary-spark transmitter for the first radio programme broadcast, from Ocean Bluff-Brant Rock, Massachusetts. Ships at sea heard a broadcast that included Fessenden playing *O Holy Night* on the violin and reading a passage from the Bible. This was, for all intents and purposes, the first transmission of what is now known as amplitude modulation or AM radio. The first radio news programme was broadcast August 31, 1920 by station 8MK in Detroit, Michigan, which survives today as all-news format station WWJ under ownership of the CBS network.

The first college radio station began broadcasting on October 14, 1920, from Union College, Schenectady, New York under the personal call letters of Wendell King, an African-American student at the school. That month 2ADD, later renamed WRUC in 1947, aired what is believed to be the first public entertainment broadcast in the United States, a series of Thursday night concerts initially heard within a 100-mile radius and later for a 1,000-mile radius. In November 1920, it aired the first broadcast of a sporting event. At 9 pm on August 27, 1920, Sociedad Radio Argentina aired a live performance of Richard Wagner's Parsifal opera from the Coliseo Theater in downtown Buenos Aires. Only about twenty homes in the city had receivers to tune in this radio programme. Meanwhile, regular entertainment broadcasts commenced in 1922 from the Marconi Research Centre at Writtle, England.

Sports broadcasting began at this time as well, including the first broadcast college football game. In 1943 the United States Supreme Court upheld Tesla's patent for radio, number 645,576, with the supreme court's justification that claim 16 in Marconi's related patent, number 763,772, contained nothing new not having been published earlier and registered by Tesla, Lodge, and others. After years of patent battles by Marconi's company, the United States Supreme Court, in the 1943 case "Marconi Wireless Telegraph co. of America v. United States", held regarding the priority of engineering advances concerning the invention of radio that "it is now held that in the important advance upon his basic patent Marconi did nothing that had not already been seen and disclosed". The decision effectively awarded priority of the invention of radio to Tesla and his 1893 presentation in St. Louis. Although Marconi claimed that he had no knowledge of prior art taken from Tesla's patents, the supreme court considered his claim false. In addition to the June 21, 1943 ruling made by the supreme court, the United States Court of Claims also invalidated the fundamental Marconi patent earlier, in 1935. This case defined radio by the statement: "A radio communication system requires two tuned circuits each at the transmitter and receiver, all four tuned to the same frequency." Because Tesla's 1897 patent for radio was intended for general transmission of energy, the court determined that Tesla's patent clearly was the first to disclose a system which could be used for wireless communication of intelligible messages and used the four-circuit tuned combination.

In contrast, related developments in the United Kingdom saw the British High Court uphold Marconi's British Patent 7,777 that was issued on April 26, 1900. This British patent held by Marconi disclosed a four-circuit system, which was strikingly similar to a four-circuit system disclosed in U.S. patent #645,576 that was issued earlier to Tesla on March 20, 1900. On the matter of invention, it is held that Marconi knowingly and unknowingly used the scientific and experimental work of many others who were devising their own radio tuning apparatus' around the same time, such as the work of American electrical engineer John Stone Stone who was issued several U.S. patents between 1904 and 1908. However, what made Marconi more successful than any other was his ability to *commercialize* radio and its associated equipment into a global business.

One of the first developments in the early 20th century was that aircraft used commercial AM radio stations for navigation. This continued until the early 1960s when VOR systems became widespread. In the early 1930s, single sideband and frequency modulation were invented by amateur radio operators. By the end of the decade, they were established commercial modes. Radio was used to transmit pictures visible as television as early as the 1920s. Commercial television transmissions started in North America and Europe in the 1940s.

In 1954, the Regency company introduced a pocket transistor radio, the TR-1, powered by a "standard 22.5 V Battery". In 1955, the newly formed Sony company introduced its first transistorized radio. It was small enough to fit in a vest pocket, and able to be powered by a small battery. It was durable, because it had no vacuum tubes to burn out. Over the next 20 years, transistors replaced tubes almost completely except for very high-power transmitter uses. By 1963, colour television was being regularly broadcast commercially and the first communication satellite, *Telstar*, was launched. In the late 1960s, the U.S. long-distance telephone network began to convert to a digital network, employing digital radios for many of its links. In the 1970s, LORAN became the premier radio navigation system. Soon, the U.S. Navy experimented with satellite navigation, culminating in the invention and launch of the GPS constellation in 1987. In the early 1990s, amateur radio experimenters began to use personal computers with audio cards to process radio signals. In 1994, the U.S. Army and DARPA launched an aggressive, successful project to construct a software-defined radio that can be programmed to be virtually any radio by changing its software programme. Digital transmissions began to be applied to broadcasting in the late 1990s.

THE SMCR MODEL

THE COMPETITION FOR AUDIENCES

In a poorly planned public communication programme, not only does the communicator stand to miss the audience entirely, either because of a poor selection of media or inadequate message preparation, but also, given the sizable charges for time and space, he or she may waste money in the process. Recognizing this waste compels business and political communicators to abandon seat-of-the-pants strategies. Over the years a good deal of practical experience, field research, and academic study have unfolded essential components of the communication process that serve to guide the business communicator in making intelligent decisions.

They assist the communicator in asking appropriate questions about the audience, media, issues at hand, and goals for the communication programme. Informed strategies enable the communicator to see important links among these components and the interrelationships that serve to explain how the manipulation of one component affects other components.

A useful starting point for an examination of the communication process is with the Berlo model, which records four principal components inherent in nearly all communication scenarios: a Source, a Message, a Channel, and a Receiver (SMCR). Certainly this is communication in its most basic form. A source sends a message through some kind of channel to a receiver. Who says what, how, and to whom? Nearly every communication event, no matter how simple or complex, involves these four components.

This elementary model is fundamentally simple yet beguilingly complex. It is accurate yet, it is not complete. Basic communication students study this model to gain an understanding of communication. We will use it here as a paradigm for complex public communication strategies.

The Source

The source, which in a majority of cases will be the company, spokesperson, or political candidate, is that individual or group who is perceived by a receiver as the originator of the message. Who does the receiver think is the source of a message?

For instance, when Bill Cosby performs E. F. Hutton's television commercials, there is a strong likelihood that Bill Cosby is considered by most television viewers to be the source of the message—not the investment firm. A senatorial candidate may hire a speech writer during a campaign, but when the candidate delivers that speech, he or she will be perceived by the audience to be the source of that message, not the speech writer.

Perceptions of the receiver, then, are critical in discussions of the source. Despite those who may be behind the scenes of a public communication, it is essential to consider audience perceptions of who the source may be.

Audience notions about the source are no small matter in the public communication process. The image projected by that source, as a composite of physical appearance, voice, demeanor, and more, may be the most critical feature of the entire communication event. That image determines the message acceptance by and the impact on an audience. A source that comes across well to audience members will promote attention and enhance the persuasiveness of the message. A source that fails to appeal to the intended audience will yield poor results.

Perhaps because the importance of the source has long been known to public communicators, a good deal of research in past years has focused on the characteristics associated with an effective source. Specifically, these studies have asked what makes a source believable to an audience and what enhances the capacity of that source to persuade an audience to accept the message. What is it that makes a source credible to an audience?

Although we will provide an in-depth examination for the purposes of this introduction we will note that in most studies three component parts constitute source credibility: trustworthiness, expertise, and charisma.

Trustworthiness deals with the inherent faith and confidence audience members place in the source. First, the source that does not have a stake in an issue and so stands to gain little from an audience's acceptance of a message will be viewed as more trustworthy. Additionally, if the source is known to audience members and has, over time, consistently provided good, honest, and accurate information, he or she will probably be perceived as trustworthy and the message viewed more positively. For years, CBS news anchor Walter Cronkite provided information that audiences perceived to be factual and believable, and so he was rated consistently as among the most trustworthy people in America.

Expertise is often measured by college degrees, years of experience in a field, awards, and citations for excellence. A source who can demonstrate expertise reveals his or her capacity to deal authoritatively with a topic. An aeronautical engineer will be perceived by audiences as having high expertise when discussing flight characteristics of a new aircraft. The president of a successful brokerage firm will be perceived as an expert on stock market matters. Note, however, that expertise is subject specific. Although the stockbroker may know Dow Jones, this investment expert is out of his or her element when discussing aeronautical designs. Audiences recognize these limitations and are quick to confine source expertise to subject areas.

Finally, charisma, or dynamism as it is sometimes called, is the peculiar quality possessed by some people that grants them special influence over others. Although this trait is ascribed to the source, it is really a matter of personality, appearance, and demeanor recognized by the receiver as compelling features of that source. Some audience members may sense strong charismatic qualities in a source, while others are unable to detect such presence. A teenager, for instance, may be driven to near hysteria by the magnetism of a rock star. The teen's parents, however, may not recognize anything remotely attractive in the same musician. Charisma, then, like trustworthiness and to a lesser extent expertise, is a trait perceived to reside in a source. Two features of source credibility emerge from this brief discussion. First, each of the component parts of credibility is imputed to the source by the receiver. It could be argued that the source may possess certain qualities of trustworthiness, expertise, and dynamism that can be measured on an absolute scale. For example, the source may have no evident stake in the issue at hand and may have consistently provided accurate information. Furthermore, this source may have college degrees to demonstrate expertise and may be an attractive person who can speak well and move audiences. Unless the intended receivers recognize and value these features, they are meaningless.

In sum, we can consider the credibility of a source only as a function of the receiver's perceptions. Therefore, public communicators should plan their strategy not only to get out the message but to get out the message about the messenger as well.

The second observation about source credibility also involves the receivers: Audience members vary considerably over what constitutes a credible source. Different receivers ascribe different levels of credibility to a source because of different value structures, exposure levels, interests, and a host of other factors that make one audience member unlike another. There is no such thing as a generic, highly credible source that can be effective with all audiences.

There are only some sources that are perceived as highly credible by some receivers. In order to maximize the benefits from selecting a highly credible source, the public communicator must carefully match source characteristics with concerns of the intended audience. Often this means the communicator must give up one audience in favour of another or develop a stratified campaign that presents different messages borne by different sources to different receiver groups. "One source fits all" may not work in any given campaign. We may need to reach young audiences with a sports figure, religious audiences with a member of the clergy, professional audiences with a respected authority in the field. To make such a determination, we must examine the group and the nature of the topic. These features of source credibility suggest a noteworthy dimension of complexity in the public communication process.

The Message

The messages you deliver as a business communicator will join the thousands of messages available to your intended receivers every day. People in this society are inundated with messages clamoring for their attention and demanding action. Everyone who has a product to sell, an idea to promote, or a candidate to elect wants desperately to get just a few moments of the receiver's attention. Public communicators must be aware, however, that public audiences are not without their defences. In order to cope with the glut of messages incoming from the media, direct mail, and other sources, people employ three psychological defences that save them from message overloads. Known as the "selectivity processes," these defences take place at three distinct stages of message processing.

First, selective exposure occurs when receivers simply choose not to pay attention to a message. They may either avoid the message entirely, for instance, by switching to another channel when the commercials come on or tossing a direct mail envelope, unopened, into the trash. They also may choose to avoid a message through a "gating" process that blocks from their awareness the information right in front of them. They simply choose not to notice it.

We have all sat in front of a television set and ignored commercials. We may talk with others in the room, pick up something to read, or just think about something else while the advertisement is underway. Indeed, the selective exposure process saves audiences from having to deal with more information than they are willing to consider.

If a receiver chooses to pay attention to a message, he or she still can defend against its effects with a selective perception strategy. Selective perception recognizes that audience members each come to a communication event with a different set of experiences, interests, and needs. Their interpretation of the message, accordingly, tends to match their preconceptions.

A speech by a GOP candidate may be viewed more positively by a Republican than a Democratic receiver because the Republican is predisposed to see good in candidates from his or her own party. Almost nothing the GOP candidate says, though, may be viewed positively by the Democrat. Each perceives the message differently because of general dissimilarities in outlook and group identification.

Finally, different receivers come away from a communication event with different recollections through a process of selective retention. We all remember what we wish to remember about a message. If the message has no particular appeal, we may choose to forget everything about it. Alternatively, we may remember only those portions of the message that hold some utility or attraction. Farmers may remember every detail of a weather forecast, while an office worker recalls only vaguely whether or not to carry an umbrella to the office. Children often remember minute details from television toy commercials long after such information has faded from adult memories.

Despite the best intentions of public communicators to get a message across, audience members have the final word on how that message is likely to affect them. Out of this discussion of messages comes this important observation: Public communication audiences are not undifferentiated masses that react in unison. Individual characteristics result in a wide array of responses. In order to have the greatest impact on the largest possible number of people in an audience, the business communicator must recognize how people process messages, anticipate their reception of and response to these messages, and develop a strategy that brings about a desired outcome within the audience. Experience and field research have disclosed a number of techniques that can assist the business communicator to develop messages that achieve desired results. Effective ways of presenting a message can help prevent receivers from blocking out the information. Techniques that take advantage of what is known about the way people process information can ensure the maximum impact of a message. Fundamental to all of these procedures is this recognition: The receiver lies at the heart of the communication process. Any attempt to impose a strategy that ignores this fact will probably fail.

The Channel

The channel is the means by which the message gets from the source to the receiver. For public communicators, this nearly always involves either the mass media or direct mail. We have already seen the extent to which American audiences are exposed to these channels where, on an average, we spend nearly ten hours every day watching, reading, or listening to some medium. Thus, public communicators do not have to encourage people to increase their media exposure. Instead, they must locate by medium the audiences they wish to reach, then use these channels as vehicles for their message.

It is helpful to recognize that people turn to the popular media for two general and basic reasons: to seek information and to seek entertainment. Of the two, entertainment seeking is for most audiences the dominant motive for media usage. Many experts believe even informational functions of the media must contain a good measure of entertainment in order to attract and retain large audiences.

The network evening newscasts, the most information oriented of television programming, are heavily adorned with entertainment features. Stories are selected for camera opportunities, and correspondents often are chosen more for their physical appearance and voice than for their journalistic prowess. Sets are bright and majestic; the new computer-generated graphics are far more elaborate than required simply to convey information. Human interest features now command large portions of the twenty two-minute newscasts. Among the accounts of hard news stories that ever make the air, most are compressed into thirty-second clips. Relatively unadorned, in-depth news programmes such as the "McNeil-Lehrer Report" have been relegated to public television stations, drawing no more than 2 per cent of American audiences.

Even news magazines, considered the highbrows of informational channels, blend into their news features a heavy measure of summaries, short analyses, quick reviews, as well as slick graphics, artwork, colour photography, and other graphic features that go beyond their informational function. We like our information short and we like it sweet.

In spite of or, more likely, because of the ornamentation of informational material, audiences continue to seek out media for information about people and events. Their motivations range from idle curiosity to a genuine need for information. In the first case, they may want to learn about events in another part of the world, not because they could possibly be affected directly, but because they find some satisfaction in knowing about things occurring beyond their immediate scope.

People also seek information because they have a direct and personal need. The media provide an ongoing catalogue of information about various products and services, the weather, local government decisions, sales at neighbourhood shops, and a host of other items that have day-to-day utility. Such information seeking by audience members is deliberate and often a matter of routine in daily media usage schedules. Businesses wishing to disseminate information will find details about customer information-seeking habits of considerable benefit in planning which media (or channels) to use in disseminating facts about their product or service. Of particular help will be details about the specific media usage patterns of different audience subgroups. Expect success only when there is a careful match between the selected medium and the desired audience.

Business communicators could solve many of their problems if audiences came to them for information. They could then become information brokers dispensing facts and figures, descriptions, and promotional material to those interested in their product or service. In such cases they would work only with those who expressed a need for information and would avoid those who did not. Such a system would be efficient and relatively inexpensive—it would also be unlikely. In today's market, business communicators must actively promote among audience members a desire for information. They must use every known technique to deliver their messages in an interesting, compelling form. Their goal is to stimulate receivers to learn about and develop an interest in their product or service, with the ultimate objective of selling goods or ideas.

Much information, then, comes to unwitting receivers. Information acquired in a forum where that information was not sought and learning was not intentional is referred to as "incidental" learning. Television viewing provides a good example. People, of course, watch television to be entertained, not to be educated (or persuaded) by commercial messages. In the process of being entertained, however, they are exposed to advertisements that attempt to persuade, inform, or in some way affect them.

An entire industry of television (and most other media) advertising is predicated on the expectation that even though audiences may have selected a medium by which to be entertained, they are nonetheless likely to learn from or be persuaded by commercial messages that accompany that entertainment. From this view, entertainment serves to lure, to attract, and to hold viewers long enough to subject them to commercial advertisements.

Information transfer from the communicator to the audience, then, may occur as a result of information seeking when receivers search actively for information or as a result of incidental learning when information acquisition is a by-product of the entertainment. Channel selection in each case may be quite different. Audiences seek certain media as a source of information.

They use others primarily for entertainment. The nature of the channel, the audience, and the message must factor into decisions by public communicators if they are to select the best media mix for the information/ persuasion task.

The Receiver

Although the receiver appears last in the Berlo model, we view public communication as a receiver-centric process. Recognizing the receiver is central to all aspects of a communication. It is not only a healthy philosophy that demonstrates concern for audience needs, it is a necessary component in a strategy that guarantees the greatest audience impact.

To underscore points made, we argue that source characteristics of trustworthiness, expertise, and charisma cannot be viewed by some absolute set of criteria but from the perceptions of receiver groups. It is more useful to regard credibility as a source characteristic inferred by the receiver than as possessed by the source. Similarly, the efficacy of a message is not absolute. Some messages work with some audiences and some work with others.

There are no guidelines one can follow to craft a message that will have an equal and effective impact on all audiences because messages are audience specific. Public communicators need to examine the specific requirements of individual audience groups and shape messages that specifically attract their attention and make an appeal to their interests and sensitivities. Finally, for purposes of public communication, the media (or channels of communication) can be defined only in terms of their audiences. A message delivered over a channel that is not attended by desired audiences misses any hope of having an impact. Costs of poor channel selection can be high in terms of programme success and budget.

Not only does the receiver have a bearing on these other components of the communication process, but also a variety of receiver characteristics, in and of themselves, are important. It is necessary to understand receiver groups along several dimensions, the most fundamental of which are demographic categories. What are their ages, income levels, and educational traits? Depending on the issues under consideration, it may be important to identify audience members' religious backgrounds and political party affiliations, their marital status, and number of children. Other demographic features may be appropriate depending on specific subject material. Beyond demographic traits that place audience members in distinct population classes, it is often essential to develop a more complete understanding of audiences with specific reference to the issues at hand. What are the general political attitudes among those who plan to vote Democratic or to support a county referendum? What do we know about those people who plan to buy a new car or take a vacation this summer or who eat at fast food restaurants at least twice a week? Answers to these sorts of questions can be important in the development of a marketing and communication campaign strategy.

THE PERSONAL NATURE OF PUBLIC MESSAGES

Differences between an interpersonal and a mass communication event involve more than just the number of people participating.

Although the size of the audience is worth considering, such a recognition neither has heuristic value to the public communicator nor does it suggest several other significant distinctions. In order to serve the purposes of communication planners, we will propose several important differences that not only distinguish interpersonal from mass communication, but also that ultimately will suggest various communication strategies.

The nature of feedback or the flow of information from the receiver to the source is one of the major differences between interpersonal and mass communication events. The principle of feedback was recognized in biological and physical sciences long before it was applied to the study of human communication. Biological homeostasis is maintained through a complex network of feedback mechanisms that report temperature, chemical balance, and other information about the status of the body.

The brain receives and coordinates this information and, in a normally functioning system, if conditions depart much from a narrow margin, responds to bring them back to normal. For instance, in the human body, when biological "gauges" detect an overheating condition, they transmit a signal to the brain that responds with appropriate directions to the sweat glands, blood vessels, and skin pores to "air condition" the system. As these measures take effect, feedback signals again go to the brain and the cooling system is turned down. This process is in constant operation, allowing the body to send continuing messages to those organs that keep the body operating properly.

Examples of cybernetics or the study of automatic feedback control systems are plentiful in the physical sciences as well. Home-heating and -cooling units utilize feedback signals from thermostats to regulate burners and refrigeration coils. Turboprop aircraft engines maintain precise speed through delicate sensors that regulate the flow of fuel and pitch of the propeller. Complex systems such as spacecrafts, submarines, and even new model automobiles rely on feedback control systems.

The quality of feedback is important in determining its value to the system. Quick, accurate feedback provides the information necessary for an appropriate and effective response to conditions. Delayed or incorrect information contributes to a breakdown of the entire interactive process. False information from sensors in rocket motors has caused more than a few catastrophes in the space programme.

Although there are vast differences among systems presented in the previous examples, the common element among them is feedback, or the transmission of information. Moreover, a unit of information (or the message) presented at one point is dependent in part on messages that precede it and will affect those that follow it. This is true for maintenance of temperature in the human body, for conditions aboard a space vehicle, and for the entire range of human communication activities.

It may be evident that the exchange of information within a physical system helps regulate functioning of that system, but how such information factors into the human communication process may not be as obvious. Imagine having a conversation over a telephone that has a broken earpiece. Under such conditions, you can talk to someone but cannot hear the response. Furthermore, you obviously have no visual cues on which to base a conclusion about the success or failure of your attempts to communicate with your "silent" partner. In other words, you are unable to obtain any information from the other party—you cannot receive any feedback. Such a one-sided conversation would soon deteriorate and the process end.

While this interpersonal communication example describes an obvious outcome of feedback deprivation, such a problem, commonplace in public or mass communication, often goes unrecognized. Public communicators—business communicators—routinely send messages to intended audiences without ever receiving or examining information from receivers, who, after all, are the other participants in the communication event. Such a unidirectional flow of information is as illogical in these mass communication settings as a conversation over a telephone with a broken earpiece. In each case the communicator has no sense about the reception of the message. There is no way of knowing if the receiver understands what is being said, is being persuaded by the arguments, or, in fact, is listening at all. In both instances messages may be ineffective or may be falling on deaf ears. No one may be listening.

Feedback lies at the heart of any communication event—mass or interpersonal. We must have some information about the reception of our messages in order to know whether or not we are successfully affecting our intended audiences. Conversations proceed incrementally. Each portion takes into account and reflects previous messages that set a tone and provide context for the interaction.

The next sentence in our conversation will be predicated largely on the previous sentence offered by the other person. Feedback from others in the conversation—or our audience—keeps us from talking to ourselves. No less is true of a mass communication event, which shares a common structure with these interpersonal settings. Both involve a message, a source, a channel, and a receiver. Both require the source to have some information about the receiver in order to initiate the communication process (even if it is just knowing a receiver is listening), and both are certain to fail if there is not ongoing feedback providing information about how well the message is being received.

It is often easier to recognize the more visible problems of inadequate feedback in interpersonal than in mass communication. First, in the interpersonal setting, results generally are more immediate.

We know quickly if another person in the conversation is listening or not. We know quickly whether or not we are being understood and often get a prompt indication about the success of our attempts at persuasion. Also, in the interpersonal context, we are able to sort out better the effects of our specific messages from the effects of other messages. Often in the mass communication setting, an assortment of messages go to our audiences, making it difficult to determine the impact of our particular message. Finally, in the interpersonal setting, we usually have available a much wider selection of cues from which to conclude reactions to our messages.

In face-to-face encounters, we can read body language, observe facial expressions, and learn a good deal of information from vocal intonations that may reveal true feelings or provide more accurate detail about a person's reactions. As mass communicators though, we may discover the quality of feedback available is not as rapid, specific, or rich with detail. So because of difficulty in obtaining feedback or interpreting it, we may ignore the need for it. Business communicators are notorious for conceiving a communication strategy based on hunches and guesswork rather than on solid information about audience needs and interests, media usage patterns, and reactions to earlier messages. In these times when people are confronted with more information every day than they can possibly take in, there is great competition for public attention. Moreover, media charges for time and space are extremely costly, contributing to a compound problem.

The business communicator may be spending a great deal of money to develop and send messages that either cannot compete with other messages and so are not heard at all, or are not particularly effective in persuading or informing an audience even if they are heard. The inherent problem with such an approach is that it ignores the audience in the following ways:

- The communicator decides what he or she wants to tell the audience (without considering what people already know or wish to know or how they feel about the topic).
- The communicator decides where the message will be disseminated (without first confirming that the audience is attending the selected medium).

- The communicator then does nothing to listen for an audience response.

Feedback information (used here in the loose sense to mean any information from receivers) before, during, and after the communication campaign has been ignored. Predictable results are, as in the one-way phone conversation, that this communication scenario will not succeed. The communicator has wasted company time and money.

For business communication this is absolutely crucial—not in any academic sense, but in a pragmatic sense. With acceptance of this premise, the entire process of business communication shifts emphasis. Business communication goals and objectives must not begin with hunches, but with feedback data from desired audiences. The communication process must begin where the messages end; or, to take this one step farther, communications end where they begin. If they originate in the imagination of a communicator and fail to involve feedback information, they will have little impact on intended audiences.

THE NATURE OF AUDIENCES

Audiences today are a complex aggregate of people, varied in their lifestyles, needs, and capacity to process information. Popular currents stream through these large populations, but on most matters there exist subgroups that hold individual views and express unique responses. Consequently, the notion of mass communication, which we, should be dispelled and replaced with the concept of targeted, directed, tailored communication. A single message cannot convey the essence of a theme to an entire population. It takes a variety of messages, each developed with a different pitch, to blanket that population.

There can be no single mass message because there is no single mass audience. There are only clusters of smaller audiences, and even these are ephemeral groups, ad hoc, coalesced around only a single issue at a single time. Business communicators must focus on these subgroups. The communicator, by obtaining feedback information, must discover these groups, learn about them, know their needs and their habits, learn what appeals to them and what repels them. The communicator must learn about the character of these groups, discover how they react and how they interact. Businesses must learn about these transitory collections of audiences, and they must move with them when they disband and re-form in new clusters around other issues.

A snapshot is not sufficient. The world these days is too dynamic. There are too many events. There is too much information competing for people's time and attention. The camera must always be kept running. The business communicator must constantly monitor the changing mood of audiences as events impact on them and they proceed through rapid evolution, day by day, event by event. The central problem faced by public communicators concerns the means they use to gain an understanding of—obtain feedback information from-their audiences. Few, if any, of us have an intuition capable of sorting among large audience populations and arriving at a formula that holds the calculus of their needs, interests, and potential responses. The complexity of this task far exceeds the capacity of any individual. Given the current state of technology, though, both hardware in the form of computer technology and social science procedures for audience measurement, the public communicator has available a wide range of techniques that can provide accurate, thorough, and timely information about potential audiences.

Information gathered through well-recognized methods can provide the feedback so necessary to begin and to sustain a communication programme. With this knowledge about desired audiences, communicators can cultivate an appropriate image of the business as a message source, shape a meaningful and effective message, and select suitable channels to reach that audience.

Beyond providing feedback information, audience assessment techniques are notably successful at identifying, defining, and characterizing subgroups in larger audience populations. In other words, these methods of audience measurement provide the specifications necessary for audience targeting. Targeting, involves the recognition that many smaller, unique, and identifiable groups comprise the general population. Targeting seeks to reach them individually with messages designed to have specific appeal. Theoretically, targeting renders public communication more like interper-sonal communication. Its considerable advantages include addressing individual needs specifically, not just general concerns with a generic, one-size-fits-all message. As competition for audience attention grows, communicators must find it increasingly important to focus their messages and fashion them to deal with individual concerns.

We will examine techniques of accessing specialized, targeted audiences, not as a supplement to reaching large, public audiences, but as an alternative to it. Some businesses, because of the nature of their product or service, may need to single out a narrow portion of the population. Targeting in such instances is an obvious strategy. Others may wish to reach broader audience sections but may choose to do so by subdividing those larger audiences for more specific handling, using the targeting techniques advocated here. Both instances involve similar procedures.

MASS VERSUS TARGETED AUDIENCES

From a theoretical point of view as well as for practical application, think about mass and targeted audiences as lying along a continuum of audience characteristics. Such a scheme places at one end audiences with a homogeneous set of traits and at the other audiences with heterogeneous traits. In the first case, audience members are all alike with regard to a particular feature. For instance, they may all be Republican or all owners of sporting goods stores or all have similar attitudes towards tax reform. In this portion of the continuum, audiences can be identified as sharing some identifiable, common characteristic that links them and provides a common bond. Audiences at the other end of the continuum represent a great blending of characteristics that hold contrasts and evident distinctions. People in these heterogeneous audiences may come from all political parties, work at different jobs in different industries, and share no common philosophies. In their issues of concern, such eclectic audiences display no apparent similarities. They are identified by their diversity and are alike only in the consistency of their differences.

For purposes of discussion and planning, we will identify homogeneous groups as targeted or narrow audiences and heterogeneous groups as mass or general audiences. In dealing with these two categories, we employ communication strategies that differ in several dimensions. First, our choice and presentation of the message source will vary. For the targeted group, we will select a source that has particular appeal to and credibility among audience members we wish to pinpoint. In source selection for the mass audience, we will attempt to appeal to the greatest portion of the group by choosing and displaying a source with the greatest general acceptance.

The topics we select and the messages we develop also vary considerably between these two audience categories. For targeted audiences we can become focused and specific and provide arguments that meet the particular needs and expectations of audience members.

The best we can do with mass audiences is to develop a generic message that attempts to embrace the largest possible number of people. Such messages are often measured by their success at having the greatest meaning and the least offence to the largest audience (which often means aiming at the lowest common denominator). Finally, the channels we employ for these audiences differ considerably.

With targeted audiences we use a prudent approach. We disseminate information through channels that appeal specifically to people of concern to us. Trade and association publications reach people in specific professions. Radio stations reach people with particular tastes in music who can often be narrowly defined by demographic features. Direct mail enables the communicator to provide specific information on a one-to-one basis.

For mass audiences we usually turn to television or newspapers that best deliver audiences that are heterogeneous or have a blending of traits. During prime time, for instance, television audiences represent a cross section of the population with people from all demographic, professional, and ideological quarters—in other words, audiences that meet the definition of heterogeneity.

Two observations underscore the approach to specialized communication adopted: First, targeted communication is nearly always more efficient and successful than mass communication; second, even large, heterogeneous mass audiences can be, and nearly always should be, subdivided into component target audiences. Targeted communication enables the public communi-cator to engage in a communication scenario like interpersonal communication. Armed with thorough and accurate audience research data (feedback information), communicators can shape their messages to meet the particular needs of homoge-neous audience blocks.

The communicator can employ precisely the arguments, techniques, and approaches that best respond to the receiver through the iterative process of two people in a conversation. Targeted communication is incisive, effective, and more streamlined than the alternative mass communication approaches, which often have enormous waste. Mass communication has some use for products and services that, like water and air, are resources used by everyone. As long as one can argue that products have differential appeal among audience members, though, one must consider dividing these general audiences into component units.

Consider, for example, a political candidate running for congressional office.

First, the candidate obviously wants the largest number of votes possible and needs support from people of all ages, races, income brackets, and political parties. Second, the candidate (or the "product," from the marketing perspective) embodies a collection of traits that may appeal differently to individual quarters of the voting population. In other words, some features of this candidate will interest some voters and other features will appeal to other voters. Although a successful candidate must attract a wide range of audiences, the best strategy to win greatest support is not by treating this audience as a single, undifferentiated unit but by dividing it into blocks for individual treatment.

Audience feedback data, for instance, may suggest that the candidate's position on social security is particularly strong with the elderly, or the position on development tax appealing to the business community, or the stand on foreign policy pleasing to conservatives. Dividing voter audiences into specific target groups for individual handling will be far more successful than running a generic campaign that treats the entire population as a single blended mass.

At the heart of targeted communication lies a recognition that receivers are the foremost factor in the equation. We must first identify receiver needs and interests before we can determine what our message should concern or how it should be presented.

We must know what our particular receivers look for in a source and what kind of source they will trust and consider credible. Only with this information can we select and portray our source in a way that maximizes audience impact. We also need to learn about specific media usage habits of target audience groups in order to determine which channels we should use. We may find a half-dozen or more target groups in the mass audience and so prepare a communication strategy that provides separate tracks for each. From this orientation arises the view of audience-based communication presented. It is essential that the business communicator recognize the logic and practical utility of beginning the process by considering the receiver.

This book focuses on the techniques of obtaining audience information and provides a thorough discussion of ways to interpret and use this information to develop successful, efficient, audience-based communication programmes.

DEVELOPMENT OF PUBLIC OPINION

The "public" in the United States is composed of all of its people, some 240 million people. In general, all we mean by "public opinion" is the views held by a majority (or very large number) of the people in the country at any one time about any event or series of events. In order to determine what public opinion is about an event, we simply ask a large number of people how they feel about a particular topic. If we find that most of the people we ask feel generally the same way, we usually can write statements that begin with "Public opinion seems to be united on this topic." If we find great differences of opinion, with some people favoring the topic, some opposed to it, and many neutral, we might find the report beginning with "Public opinion is divided on this topic."

Knowing the level of public opinion, however, is not enough. We still need some insight into how the opinion process works. For that understanding, we turn to the individual and examine the process of attitude formation. All we mean by an "attitude" is the feelings of liking or disliking we all have towards people, places, events, and ideas.

We have attitudes about dogs, cats, gasoline, rationing, and businesses. We have attitudes about friends, coworkers, wives, children, and legislators; about movies, education, politics, and religion. We form attitudes about all of the events that occur in our daily lives. The actual attitudes we hold will generally be the result of our experiences with people, ideas, and events. If we meet a teacher who is helpful to us, we are likely to hold favorable attitudes towards teachers. If we were bitten by a dog when we were very young, we may have a negative attitude towards dogs.

Attitudes can range from highly favorable to neutral to highly unfavorable. They can also be held with various degrees of intensity. I may be highly favorable towards a certain product, but it does not fill all my thoughts. I do not try to sell the product to others, do not try to have it adopted by my company or to convince others to use it.

I just do not hold a very intense attitude towards the product. In another case the situation might be different. I might be highly unfavorable towards abortion and also feel highly intensely about the subject. I might well write letters to the newspaper, try to get a new law passed prohibiting abortion, avoid socializing with people who favour abortion, and vote only for candidates who favour antiabortion legislation. Clearly, it is important to distinguish between the nature of the attitude held, that is, favorable or unfavorable, and the degree of intensity with which the attitude is held. As managers we might become concerned if we found that a large number of people held unfavorable attitudes towards our company. But we would become greatly concerned if we found that many of those same people were filing petitions to increase our taxes by increasing our assessed valuation. The latter group is not only unfavorable, but holds its attitudes intensely enough to operate in accordance with them.

We have said that individuals hold attitudes towards all of the people, objects, events, and ideas that they meet in their daily lives. Those attitudes do not seem to be held completely in isolation from one another. Instead, we tend to "group" attitudes into larger sets that we can term "frames of reference." When individuals build up a pattern of attitudes towards a set of objects or ideas based on past experience, they then tend to use this frame of reference as a way of assessing events or experiences or messages that may appear in the future. Thus, we might expect that an individual would develop a reference frame based on all the experiences he or she may have had with similar businesses.

There may be some favorable experiences and thus favorable attitudes towards the water company. There may be favorable attitudes towards a telephone company repairman. There may be unfavorable attitudes towards a service representative at the telephone company. That total set of attitudes towards utilities can be called the individual's frame of reference about utilities.

Why is the frame of reference important? There are two main reasons why behavioural scientists think this is so. First, the existing reference frame that an individual possesses tends to govern the ways in which new experiences are perceived. Thus, the individual who has had a whole series of negative experiences with one supermarket is very likely to approach any new contact with that supermarket in a negative manner. Such an approach may be neither logical nor rational, but behavioural scientists are inclined to think that rationality is not as important to attitude development as the kind of past experiences we have had. The obvious implication for a manager, for example, is the importance of long-range programmes. It is not enough to make an individual happy on the first visit to a store or when a product or service is first purchased. Efforts must be made to continue the flow of favorable experiences to the customer.

The second major reason why frames of reference are important is that they tend to govern future behaviour. The frame of reference is composed of a set of attitudes. An individual who is exposed to a new situation and who has a favorable attitude towards the situation is likely to behave favorably. An individual who approaches a new situation with an unfavorable attitude is likely to behave by avoiding the situation.

A simple example will illustrate this relationship between attitudes and behaviour. Imagine two children. One child was bitten by a dog when he was three years old. The other was given a puppy for Christmas when she was three and has always loved it. What happens when the two children are approached by a large police dog on the streets? The child who was bitten is likely to run away. The child who loves her own dog is likely to pet this new dog. Note that neither behaviour may be "rational." This dog might be friendly, in which case running away is not an appropriate behaviour. Or the dog might be unfriendly, in which case attempting to pet the dog is not appropriate. But the children behaved as their set past attitudes dictated. The frame of reference they had developed helped govern behaviour.

We must hasten to note that not all behaviour is directly governed by attitudes. Many people are prejudiced against members of minority groups. But that does not mean that someone meeting a member of a minority group on the street will automatically run over and hit the person. Our behaviour is also determined by laws, customs, fear of retaliation, and other influences. That we may not always behave as our attitudes would indicate, however, is important to the individual attempting to make an assessment of public opinion and its possible consequences. For example, suppose we hold a series of public meetings and find very few people who say anything negative about a bond issue.

But when the vote is taken, the bond issue fails miserably. What happened? The fact is that few people are willing to express themselves in public meetings. They worry that they may be the only ones opposed to the bond issue, so they keep quiet. They may not want to offend the individual conducting the meeting, so they say nothing. In the privacy of the voting booth, their behaviour is governed more directly by their attitudes.

The fact that not all attitudes lead directly to behaviour should not lead to the conclusion that attitudes are not important. Making a careful assessment as to the state of individual attitudes, and thus the attitudes of a population, is one of the best ways we have to predict the eventual outcome of a proposal, a law, a bond issue, or a price increase.

One other matter should be understood about the frames of reference we possess. We have said that we tend to group all of the attitudes we hold about the ideas, events, or people associated with an area into similar reference frames. Thus, we might expect an individual to have attitudes about a product, about the manufacturer, and about expenses incurred from purchase of that product. The same individual might not have strong attitudes towards managers of that company, if only because there may never have been an association between a manager and the company he or she represents. However, if that association is made, and the manager is featured in a newspaper story or radio feature or television announcement, it is likely the manager will now be perceived in a fashion similar to that used to perceive the other events in the frame of reference. If the individual has a generally favorable reference frame, the likelihood is that the manager will be initially perceived as favorable. If the frame of reference is negative, the likelihood is that the manager also will be initially perceived as negative. In other words, new ideas, new events, and new people are viewed against the backdrop of the reference frames that people possess.

This is one of the central reasons why it is important to send messages stressing the positive aspects of everything connected with the affairs of a business. If someone is exposed to a series of messages in the local newspaper that are constantly negative towards a business, its employees, and operation, it is not likely that one or two positive contacts with that business will be able to undo all of the negative information. However, if that same person picked up the local newspaper, found the negative stories, but had a positive frame of reference for the business based on a long history of positive contacts, the effect of the newspaper story should be quite different. The positive frame of reference should mean that the negative story will not have the same effect on the reader as it might if the reader had a negative frame of reference or had not developed a strong reference frame.

We are now ready to move to a discussion of public opinion and of ways of helping to modify or to maintain certain levels of public opinion. We know individuals form attitudes as the result of contacts with their environment. We know people tend to group their attitudes into reference frames. And we know that people tend to react to new ideas, new experiences, and new people in ways that are dependent on their reference frames.

PUBLIC OPINION

The term "public opinion" has a long history. In 1922 Walter Lippmann published his famous book entitled Public Opinion. Lippmann utilized the concept of a stereotype to build a definition of public opinion. People utilize the experiences they have, the books they have read, and the messages they have received to build a "picture in their heads" of how the world is. The picture may be right or wrong, but it is this individual picture that people use to govern their behaviour. Only when sufficiently strong contradictory information is encountered will people change their stereotype. Lippmann suggests that those people who have had similar experiences will tend to have similar stereotypes, and thus public opinion can be determined by looking at people of similar socioeconomic class, similar education, and similar geographic area. Lippmann's concept of stereotype, of course, is very much like the frame of reference concept we have already used. We prefer "frame of reference," because the term "stereotype" has come to have a negative connotation.Today, there are many ways of measuring or assessing what attitudes are held by individuals within the society (Scott, 1968). We can use those methods to get an estimate of the attitudes held by a random sample of the people in a community, a state, or the entire country.

We define public opinion as the majority opinion or set of attitudes held by the members of a population. This procedure is used every day by market opinion research firms, political polling firms, and social psychologists. Many of these studies are done on a national basis, and are intended to give a picture of what the general public may feel about governmental policies, political issues, or foreign affairs.Many managers, of course, will not find these general studies very useful in the daily business of managing a supermarket, a plastics-manufacturing plant, or a restaurant. For example, presumably we could ask a number of people about their attitudes towards coffee tables, or sliced bread, or blue rugs. We would certainly be able to determine what the majority attitudes were towards each of these three objects. But the probability is that none of these attitudes will be held with any degree of intensity.

It is also likely that most people will be either neutral towards these topics or only very mildly favorable or unfavorable. Unless we happen to be in the business of selling blue rugs, the time and expense of trying to find out what public opinion is for relatively minor topics or issues are seldom worth it.As managers, the fact that people are seldom interested about blue rugs or any other events that are not of crucial importance poses a dilemma. If we do not monitor public opinion in some way, before we may recognize it, a very minor matter may be blown into a major event. On the other hand, spending the money to make constant analyses of public opinion in a community may not be justified. What is needed is some way of cheaply monitoring public attitudes such that potential crises can be identified in time for more adequate measures to be taken. Below are offered some specific suggestions for any managers interested in such monitoring:

- Set up a Procedure for Systematically Logging and Classifying Letters and Telephone Calls from Clients, Customers, or Citizens.
- Most of these calls and letters will fall into common patterns and will deal with service or rate or payment problems. But problems of a potentially more serious nature can sometimes be identified by changes in the flow of letters and calls. When this happens, the manager can implement more accurate research about the state of public opinion in the community.
- Encourage Public Comments by Providing Space on Monthly or Quarterly Bills. You will typically receive very few such comments, but those that are received can sometimes lead to the identification of emerging issues before they become a major problem.
- Use Suggestion Boxes or Feedback Letters to Solicit Comments. Many motels and restaurants provide forms that people can mark

and send back to evaluate the nature of the service. Relatively few people ever send back such forms, but those who do usually identify problems previously unknown to managers, who can make corrections. There is no reason why such suggestion boxes and feedback forms should be confined to hotels and restaurants. Many businesses would benefit from these attempts to tap into public opinion.

- Monitor the Opinion Leaders in a Community. Every community has individuals who are influential with certain groups of people. They may be ministers, labour leaders, local store owners, or even local politicians. They are members of the community who see and talk to a lot of people. Frequently, problems that may arise in the community are identified and passed on by opinion leaders. Attendance at civic functions, labour picnics, church groups, and other such meetings can frequently provide information of real value about the potential state of public opinion in a community.

One caution needs to be added. One of the most frequent mistakes made by managers is attending only those functions where they know everybody and are, in fact, opinion leaders for those groups. Such groups are comfortable places to be, but will probably add little new information and almost never provide disturbing information. An attempt must be made to get information from all segments of the community.

MONITOR THE LOCAL MEDIA IN A SYSTEMATIC FASHION

Many large companies subscribe to a monitoring service that provides newspaper clippings. I urge all companies to do the same even if the service is on a smaller scale. Stories in news columns, editorials, and letters to the editor will frequently be forerunners of major problems that can arise in a community. The business that has a carefully planned monitoring service may well be able to anticipate problems from the local, state, and national news and comments. Monitor Legislative Bodies and Potential Legislation. Many large companies already monitor such activities, but there is no reason why even small businesses should not do so.

It may be possible for a number of interested firms to join together to hire an analyst who will inform member firms about potential legislation that could affect business success or failure. The activities of legislators may not seem directly related to public opinion. Usually, however, there is a fairly direct relationship between legislative activity and the state of public opinion about an area. Legislators do have their fingers on the pulse of the majority of the voters or are influenced by those voters in a city or state who are most influential. Activity on the legislative front is almost always an excellent barometer of public opinion about any topic.

These suggestions are designed to let managers identify potential changes in public opinion before they emerge as serious and difficult problems. This kind of monitoring effort, however, cannot exist in isolation. If companies are to establish a favorable image and thus have potential problems viewed from positive frames of reference, communication and public information campaigns must be conducted on a continuing basis. Most frequently, that is not what is done. The company "goes into action" when a price increase is needed or when something negative appears in the press. Much of the rest of the time, there are relatively few efforts to establish dialogue with a community.

A real example, but with the name of the company omitted, illustrates the situation. A major utility was in the midst of requesting a major rate increase because of the increased cost of supplies. The case generated considerable public interest, and the public response to the increase was strongly negative. The response included marches on the Public Service Commission, threats of lawsuits, organized letter campaigns, and the other accompaniments of aroused public opinion. The outcome of the case is still in doubt, but the utility's behaviour leading to the rate increase request was not. I examined every local newspaper for a two-month period prior to the news release announcing the request for a rate increase. I found exactly three stories that pertained to the utility itself. One announced a minor change in personnel. Two were good public relations stories about the company, picked up by several area weekly newspapers.

In none of these stories was there any mention of activities of any company top management or any suggestion of problems that might cause a rate hike.The point is that this company went into a major rate situation with a public image that could, at best, be described as "neutral." In such a situation, the announcement of a major rate increase cannot help but be viewed as negative by the public. There was no backlog of goodwill built up. There were apparently no credible individuals within the utility that could have explained the situation. If a steady public information campaign had taken place over the three- or four-month period prior to the announcement, the probability is that the public furor would have been far less. I would not want to argue that some negative public reaction would not have taken place at all, but I will argue that the level of objections might have been considerably lessened if the company had engaged in an effective public information campaign before making the rate announcement. Below are some suggestions that managers might use in considering efforts at modifying public opinion:

MAKE USE OF ALL THE LOCAL MEDIA IN A COMMUNITY TO GIVE INFORMATION TO THE GENERAL PUBLIC

This is a principle that is frequently forgotten. The local daily newspaper is flooded with feature stories and announcements. Much of what is sent to them is tossed away. But in almost any community of even fair size, there are weekly newspapers, "shoppers" of various types, union newsletters, college papers, local magazines, board of education publications, local library bulletin boards, and other potential outlets. Many of these are excellent sources for stories about local people and local companies. Local television stations are usually inundated with stories. But the local radio station may well use feature stories and do local interviews. The local cable network is frequently open to local industries. The communications specialist should attempt to make use of all potential media.

Become as Publicly Visible as Possible. What we know about attitudes and attitude formation suggests that people form stronger attitudes about people than they do about ideas or events. But when there are only weak attitudes held towards people associated with an idea, an event, or a company, the evidence suggests that the negative idea can also "rub off" negatively on individuals associated with it. If, however, there are strong positive attitudes towards the individual, it is possible to propose even negative ideas and have them accepted without seriously damaging the credibility of the individual. For many managers this is an unusual idea to accept. Individuals are usually selected for top management positions because of their technical expertise, and not because of their ability to "make friends and influence people." I am suggesting we ought to encourage top management to take stronger interests in civic affairs, be willing to make speeches and be interviewed by the press, be available for interviews, and take a stronger interest in the state of public opinion within their community. Only in such fashion can individuals build personal credibility and have at least a chance of overcoming negative publicity.

MAKE POSITIVE USE OF ALL EMPLOYEES AS CHANNELS OF PUBLIC INFORMATION

Many companies recognize this principle and systematically give their employees information about upcoming events, problems, and proposals. Many other companies do not, and employees read about a new idea in the local newspaper along with their neighbours. This failure to inform employees is a mistake. Imagine the attitude of an employee who goes home after work and is greeted by his next door neighbour with the words, "Hi Jim. I see in the paper where you guys are going to raise prices again." If the employee knows nothing about the increases, he is made to feel like a dunce in front of his neighbours. A far better situation would obtain if the employee could answer, "Yes Bob, but they aren't going to start until next month, and we're going to have a sale next week. The cost of raw materials just won't stop climbing." This ability to answer makes the employee more credible to the neighbour, and also increases the employee's loyalty to the company. It is difficult to see why more companies do not make better use of their employees.

Up to now, our suggestions have been concerned with attempts to conduct ongoing public relations campaigns in such a fashion that a company can build its credibility and thus mitigate the effects of negative actions. However, events may still occur that will be perceived as negative by the public, and public opinion may be expressed through negative attitudes on the part of the general public. What should the stance of the manager be? Below are several suggestions for handling such situations:

WHENEVER POSSIBLE, HANDLE THE RELEASE OF ANY INFORMATION

It is seldom the case that any given piece of information is entirely negative. Frequently, there are positive aspects to any event. If the news media are allowed to make the presentation through the mechanism of a press conference, the manager has very little control of what they will present. If, however, a manager can release the information through a press release or a personal appearance, there is some opportunity to present positive as well as negative aspects.

MAKE USE OF CREDIBLE SOURCES TO RELEASE NEGATIVE INFORMATION

Too frequently, the company president announces only positive things, and negative announcements are relegated to the public information officer. In my judgement, this is a mistake. If the president has built up credibility over time by participation in civic affairs, help to the community, and announcement of positive measures, that same credibility can be used to "soften" the blow of having to announce a price increase or a serious accident. The president may well lose some credibility, but that temporary loss can be made up.

- Whenever Possible, Involve Community Opinion Leaders. It can be very helpful to give briefings to labour leaders, church leaders, city council members, and other influential groups. Opinion leaders are inclined to talk to anyone who asks their opinion. If they do not have any special information, they are most likely to reflect that frustration in a complete lack of support for a new idea. If, however, they have been briefed ahead of time, they can give more accurate information. This tends to increase their credibility with their followers and to make them more receptive to further announcements. Obviously, care must be taken in using opinion leaders, but they can prove of immense benefit to a company manager who must transmit information to the general public and have most of that information understood and accepted by the public.
- If Possible, Time the Release of Negative Information to Coincide with the Announcement of a Positive Piece of Information. If a natural

gas utility has to raise rates, it may help to mitigate that announcement if the utility can also announce the discovery of a new gas source that will have positive effects on customers. Certainly, this combination of announcements is not always possible, but when it is, the company should take advantage of it. It may not eliminate the formation of negative attitudes on the part of the public, but it may help soften the blow.

USE EMPLOYEES TO TRANSMIT INFORMATION

We have suggested this for longrange public information programmes. It is even more useful when a company has a public relations problem. Members of the general public usually want to hear "the inside story" after reading a general news story about a problem or viewing a television account. Many people do not read their newspapers carefully, nor do they always trust them. If they know that their next door neighbour works for a certain company, they will turn to that source for information. If the employee has no idea what is going on, his or her answer is likely to be one that blames the company and its managers for not telling him or her what is happening. In such a situation, the company takes a double blow—once from the bad news and then from its own employee.

USES OF COMPANY RESOURCES

Many companies can use inserts that are sent with the monthly bills. Others have newsletters that are sent to customers. In many cases it is possible to use these means to transmit new information to the public.

This list is not exhaustive, but it should give some indication of the ways in which companies might help meet demands for public information in situations where negative information has to be given to the public or in which a high level of public concern has been voiced. I must offer one final bit of information about public opinion. Although the management of a company may feel that the "public" will become outraged about information that appears to be inimical to their interests, the chances are that most of the members of the public feel far less strongly than do the managers. We are all inclined to react strongly to anything about ourselves that seems to be going badly.

The fact of the matter is that most members of the public will feel far less concerned than will company managers. There are always a few who will raise their voices, but most people simply accept change without reacting in a negative manner. This is particularly true when a company has established goodwill through a long campaign of public information activities before negative ideas or proposals must be transmitted to the public. If the company has done its job well, the intense pressure placed by a few members of the public can be overcome by the larger mass of real public opinion.

4

Communication in Business

AN OVERVIEW

To understand communication in a corporate setting, one can explore any of several defining characteristics. One characteristic has to do with time: Communicative acts are embedded within a flow of prior and subsequent interaction. Indeed, in a business setting, a document may not have any more intrinsic importance to that community than the process that created it; that is, the real value in the process may come from negotiating a consensus for the final text. Another characteristic relates to form, as the ideas constructed over time may move through many communicative forms: Informal discussion may lead to an agenda item in a meeting, which may result in a request for a document, which may in turn be presented orally in another meeting.

An almost endless variety of forms are possible—from formal documents to review comments, from hallway conversations to lengthy presentations, from scrawled notes to multimedia. Not only is the relationship between oral and written texts important, but also the plethora of technology-mediated forms that confound traditional definitions of text. Even with so many possibilities, form is a relatively straightforward characteristic in describing communication after the fact.

Form, on the other hand, is considerably more complex for the individual doing the communicating. In a business setting, individuals choosing the form of a communicative performance must balance a whole range of contextual factors from access to timeliness to appropriateness. In short, the flow of communication over time and the form communicators choose to give it are embedded within a social framework a set of cultural expectations—that largely define how the individuals within a particular setting interact.

FUNDAMENTALS OF BUSINESS COMMUNICATION

Fundamentals of Business Communication distills the basic concepts and information from Ober' s "Contemporary Business Communication and places greater emphasis on grammar and mechanics.

This brief text combines the traditional textbook format with a workbook and allows students to immediately test, apply, and reinforce the basics of business communication. Each chapter opens with an interview profiling managers from multinational companies (such as 3M), small entrepreneurial companies (such as village), and non-profit organisations (such as The Wilderness Society).

These discussions with industry insiders set the stage for key topics covered in the chapter. Language Arts topics appear in every third chapter to introduce or review basic grammar and mechanics. Ongoing examples provide a consistent thread of instruction, illustrate business communication in context, and reinforce the importance of audience analysis.

After each major topic, "Checkpoints allow students to immediately review and test their understanding of the material just covered.

Progressively increasing in degree of difficulty, these features ask students to recall, define, apply, and then critically analyse what they have learned.

Activities and end-of-chapter exercises that follow the "3Ps model guide students through the assessment of a "problem or a typical business scenario involving effective communication, the process of determining how to respond to the situation, and the final "product—such as an e-mail or memo—created in response. Seven "Portfolio Projects allow students to demonstrate their communication skills to prospective employers. Students prepare: a routine informational message; claim; bad-news message; persuasive request; situational business report; videotape of an oral business presentation; and a resume, cover letter, and videotape of a practice interview.

THE IMPORTANCE OF COMMUNICATION

When he first started taking projects on RAC, he passed through a typical period of lurking; poking around and looking at all the details for various projects. He was even reading the comments from coders to buyers and vice versa, in their online resumes. It seems to me that there was a word that was present in most of the comments: "Excellent Communication", "Good Communication", "Communication is superb.

It is clear that many people were evaluating someone by his/her communication skills. Being a hardcore coder for many years I always believed that he must be judged by the final outcome of the project. In RAC, he discovered that this is partially true. A great implementation of a project will make the buyer accept the project 100per cent but if the communication is pour during the development of the project, neither the buyer nor the coder would like to cooperate again. Good communication will ensure repeating work between the same buyer and coder.

He strongly believe that the secret of successful projects is "Communication" If the buyer and the coder can communicate well, the project is only a matter of time to finish. Communication doesn't only mean that both parties have to speak the same language. It means more than that. It has to do with the wealth of information that is exchanged between them. Communication must be fluent, clear and enriched with meaningful information.

Many projects have failed to be completed and went to arbitration because the buyer and coder failed to communicate efficiently. Here is an example from my own personal experience. During the development of a project, the buyer was constantly sending me short, cryptic e-mails. I always had to reply back and clarify even minor details. Chatting with him online wasn't proved useful either.

He didn't really know what he wanted. Sometimes, when he replied to my long e-mails it was hard to read his replies because he didn't even use paragraphs to separate my text from his.

When he finished the project, I got a 10 and a nice comment but only I, knew how hard it was to complete it. It was a nightmare. Most of my time on the project was spent trying to communicate with him. He estimated that I spent double the time that it was worth for this project.

Do you think that this was an extreme example. Think again. It is very possible to happen to you if you fail to communicate.

Buyers must clearly specify their needs before they post a project. You don't have to be a system analyst in order to do this efficiently. Write as many details as you can and give examples. Coders are not magicians.

They can't guess what you want. During the development, constantly comment on the work. Always check the various steps and make sure that you are moving into the correct direction. Praise the coder if he finishes a nice tricky part of the project. Most coders are take pride in their work. Reward them if they take the extra mile for you.

Coders must have patience. Buyers aren't always experts in technical terms. Don't use technical lingoes to show off. It is better to explain things in simple words, one step at a time. In the long run this is going to save you time. If the buyer has a strong technical background about the project then you can use the appropriate terminology.

During the development, keep a constant communication flow. Be sensitive about the buyers needs. Don't keep him in the dark about what you are doing. It is always a good idea to send daily short reports even for the smaller projects. This will assure that you are on the right track. A successful project completion depends on many factors. "Communication" is the most important one. You can't go wrong if you make a lot of effort to communicate the best you can.

FORMS OF COMMUNICATION

Effective communicators have many tools at their disposal when they want to get across a message. Whether writing or speaking, they know how to put together the words that will convey their meaning. They reinforce their words with gestures and actions. They look you in the eye, listen to what you have to say, and think about your feelings and needs.

At the same time, they study your reactions, picking up the nuances of your response by watching your face and body, listening to your tone of voice, and evaluating your words. They absorb information just as efficiently as they transmit it, relying on both non-verbal and verbal cues.

NON-VERBAL COMMUNICATION

The most basic form of communication is non-verbal. Anthropologists theorize that long before human beings used words to talk things over, our ancestors communicated with one another by using their bodies. They gritted their teeth to show anger; they smiled and touched one another to indicate affection. Although we have come a long way since those primitive times, we still use non-verbal cues to express superiority, dependence, dislike, respect, love, and other feelings.

Non-verbal communication differs from verbal communication in fundamental ways. For one thing, it is less structured, which makes it more difficult to study. A person cannot pick up a book on non-verbal language and master the vocabulary of gestures, expressions, and inflections that are common in our culture. We don't really know how people learn non-verbal behaviour. No one teaches a baby to cry or smile, yet these forms of self-expression are almost universal. Other types of non-verbal communication, such as the meaning of colours and certain gestures, vary from culture to culture.

Non-verbal communication also differs from verbal communication in terms of intent and spontaneity. We generally plan our words. When we say "please open the door," we have a conscious purpose. We think about the message, if only for a moment. But when we communicate non-verbally, we sometimes do so unconsciously. We don't mean to raise an eyebrow or blush. Those actions come naturally. Without our consent, our emotions are written all over our faces.

Functions of Non-Verbal Communication

Although non-verbal communication can stand alone, it frequently works with speech. Our words carry part of the message, and non-verbal signals carry the rest. Together, the two modes of expression make a powerful team, augmenting, reinforcing, and clarifying each other. Experts in non-verbal communication suggest that it have six specific functions:

- To provide information, either consciously or unconsciously
- To regulate the flow of conversation
- To express emotion
- To qualify, complement, contradict, or expand verbal messages

- To control or influence others
- To facilitate specific tasks, such as teaching a person to swing a golf club.

Non-verbal communication plays a role in business too. For one thing, it helps establish credibility and leadership potential. If you can learn to manage the impression you create with your body language, facial characteristics, voice, and appearance, you can do a great deal to communicate that you are competent, trustworthy, and dynamic.

For example, Wal-Mart founder Sam Walton has developed a homespun style that puts people at ease, thereby helping them to be more receptive, perhaps even more open. Furthermore, if you can learn to read other people's non-verbal messages, you will be able to interpret their underlying attitudes and intentions more accurately. When dealing with co-workers, customers, and clients, watch carefully for small signs that reveal how the conversation is going.

If you aren't having the effect you want, check your words; then, if your words are all right, try to be aware of the non-verbal meanings you are transmitting. At the same time, stay tuned to the non-verbal signals that the other person is sending.

Verbal Communication

Although you can express many things non-verbally, there are limits to what you can communicate without the help of language. If you want to discuss past events, ideas, or abstractions, you need words—symbols that stand for thoughts — arranged in meaningful patterns. In the English language, we have a 750,000, although most of us recognise only about 20,000 of them. To create a thought with these words, we arrange them according to the rules of grammar, putting the various parts of speech in the proper sequence

We then transmit the message in spoken or written form, hoping that someone will hear or read what we have to say. It shows how much time business people devote to the various types of verbal communication. They use speaking and writing to send messages; they use listening and reading to receive them.

Process of Communication

Communication is the process of sharing thoughts, ideas, and emotions with others, and having those thoughts, ideas, and emotions understood. You need a sender, a message, and a receiver for communication to take place. Here are some other things that help communication to be effective:

Attention: The sender needs to pay attention to what he/she is trying to communicate, and choose the best words and body language to communicate with; the receiver needs to pay attention to what is being communicated by listening and watching.

Attitude: Both sender and receiver need to have a positive (and respectful) attitude. They should want to communicate, and be willing to work to see that communication can take place. Using negative or blaming words shows a poor attitude - using "I" messages and trying to understand the other's point shows a good attitude

Feedback: Both sender and receiver can give feedback to each other, either by using words or by body language. This helps to show whether the communication is being understood correctly or not.

BARRIERS TO COMMUNICATION

There are many things that can hinder or prevent good communication. Here are some of the most common barriers:

Distraction: It is hard to understand if you are distracted by something else. When you are trying to communicate, make sure there is no competition for your attention like exciting things going on nearby or other people talking (cellphones, IMs, chat rooms, e-mail, *etc.*)

- *Blocks*: Sometimes it's hard to communicate simply because you cannot send or receive the message. Loud noises can block communication, and so can things like lost phone signals and computers not being able to interface.
- *Poor Skills*: Some people have not learned how to effectively listen, and do not understand what you are trying to communicate.
- *Attitude*: Communication can also be affected by a poor attitude towards the other person, towards the subject, or just because the sender or receiver is having a bad day. Fear and mistrust can impede communication, as can boredom or lack of interest in the subject. For best communication, try to keep the emotions out of the way until you understand what is being communicated.
- *Poor Understanding*: Sometimes the sender uses words that the receiver does not understand, or refers to cultural experiences that the receiver has not grown up with, so that communication is less effective. Try to use simple words if you are communicating something complicated, and make sure that both of you understand the context or cultural references.
- *Lack of Feedback*: If the receiver does not give feedback, the sender does not know if the communication is effective or not; also, if the sender is not paying attention to the feedback, the communication will not be effective.

The best way to insure good communication is for both the sender and the receiver to use "I" messages - instead of saying "You hurt my feelings," or "That's stupid," you let the other person know how you feel by saying things like "I feel hurt when ___ happens," or "I feel angry when I hear someone say ____." Pay attention to how your voice sounds when you speak, and try to avoid sounding angry or condescending to the other person. Avoid making hateful statements, insulting others, and complaining - instead, try to make helpful statements that can change the situation from negative to positive.

Dealing with Communication Barriers

No matter how good and effective a communicator one maybe, yet the fact is that one does face certain barriers, from time to time, which forces them to work on becoming even more effective in their skills to communicate. Given here are the communication barriers that occur while listening, speaking and in the case of non-verbal communications...

Listening Barriers

- Interrupting the speaker
- Not maintaining eye contact with the speaker
- Rushing the speaker to complete what he/she has to say
- Making the speaker feel as though he/she is wasting the listener's time
- Being distracted by something that is not part of the on going communication
- Getting ahead of the speaker and completing his/her thoughts
- Ignoring the speaker's requests
- Topping the speaker's story with one's own set of examples
- Forgetting what is being discussed
- Asking too many questions, for they sake of probing

Barriers While Speaking

- Unclear messages
- Lack of consistency in the communication process
- Incomplete sentences
- Not understanding the receiver
- Not seeking clarifications while communicating

Other Barriers

- An individual's subjective viewpoint towards issues/people, which leads to assumptions.
- An emotional block, which can lead to an attitude of indifference, suspicion or hostility towards the subject.
- An emotional block or bias that is based on a third party's view point, or on what you have read/heard.
- Words can have different meanings to different people, thus blocking communication.
- Use of negative words

Well before the current world financial crisis struck, organisations have sought inventive ways to engage in face-to-face meetings without the need to travel.

Companies have turned to services such as Adobe Acrobat Connect Pro, Cisco WebEx, Citrix Got Meeting, and Microsoft Live Meeting as a means for workers in multiple locations to share presentations and otherwise collaborate.

No question, these tools greatly reduce costly, productivity-sapping travel, with the added benefit of lowering a company's carbon footprint. Yet scratchy audio quality, out-of-sync slides, and tiny, Webcam-quality video often diminish these solutions' usefulness.

Prediction: Google Announces Twitter Acquisition

Similarly, more traditional videoconferencing systems (which have been around for decades) suffer from low utilization rates — partially because of complicated, unreliable technology. The door has now opened for telepresence solutions: a conferencing environment that seeks to mimic the in-person experience as much as possible.

Several technologies make telepresence possible. High-definition video cameras and large, flat-panel monitors clearly display participants in life size. Optimized networks — making use of QoS and even application-aware protocol acceleration — help eliminate audio and video delay over long-distance and high-latency WANs. As such, participants can make eye contact with colleagues and immediately pick up on all-important visual cues — such as how someone reacts to an offer. Moreover, operating the systems can be as simple as using a television remote control or telephone.

Something for Everyone

In general, telepresence systems fall into three configurations. First, there are formal group setups, purpose-built rooms that accommodate four to eight participants.

Here you'll find warm wall coverings, soft lighting, three or four wall-mounted monitors, and a conventional conference room seating arrangement. In use, it's as if remote participants are sitting across the table from you. Second, you'll find small-to-midrange setups, which comprise a single monitor and one camera, suited for handling one to four users.

This option works well in executive offices, and some systems are mobile enough to be ferried among regular conference rooms. These less-costly systems work over existing networks, yet the picture and audio quality surpass that of early-generation videoconferencing solutions.

None come with amenities such as plush suites, but they closely match expensive systems' picture quality and usability.

Finally, there are classroom-style rooms that can hold 30 participants or more.

These facilities, which are used by corporate and educational institutions alike, usually have multiple monitors or video projectors.

The Cost of Collaboration

Even with falling hardware costs, a telepresence system doesn't come cheap. A group system at a single site that can accommodate 18 to 36 users can go for $350,000. One reason for the expense is that you typically don't install telepresence systems in any old room. An immersive face-to-face environment requires special lighting, acoustics, and furniture, which all factor into the price. And that doesn't count in-house (or contracted) network and support costs. But before you despair, take a serious look at how much money you're spending on employee and executive travel among your various offices: airline tickets, food, accommodations, and the like. Factor in how much productivity is lost during travel, as well as how much time that travel can add to moving forward with a project or deal. In the end, you may find fast payback on your investment. For instance, Cisco representatives say that their customers often recover a telepresence investment in six to nine months, according to independent audits.

Notably, there are ways to reduce telepresence costs, including equipment leases and renting time at conferencing facilities. If price is still a barrier, you could consider one of the lower-end, high-performance systems, which run for less than 10,000. Moreover, video chat applications are improving, too, though it's a real stretch to put them in the same category as fully developed videoconferencing solutions. Still, for little (or no) cost they let several people connect with very usable audio and visual quality.

EFFECTIVE BUSINESS COMMUNICATION

A two way information sharing process which involves one party sending a message that is easily understood by the receiving party. Effective communication by business managers facilitates information sharing between company employees and can substantially contribute to its commercial success.

Face-to-Face

Face-to-face communication helps to establish a personal connection and will help sell the product or service to the customer. These interactions can portray a whole different message than written communication as tone, pitch, and body language is observed. Information is easier to access and delivered immediately with interactions rather than waiting for an e-mail or phone call. Conflicts are also easily resolved this way, as verbal and non-verbal cues are observed and acted upon.

Communicating professionally is very important as one is representing the company. Speak clearly and ask questions to understand the needs and wants, let the recipient respond as one resolves the issue. Decisions are made more confidently during a face-to-face interaction as the recipient asks questions to understand and move forward with their decision.

E-mail

When using e-mail to communicate in the business world, it is important to be careful with the choice of words. Miscommunication is very frequent as the reader doesn't know what non-verbal cues one is giving off, such as the pitch, tone, or expressions. Before beginning an e-mail, make sure the e-mail address one is using is appropriate and professional as well as the message one is going to send. Again, make sure the information is clear and to the point so the recipient isn't confused. Make sure one includes their signature, title, and other contact information at the end.

Telephone

When making a business call, make it clear who is on the line and where one is from as well as one's message when on the phone. Smile and have a positive attitude as the recipient will be able to read the caller and that will affect how they react. When leaving a message, make sure one is clear and brief. One should state their name and who they are and the purpose for contacting them. If replying to a voice-mail, try to respond as soon as possible and take into consideration the time of day. Don't call too early or too late, as it is important to respect other's time. Also be mindful of where one is and the noise level as well as the people one is around when trying to reach someone by phone.

When making a sales call, hope for the person one are trying to connect to does not answer the phone. Leave up to five enticing messages and one's target audience will be ready to speak when one either gets a call back or one calls and reaches the person. The enticing message prepares the person to speak to the representative. It may be that the person is not interested based on what one had said in each voice message. Always be polite and accept that one may have many more to call. If the individual is reached, one might ask if there might be someone better suited for the advertised programme.

If one is calling and leaving voice messages, include time of availability for callbacks. There is nothing worse than a callback coming to one when one is not available. Use the telephone as a great communication tool. Be polite and always put oneself in the other person's position.

Listening

When listening to another employee or customer speak it is very important to be an avid listener. Here are some obstacles that you might have to overcome:

- Filters and Assumptions

- Biases and Prejudices
- Inattention and Impatience
- Surrounding Environment

A good way to overcome these factors is by using LOTS Better Communication method. This method includes four steps in order to produce good listening skills and the ability to respond with an educated statement. The four steps to this method are:

- Listen
- Observe
- Think
- Speak

Doing all of these things while showing good eye contact and body posture will assure the speaker that he/she is getting full attention from the listeners.

CHOOSING COMMUNICATION MEDIA

When choosing a media of communication, it is important to consider who are the respective audience and the objective of the message itself. Rich media are more interactive than lean media and provide the opportunity for two-way communication: the receiver can ask questions and express opinions easily in person.

Subliminal Method of Communication

Subliminal perception refers to the individual ability to perceive and respond to stimuli that are below the threshold or level of consciousness, which proved to influence thoughts, feelings or actions altogether or separately. There are four distinct methods of communicating subliminally.

These are visual stimuli in movies, accelerated speech, embedded images in a print advertisement, and suggestiveness which is not normally seen at first glance.Focussing on Subliminal Communication through visual stimuli, Marketing people have adopted this method even incorporating it films and television shows.Subliminal method of communication first made its debut in a 1957 advertisement, during which a brief message flashed, telling viewers to eat popcorn and drink Coca-Cola. Since that time, subliminal communication has occupied a controversial role in the advertising landscape, with some people claiming it's omnipresent, while others emphasize it's not real.

As of publication, there is still an ongoing scientific debate about whether subliminal advertising works. Subliminal messaging is a form of advertising in which a subtle message is inserted into a standard ad. This subtle message affects the consumer's behaviour, but the consumer does not know she's seen the message. For example, a marketer might incorporate a single frame telling consumers to drink tea in a movie. In print media, advertisers might put hidden images or coded messages into ad text.

Arguments for Effectiveness

A 2009 study at the University College of London found that people were especially likely to be affected by negative subliminal communication. For example, a cosmetic advertisement conveying to a consumer that she is ugly might be more effective. Subliminal ads "prime" the brain to seek out stimuli that match the message in the advertisement, according to a 1992 study published in "Personality and Social Psychology Bulletin." This can affect behaviour, particularly when a message addresses an individual's insecurities or behavioural tendencies and when a consumer is in a context that allows her to act on the ad's message.

ORGANISATIONS

- Founded in 1936 by Shankar with the Association for Business Communication (ABC), originally called the Association of College Teachers of Business Writing, is "an international organisation committed to fostering excellence in business communication scholarship,research,education, and practice."
- The IEEE Professional Communication Society (PCS) [2] is dedicated to understanding and promoting effective communication in engineering, scientific, and other environments, including business environments. PCS's academic journal, is one of the premier journals in Europe communication. The journal's readers are engineers, writers, information designers, managers, and others working as scholars, educators, and practitioners who share an interest in the effective communication of technical and business information.
- The Society for Technical Communication is a professional association dedicated to the advancement of the theory and practice of technical communication. With membership of more than 6,000 technical communicators, it's the largest organisation of its type in North America.

BUSINESS PROCESS DISCOVERY

Business process discovery related to process mining is a set of techniques that automatically construct a representation of an organisation's current business processes and its major process variations. These techniques use evidence found in the existing technology systems that run business processes within an organisation. Business process discovery techniques embody the following properties:

- *Emergent paradigm*: Current methods are based on top-down structured manual interviews relying on second-hand representations of the business process/system behaviours. An automated discovery process relies on collecting data from the information system over a period of time. This data can then be analysed to form a process model.

- *Automated process discovery*: By automating the analysis of the data, the subjectivity of current manual process analysis techniques is removed. The automated system has an ingrained methodology that — through repeated trials — has been shown to accurately discover processes and process variations without bias.
- *Accurate information*: Since the information is collected from the actual source it cannot be inaccurate, as opposed to gathering it from second party representation.
- *Complete information*: An automated process captures all the information that is occurring within the system and represents them by time, date, user, *etc*.... Since the information is collected from real-time interactions, it is not subject to lost or selective memory issues. This includes completeness regarding exceptions in the processes. Often, exceptions are treated as statistical "noise," which may exclude important inefficiencies in business processes.
- *Standardized Process*: The automated collection of information yields process data which can be grouped, quantified and classified. This supplies a basis for the development and monitoring of both current and new processes, to which benchmarks can be assigned. These benchmarks are the root of both new process design and the determination of problem root cause. Additionally, standardized process data can set the stage for efforts at continuous process improvement.

Business Process Discovery compliments and builds upon the work in many other fields.

- Business process discovery is the next level of understanding in the emerging field of business analytics, which allows organisations to view, analyse and adjust the underlying structure and processes that go into day-to-day operations. This discovery includes information gathering of all of the components of a business process, including technology, people, department procedures and protocols.
- Business process discovery creates a process master which compliments business process analysis. BPA tools and methodologies are well suited to top-down hierarchical process decomposition, and analysis of to-be processes. BPD provides a bottoms-up analysis that marries to the top-down to provide a complete business process, organized hierarchically by BPA.
- Business Intelligence provides organisations with reporting and analytics on the data in their organisations. However, BI has no

process model, awareness or analytics. BPD compliments BI by providing an explicit process view to current operations, and providing analytics on that process model to help organisations identify and act upon business process inefficiencies, or anomalies.

- Web analytics are a limited example of BPD in that web analytics reconstruct the web-user's process as they interact with a Web-site. However, these analytics are limited to the process as is contained within the session, from the users perspective and with respect to just the web-based system and process.
- Business triage provides a framework for categorizing the processes identified by business process analysis based on their relative importance to achieving a stated, measurable goal or outcome. Utilizing the same categories employed by military medical and disaster medical services, business processes are categorized as:
  - *Essential/critical*: Process essential for achieving outcomes/goals
  - *Important/urgent*: Process which speeds achieving outcomes/goals
  - *Optional/supportive*: Process not needed to achieve outcomes/goals

Resources are allocated based on the process category with resources first dedicated to red processes, then yellow processes and finally green processes.

In the event that resources become limited, resources are first withheld from Green Processes, then Yellow Processes. Resources are only withheld from Red Processes if failure to achieve outcomes/goals is acceptable.

STRATEGIC BUSINESS PLANNING

Strategic planning is a team effort, one that draws on the particular skills and expertise of employees in the organisation. Early on in the planning process, the organisation should start identifying several key players who will help create the plan. These players should include professionals with experience in the field or region that the institution will find itself in, and who can speak to the particular needs of that area.

Incorporating players from all levels of the organisation helps determine if the programme is appropriate to the social and economic context of the clients and the realities of the informal sector that the programme will serve. Research has shown that individuals in an organisation work harder at achieving a goal when they help in setting the goal. In other words, the process that a microfinance institution employs in the early planning stages determines the quality of the plan and its final outcome. Considering the interests and visions of several key stakeholders in order to achieve the goals of the organisation, outreach and profitability, is vital. These stakeholders include:

- The institution's board members
- Staff members
- Clients

"Involving those responsible for implementing the plan helps ensure broad endorsement, essential for successful implementation." In fact, researchers have discovered several barriers to the effective implementation of strategic business plans. These barriers generally arise from conflicting priorities among managers and staff, but also from poor communication of programme goals.

Strategic business planning is also helpful (especially in the early stages) in determining which factors are vital to the microfinance institution's success. While the primary goal of a microfinance institution is to serve client needs, it is also necessary for managers in an organisation to determine how to efficiently maximize the resources available to them.

Financial projections can be a very useful operating tool for an institution's managers. Comparing actual performance results with those projected, managers can determine if the institution is keeping the "right pace" towards the goal reflected in the business plan. Other issues such as the sustainability of the organisation and its longevity can be revealed in examining the financial components of a business plan.

AN ONGOING PROCESS

Finally, strategic planning must be viewed as an ongoing process, one that must be revisited periodically and revised as real-life experiences reveal areas of the plan that can be improved upon. When considered as a continuous procedure, an organisation can regularly evaluate its stated goals and mission, adjust them as needed, and better respond to environmental and institutional changes. This idea of a cyclical planning process can be illustrated in the following:

- Articulating MFO's mission and goals
- Defining the institutions markets, clients and other stakeholders
- Performing an environmental analysis
- Performing an institutional assessment
- Choosing the appropriate strategy
- Defining the objectives and general activities

As the model illustrates, the steps taken in establishing a strategic business plan are not linear. As an organisation performs the various steps in the planning process, it is important to determine if the stated mission and goals are appropriate. Revising your strategy when needed is key to a strong business plan.

ARTICULATING THE INSTITUTION'S MISSION AND GOALS

Successful management of a microfinance institution requires many business skills. Yet, before these can be put into action, an organisation must define its mission and goals. Defining a mission helps to lay the foundation of an organisation, providing the basic direction that the institution will follow. In essence, creating a mission statement establishes why the organisation exists and what it hopes to accomplish. The mission should succinctly state the target market, objectives, and guiding principles that will be used to reach the objective. The mission and goals should be the basis for all activities that the institution will be involved in. It should be viewed as a source of motivation for its board and staff members, bringing them together with a clear, unifying vision.

Developing the Mission Statement

In general, when developing a clear and complete mission statement, there are several things that a planning team must consider.

What is the problem that the organisation wants to address? There are several questions that you can ask that will help you to determine this, these include:

- Is it the lack of access to financial services among rural poor; or the alleviation of poverty?
- Not only does an organisation need to determine the problem area, but it also needs to decide on what level they plan to address the issue.
- It is vital that the organisation clearly understands the problem and how a microfinance project can help solve it.
- Who is the organisation assisting?
  - A clear idea of this group cannot be overlooked, as the characteristics of the target group will directly influence the design of the institution's services.
  - An organisation must have an understanding of the economic activities that the target group participates in, their demographic, and their cultural characteristics. These traits all influence the activities, and therefore the mission of the microfinance organisation.
- How will you reach the client, and what services will your organisation be providing?
  - Given the particular characteristic of the target group, what outreach method is most likely to engender trust in your organisation?
  - What microcredit model is most suitable for this particular group and its needs?
  - Is a solidarity group-lending model more appropriate than an individual lending programme?
- What are the institution's ultimate goals?
  - What would you like to achieve in five years?
  - How will your organisation measure success?
  - Will it be through the number of clients served, repayment rates, or another measure of impact on the client's well being? This should be stated somewhere in your mission.

- Does your organisation have a plan for sustainability and self-sufficiency?
  - Have you considered ways to reduce your dependency on outside funding sources?
  - Do you have a plan in place that ensures the services you provide to your target group will be available to them for the long term?
  - Are you considering expansion plans to provide your services to a broader range of people?

Mission Statements Motivate and Clarify Purpose

The importance of a clear, well thought out mission statement cannot be overemphasized. Not only does it force an organisation to think critically about its objectives, but it also requires the organisation to start thinking realistically about how the objectives will be met. A mission statement can serve as a motivating factor for workers, board members, and funders alike, especially if the goals are clear and attainable. Finally, by working through a series of detailed steps at the start of a programme, an organisation can begin focusing in on a particular area of work and design solutions that will effectively serve its target group.

Examples of Mission Statements

While the process of developing a mission statement requires that the organisation undergo in-depth analysis of its operations, the final statement produced should be simple and to the point. Some examples of mission statements include:

- Rural Finance Facility of South Africa's mission is to Facilitate investment in rural communities by the provision of professional financial services.
- The Microfinance Capacity Building Programme in Africa (AFCAP) also provides a good example of a succinct mission statement:

To build a core group of internationally competitive African professional service providers from the private sector who in turn will deliver appropriate, high quality products and services to the microfinance industry.

- The mission of Friendship Bridge is

To work with mutual understanding and respect to connect persons of the United States with those of Southeast Asia. We hope to promote sustainable healing of the injuries to the body and spirit that were caused by the ravages of poverty, disease, ignorance and war, so that we may all share in peace, joy and hope for our future in the global community.

- Another example of a mission statement is Opportunity International's statement, which is short and precise:

Our mission is to provide opportunities for people in chronic poverty to transform their lives.

A microfinance institution's mission statement can be as short or as long as necessary, depending on the desire of the organisation, and on the depth of its specialisation and commitment. Yet, it should be clear to the reader of the statement, exactly what an organisation is trying to accomplish. It should also "define the institutional culture of your organisation". Many missions are hard to accomplish, and the goals of an organisation should be phrased in a way that illustrates how your organisation plans to make the mission a reality. For example,

- "To provide access to microfinance services to over a certain number of households by the end of a certain year.
- "To reduce donor dependency of an organisation by 50per cent"

Final Thoughts

Goals will differ depending on the stated timeline, and of course your organisation. Through the course of developing a mission statement, the feasibility of meeting various goals may change. It is important to continually review and revise your mission and goals, as further research or experiences reveal that previously determined timelines are not attainable. Your organisation may also decide, after spending some time in the field, that there are other areas or issues that it is better able to address. The organisation is considered effective if it sets and reaches measurable and attainable goals, not if it adheres to its original mission without revision.

DEFINING THE INSTITUTION'S MARKETS AND CLIENTS

Understanding Your Clients

Microfinance institutions exist to serve clients, so it is vital that the organisation has a clear understanding about the demographics and cultural characteristics of the group that is being served. In addition, recognizing the economic needs of the group, and how your organisation can assist them in furthering their goals is an important part of understanding your clients. Once you have identified your target group, members of the group can provide valuable feedback on your products and services, as well as the design of future services.

IDENTIFYING YOUR MARKET

When a microfinance institution decides to operate in a community, it is important to recognise that it is not possible to serve everyone in the community. Instead, an organisation should identify a target market within which it will work, and begin focusing its resources there. In order to choose the proper market for the services provided, an organisation should consider operating in communities that have the following:

- Good access to the services that you are providing
- A demonstrated interest in your assistance
- Committed and capable community leadership that will support your organisation's efforts in the community
- An identifiable and real potential for the success of your organisation in the community

Market Segments

Markets can be divided into market segments, which are usually classified by location (for example, a particular neighbourhood, a semi-rural market town, or the area within a 15-mile radius of a branch office). These can be further segmented according to the economic activities located within them, such as market vendors, producers, or farmers.

The potential clients within each segment generally have many common characteristics. As a result, when an organisation chooses to operate within a specific market segment, the institution increases the likelihood of reaching its clients and providing its products and services to meet the needs of those particular clients.

Market Analysis

Before an organisation decides to enter a new market or expand further into its existing market, the market should be carefully analysed, and the following factors need to be considered:

Considering the size of the market and the number of microentrepreneurs that operate in it. The size of the market is important to know in order to do things like forecasting, financial planning and budgeting, and calculating the risks and abilities of other potential MFOs entering this specific market or area.

What is the expected demand for financial services? This is the most important issue in market analysis, because it specifically demonstrates the market potential. Understanding the potential for your services is important for a microfinance institution in order to establish whether it is worth creating an MFO in the area. This information is also vital in determining the size of an organisation, and the amount of resources needed in order to start an MFO, or to develop it further. A microfinance institution should track the expected demand in order be ready to react to changes to it.

What market penetration can be reasonably achieved? In other words, what is the portion of all potential clients in the market that you estimate that your services can reach? This is related to the point above about expected demand.

An organisation should not expect that it will reach all potential customers, but having a realistic sense about whom you are likely to reach is valuable, especially when you are forecasting revenues and expenses in the budgeting process.

Consider the key market trends, such as the growth in market demand for the goods produced by the entrepreneurs. Tracking key market trends is important to predict the change in demand, economic activity, and economic situation. An organisation can use this information in order to adjust its pricing policies, therefore better serving its customers.

How does an organisation gather this type of information? There are generally two types of market analysis that can be performed: formal and informal.

- Informal analysis may include a casual discussion with potential or current clients
- Formal analysis is usually a more structured process that might involve conducting a detailed market study.

For example, your organisation may decide to conduct formal interviews with potential clients, asking them questions about the type of work that they do, to get a sense of the services that they may require.

Based on the results of evaluation, the institution can decide whether the market has opportunities for expansion, or may require more in-depth research.

Where else can one find information about the market? The organisation may use primary and secondary sources of information. The local bureaus of statistics, as well as other banks of information, are a valuable source.

However, it is possible that this information might not be up to date, as may be the case now in Russia, where the external environment is changing very rapidly. Information that was relevant two years ago may no longer be useful in decision-making today.

IDENTIFYING YOUR CLIENTS

If a market segment meets the initial selection criteria, the organisation will want to conduct a more detailed analysis. This analysis can help the institution understand the economic, social, and personal characteristics of the entrepreneurs that operate within the segment, as well as the kinds of products and services that most appropriately satisfy their needs. The analysis consists of two parts – the analysis of the key economic indicators and of the personal traits of the customers. Economic traits primarily deal with inherent risks. This analysis addresses questions like: Will the customer be able to pay back her loan? How will he or she pay it back (from what sources) in case of an emergency? Does she have enough work experience to manage her business and take on the responsibility of paying off her debts?

Economic Indicators of Clientele

Key economic traits include: *The nature of the enterprises e.g.*, relative proportion of commerce, service, production and agriculture. Production and agriculture have historically been fields where microfinancing has been most prevalent. It was the most popular way of self-improvement among the poorest people with very small businesses; while services were the prerogative of other, larger business units.

The demand for specific financial services, i.e. credit or savings, working capital or equipment loans. Identifying for what purpose clients wish to borrow money is important. Loans for working capital are different from equipment loans with respect to their liquidity and risk.

Analyzing the intended use of the loans is suggested, in order to build appropriate loan policies and pricing strategies. This market information might vary greatly in different areas, and organisations would have to encompass different pricing strategies within one area for different client segments.

What are the income and assets of both businesses and households? Understanding the amount of clients' income and assets is important to secure the loans. How will the client be able to repay the loan if he fails in his business? This involves determining if the client will have the ability to pay back the loan.

The diversity of income sources is another economic trait to consider. This economic trait is related to the previous one and is primarily an issue related to risk. If a client's income is based on what she earns from selling handmade matryoshkas and a wage paid at a plant, and she loses her job, will she be able to pay back her loan? Diversity of income sources is one way to reduce risks to both sides – to an MFO and a client. Finally, it is good to consider the presence of other wage earners in the household, which can influence the rate of repayment.

Recognizing the work experience of your client. The more work experience the customer has within her business field the more likely the entrepreneur will be successful in his venture. An organisation should analyse the chances that the borrower will be able to pay back his loan.

Demographic Characteristics of Clientele

In addition to the economic indicators, a microfinance institution must also note the demographic characteristics of the clients it will serve. These include:

The gender of your client is an important economic indicator. When considering the design of a credit programme, an institution must factor in the gender of the clients that it will serve, for example, women are more likely to use the services provided by a microfinance organisation. Social and cultural conditions in many poor countries result in women being generally excluded from the formal and informal financial sectors. Careful programme design will include strategies to extend services to women in ways that they will be effective for them, for example peer group lending methodologies.

The age of your client is also an important consideration. If a specific age group is being targeted as a client group, it is necessary to determine any existing barriers to extending loans to them. You will want to consider whether there are laws requiring a minimum age before a person can enter into a loan agreement? Similarly, assessing whether there are any risks involved with loaning money to elderly clients, *i.e.* a lower life expectancy in an area might lower the chances that your organisation will receive repayment.

What is the main language of your client and her level of literacy? What is the literacy rate in the area that you are working? How does this influence how you will deliver your loan services? If a significant portion of your target group is illiterate, this will influence whether you require written loan agreements. Does the region that you are working in have laws that govern how to deal with legal agreements entered into by illiterate clients?

The citizenship of your clientele may also be a factor that you should be considering. Will your organisation have requirements for citizenship or residency in order for a client to be eligible to receive your services? There are practical considerations when determining whether to establish these criteria. Chief among them is the idea that residency or citizenship represents a sense of stability and therefore the greater potential for the repayment of a loan. Your organisation may also have determined in its mission statement that it will specifically serve the needs of residents or citizens of the country that you are operating in.

It is important to understand that the nationality of a potential borrower is not an obstacle in communicating with an MFO, but is an important issue that should be used to create special product mixes for this specific client, to better serve his or her needs. Due to the fact that the Russian social environment is very diverse, an organisation will succeed if it takes national and cultural differences into consideration. In other words, a seeming challenge can become an opportunity.

By understanding the economic and personal traits of your clients, you can develop the products and services to effectively meet their needs. However, an organisation should not simply identify the key trends in clientele, but also be willing to orient its services towards the needs of the clientele.

CONTEXT AND NON-ACADEMIC WRITING

The connection between context and non-academic writing has been fruitful territory for research. Non-etheless, it is a difficult concept to generalize. Witte presents a useful definition of context not tied to a specific research site, which (to paraphrase mightily) focuses on the writer's projected self in light of the writer's understanding of external reality. Context and the social perspective have much to offer in understanding the role of texts in constructing meaning, but they also raise challenging questions when applied to non-academic research sites. The essential difficulty can be stated briefly: How can we know an unfamiliar context?

Returning to the ideas of flow and form help emphasize this difficulty. As a researcher, we can fairly easily characterise the form of a text; we can also, through various means, explore its flow in terms of precedents and antecedents. Thus, we can describe what a communicative performance is and where it fits into the overall conversation. But context, in one simple word, embraces the localized social complexity of communication and all that suggests in terms of what is knowable and what transformations take place in representation.

The crux of the difficulty may lie in moving from the familiar to the unfamiliar. In researching writing in the classroom, a familiar setting for many researchers, the barriers to understanding context may not be insurmountable to the extent that we can really understand the context of classroom communication from external points of view. But in many non-academic settings, writing researchers may find themselves on alien turf.

Context in a business setting may involve anything from the competitive climate for an entire industry to relations among employees assigned to the same project; from the formal power relationships defined by organisational charts to informal power hierarchies based on information distribution; from managerial attempts to create unified corporate cultures to the unique aspirations of individual employees.

Context, in any setting, is layered: The difficulties in its characterisation are exacerbated by unfamiliar value systems and distinctly different institutional goals. Yet context can charge texts-even fairly mundane business texts such as memos and meeting minutes—with subtle ironies, implied put-downs, challenges, celebrations, and humour—all difficult to detect for the cultural outsider. For the purposes of this study, however, we chose to impose some boundaries on the idea of context.

Non-academic writing researchers have most often used qualitative research methods to understand context, generally focusing on individuals or relatively small groups of employees. My own approach is similar but perhaps foregrounds the sources of contextual knowledge to a greater extent in that we asked employees specific questions about context (defined as three layers of corporate culture), supplemented with research into the history of the corporation, where the research took place, and the industry in which it competes. It may be that making explicit the sources of contextual knowledge and relying where possible on the words of cultural insiders to describe their perceptions of context reduces some of the difficulties with representing an unfamiliar culture.

This approach, of course, has its limitations: Perceptions of context will differ among any set of cultural informants so that any claim for an overall characterisation of context becomes suspect; the selection of which details to present, although in informants' own words, reflect the researcher's institutional biases. Still, as cultures are dynamic, context may be best described as a phenomenon based in individual perception. Construction of meaning ultimately begins in the interaction among and between individuals and small groups.

TECHNOLOGY AND CONTEXT

The balance focuses on the relationship between context and technology (a major influence on both form and flow), providing a socio technological perspective on communication at a specific site.

We chose this focus for several reasons. First, as noted earlier, connections between text and context are well established, as are links between context and texts over time. Connections between context and use of technology—from a communications point of view—are not as well understood. Third, choice of technology provides a useful site to emphasize a relationship between context defined as perceptions of corporate culture and decision making about communication. Many decisions about communication are fleeting, recoverable only through means such as protocol analysis.

Decisions about choice of technology, on the other hand, are observable and recordable, and other means of gathering information still apply.

Finally, like understanding context in unfamiliar settings, understanding the use of technology in a corporate setting presents its own challenges.

In composition and other fields concerned with communication, researchers have tended to study technologies as discrete entities, starting with a focus on personal computers and word processing software in the early and mid-1980s, through recent scholarship focusing on new or emerging technologies such as electronic mail over local area networks, hypertext, and multimedia.

In many workplaces, and in contrast to the college or university computer lab, employees often choose among many available computer-based technologies to communicate a particular message. In terms of technology, then, this research had two goals: first, to explore how people chose among many technological options; and second, to investigate links between employees' perceptions of their context and their use of technology to interact with other employees. And there were links. At the corporate site where we conducted my research, social factors defined the use of communication technologies. Specifically,

- Communication technology options were determined by contextual factors at the organisational level. That is, technology deployment echoed the organisation's goals, values, and conflicts.
- Choice among the options reflected local culture. For example, widely held perceptions of uncertainty or distrust of management affected which technologies employees used to communicate.
- Not surprisingly, individual factors, such as an employee's interest in new technology, a need for control, or a dislike of writing further affected choice among communication media.

TYPES OF BUSINESS COMMUNICATION

There are two types of business communication in an organisation:

INTERNAL COMMUNICATION

Communication within an organisation is called "Internal Communication". It includes all communication within an organisation. It may be informal, formal function, or department providing communication in various forms to employees.

Effective internal communication is a vital mean of addressing organisational concerns. Good communication may help to increase job satisfaction, safety, productivity, and profits and decrease grievances and turnover. Under Internal Business Communication types, there come.

Upward Communication

Upward communication is the flow of information from subordinates to superiors, or from employees to management. Without upward communication, management works in a vacuum, not knowing if the messages have been received properly, or if other problems exist in the organisation. By definition, communication is a two-way affair. Yet for effective two-way organisational communication to occur, it must begin from the bottom. Upward Communication is a mean for the staff to:

- Exchange information
- Offer ideas
- Express enthusiasm
- Achieve job satisfaction
- Provide feedback

Downward Communication

Information flowing from the top of the organisational management hierarchy and telling people in the organisation what is important (mission) and what is valued (policies). Downward communication generally provides information – which allows a subordinate to do something.

For example, instructions on how to complete a task. Downward communication comes after upward communications have been successfully established. This type of communication is needed in an organisation to:

- Transmit vital information
- Give instructions
- Encourage 2-way discussion
- Announce decisions
- Seek cooperation
- Provide motivation
- Boost morale

- Increase efficiency
- Obtain feedback

Both Downward and Upward Communications are collectively called "Vertical Communication"

Horizontal/Literal communication

Horizontal communication normally involves coordinating information, and allows people with the same or similar rank in an organisation to cooperate or collaborate. Communication among employees at the same level is crucial for the accomplishment of the assigned work. Horizontal Communication is essential for:

- Solving problems
- Accomplishing tasks
- Improving teamwork
- Building goodwill
- Boosting efficiency.

EXTERNAL COMMUNICATION

Communication with people outside the company is called "external communication". Supervisors communicate with sources outside the organisation, such as vendors and customers. It leads to better:

- Sales volume
- Public credibility
- Operational efficiency
- Company profits

It should improve:

- Overall performance
- Public goodwill
- Corporate image

Ultimately, it helps to achieve:

- Organisational goals
- Customer satisfaction

5

Prospects of Information Technology, Communication and Entertainment for Development

INFORMATION, TECHNOLOGY, AND KNOWLEDGE SHARING IN GLOBAL ORGANIZATIONS

By all accounts, the trend towards using information and communication technologies for the global expansion of organizations is growing swiftly. Many organizations have moved into global operations through captive offshoring. In fact, a 2005 report by the McKinsey Global Institute has predicted that, by the decade's end, US companies will employ more than 2.3 million offshore knowledge-intensive workers.

From the perspective of organizational communication research, increases in the captive offshoring of knowledge-intensive tasks that rely heavily on the use of ICTs are hardly surprising. Recent studies have consistently shown that technologies enable the global distribution of knowledge-intensive work by providing individuals access to crucial information improving knowledge transfer capabilities among corporate units in different countries and permitting new organizational forms that more effectively handle spatial and temporal dispersion.

A good number of authors who study organizations in which people in different parts of the world are working on highly interdependent tasks have concluded that global knowledge sharing is fraught with difficulties. The problem, as they often argue, is circular in nature. ICT infrastructure, such as telephone lines and the Internet, and software applications that run on them, like groupware, group decision support systems, and even complex computer simulation technologies, enable organizations to internationalize; they create the conditions that make it possible to offshore interdependent knowledge-intensive tasks. But those same technologies also pose major obstacles for global knowledge sharing. This circular problem is often implicitly understood in terms provided by the transmission metaphor of communication. ICTs create an easily accessible channel for information to flow through space and time. Channels are always limited in their carrying capacity. Only a small extract from the entire body of knowledge necessary to perform a task can flow at a given time.

Further, as the knowledge leaves its source it becomes de-contextualized and uprooted from the practical space that defines the contours of its meaning, and can best be termed "information." Consequently, when such information arrives at its terminus it appears only in bits and pieces, and is abstracted from its original context and key referents. Because channels are limited in the types of content they can transmit, some amount of information must be left behind. Researchers of computer- mediated communication have long suggested that because the channels created by ICTs support text and voice predominantly, non-verbal cues are often omitted from transmission.

The omission of non-verbal cues has been shown to impede mutual understanding by reducing personal self-disclosure and increasing conflict. Further, channel limitations can preclude the transfer of entire spaces of knowledge. Knowledge gained from touch, smell, taste, or lived experience cannot be transferred through most ICTs available for use in today's global organizations.

A good deal of knowledge is acquired through these sensory stimuli, and when senders attempt to translate this knowledge into text and voice, receivers are not often able to acquire the contextual understanding necessary to use that knowledge in meaningful ways. Limitations of the transmission metaphor also direct our attention to problems that arise when knowledge is, at one time, encoded into a channel by someone with a particular constellation of socio-cultural understandings and later decoded by someone who does not share those same orientations.

A persistent concern is that a sender from one culture might encode knowledge in a way that will not be decodable by someone from another culture. If such cultural misalignment occurs, knowledge is not transferred. A related concern is that culture shapes the way individuals cognitively process information. As a consequence, individuals who encode or decode information will sample it in different ways, assign different weights to what is sampled, and make distinct associations between different pieces of knowledge.

The result is that the entirety of knowledge sent from one shore via ICTs may not be received on the other. Such a practically grounded and communicatively situated conceptualization helps us to explain why so many problems arise when knowledge is extracted from the context that defines it, forced into an ICT that mutates it, and decoded by someone who has neither the practical nor cultural experience to apprehend it.

It is striking that, despite the subtlety with which these accounts are constructed, few researchers seem to consider that people who are attempting to transfer knowledge and share it with others may not even agree on what knowledge is. Imagine the following scenario. Person A wants to transmit a dog to person B. Person A finds a teleporter that breaks the dog down into sub-atomic particles, which are sent across space and time and reassembled on the other side.

He puts the dog in the transporter and presses the "send" button. In our current conceptualization of knowledge transfer, we say that a problem of transmission occurs if person B receives the dog but it has only three legs, it has no tail, or it has two heads. Indeed, our theories can explain, in intricate and varied ways, why the dog that went into the transporter is not as complete as the dog that came out on the other end. But what if person B receives a monkey? She calls person A and says, "I thought you were going to send a dog, but I got a monkey." Person A responds, "I did send a dog, check it again." She checks. The monkey is the same weight, the same size, and the same colour as the dog person A says he sent–but it's a monkey. In this scenario, the problem is not with the transfer process; no content was atrophied in the transmission.

The problem is that persons A and B do not agree on what constitutes a dog. If they continue to have different ideas of what a dog is, no amount of refinement or improvement in the transfer process that eliminates channel noise will help. Where one person sees a dog, the other person will see a monkey. The knowledge-sharing problem that this metaphor raises is one of semantic incompatibility.

It comes as no shock to most that people from different cultures often have markedly distinct understandings of concepts like family, fidelity, faith, and friendship. So why wouldn't people from different cultures also have divergent understandings about what counts as knowledge? If people have unique understandings of what knowledge is, an important attending concern is that they will have different perceptions of where knowledge lies. Just as dogs lie on the ground and monkeys lie on branches, thing X, which is considered to be knowledge by person A, is likely to lie in a different place than thing Y, which is understood to be knowledge by person B.

The issue of where knowledge lies is of great importance for theories of knowledge sharing in global organizations, particularly those engaged in offshoring. In most offshoring arrangements, there is little direct interpersonal exchange of knowledge. Instead, people on one shore simply point each other to locations where they are likely to find the knowledge they need to do their tasks.

Research shows that people variously point to images or models, knowledge management systems or written documentation and contracts as loci for knowledge. But if people from different cultures have distinct conceptualizations of what counts as knowledge, and, consequently, unique beliefs about where knowledge lies, one person may look in a location designated by another and find nothing there that she considers knowledge. Or worse, when pointed towards a particular location by a colleague on a different shore, she might grow frustrated, thinking "of course there is no knowledge here," and form disparaging opinions about that colleague's competence, which, consequently, can cause her to question the soundness of the organization's offshoring plan altogether.

The goal of this chapter is to explore how cultural differences in perceptions of where knowledge lies can have adverse effects on global knowledge sharing in organizations. Rather than take for granted that people on different shores each conceptualize knowledge similarly and look for it in the same places, I begin with the assumption that cultural differences may compel workers in the same company to think of knowledge in distinct ways and to look for it in diverse places.

This approach focuses attention on how people within the same organization come to think about knowledge in varied ways. Drawing on empirical examples from a large automotive engineering firm, I explore how different conceptualizations held by engineers in the US, Mexico, and India about what knowledge is and where it lies stifled sharing, impeded learning, and led to general animosity among members of the organization who needed to work collaboratively to design and test vehicles. I conclude this chapter by discussing the implications of these findings for theories of technology, knowledge sharing, and organizational communication.

INFORMATION TECHNOLOGY AND OFFSHORING IN AUTOMOTIVE ENGINEERING

The International Automobile Corporation is a large automobile manufacturer headquartered in the United States. IAC is one of a growing number of companies, such as Intel, Dell, General Electric, Microsoft, and others, who have formed captive offshore facilities in a number of countries around the world. In contrast to offshoring-sourcing a captive offshore arrangement is a company-owned offshore operation in which the individuals who work at the offshore sites are full-time salaried employees of the focal organization. In this chapter, I focus on the work of performance engineers who are responsible for using simulation tools to validate and test parts as they are assembled into complete vehicles. Performance engineering work is comprised of two major tasks: model building and model analysis. To build simulation models, PEs convert computer-aided drawings into finite element models by dividing the geometry of a part into a collection of discrete portions called finite elements.

The elements are joined together by shared nodes. Nodes are the locations where values of certain load cases will later be approximated. The collection of nodes and finite elements together is known as the "mesh." This mesh is programmed to contain the material and structural properties which define how the structure will react to certain loading conditions. Once a mathematical finite element model is built, PEs begin to analyse it by submitting the model to a solver–a software package that performs computational analyses on the finite element models. I chose to study the work of PEs because they are the engineers who are most active in using information technologies that permit the offshoring of tasks to foreign locations.

In the eyes of IAC managers, the mathematical nature of model building and analysis, paired with the availability of advanced technology applications, VOIP, FTP sites, instant messaging, collaboration tools, and networked databases, means that PEs should be able to easily share work over geographic distance.

As one senior manager commented:

- We've paid lots of money to get technologies in place to help support our global work. We've got very expensive infrastructures that are among the best in the world. So we shouldn't see many problems with transferring work back and forth. The tools are all in place to share work, knowledge, and learning. In other words, we've been careful to get the right technologies in place so now all people need to do is use them to collaborate effectively across the globe.

As IAC managers regularly noted, offshoring is made possible, in large part, by the move away from using physical models for analyzing vehicle dynamics and towards the use of mathematically-based simulation technologies and the use of advanced ICTs. This chapter focuses on the ways that PEs at IAC engineering centers in the US and Mexico offshored work to engineers in India.

Apart from their size, the US and Mexican centers were quite similar. Both locations were responsible for the development of vehicle platforms. A vehicle platform is a common architecture upon which different models for various automotive brands can be based. PEs at both engineering centers were grouped into identical functional organizations that were responsible for various aspects of vehicle performance.

In 2003, IAC decided to begin its own captive offshoring operation in India. The India center was explicitly created by IAC to be a captive offshore service provider for engineering centers that worked on their own vehicle programmes. The India center had neither its own vehicle platforms nor production facilities.

As programme-based engineering centers, both the US and Mexico centers sent tasks offshore to the India center. Although the task assignment was unidirectional, knowledge sharing was not. To complete work successfully, the India center had to obtain knowledge from either the US or the Mexico center. In addition to the knowledge they acquired from these two centers on how to do the task, the India center gained important knowledge about the vehicle's performance in the context of actually conducting the task.

This knowledge had to be sent back onshore along with the completed task so that the engineers in the US or Mexico could make recommendations for improved vehicle design. This meant that the flow of knowledge was bidirectional. In the following sections, I demonstrate that each of the three engineering centers had a unique understanding of what constituted knowledge and, consequently, where that knowledge could be found. I explore how cultural norms for communication and interaction helped to shape these conceptualizations of knowledge and where it lies, and I then consider how these differences among the sites made difficult the collaboration between these globally distributed centers.

CULTURAL DIFFERENCES IN PERCEPTIONS OF WHERE KNOWLEDGE LIES

US Center: Knowledge Lies in the Head

Over the years, many scholars in the organizational sciences have given prominence to the individualism–collectivism distinction between national cultures. Individualism can be defined as a communicative pattern that consists of loosely linked individuals who view themselves as independent of collectives, and who are motivated by their own preferences. Collectivism, by contrast, is often defined as a communicative pattern that consists of closely linked individuals who see themselves as belonging to collectives, and who are motivated by the norms imposed by those collectives.

Following the work of Hofstede scholars have argued that the individualism–collectivism dimension of cultural variation is the major distinguishing characteristic in the way that various societies of the world analyse social behaviour and process information. Scholars frequently characterize the US as a highly individualistic national culture. At IAC, one need only walk around the offices occupied by PEs to see vestiges of this individualistic orientation towards knowledge.

A good number of PEs display diplomas from undergraduate and graduate studies, and many more proudly exhibit certificates earned for the completion of in-house training courses. There are also many signs hung in jest on the walls of people's cube that read "Weld Guru" or "Brake Booster Boss."

When asked why PEs were so eager to display these indicators of individual accomplishment, one informant responded:

- You know, this stuff just tells other people what you know. It's all sort of like displaying your credentials so other people know if you have some knowledge or some kind of expertise that other people need. I mean, no one really says that, but if you see someone got their [mechanical engineering degree] from MIT and you know that he's got lots of experience in vehicle dynamics, you might say, "hey,

I'll go to him if I need to learn something about a problem I'm having." It's all subtle, but it helps to just point out who knows what.

As this PE regularly observed, engineers at the US center were very clear in their understanding that knowledge was something that belonged to people. Banal though this observation may seem, PEs' belief that knowledge existed in the heads of people who were experts directly influenced the way they went about acquiring knowledge. PEs often sought knowledge from other people through both face-to- face and mediated communication.

In most instances, PEs were working on solving a vehicle analysis problem alone at their workstations. When PEs grew frustrated enough to seek help, they would often turn to me and say something like the statements made, at separate times, by three PEs:

- "I can't figure this out. I better go find someone who knows it."
- "The file has some penetrations in it. I need to talk to [the DE]. He probably knows why this is happening."
- "The last three iterations of the model haven't produced any better results. I'm going to talk to [another PE] because he might know how to fix it. He's really knowledgeable about this."

In each case, the PE was certain that the knowledge he or she was seeking lay in some other PE's head, as opposed to a book, a set of routines, or a communal data repository. To build and analyse a complex simulation model required a considerable amount of technical and domain knowledge. Once a model was complete, the technical knowledge that was used to produce the model remained with the PE who built it. However, the domain knowledge used to produce the model became embedded in the model itself.

To give a concrete example, a knowledgeable PE might know from his training and experience that to build an effective frontal crash model he needed to use a dense finite element mesh. The technical knowledge he used to build the model with a software programme could not be deciphered by dissecting the model later on, but the domain knowledge that the model should have a dense finite element mesh could be seen by examining the model.

For this reason, one might expect that PEs who wanted to gain the domain knowledge possessed by someone else might not have to talk with them directly, but could instead look at the models they built. But due to the strongly individualistic culture of the US center, PEs were very territorial about their models.

As one PE commented:

1. When I build a model it's like my intellectual property. Ok, ultimately it belongs to IAC. But I'm the one that built it. I don't want anyone just being able to go and look at it and use it how they want. I mean, I'm happy to share and explain it but they just need to come and talk to me.

Institutional IT policies at the US center reinforced this individualistic orientation that favored individual ownership of models. Each PE was assigned a unique user name and password, and was required to store his models in password secure drives. PEs were strictly forbidden from sharing their passwords with one another, and IT policy precluded the creation of group-level passwords such that any one member of a workgroup could log in to any other member's files.

Thus, if one PE wanted to look at another PE's model, he would have to ask him or her to fetch the model and then send it to him by e-mail or FTP server. Obviously, this policy and its attending practices encouraged PEs to talk directly to others and, for all intents and purposes, make fact out of the belief that knowledge only existed and was accessible by extracting it from someone else's head.

Mexico Center: Knowledge Lies in the Output

In contrast to the US, Mexico is often considered to be a prime example of a country whose culture is defined by a strong collectivist orientation. Studies have also shown that workplace cultures in Mexico carry strong overt preferences for collectivist action. PEs at IAC's Mexico center were acutely aware that anthropologists, psychologists, and communication theorists viewed them as members of a communally-based society.

As one informant commented on my first visit, after he learned that I had spent time observing engineers at the US center:

- I bet you'll find that we're much closer and more group-centered than the engineers in the US. All of the studies say that about us, right? We'll I think they're true. You'll find that there is much more talking going on here and we're all a lot closer and more friendly than if you are in the office in Michigan.

At first glance, the evidence seemed to corroborate this bold proclamation by the Mexican informant. The data reveal that PEs at the Mexico center did actively share knowledge with one another. However, unlike their US counterparts, they had a strong understanding that knowledge lay not in people's heads, but in the outputs of their labour. For PEs working on vehicle analysis, the outputs that they normally referenced were simulation results and finite element models.

Informants commented that they could typically gather greater domain-specific knowledge by examining the models a colleague had built as opposed to talking with that colleague directly:

- If you want to learn something it's best to look at someone's work. Find out someone who did something similar to what you need to do and go look at his model. You can examine the model and that is going to be more effective and more efficient. For example, if someone tells you that they found that some certain shape of a part gave the best performance that's helpful. But maybe your problem is a bit different. So if you can look at their models and see the steps they went through–I mean the different iterations of the test–then you can start to pick up some trends that will help you to design your parts better.

In addition to the perceived advantage of following a particular design solution through a series of iterations, Mexican PEs also believed that knowledge had a comparative basis. In other words, if one talked to another PE directly, that PE was likely to tell you what worked for her. Another PE would discuss what sorts of solutions had met her needs.

But without direct comparison of these described solutions to performance metrics, Mexican PEs felt that they could not tell which engineer's knowledge was better, or whose was most pertinent to the problem at hand:

- It's like everyone can tell you a different answer and everyone can seem to be very knowledgeable. But if you don't look at their results, you can't tell who is really the most knowledgeable. So it is better to look at their models than to talk to them. Get a model from person one, and a model from person two, and compare them side by side. See whose solution gave you better performance given the parameters you've set and then you can really tell. The knowledge that is in the models is more objective than the knowledge you get by talking to people.

This strong statement underscored a common distinction made by PEs at the Mexico center between what they called "espoused knowledge" and "demonstrated knowledge." To be sure, PEs valued demonstrated knowledge over espoused knowledge, and believed that the former lay in the output of people's work and it is there that one should go to uncover it.

The collectivist orientation permeating the Mexico center had, over time, diffused into a number of shared practices and policies. Among the most important for knowledge sharing was open access to others' models. It was a strong norm at the center for PEs to enter each other's files without permission and review each other's simulation results. Although PEs had their own unique user names and passwords to protect their documents, it was common practice for informants to store the results of their simulation analyses on a shared drive. The IT department at the Mexico center provided common passwords to these directories so that they could be accessed by anyone at any time.

Indeed, PEs espoused a very different relationship with their models and the results of their analysis than did their compatriots at the US center:

- When you build and analyse a model it's an opportunity for you and for other people to learn what works and what doesn't. You should share your model around if other people want it. But most of the

> time we're too busy to do that so you can just put it in the [common directory] and then if someone needs it they can look at it later.

Thus, a common collectivist belief in the value of sharing work and the notion that models belonged to the group rather than to any individual encouraged and was reinforced by IT policies that made it easy for PEs to share the outputs of their simulations.

The chatter and informal talk that took place in the office provided a useful venue for PEs to learn about who had done what kinds of jobs in the past, even if they didn't learn any specific domain knowledge from those conversations. But knowing who did what allowed PEs to form a mental directory that later helped them to navigate the electronic directories to find a person's output and examine it.

During my tenure at the Mexico center, I routinely observed PEs opening each other's models and studying their outputs. On occasion, PEs would add documentation to their output in anticipation of others examining it later and wanting to learn from it. Together, the collectivist orientation prevalent at the Mexico center encouraged and endorsed an understanding that knowledge lay in the products of people's work. As one PE put it so succinctly: "If you look, all the things you see are arrangements of knowledge in some form or another. You just have to look at them to learn yourself what the builder knew. Knowledge belongs to a community."

India Center: Knowledge Lies in the Position

While India is often viewed to tilt in the direction of a collectivist culture most observers agree that the cultural dimension that most strongly pervades everyday life, whether on the street, in the home, or at the workplace, is the ingrained respect for social hierarchy. As Mines notes: "In India, hierarchy structures all relationships and proscribes autonomy." Research conducted in Indian organizations has described, for more than half a century now, the pervasive effects that the cultural inscription of hierarchical thinking has on working relations.

Such a cultural sensitivity towards and respect for hierarchy is enabled and perpetuated by a deeply seated Hindu caste system, which has been shown to lead Indian nationals to be cognizant and respectful of the status differences inherent in any social relationship. At IAC's India center, PEs were acutely aware of where they stood in the center's status hierarchy. During my two months at the India center, I often encountered PEs running into problems building or analyzing simulation models. The reasons for these problems were varied. In some cases, the Indian PEs simply did not have enough information from the requesting engineer in order to complete the assigned task.

In other cases, the Indian PE did not have enough domain knowledge to effectively build or analyse the model. If this were the case, it was often because the engineer in India had never seen or worked with the kind of analysis that the engineer in the US or in Mexico was requesting.

When Indian PEs found themselves in a situation where they did not have the domain knowledge to solve a particular problem, they were often quite candid with me, the observer. They would say things like, "I don't know how to do this," or "this problem seems to be more complex than I can know how to solve." I would often ask them who they believed did have the knowledge to solve the problem.

Consider the following responses:

- "Oh, my manager will know the answer to this."
- "It's definitely my manager. I will talk to him about this."
- "My manager will be able to figure this out."
- "I will have a conference with my manager. He can give me some knowledge about how to do this."

Such statements contain an unwavering belief that someone of a higher status position will have the knowledge to solve the particular problem at hand. After conducting research at the US and Mexico centers, I was quite surprised to hear this type of response. It was a norm, rather than an exception, for PEs in the US and in Mexico to verbally denigrate the skills and knowledge of their managers.

In India, by contrast, PEs seemed quite assured that their managers could solve most engineering problems, and that they were key holders of important domain knowledge. This tendency to believe that knowledge lay in one's position had consequences for PEs' daily work. For example, I spent time observing a PE in the HVAC group who was conducting an airflow analysis.

The analysis used a simulation to determine whether the force of air emanating from the vents on the dashboard was sufficient to cool the driver and the front passenger. After running the simulation, the PE opened a 3D rendering of the mathematical model, which depicted air flowing out of the dashboard vents and through the passenger compartment.

After spending some time looking at the 3D rendering, the PE turned to me and commented:

- Basically, these are the flow lines. What happens is that when the flow comes it will go through the ducts and from the outlet it will come out. But we need for people to be at certain angles so that the air either it hits chest, face or lap position which are our target points. So, to cool it effectively, rotation of the vent should meet the target–that is head, chest and lap. So if it's not meeting the target it won't hit you on the face or lap, you won't get cold air, so that is the reason. So we cannot run the analysis with just this vent, because what will happen is the place where this is happening it will show regulation of the temperature because when you, this is just for the flow when you do it with the temperature, see, the velocity here it is very high. So this is a problem.

The problem that the PE referred to is that the model was run by simulating airflow from only one vent in the center of the dashboard. As the PE observed, this particular model would not give an accurate representation of the force of airflow because it omitted an analysis with the other vents.

The implication of such an omission on the model was that if a decision about the force of the airflow was made on this analysis alone it would be incorrect, because it failed to consider the alternate sources of airflow in the passenger compartment. The PE copied the 3D rendering into a Power- Point presentation and wrote several notes in the margin indicating that the analysis was run with only airflow from one vent modeled.

He sent the PowerPoint deck via e-mail to his manager. The next day, the PE and his manager sat down to review the results of the airflow analysis. They began by opening the PowerPoint that the PE had created the day before.

The manager looked at the image and commented:

- *Manager*: Why was this run done with only the vent in the center stack operating?
- *PE*: This vent was the only one included in the geometry that was sent from the US center.
- *Manager*: It is not a sufficient analysis because it is missing the other dash vents, so this model of the airflow will not be accurate.
- *PE*: Yes, I see.
- *Manager*: Did you notice this when you were running the analysis?
- *PE*: Yes
- *Manager*: Why didn't you fix it then?
- *PE*: Yes sir. I thought I should review it with you before I made any changes.
- *Manager*: But you knew it was a problem?
- *PE*: Yes.
- *Manager*: So now we've lost a day because you did not repair the model before running it.
- *PE*: I just thought it was best to ask you because you might be knowing better whether this should be adjusted instead of me just doing it without asking.

What is striking about this interchange, and the many more like it that I observed, was that the PE indicated just the day before that he knew the model was inaccurate and that it needed to be fixed. Despite this knowledge, he was reluctant to make any changes without the explicit consent and recommendation of his manager.

The PE felt that because his manager had a higher status position, he would be more knowledgeable about the analysis and would be in a better position to determine whether or not the model needed to be changed. The interchange, however, shows the tension that can arise when a PE has sufficient domain knowledge to complete the task but does not believe that he is as knowledgeable as someone with a higher status position.

To wit, we see the manager growing frustrated that the PE did not take more initiative to complete the task on his own. This problem was common, even between PEs and managers who were both Indian nationals. The hierarchical nature of the work at the India center led to very clear culturally-bound understandings that knowledge was not the province of individuals but that knowledge lay in one's position in a status-driven hierarchy of relations.

COMPUTER COMMUNICATIONS

We have thus far avoided mention of the budding computer communication industry that, without doubt, will have a major impact on the ways businesses communicate among themselves and with clients. Cost of equipment necessary for computer communication is beyond reach of the average person, and applications for such a service are limited to professional settings. Nonetheless, there are two reasons why this discussion is relevant to our purposes. First, there are immediate uses for computer communications among many specialized audiences.

Businesses, educational institutions, political organizations, and others have already adopted the equipment necessary for computer communication and are now in a position to utilize computer-based interpersonal programmes. Second, as costs are reduced for computer equipment and the technology diffuses further into the population, audiences and uses for such programmes will expand. The design we describe here is only an early prototype that will probably go through many modifications to accommodate expanding audiences and improvements in technology.

This example draws positive features from several existing computer communication programmes and thus represents an amalgam of the best components rather than a single programme currently in operation.

SETTING AND BACKGROUND

A political consulting firm in Arlington, Virginia, spotted a trend in the use of professional campaign assistance by candidates running for small state and local offices. As campaigns have become more sophisticated with extensive use of mass media, direct mail, and polling technologies, candidates have had to supplement their small campaign staffs with help from professional consultants.

Market analysis revealed that candidates often had difficulty locating such help, and when they did hire these specialists, they often had to pay for more services than their small campaigns really needed.

The firm decided there was a national market for one-stop shopping for campaign consulting services. Candidates around the United States could turn to this outfit for assistance in audience measurement, campaign strategy design, media purchases, fund raising, and other political campaign features. They could buy an entire package or use only those services they needed at any given time.

Moreover, the company believed it could provide most of its services directly from Arlington and avoid spending a great deal of time on site. Although company specialists would travel to the field if necessary, the plan called for most of the work to be done from the main office in northern Virginia.

The essential communication link between the company and clients would be the computer.

Data could be sent back and forth, problems could be examined and discussed, budgets could be debated, media could be planned. In fact, communication required for all activities could be accomplished quickly, accurately, and efficiently by exchanging information between computers over the telephone lines. For instance, a client in Missouri could send telephone survey data to Arlington where they would be processed and analyzed. Within hours, results complete with charts, graphs, and recommendations could be sent back to the client.

The computer system would allow transmission of complex material that could otherwise be sent conveniently only by mail. In the heat of a political campaign, even overnight mail is too slow. The computer links made this consulting plan possible. Information could be exchanged quickly with virtually no limitation on the complexity of data that could be sent. Since computers were so important in the operation of this service, the company decided to involve them in the interpersonal portions of the promotion. This consulting firm established initial contact with potential clients through mass media and direct mail. They would then demonstrate the capacity of their system to engage in an interpersonal dialogue using the computer connections.

Programme Design

It is typical for such consulting firms to work exclusively with one political party. Such was the case in this instance. Consultants who work exclusively with one party enjoy the confidence of candidates and party officials. They also find it easier to obtain general information about people who plan to run on that party's ticket. With its party connections, the Arlington firm was able to get a mailing list for the direct mail portion of the campaign. The company firm generated personalized letters to several thousand announced candidates. It prepared several versions of the letter based on the office sought, incumbency status of the candidate, region, previous party successes in the area, and probable campaign issues. Computer-typed letters were addressed to each candidate by name, and letters were further personalized by using the candidate's name throughout the text.

Mass media (only magazines in this case) were used in the following way. The firm advertised this service in political party magazines received by large numbers of party regulars, officeholders, and staff members. Interested readers were given an address to which they could write and a toll-free number to call if they wished additional information about the company's services. Through either channel, the receiver was placed on a list that would bring a copy of the personalized letter (the same one sent out in the direct mail phase). Only the letter, and not the mass media ads, contained specific information about the interpersonal portion of the programme. Significant programme costs made it necessary for the company to limit enquiries, where possible, to serious prospects. If a receiver was sufficiently stimulated by descriptions in the letter to make the enquiry, he or she would have some reasonable level of interest in the service.

The letter provided simple step-by-step instructions for the receiver to become involved in the interpersonal communication programme—called the "demonstration." Receivers were told what hardware and software they would require and what they should expect when they had established contact for the demonstration.

First, they were to call an 800 number. A company representative would answer and review with the caller the basic design of the consulting services being promoted. In other words, the caller was given a standard sales pitch. But the programme went beyond that.

The caller was prompted to ask questions, discuss problems, or deal with any relevant aspect of these consulting services. When this interaction played out, the caller was asked for several items of information that were used by the representative to prepare the demonstration programme.

The caller was asked to turn on his or her computer, printer, and modem (equipment that enables computers to communicate over phone lines), load the communication software, and then observe the computer screen.

Using the information provided by the caller, messages appearing on the screen showed colour charts, budgets, and other information selected for their substance and visual appeal. For the grand finale, a message on the screen instructed the receiver to turn attention to the printer that typed out three pages of statistics, charts, and a radio script.

The printer then produced a final message wishing the candidate (by name) success and expressing the consulting firm's desire to assist in the campaign. A message flashed on the screen directing the caller to pick up the phone for further conversation with the company representative. At this point, talk turned to specific commitments to the service, follow-up demonstrations, and additional discussions. This computer communication system is an example of a truly specialized, interpersonal communication approach, posses-sing many of the features we look for in one-on-one communi-cations:

- It provides for feedback. Interactants first make verbal contact and establish a rapport, then they communicate through computer keyboards and other computer devices (such as sending data contained on a disk) in an iterative fashion. The same channel allows information to flow back and forth between sender and receiver.
- Information exchange is rapid. People can send and receive information instantaneously, avoiding the serious problems that result from delayed transmis-sions. In some applications this feature may be critical.
- Receivers are self-selected. Clients who use the computer to interact with a business choose to do so. They are inclined, therefore, to have a particular interest in the topic and so are stronger business prospects.

As we said at the beginning, the use of computers is just now being explored for interpersonal business communica-tions. Technology within the next decade will no doubt considerably expand these uses for specialized interpersonal programmes. Businesses stand to save time and money. They will be able to do a great deal of work from a single location, reducing travel requirements and enabling a single employee to handle a greater number of accounts. An accountant in New York can work on the books of a client in Seattle without leaving his or her desk. Moreover, he or she can discuss intricacies of these books with as much ease as if everyone were in the same room. A small automotive engineering firm in Albuquerque can review details of its new windshield design with prospective clients in Detroit who have decided to see what the distant firm has to offer. Companies may conduct sales, respond to queries, and generally engage in the give-and-take we have come to expect with interpersonal communications.

Although there will still be need for other forms of interpersonal contact, we expect computer communication to be an increasingly important addition to the available repertoire of approaches.

THE CHANGING NATURE OF TECHNICAL COMMUNICATION PROGRAMMES

THINKING IN BROADER TERMS

In the last half of this decade, the questions that we have identified have begun to influence the ways in which educators prepare students to enter the U.S. workforce. Faced with these unsettling issues, many educators have been forced to reconsider their own responsibilities and identities, as well: to see themselves less as instructors of writing skills in a narrow sense and more as teachers of communication in a field that has broadened considerably in its scope.

During this time, teachers of business and technical communication have expressed increasing interest in social theories that help them and the students with whom they work come to a broader understanding of discourse and its roles in shaping cultural formations (*e.g.*, feminism, Marxism, radical democracy, socialism); and address the role of writing and other discursive practices in formulating, examining, and enacting civic responsibilities within broader social arenas. Teachers of business and technical communication have also begun to explore how their own educational responsibilities relate to the expanded programme of democratic social action that now informs critical pedagogy, liberatory pedagogy, rhetorical theory, composition studies, and cultural studies.

As a result of these explorations, the teaching of professional and technical writing, of non-academic writing, has also begun to expand in dramatic ways. Many programmes now include the study of ethics, decision making, social policy formation, rhetorical theory, or risk communication. Increasingly, professional writing courses within these programmes are designed to impart to writers not only a sense of responsibility within corporate contexts, but also a sense of responsibility within broader social and civic spheres.

Inspired, further, by the direct connections that have been established between the professional practice of technical communication and the social/ political decision making in cases such as the Challenger disaster and recombinant DNA research, professional educators are beginning to perceive their responsibility not only as teachers of writing skills, but also as transformative intellectuals who must pass along to communicators both a sense of "public responsibility" and "civic courage".

These perspectives, it is clear, may require communicators to undertake political or civic action that is radically opposed to the official status quo or to a narrow sense of corporate interests. Given this recognition, educators have begun to reason that technical communicators need the ability to think against the grain of prevailing thought as well as with it.

Without this ability, technical communicators, and indeed all students who populate our schools, may prove unable to influence, shape, or change technological and political decision making within the public spheres they inhabit as workers and citizens. As a major part of this expanded course of study, teachers of professional and technical communication are recognizing the need to pass along to students an expanded vision of democratic citizenship and involvement, a sense of the importance of public debate over science policy, and an critical consciousness about the role of language in weaving the cultural fabric of a democratic society.

Enacting such new pedagogical directions in a meaningful way, however — especially within traditional professional writing or technical writing classrooms — has proven difficult, given the general influence of dominant cultural tendencies, the constraints of traditional classrooms, the dynamics of the larger educational system, and the expectations of industry. Faced with these tendential social forces, both teachers of written communication and students may find it easier to think and to write within the bounds of conventional thinking than outside of them.

Educating students to question decisions, to involve themselves in broader social programmes, to engage in debates concerning public policy often creates problematic educational feedback. Such feedback comes from parents, who are understandably concerned about the expanded course of study and the effects it will have on their children's future in the workforce; from the public, which may be exposed to students practicing their craft in less that skillful ways within high-stakes arenas; from administrators, who must cope with the institutional costs of an expanded curriculum in technical communication programmes.

Similarly, practicing communicators — like Jackie in our earlier example — often find it easier to practice written communication that supports the existing goals of a company, an organization, or an assignment than to resist and interrogate these goals. As Jackie found out, the task of identifying and gaining access to spaces in which writing is recognized and practiced as an activity involving larger social and political dimensions is difficult, albeit possible. At the time of publishing, Jackie had not only kept her access to the technical writing discussion group on Internet, but, by her own admission, made inroads with her supervisor who modified his concept of the corporate good.

Equally difficult is the task of coping with the related responsibilities of reflecting on the complexities, subtleties, and challenges of such writing. Often, writers in non-academic settings perceive themselves as caught in webs of social, economic, and political forces that work against productive social action or involvement — in discursive situations that take place both on and off computers. These individuals may, indeed, avoid talking about writing as a means of participating in expanded social projects because such talk is perceived as dangerous, contentious, or disloyal within existing organizational settings.

TURNING TO THE NETS AS LANDSCAPES FOR AN EXPANDED CURRICULUM: PROMISE AND PROBLEMS

As we have indicated, one area that indicates some potential for supporting an expanded conceptual framework for technical and professional writing is that of computer networks. For the last 8 years, technical communication and composition specialists have devoted increasingly large portions of their scholarly attention to the study of electronic forums — discursive spaces created on local-area networks and wide-area networks -as alternative communication spaces for professional writers, and for teachers and students of writing.

The primary focus of the interest in these forums, to date, has been on the value of the virtual landscapes of networks as alternative communication spaces that have the potential for supporting learning and discursive practices that can be different from, and-some claim — more democratic than, those occurring within traditional corporate or classroom settings.

Claims made for networks in industry, for example, have indicated that they may provide a low-cost, time-efficient forum for communication among expanded communities of individuals and groups; that they may increase the opportunities for democratic participation in problem-solving tasks; that they may encourage individuals to share information across corporate sites in increasingly altruistic ways; that they may encourage expanded opportunities for professional development; and that they may support more responsive, intimate communication environments than do conventional settings for exchange.

Related claims for computer networks as alternative learning environments in educational settings indicate that they can be structured to provide for student-centered, online discussion groups in which individuals discover their own motivations for using language through actual practice; for online conferences in which writers' race, gender, age, and sexual orientation may not figure in the same ways that they do in more conventional face-to-face settings; for collaborative groups and online editing groups in which students learn to negotiate discursive power for themselves; and for self-sponsored written exchanges among expanded social communities.

Through this work, we have come to recognize some of the potential of computer-supported forums, to see them as intriguing micropolitical spaces within which technical communicators, and teachers and students of technical communication, can seek to address, on a relatively localized level (within a particular classroom or business setting, for example), some of the problems currently plaguing our educational system and corporate culture. Given this set of circumstances — educational, social, corporate the widespread exploration of these electronic discursive spaces has become important not only for many technical communication teachers and students, but also for writers and technical communicators in corporate environments.

Importantly, however, we have not yet paid enough attention to the many problems associated with educational and professional discourse within virtual landscapes or to the complicated political issues that permeate and shape communication on networks. Frequently, we have been content to portray these electronic landscapes as one-dimensional, utopian spaces-open to progressive and reformist influences, but not to conservative forces.

It is becoming increasingly clear that if these virtual landscapes are conducive to productive discursive involvement in larger social and political arenas, they are also complex, hotly contested public territories shaped by a set of dominant social forces which generally influence and limit this involvement in certain directions and for certain purposes. Given this recognition, teachers of technical communication and professional communicators are beginning to see that electronic landscapes need to be explored with an increasingly critical sense of the ways in which they are constituted and the ways in which they operate.

One important area of concern, for example, is the extent to which these electronic spaces — and the discursive practices that occur within them — are already controlled and shaped by official interests: those of government, business, the military, and educational institutions that conduct research for these entities (sometimes identified collectively as the State or as the military-industrial complex).

The combined interests of these groups may serve not to support discursive changes that result in social action and democratic reform, but rather may serve to reproduce forces supporting the status quo. For evidence of this claim, among many other sources, we can point to current work on the National Research and Education Network, a project being discussed and designed primarily by governmental agencies such as the Defence Advanced Research Projects Agency (DARPA), the Department of Energy, the National Aeronautics and Space Administration, and the National Science Foundation (NSF), and national research universities which do contract work for these agencies. We can also point to increasing restrictions on agricultural database information by the Office of Management and Budget and the Department of Agriculture, and to the work on "weaponized virus" programmes by the United States Army.

These examples represent only a fraction of those computer-based projects currently being funded by that collection of corporate, educational, governmental, and military forces. And, although we certainly cannot assume that all such efforts are problematic in terms of their democratic or social goals, we can assume that they are shaped by the same widely dispersed set of complex, shifting beliefs, signification, and material relations that sustains existing social inequities and differentials of power and resources within our government, economic, military-industrial, educational, and welfare systems.

What these examples do confirm is the need to understand virtual landscapes as the ground for multiple, ongoing struggles — among them, struggles between official entities that generally have a vested interest in sustaining the current social, educational, political, economic status quo, and the competing interests of citizen groups (some consisting of technical writing teachers and workplace communicators) who are committed to a programme of expanded democratic political action that alters the status quo.

The examples we have provided, however, are more complicated than a simple oppositional relationship indicates. They also illustrate the recognition that teachers in state-run, state-sponsored, or state-supported institutions and practitioners in corporate contexts — that is, many instructors of communication and professional communicators — are themselves often representatives of the interests of the military-industrial complex and the State, even as they are simultaneously opposed to many of the goals or practices of these entities.

These facts as scholars such as Laclau and Mouffe, and Virilio might point out — seriously complicate the ways in which we conceive of communication within electronic spaces, the ways in which we see our roles in shaping and reproducing these spaces, the possibility of undertaking democratic reform within these contexts, and the ways in which we understand our own motivations for civic action.

WHERE WE START

Public Sheres as Discursive Landscapes and Sites for Civic Action

To understand how and why the particular discursive spaces of computer networks have come to assume such importance and power as intellectual and political territories for teachers of written communication and for writers in workplace settings, it may be useful to first examine, in a general way, the power of discourse as a force for political action when it is deployed in public spheres inhabited by members of a body politic. Certainly, scholarship on this subject is abundant in fields as diverse as literary theory, critical theory, radical pedagogy, feminist theory, and cultural studies.

Rhetorical theory, however, may provide the most immediate entry into this conversation for teachers and practitioners of technical writing, given the value it has traditionally placed on civic discourse and its role in political affairs. In the field of rhetoric, a great deal of attention has been paid recently to the role of classical rhetorical studies within the modern academy and the public spheres of civic involvement. Generally, work in this area points to the need for a resurgence of rhetorical study as civic discourse aimed at social action, as a theory-laden practice that reconnects textual invention, arrangement, and analysis to political, legal, religious, educational, and commercial contexts.

Central to these works are two tenets: that the modern study of rhetoric needs to become more "practical" and "politically oriented", and that citizens should learn to use rhetoric to increase their effectiveness as "critical thinkers" capable of social and political action. This work which Kinneavy, Miller, and other scholars trace back to rhetoric's classical roots foregrounds the importance of public spheres that are poised, in Eagleton's words, "between state and civil society", spaces in which individuals employ symbolic and rhetorical systems to discuss, analyse, and transform the complicated forces affecting their lives as workers and citizens.

This notion of rhetorical study departs from the concept of rhetoric — and written communication — as areas of study limited exclusively to the academy. Further, it suggests to teachers in disciplines like professional writing and technical communication — and to writers within non-academic settings —

the importance of entering and working within larger public spheres, taking responsibility for engaging in social and political action, acting as citizens who can be "persuasive in a political environment". Such a system, Kinneavy pointed out, recalls the essential connection among discursive practices, discursive spaces, and political action so fundamental to Athenian culture during the 5th century B.C. where "the implementation of a programme by laws and assemblies presuppose[d] individuals speaking freely in a society, the conceptions of freedom, free speech, the city, and an individual's right to make decisions" as "necessary axioms". The essential components of these arguments are the study and practice of rhetoric and its extension into public spheres with a stated commitment to individual or collective civic action and meaningful political involvement on the part of workers and citizens.

Eagleton and Habermas, in related cases from different perspectives, also argued for a return of open and critical discourse to public spheres. Eagleton, talking about the role of literary critics as it developed in the late 17th and early 18th centuries, describes the discursive spaces of "clubs, journals, coffee houses, periodicals" in which "private individuals" of the European bourgeoisie assembled for "the free, equal exchange of reasonable discourse, thus welding themselves into a relatively cohesive body whose deliberations" assumed "a powerful political force". The critical discourse within this public sphere, as Eagleton noted, also assumed a collective political force that "served the emancipation movement of the middle class as an instrument to gain self esteem and to articulate its human demands against the absolutist state and a hierarchical society". Habermas provided a related analysis of the public sphere that emerged with the growth of the bourgeois in Europe, "a sphere of public authority, a forum in which the private people, come together to form a public, readied themselves to compel public authority to legitimate itself before public opinion".

The essential argument in both cases — that of the rhetoricians, and of Eagleton and Habermas-is that this public discursive forum, in which people engaged in "debate over the general rules governing relations" allowed for a "public use of... reason". As Eagleton continued, a "ceaseless circulation" of public discourse, of civil and political exchanges within public spheres can serve workers, writers, and citizens who want to form a political collective, a "power bloc at the level of the sign". In short, public spheres as discursive spaces can also serve as powerful political landscapes, and ones that teachers of written communication and professional communicators may not be able to afford to ignore.

Eagleton also pointed out, however, some of the contradictions and complications connected with the concept of the public sphere, particularly that the exercise of rhetorical power and democratic involvement within these spaces is complicated by the exercise of power and ideology that shapes their nature. The public sphere of the 17th and 18th century, as Eagleton noted, contained a "concealed problematic" in that it established its own boundaries of rational discourse on the basis of participants' "capacity to articulate" a case through rational conversation, an exercise of power limited to those with property, education, and a certain social status. As Eagleton quoted Saunders, membership within the public sphere of clubs, journals and coffee houses in the 17th and 18th centuries was limited to "politicians, diplomats, lawyers, theologians, scientists, physicians, surgeons, actors, and so on, besides the poets and other writers".

Hence, the legitimacy of the discourse within this particular public sphere in Europe belonged only to propertied classes and was denied those without money and education, people like "farm laborers or domestic servants".

As a result, the legitimating of discourse within this community, Eagleton commented, was ideologically constrained within "a certain paradigm of reason inscribed in the very event of saying". Given these circumstances, then, free exchanges were possible, but only within a localized "ideal discursive sphere." The ideological apparatus of this sphere allowed what seemed to be the free exchange of civil and political discourse without apparent "domination," "without a breath of exploitation", just as long as participants could ignore those classes outside the political and ideological boundaries of their discursive space. Hence, in Eagleton's words, irony was inherent in this public sphere during the 17th and 18th centuries: Although it embodied, in one sense, the potential for resistance, democratic change, and a productive "discursive reorganization of social power", it typically proved "conservative and corrective". Given the ideological constraints woven into its fabric, discursive exchanges within this space simply served to redraw "the boundaries between social classes" along different lines, and, hence, to preserve many of the inequities that rested at the heart of social problems characterizing the period.

If we wanted to go back to the roots of classical rhetoric, we could also find, in 5th-century Athens, a similar, localized exercise of free rhetorical exchange, one shaped and constrained within ideological boundaries of another public sphere. Although this period is often heralded as the Golden Age of classical rhetoric and democratic discursive participation, women and slaves — partially because they did not have property rights — were not considered citizens in the fullest sense of the word and were, thus, never allowed to vote on political matters or to sit or deliberate in the ekklesia or assembly, the very foundation of Greek citizenship.

Hence, the notion of public spheres as forums for democratic discursive exchanges — places for the critical analysis of social issues, for amassing and deploying individual and collective political force — may present an attractive concept to teachers of writing and to writers practicing in non-academic settings who are committed to an expanded democratic project. But if this concept is attractive, it is also problematic and highly complicated. If citizen rhetors, citizen critics, workplace writers, and even teachers of professional or technical writing can find within these public discursive spaces opportunities to exercise power, through discursive strategies to "reconnect the symbolic to the political," and to wield individual and "collective political force" they also find themselves operating within an existing ideological landscape shaped at fundamental levels by regularly dispersed discursive formations and leveled, at least currently, by our "commodity culture" and its accompanying ideologies. Within such ideological constraints, the potential of fundamental change is clearly limited and controlled influenced by dominant ideologies which generally serve the interests of the status quo.

However, as Laclau and Mouffe help us see, social contexts are composed of complicated sets of relations among discursively constituted identities, and cannot be either simply or fully articulated by terms like State, the status quo,dominant ideologies, or expanded democratic project, which we have employed thus far. The relations among these social elements, the authors pointed out, are overlapping, "polysemic", dynamic, and continually shifting. Hence, dominant ideologies that broadly support the continued functioning and reproduction of military-industrial or state interests, never exert complete or totalizing control over social identities which oppose these constructs. Nor, at the same time, can opposing, or reform-based, forces hope ever to define themselves in the complete absence of these dominant systems.

Such complicated sets of cultural relations deny "the conception of 'society' as a founding totality", and illustrate the partial, fragmentary, "precarious" nature of all power and its exercise. If the discursive practices of public spheres can contribute to "the maintenance and reproduction" of the status quo — this reasoning suggests — the same practices shift continually in "unstable oscillation" and never crystallize as a "moment" of "unified discourse" that would entirely preclude effective action or change.

Rather, as Laclau and Mouffe pointed out, the contradictions in the "space of hegemony", the "antagonisms" fundamental to discursively constituted identities within cultural and social spaces, the necessary presence of continual subversion and contradiction attest constantly to the possibility of such action. In fact, it is through the exploitation of these discursive antagonisms, through the exploitation of ruptures and gaps in political spaces (and, here, Jackie's efforts come to mind) through the continual transformations of unstable limits and frontiers that "democratic struggles" find life.

ASPECTS OF THE COMMUNICATION (MESSAGE)

The studies reviewed to this point have all dealt with the influence of the characteristics of a source of a communication and the setting in which the communication was delivered on attitude change. The source and the channel or setting in which a message is delivered, constitute two of the four broad classes of stimuli viewed as central to the persuasion process.

Another aspect of the communication situation that has a major influence on attitude change has to do with the general form of the message itself, a central feature of the SMCR model. Message form encompasses a wide variety of communication characteristics, but two critically important features, discrepancy (between a communication and a receiver's attitude) and the emotion-arousing nature of the message, are discussed in the sections that follow.

SOCIAL JUDGEMENT THEORY

In any persuasion attempt, the communicator is faced with the question of the optimal distance to interpose between the message and the receiver's established attitude. Should the persuasive message be very inconsistent with, or very close to, the position of the receiver? If the communication is extremely discrepant from the receiver's attitude, and if it is accepted, then the source has induced the maximal amount of change for the smallest investment.

On the other hand, a message can be too distant from a receiver's established attitudes, and thus is rejected. In this circumstance the maximally discrepant communication would prove 'minimally effective. Under such conditions a somewhat less discrepant message would prove more influential. Although the degree of attitude change that such a message produces might not be great, such a communication might prove more effective than more extremely discrepant appeals.

An extension to the standard theory of attitude change. Called "social judgement theory," this approach borrowed from classic psychological research on perception to develop a predictive model of attitude change that is not only simple, but also based firmly on well-established psychological principles. To present social judgement theory properly, we first must introduce a few novel terms, and will do so in the context of a psychological demonstration.

Suppose that you were given a set of small blocks of lead, and asked to estimate their weight. To assist you in this task, you were provided with the heaviest weight, and informed that it weighed five hundred grams. On the basis of considerable prior research on topics of this nature, we know that this information would influence your judgement of all the other stimuli in the series. The known weight would act as an anchor, which is a stimulus that exerts a large influence on the judgements of other similar stimuli.

Interestingly, the position of the anchor in the stimulus series determines the manner in which it affects judgements. If the anchor falls at one or the other extreme of the series of weights, judgements of the other weights are displaced away from it. In the present instance, you would have a tendency to judge the other weights as lighter than they actually were. This type of anchor-induced bias on judgements is called a "contrast effect," which refers to an influence on one's judgement in a direction away from the anchor.

Baseball players make use of the contrast effect when they swing a leadweighted bat before stepping up to home plate. Why do they do this? Because after swinging a very heavy bat, the one to be used at the plate feels much lighter than it would otherwise. They feel that they can bring this "lighter" bat around more quickly, and thus hit the pitch with greater velocity.

A contrast effect also would have occurred if the ten-gram weight, the lightest of the seven lead blocks, were used as a comparison in forming judgements of all of the other weights. However, the shift in judgements away from the anchor in this instance would have resulted in the other weights being perceived as heavier than if no anchor were used.

There is yet another way in which your judgements could have been biased in the weight-judging task. Suppose that you were given the weight of the lead block in the middle of the series (the two hundred fifty-gram weight) and asked to use it when judging the other blocks. In this instance your judgements would shift towards the known weight. This shift in judgement towards an anchor is called an "assimilation effect," and it occurs when the anchor lies somewhere within the range of stimuli to be judged.

The findings concerning the effect of anchors and their placement on people's judgements are well established and were used to form the basis of social judgement theory. The task of demonstrating the relevance of these fundamental psychological findings for communication and persuasion was simplified in a series of studies that showed that anchors need not necessarily consist of physical, external stimuli such as blocks of lead. Anchors also can be internal to the perceiver, and such "internal anchors" can bias judgements just as surely as external ones.

For example, suppose you are asked to rate each of twenty-five pieces of construction paper of different colours in terms of the "pleasantness" of their colour. After going through this task once, you are asked to think of the most pleasant colour imaginable and to concentrate on this image for a few moments. Following this exercise, you once again judge the pleasantness of each piece of colored construction paper.

If you guessed that your evaluations of the paper the second time would be less positive than the first, you would be correct. The "most pleasant colour" acts as an internal anchor, which is at the extreme (pleasant) end of all colours. When this anchor is made salient, a contrast effect will result when the other colours are presented a second time. Ratings of these other colours will be displaced in a direction away from the extreme anchor. Since this anchor represents the most pleasant colour you could imagine, the "pleasantness" ratings of the other colours will decline. While this study might strike the reader as somewhat implausible, it must be stressed that the expectations discussed here were confirmed in a study conducted nearly a half century ago and have been replicated in innumerable classroom demonstrations since then. Anchors that are internal to the perceiver do exist, and they do influence judgements.

Anchors an.d Attitude Change

The relevance of this observation for attitude change is clear: If attitudes are considered internal anchors, then persuasive messages that foster positions at variance with such attitudes are likely to be displaced judgementally as a consequence of the distance between the anchor and the position being advocated. Contrast effects are likely in situations involving a large discrepancy between the anchor and the communication.

In other words, if a message advocates a position that is extremely discrepant from a receiver's established attitude, a contrast effect is likely. In such a circumstance, the message will be viewed as even more threatening than it actually is, and tenacious counterargumentation can be expected. Little, if any, attitude change is likely under such conditions; indeed, in some situations of this type, people have been found to change their attitudes in a direction opposite to that of the communication (such reversals sometimes are given the graphic term of "boomerang" effects).

On the other hand, if a message advocates a position that is relatively close to the internal anchor (that is, the receiver's attitude), it is likely to be viewed as being closer to this position than it actually is. Under such circumstances the message will stimulate little need on the part of the recipient to counterargue.

As such, the information presented in the message should prove persuasive; assimilation will occur, and attitude change will result. However, since the position advocated in the message is not too discrepant with the receiver's established position, the actual amount of change that occurs will not be great.

Given the theory of social judgement as presented to this point, we can make some reasonable, if gross, predictions about the likely outcome of an attempt at persuasion if we know a receiver's established belief and the discrepancy between this attitude and the position advocated in the persuasive message.

Latitudes of Acceptance, Rejection, and Non-commitment. Suppose a person held a negative attitude towards a company or product. We could conceptualize this attitude as lying near the negative end of a scale that is representative of all possible shades of attitude towards such concerns. (The person's position is marked with an X on the scale.) If a message only slightly contrary to this view were introduced (let us call this "message A"), it might be assimilated by the person, whose attitude might change slightly in the direction of the message. On the other hand, if the message were extremely discrepant, a contrast effect is likely, and no change, or a change opposite to that urged in the communication, would occur.

From personal experience we know that most attitudes are not discrete points on the continuum of all possible beliefs surrounding an issue; rather, our attitudes might be described more accurately as summary statements of the range of positions or statements about an issue that we are willing to accept. This fact and acknowledged this view in their theory. In doing so, they defined the range of positions that an individual might find acceptable as that person's "latitude of acceptance."

Just as there is a range of positions on an issue that an individual might find acceptable, there also exists a range of positions on a topic that one might find completely unacceptable. This range is called the individual's "latitude of rejection." The concepts—latitude of acceptance and latitude of rejection. The latitudes of acceptance and rejection embrace a range of possible acceptable and unacceptable positions.

Not all attitude-relevant positions on an issue are subsumed within the latitudes of acceptance and rejection. The remaining possibilities on the attitude continuum are called the "latitude of non commitment," which represents positions that an individual neither accepts nor rejects automatically. Such positions are viewed by the individual as neither particularly laudable nor particularly odious.

FLatitude of Acceptance | FLatitude of Noncommitiment | Latitude of Rejection

[X] [ ] [ ]

Fig. Possible Range of Opinions Towards Some Issue or Object

The relevance of these concepts for the practice of persuasion is that messages falling within a person's latitude of acceptance will be assimilated, while those falling in one's latitude of rejection will stimulate a contrast, or boomerang, effect. To achieve maximum attitude change, a communicator ideally would target a persuasive message so that it fell somewhere within the boundaries of a receiver's latitudes of non- commitment.

Such a message would avoid the latitude of rejection and as such would not maximally engage the receiver's defences. The receiver would probably counter argue in this instance, but would still be susceptible to attitude change. Messages falling within the person's latitude of non- commitment provide the possibility for the most extensive attitude change. When people change their attitudes on an issue, the positions that once were within their latitudes of non- commitment often are displaced to their latitudes of acceptance or rejection.

FLatitude of Acceptance | FLatitude of Noncommitiment | Latitude of Rejection

[X] [C] [ ]

Fig. Latitudes of Acceptance, Non- commitment, and Rejection

Ego Involvement and Latitude Width

There remains yet one additional feature of social judgement theory that should be discussed, and this feature has to do with the width of the boundaries of people's latitudes of acceptance, rejection, and non- commitment. The latitudes need not be of equal size—indeed, such an occurrence is unlikely. What, then, determines the varying widths of these three regions? The extent to which an individual is involved in the issue under consideration will play the central role in determining the width of the various latitudes. Ego involvement is defined as "the intrinsic importance of the issue" for an individual, reflecting that person's "abiding stand on the issue."

In circumstances of extreme ego involvement, the theory predicts a broadened latitude of rejection and a constricted latitude of acceptance. Under conditions of low ego involvement, the opposite is expected—a wider latitude of acceptance relative to the latitude of rejection is postulated.

A pictorial representation of variations in people's latitudes of acceptance and rejection. From this illustration it should be clear that highly involving attitudes will be the most difficult to change. In these conditions a receiver's latitude of rejection is wide, and the latitudes of acceptance and non-commitment are correspondingly narrow. As such, there is a much greater possibility that a persuasive communication will fall within the receiver's latitude of rejection when highly involving attitudes are the focus of the persuasive message. The usefulness of this theory in a mass communication application rests on the satisfaction of two conditions. First, it is necessary that the receivers of the persuasive message share some generally consistent attitude about the issue of concern. Further, while the audience might be involved in the issue, there must be some room for persuasion—that is, that the members of the audience are not so involved that there is no possibility for modification of attitudes.

Both of these necessary conditions presuppose some form of audience assessment. In our terms, "needs assessment" is necessary before the insights of social judgement theory can be brought to bear in a communication programme. Therefore, the business communication expert intent on making use of this model first must determine that there exists in the audience a relatively homogeneous attitude on some issue of relevance, through appropriate forms of needs assessment. In addition, some estimate of the degree of involvement in the issue is also necessary. Having done this, the communications expert then can tailor the message so that it falls somewhere within the latitude of non-commitment of the general audience.

Ego Involvement, Discrepancy, and Change

In its most simple form, social judgement theory predicts an inverted U-shaped relationship between communication discrepancy and attitude change.

At very low levels of discrepancy between a persuasive communication and a receiver's attitude, an assimilation effect is expected, and hence little change is anticipated. As the communication moves into the receiver's latitude of non-commitment, increasing change is anticipated until the person's latitude of rejection is reached. At this point the change value of the communication is minimized by the contrast effect.

The research undertaken in the investigation of the predictive implications of this model has provided generally supportive evidence. A review of a few of the many studies in this area will supply some insight into the general trends in this field. In one of the earliest studies of the effect of ego involvement and the relative widths of respondents' latitudes of acceptance and rejection, a series of nine statements that summarized a wide range of possible attitude positions regarding the prohibition of alcoholic beverages in their state (an issue on an upcoming ballot).

People were asked to indicate which statement best represented their attitude, which of the others were acceptable to them, which was most unacceptable, and which of the others also were unacceptable. This research indicated that the more extreme the respondent's most acceptable position, the wider the latitude of rejection.

Source Credibility, Discrepancy, and Attitude Change

There is a limit on the extent to which greater message-attitude discrepancy results in increased attitude change, and this limit appears to be imposed by a variable that has been shown to play a major role in other areas of attitude change research, namely, source credibility. A summary observation that appears justified on the basis of considerable research is that the greater the credibility of a source of a communication, the stronger the relationship between discrepancy and attitude change. When source credibility is not high, there is little relationship between communication discrepancy and attitude change.

At moderate levels of source credibility, the relationship appears U shaped (or "curvilinear"); that is, discrepancy and attitude change are positively associated up to a point, with greater discrepancy resulting in greater change. After this point is reached, however, increasing messageatti-tude discrepancy typically results in less and less attitude change.

In this idealized illustration, we see that the perfectly credible source is totally effective in inducing attitude change. The more change suggested by such a source, the greater the change induced. This is reasonable, as the very definition of perfect credibility demands an identity between suggested and observed change.

Similarly, the complete lack of relationship between discrepancy and change when the source of the discrepant message is perfectly incredible also is set by definition.

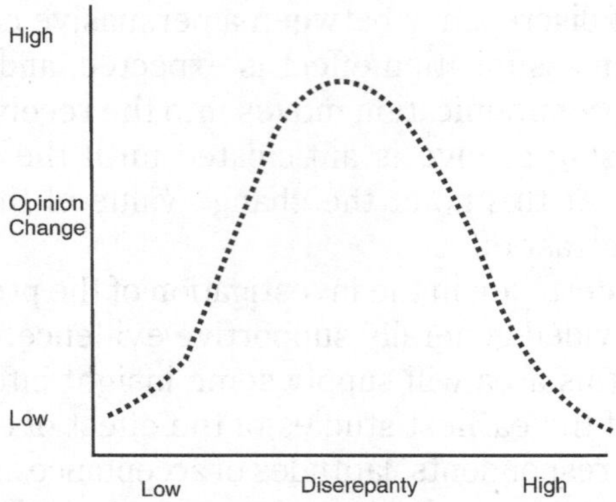

Fig. Hypothesized Relationship between Discrepancy (between a Message and a Receiver's Opinion) and Opinion Change

If one cannot believe anything a communicator says, then no relationship will exist between message discrepancy and attitude change for communications produced by such a source. Finally, at moderate levels of source credibility, we expect a gradual increment in attitude change as message discrepancy increases; however, at some point, the receiver will begin to refuse to accept the source's influence. As discrepancies beyond this point grow, the receiver will question more and more intensely the expertise or objectivity of the source. Eventually, at extreme discrepancies, the impact of the source's message on the receiver will prove counterpro-ductive.

Fear-Arousing Communications

Another variation in message form or organization that has stimulated considerable research in theoretical and applied communication and persuasion settings is concerned with the effects of fear- or emotion-arousing communications on attitude change. In this area the central issue has to do with the relative differences in persuasiveness of emotionally arousing versus non-arousing communications.

The investigators presented their respondents, high school students, with one of three different communications regarding dental hygiene. The messages, which combined slides with verbal instruction, were the same, except in the degree to which gory details and personalized threats ("Brush your teeth properly, or they're liable to fall out") were included as part of the communication. In the high-fear arousal condition, respondents were informed of the painful difficulties they would experience if they did not brush their teeth properly, use the appropriate type of toothbrush, etc. In addition, a series of gruesome slides depicting the consequences of poor dental hygiene were presented along with the verbal message.

At the other extreme, respondents receiving the low fear appeal learned of the development of teeth, etc., and were shown slides of healthy teeth, xrays of cavities, etc. A middle group employed a moderate approach to the topic.Assessment of respondents' recall of the factual materials revealed no differences among the three message conditions. However, there were differences between the groups in the amount of fear induced. As expected, the gory, personalized threats of the high-fear message did induce greater anxiety than the moderate- or low-fear-arousing communications.

One week after this session, respondents were tested again. This followup revealed that the students who had been subjected to the high-fear-arousing message were the least likely of all three of the groups to have followed the advice presented in the first session. In addition, they were most susceptible to a countercommunication that argued against the major premise of the original message. In explaining their results, the experimenters argued that the high-fear message caused people to respond defensively to it, and thereby to avoid thinking about it. Over time, such defensive reactions would offset the possible impact of the persuasive message on receivers' behaviour.

This interpretation was consistent with a further series of findings by Janis and Terwilliger, who provided groups of smokers with one of two communications regarding the dangers of smoking. In the low-fear communication, respondents were given fifteen paragraphs, attributed to medical authorities, which argued that a serious form of cancer caused by smoking could be avoided if smokers reduced their use of tobacco. The high-fear message contained seven additional paragraphs that detailed the life-threatening aspects of lung cancer.An intriguing aspect of this study concerns the measures that were gathered as respondents read each of the messages. After each paragraph, people were asked to verbalize their reactions to the information that it contained. An analysis of these reports revealed that those people in the high-fear condition

- Were more frightened than their counterparts—in other words, the arousing communication worked
- Were much more likely to reject the information presented them
- Were consequently less likely to change their attitudes regarding smoking

These results supported their "defensive reaction" explanation of the effects of fear-arousing communications. Apparently, a very frightening or threatening message results in a rapid and tenacious counter argumentation response. This reaction in turn weakens the effect of the communication on the attitude of the receiver.

The consistency of results of the two studies by Janis and his co-workers presents a somewhat misleading picture of the consensus of scientific opinion in this area of research. In fact, social psychologists and communications specialists are far from agreement on the issue of whether high- or low-fear arousing messages are more persuasive. Indeed, if consensus exists on this issue, it is that the greater the level of fear arousal, the more persuasive the message. Some idea of the reasons underlying the uncertainty of results in this area can be gleaned from a consideration, which in many respects was very similar to that of Janis and Terwilliger. In the study by Insko and co-workers, a group of non-smoking junior high school students served as respondents and were exposed to either a high- or a low-feararousing antismoking message. Contrary to the results of Janis and co-workers, these investigators found that the high-fear arousal message had a greater effect on respondents' attitudes than the low-arousal communication.

In his discussion of this study, Insko reported that respondents who had been exposed to the more arousing message were much more likely to respond negatively to items such as "Will you ever try smoking cigarettes?" and "Will you become a regular smoker?"

The communications varied considerably with respect to the fear-arousing nature of the materials presented. The high-fear arousal message, for example, included colour pictures of a tracheotomy, pictures of tetanus patients with tubes inserted in various parts of their bodies, etc. The results of this study disclosed that those who had received the high-fear-arousing message were more fearful about tetanus; in addition, they had more favorable attitudes towards tetanus injections than students who had read the low-arousing message.

Results such as these have been viewed as inconsistent with those of the Janis group, and on the surface such an interpretation appears justified. However, these divergent findings can be integrated. In considering these apparently contradictory findings, it is useful to concentrate our focus on the research of Janis and Terwilliger and to contrast aspects of their research operations with those of Insko, Arkoff, and Insko. While similar in many major respects, one crucial difference did exist between these studies, and this difference provides an important clue to the interpretation of this research literature. In Janis and Terwilliger's experiment, the sample consisted of a group of long-term smokers; in the study by the Insko group, the respondents were non-smoking seventh-grade schoolchildren.

While the age difference between the samples is obvious, it is not this feature that is crucial; rather, respondents' differential experience with the activity in question, smoking, appears to be the major determinant of the variations in the results. Respondents in the Janis and Terwilliger study were smokers.

Consequently, it is reasonable to hypothesize that they might have been more than a little concerned about the implications of this practice for their health, even before the experiment began. Given this circumstance, it is arguable that a large increment in this arousal level—which would be evoked by the high-fear arousal message—would prove extremely noxious, since it would add to an already uncomfortable level of anxiety. If this were the case, then respondents in the high-arousal condition of the study would be expected to counterargue the persuasive communication with a good deal of vigour, for in doing so they could counteract the threatening implications of the communication. Smokers in the low-arousal condition would not be expected to raise such a strong defence against the message, since that message would not be expected to raise anxiety to noxious or intolerable levels. Accordingly, the low-fear arousal communication would be expected to be the most persuasive in this study, since it would not stimulate extreme defensive counterargumentation. This was the result obtained by Janis and Terwilliger.

The persuasion context was very different in the Insko group experiment. In this study, respondents all were non-smokers. As such, they probably were not worried about the impact of smoking on their health. As such, a motivating high-fear arousal message would be expected to prove more effective, and this is the result that was observed.

These findings in combination suggest that the pre-existing level of a person's anxiety will affect his or her response to a fear-arousing communication. If an individual already is deeply concerned about an issue, then a message designed to evoke fear will prove counterproductive. Such a message will be punishing to the receiver, who thus will be stimulated to reject its contents. If the receiver is not already in a highly anxious state, then a highly arousing communication will prove more effective than a non-emotional message.

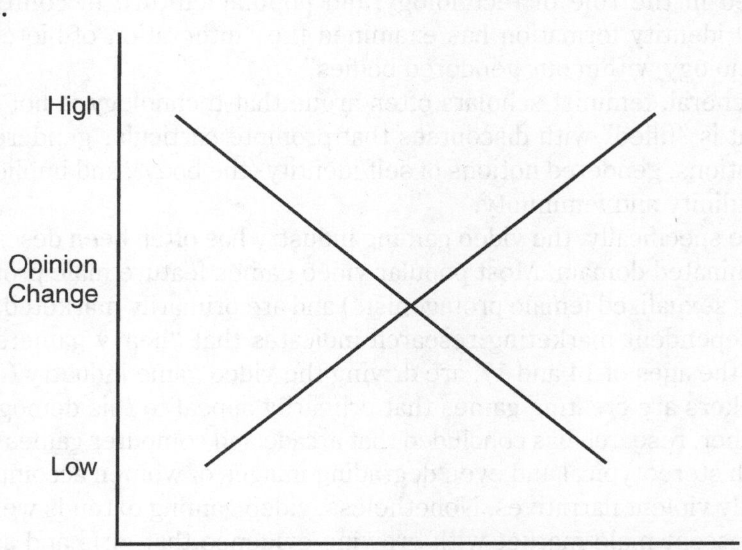

Fig. Relationship between Receiver Anxiety and Threat Level of a Communication on Opinion Change

The impact of a fear-arousing communication does not depend totally upon the level of threat provided in the message itself, but operates in concert with the level of anxiety or fear that already exists within the receiver.

The practical applications of these findings for the communication specialist are straightforward. First, the literature suggests that emotional communications need not always be avoided. Indeed, such messages do have a place in the communicator's fund of potentially employable techniques of persua sion. It is critical, however, to understand the level of anxiety that surrounds the issue of concern.

If the audience already is worried about the issue to be discussed, then it is in the best interests of the communicator to avoid adding to this anxiety. To do otherwise would stimulate avoidance of the message, thus rendering ineffective the attempt at persuasion or information diffusion. On the other hand, if the issue is one about which there is little concern, then a fear-arousing message, if justified, can prove effective in alerting the audience to the problem and in motivating an appropriate action.

GENDER AND VIDEO GAMING

Built upon the language and discourses of science, pervasive communication technologies play a unique role in contemporary cultural processes, particularly conceptualizations of gender. Previously, feminist scholars have identified mastery and control as primary values of both masculinity/patriarchy and science/technology. For instance, feminist critics interested in the role of technology and popular culture in contemporary gendered identity formation has examined the "integration of biotechnology and technology within our gendered bodies".

In general, feminist scholars often argue that technology is not a neutral "tool" but is "filled" with discourses that promote particular gendered power configurations, gendered notions of self/identity (the body), and implicit values for masculinity and femininity.

More specifically, the video gaming industry has often been described as a male-dominated domain. Most popular video games feature male protagonists (or highly sexualized female protagonists) and are primarily marketed to young men. Independent marketing research indicates that "heavy gamers," males between the ages of 14 and 17, are driving the video game industry (*i.e.*, video game makers are creating games that primarily appeal to this demographic).

Further, research has concluded that arcade and computer games are often filled with stereotypical and even degrading images of women accompanied by graphically violent narratives. Nonetheless, video gaming extends well beyond this adolescent male market with growing evidence that girls and adult men and women are increasingly playing video games—as many as 56 million people between 35 and 50 are playing video games and around one-third of console-game players and 40 per cent of computer-game players are female. The diversity of video game players does not appear to be changing the types of games produced by the video game industry. In fact, "the bikini babes" and "damsels in distress" that pervade video gaming alienate many women who enjoy playing computer games.

For instance, many video games' narratives and imagery fit well with adolescent male fantasies—*e.g.*, the packaging and images of popular games like Blood Rayne and Xtreme Beach Volleyball depict young women in revealing clothing in poses conventionalized in "soft core" pornographic magazines such as Maxim and Playboy with the clear intent of attracting the gaze of the adolescent, heterosexual male consumer.

This "male-dominance" of the video gaming context also emerges from the social norms surrounding video game players. As Lucas and Sherry (2004) concluded, "Based on established social norms, video games are perceived to belong in the male domain, and female players and male players alike experience greater social acceptance by staying within sex-role expectations".

The adolescent (heterosexual) male emphasis of the video game industry is perhaps best exemplified in the cable network G4's television series "Video Game Vixens," an awards show for female video game characters which aired in the summer of 2005. The programme was promoted by the network as "The hottest, sexiest and most lethal videogame babes will get your heart racing and your palms sweating in G4's irreverent new awards show". The "awards show" included categories such as "dirtiest dancer," "best booty," and "most dangerous curves." Some video game advocates defend these sexualized and violent female video game characters (or "avatars") as empowering to women—while virtually always scantily clad and with the impossible proportions of a Barbie doll (or perhaps, more appropriately, a Playboy playmate), these women are "fighters" and therefore "empowered". The notion that this quasi-"girl power" is positive for women is highly problematic, bell hooks clearly identified the inconsistencies of the messages in these video games—rather than challenge patriarchy:Now women can be killing machines, but adolescent about everything else That is what one sees in 'Charlie's Angels,' the women kill as ruthlessly and as brutally as any men, but when it comes to sex that drops out and they are little girls.

It is a tremendous burden. (online document)Frankly, to view these depictions of women in popular video games as "empowering" is a rationalization based upon a distorted "it could be worse" logic. While women can offer resistive, alternate readings of these characters, the dominant reading (particularly by most gamers) is clearly promoting patriarchy by reproducing images of highly sexualized and childlike women performing for a heterosexual male gaze. On the other hand, not all representations of women in video games rely on sexist stereotypes. In popular games such as Half-Life, Radiata Stories, and Elder Scrolls, women are not sexualized and often are represented as competent, intelligent, and assertive. Unfortunately, in an industry courting the young male consumer (gamers), these representations remain a minority. As Jansz and Martis concluded:

Gender stereotypes are particularly robust with respect to physical features. Men are still represented as hyper muscular characters, and women hyper sexualized characters. In other words, quite a few women became leaders in games, but they continue to function as 'eye candy' for their consumers, the gamers.

Further, popular video games usually involve narratives of violent conquest. For instance, of the 83 games with nine or higher ratings (with ten the highest rating) by the most popular gaming publication, Game Informer: 18 were sports simulation games (games such as NCAA Football 2005 and Gran Turismo 4, which reproduce sporting events), 7 were "puzzle" oriented games (*e.g.*, games such as Super Mario Bros and Lumines in which the player moves through layers of a puzzle), and 58 were "violent conquest" games (games such as Halo 2 and Doom 3 in which the primary objective is to violently defeat and/or kill enemies to advance through missions or stages).

Like other forms of entertainment media such as television and film, video games typically involve characters who perform actions within stories. In fact, often the narratives of video games are taken directly from feature films, books, and television programmes (*e.g.*, Spiderman, The X-Files, The Lord of the Rings)—and, increasingly, the inverse is also true (*e.g.*, Resident Evil, Final Fantasy, Tomb Raider). In some respects, the narrative form of video games follows the conventions of other entertainment media such as films and comic books.

These consistent patterns within video gaming narratives have fostered generic conventions and expectations that consistently emphasize violent conquest. A journalist describing a video game convention in 2003 observed, "A few genres dominate: first person shooting games, fantasy multiplayer games, sports re-creations, movie fie-ins".

Based upon the reviews of the most highly rated games by Game Informer, the narratives of these "violent conquest" games are remarkably consistent. While there is variability in the "specific objective" such as tracking down a terrorist as a spy (Splinter Cell: Pandora Tomorrow) or defeating a criminal as a super hero (City of Heroes) or killing monsters in a fantasy world (Fable), the template of the story is essentially the same: Violently defeat the "enemy" and progress to the next "stage."

The reviewers consistently described the process of reaching these violent objectives as the primary source of pleasure derived from playing the game. For instance, the review for Devil May Cry 3 stated: "The sense of accomplishment you get when you master your skills and beat one of the insane bosses into submission makes all the toil worthwhile". As this example demonstrates, the general emphasis of many of the reviews was the "technique" for killing the enemy. The review for Resident Evil 4 described the game's most appealing characteristics as:

This time around, everything that so much as raises a finger at you must die—preferably by a nicely placed headshot. A remarkable new targeting system allows this feat to be handled with the utmost precision. On this note, I've never seen so many heads explode in my life.

The new over-the-shoulder perspective coupled with abeautifully crafted laser sight makes for a lethal and satisfying combat experience.

Further, even in the sports-related games, the "techniques" for dominating the "enemy" (the other team, the other drivers, etc.) were still the primary focus of the reviews. The reviewers referred to the application of these techniques as "control." Previously, scholars have argued that the "interactivity" of video games provides the player pleasure because the game makes "it possible for players to gain control over the elicited arousal". This control is a source of pleasure for the gamer. As the review for NCAA Football 2005 stated:

I loved scoring first as an away team and causing the crowd to eat a big plate of shut the hell up. You can also get things under control by calling a timeout, during which your coach boosts the morale of a particular segment of your team, such as the WRs. This is what a big-time NCAA game feels like, and I love it. The game also contains some nice brutal hits, including user-controlled ones by pressing the L2 button.

In general, the themes of the vast majority of the most popular and "well-respected" games are remarkably consistent: dominate the "enemy" via skillful (usually violent) techniques. At this point in the discussion, I should note that not all popular video games follow these conventions. More specifically, not all popular games have a win-state or the goal of ultimate victory.

Frasca (2003) distinguished between "the most widely popular" ludus video games which provide "us with two possible endings: winning and losing" and much less pervasive paidia video games which leave "its main goal up to the player".

Games such as The Sims, SimCity, Nintendogs, and Animal Crossing do not involve violent conquest or competitive conflict. As I examine in the conclusion of this analysis, these non-violent, non-competitive, more "open-ended" gaming conventions may offer viable alternatives for the gaming community.

While both conservative and liberal critics have been quick to point out the violence and sexism that is ubiquitous in video gaming, social critics and scholars have rarely offered an explanation concerning the underlying motivation to play these sexist and violent video games.

In the following analysis, I argue that the discourses of these games create an entelechial motivational system drawing players towards a perceived state of perfection. Further, video games' patriarchal and sexist discourses emerge from the pursuit of an entelechial state of perfection that ultimately encourages subjugation via dehumanization.

VIDEO GAMING AS AN ENTELECHIAL MOTIVATIONAL SYSTEM

In the reviews of the 83 top rated video games (9.0 or higher) from Game Informer between December 2003 and August 2005, two words were recurring: "addictive" and "master." First, variations of "addiction metaphors" were sprinkled throughout the reviews of all types of games with statements like, "absolutely addictive gameplay" and "one of the most addictive and rewarding time sucks in recent memory".

As these statements suggest, these addictive qualities were not characterized as negative but as the highest compliment the reviewer could offer a game. As the review for the game Max Payne 2 stated, "At its heart, this is a shooting gallery—the world's coolest, most stylish, and addictive shooting gallery".

In fact, both inside and outside the gaming world, video gaming is often descibed as a compulsive or "addictive" activity. For instance, on Thanksgiving 2002, Shawn Wooley committed suicide while sitting in front of his computer playing the multi-player fantasy video game, EverQuest. Publicly, his mother blamed his suicide on an "addiction" to EverQuest.

This incident drew tremendous media attention and fed an already growing perception that video games were addictive. Popular periodicals ranging from Newsweek to The Washington Post to National Public Radio reported stories concerning the "addictive" quality of EverQuest or "EverCrack"—a term popularized by the game's players. Recently, an online support group for "EverQuest Widows" (*i.e.*, significant others of EverQuest "addicts") has attracted over 6,000 members.

This perceived video game addiction is closely tied to the gamer's pursuit of "higher scores" and "new levels." For gamers, status is measured precisely and numerically. Once the gamer has "completed" all levels or reached the "high score," he/she has "mastered" or "beaten" the game. Again, this status relies upon the mastery of the "skills" of the video gamer's avatar.

For instance, the review for Jade Empire stated, "By game's end I had dabbled in or mastered over a dozen different fighting styles". Similarly, the review for Doom 3: Resurrection of Evil stated, "once you become proficient in the use of your environment and the new toys, RoE will suck you in and keep you enthralled until the last demon lies gibbed at your feet". Game reviewers characterized the video gaming experience as mastering skills to ultimately "beat" the game: "While I beat the game in about 12 hours, much of my time was spent repeating a handful of tough stages scattered throughout the game".

The more "skills" (*e.g.*, accurately shooting a gun, timing a punch) the video gamer masters, the greater status the video gamer achieves.

This is referred to as "deep play" or the "near-obsessiveness" with "gaining points, devising a winning (or at least a spectacular) strategy, and showing off their prowess to other players during the game and afterwards, during replay".

The review for Onimusha 3: Demon Siege described this process: "Each character will upgrade their weapons and skills through the course of the game Without a combo-laden combat system, Demon Siege relies heavily on timing and strategy to master each of the three warriors". Ultimately, these techniques or skills allow the player to advance to new, increasingly challenging game stages.

In many respects, the perceived addiction derives, in part, from the desire to "see the end" and "beat" the game. This is a distinctly entelechial process based upon a desire for completeness, finishedness, and perfection. As the review for Halo 2 stated:

- You begin this roller-coaster ride, and you just want to keep playing till you reach the end (and even then I instantly restarted the game on its Heroic and Legendary levels—which offer a whole new level of death and destruction).

In the gamer vocabulary, advancing to new stages in the game is considered "leveling." Leveling is often based on what Gee (2006) calls challenges that "feel hard, but doable" or each task becomes slightly more difficult but always within the reach of the player. Players continue developing more and more complex skills until they achieve, in Gee's words, "mastery".

In violent conquest games, leveling generally occurs by reaching a particular "objective" (which typically requires the skillful execution of enemies). In sports-oriented games, leveling occurs when players "master" the skills associated with driving the car, throwing the football, shooting the ball, etc. The pleasurable experience of developing skills to reach a new level was clearly described in the review for Ninja Gaiden:

- Each weapon (and its upgrades) brings with it a different set of moves and strategies. When you begin the game, you have a standard set of attacks at your disposal. A few stages later, you'll find yourself with more moves than you know what to do with.

You'll be bouncing off of enemies' heads, tossing them into walls, launching into the sky and spearing them, and even summoning the power of the gods to create a whirlwind of ice With 16 lengthy stages, Normal and Hard difficulties, and secrets buried around every comer, Ninja Gaiden is capable of keeping you hooked for the better part of the year.

From start to finish, this game captivated me to no end and wowed me like few others have. The more skillful and knowledgeable the player becomes, the more the player can control aspects of the game with advanced combat skills, magic, weaponry, etc.

The convention of leveling originally emerged from the video game producers' desire to have players plug "more and more quarters in the arcade machine" with "the revelation of the new level the reward for having survived and mastered the previous environment".

Even though 21st century gamers usually play video games from their homes on console machines and PCs, these "quarter plugging" conventions remain. Today, in most games featuring avatars, gamers seek to develop the "best" or "strongest" characters possible—this is the central purpose of the game. In fact, the intense desire for the strongest character has fostered online auctions for already created, highly advanced characters. By purchasing powerful characters, gamers can more quickly advance to new levels in the game and achieve greater status in the video gaming community.

An organization entitled "Twin Galaxies" compiles the "high scores" for hundreds of video games. On its web site, the organization describes its mission as "to verify 'official' world record high-scores and crown new world champions." For instance, according to Twin Galaxies, only four video gamers have played a "perfect" game of Pac-Man reaching the score of 3,333,360, the maximum number of points allowed in the game. As the highest plateau on the hierarchy, these "word champions" represent the absolute, "perfect" completion of the game. This hierarchy resides in the inherent "gameness" of video games: "quantifiable outcome means that the outcome of a game is designed to be beyond discussion". The gamer's primary objective is to reach the highest level of the hierarchy (moving up each "level") in order to reach a teleological endpoint. In fact, Burke's articulation of the entelechial principle in Language as Symbolic Action almost seems to be specifically describing the gamers' discursive system: The principle of perfection (the "entelechial" principle) figures in other notable ways as regards the genius of symbolism. A given terminology contains various implications, and there is a corresponding "perfectionist" tendency for men (humans) to attempt carrying out those implications.

Thus, each of our scientific nomenclatures suggests its own special range of possible developments, with specialists vowed to carry out these terministic possibilities to the extent of their personal ability and technical resources. For Burke, the ultimate objective when analyzing an entelechial system is "the tracking down of implications within a particular vocabulary". In the case of gamers' discourses or vocabularies, the implications stem from the technical pursuit of a "perfect" state of mathematical mastery.

6

Information and Communication Technology

Incorporating dimensions of the metaphor of information ecology in an analysis of the role of the LIS professions in community development helps to identify the close relationship of social equity with ecology and economy in specific contexts. Connecting economy, ecology and social equity as overlapping, interdependent, and mutually encompassing spheres helps LIS professions participate in community development in ways that are more inclusive of people and impacts their lives in more meaningful ways.

Historical evidence suggests that efforts to encourage community development are successful only if there is active participation from people in local communities, and they have a significant stake in community building. In the coming years, use of emerging information and communication technology (ICT) can potentially lead towards an increased transfer of authority and responsibility from higher-level agencies to the neighbourhood or community.

This transfer will significantly engage and empower people and provide wider benefits to the community's well-being. ICTs can also strengthen the role of the library and information science (LIS) professions in this process of community building for achieving sustainable community development in terms of economy, ecology, and social equity. This paper will discuss different service-oriented examples in which libraries, library practitioners, and information professionals have played a significant role towards ICT-related community development to promote an equitable distribution of society's resources to disadvantaged users. The aim is for community development practitioners to recognize the efforts of LIS professionals and integrate them in community development efforts.

Libraries are viewed as an information ecology that consists of a system of people, practices, values, and technologies in a particular local environment. Such a vision helps to develop our understanding of information not only in terms of the institution or the technology that helps in its creation, organization, dissemination, and access.

The metaphor of information ecology places information in the context of use of the information, in the context of the people who need the information and who are impacted by the institution and its technologies, and in the context of the embedded community and its "messy" realities. This paper interprets the idea of information ecology in the context of a holistic vision of communities. The goal is to identify some potential characteristics of information ecology (in the context of communities) that are important requisites for sustainable community development.

The discussion addresses the expanded function of the LIS professions in community development initiatives to use ICTs to enhance social equity in communities. Incorporating dimensions of the information ecology metaphor in an analysis of the role of the LIS professions in community development helps identify the close relationship of social equity with ecology and economy in specific contexts. In traditional conceptualizations, the notions of economy, ecology, and social equity offer three different domains in which libraries have an impact on communities.

This paper takes a contrasting position where even though the focus is on the social equity component in community development yet the underlying assumption is that social equity, ecology, and economy are intrinsically intertwined. The line of thought emerges from the understanding that LIS professions are valuable partners in building local assets in community development, based on several interrelated factors associated with human, physical, social, financial, and environmental capital to meet community needs.

LIS AND COMMUNITY DEVELOPMENT

As community information providers, libraries have a long history of involvement in community development efforts by creating convivial cultures and providing mechanisms for information delivery and community services. Yet, there is tremendous potential for developing these ties further in the future, especially in the context of the "digital divide" and the specific needs of "marginalized" communities. In recent years, based on the tradition that libraries provide democratic access to communities, scholars have recognized that libraries are among the best places for provision of ICT.

As a result, the entire LIS profession is attempting to extend their roles in community development as information providers to disenfranchised populations. This attempt means incorporating cutting edge ICT and advanced computer systems in community development. The first library-based online community information system in the United States, developed by the Pikes Peak Library System in Colorado, began providing dial-in access to community information in 1978. Some of the earliest library-based community networks are still operating, such as the Sacramento Public Library's nearly twenty-year old Community Information Centre.

The networks provide a range of facilities and services for community development such as public Internet access, computer-based community information and referral services, online calendar on community events, employment listings, and information about local business resources, amongst others. Another direction of growth of the LIS professions in community development has involved collaborations and partnerships with community networks to make local information accessible to disadvantaged users. Strategies have incorporated broad-level application of ICT for tasks and applications considered relevant to the everyday lives of lay people, as well as development of training and support infrastructures within particular disenfranchised communities. For example, the overlapping and shared functions between a Free-Net and a public library benefited the community as a whole in the example of The Three Rivers Free-Net (TRFN), a service of the Carnegie Library of Pittsburgh (CLP) that provides Web space, training, in-house equipment, e-mail accounts, and support for developing Web sites.

Such collaborations have been especially significant in the context of recent struggles for survival by community networks that face severe economic cut-backs and limited financial support, unreliability of a volunteer-based workforce, lack of a permanent social and technical infrastructure, and competing pressures from commercial and business-oriented enterprises. Such collaborations have led the LIS professions to extend their outreach capabilities to provide services to local users on the margins of society. Recent work by leaders in the LIS professions argues for greater recognition of libraries in community development. These leaders note that LIS professions (including libraries) have historically supported "social justice values" and provided service towards "social and community development and the empowerment of groups and individuals".

"Community librarianship" is one area of involvement in which librarians and LIS professionals advocate "a more flexible and diversified form of public library provision which would enable resources to be targeted at the disadvantaged". Community librarianship addresses not only the development of "sophisticated, qualitative research into the complexion and needs of local communities (community profiling), but also the pro-active involvement of the LIS professions in these communities, along the lines of contemporary practice in community work". "Civic librarianship" is a domain that captures the potential role of the LIS professions to support education for a democratic society and strengthen communi-ties and civic society.

Reaching out to under-represented communities, civic librarianship incorporates "participatory community involvement" and civic virtues as a starting point to build "social capital that supports active citizen participation, public problem-solving and deliberative dialogue".

In response to contemporary needs in a networked society, LIS professionals are applying values of community and civic librarianship in new directions. Such efforts involve addressing social equity via the support of ICT use and developing user-centered services for disenfranchised communities. These initiatives have potential to further ICT-related support for culturally appropriate programmes that reach out to marginalized people in ways that lead to the empowerment of diverse minority and under-represented populations. An important factor in this vision is the role of the LIS professions in the organization of the "dynamics of technology" to sustain community development so that "individual and collective action be taken to help orchestrate the integration of community resources—human and informational—into a new dynamic continuum of developmental services".

The importance of understanding the human, physical, social, and cultural environment in terms of linkages between social equity, local economies, and the complex realities of communities as ecologies, is essential in this regard.

COMMUNITIES, COMMUNITY DEVELOPMENT, AND LIS

The following section discusses the role of the LIS professions in reaching out to disadvantaged local communities via ICT use. Holistic characteristics of communities are identified that can be supported by the LIS professions to nurture connections between social equity, ecology, and economy and promote sustainable community development. These connections will draw attention to the role of LIS professionals in community building and will apply this information towards fulfillment of other community development initiatives, strategies, and programmes in diverse settings. Components from the metaphor of information ecology in the analysis help us understand the complex interdependent relationships between social equity, economy, and ecology in the different contexts. Broadly, social equity simply means that which is fair and just. However, it is often problematic to arrive at an understanding of what this implies, especially in cross-cultural situations in which value systems and perceptions of rights, obligations, and duties differ. Such a setting "requires that we recognize the values and norms of other peoples" and that our decisions and actions must be "guided by notions of justice and fairness that accept the integrity and validity of other cultures and lifestyles". This recognition is important for social justice and social equity for minority and under-represented populations in the United States particularly in the context of their use of ICT. As isolated applications, completely disconnected from the realities of holistic experience of the disadvantaged, ICT is not the solution. Understanding ICT in relation to larger social, cultural, economic, political, and other forms of experiences of under-represented users is necessary to make applicable impacts that may be meaningful to them in their everyday lives.

Consequently, the concept of ecology must be applied in the context of communities. An ecological perspective includes recognition of: the interdependency between parts, the relevancy of local initiatives, the situatedness of efforts, and the acknowledgement of local capacity, as well as diversity and empowerment and the promotion of inclusiveness. Economy is an important and intrinsic feature of sustainability in the specific projects. The metaphor of information ecology helps advocates to see the intersections between the constructs of social equity, ecology, and economy as expressed in the context of community development. "The complete information environment" definition of information ecology as related to communities addresses all of "[the community's] values and beliefs about information (culture); how people actually use information and what they do with it (behaviour and work processes); the pitfalls that can interfere with information sharing (politics); and what information systems are already in place (yes, finally technology)".

INTERDEPENDENCY AND COLLABORATION BETWEEN THE "PARTS" OF THE "WHOLE"

Bringing in various voices that represent different stakeholders is essential to the success and sustained implementation of community development efforts. Stakeholders include local community organizations and potential users of the ICT to be designed. The underlying assumption is that all who are directly affected "own" the problem, and should be involved in understanding and addressing it. Lessons learned in projects that employed ICT in rural Canada and East Africa recognized the importance of efforts with clear activities, as well as goals and outcomes that are "identified by stakeholders themselves as critical and representative of what can help them be better off".

Multiple stakeholders bring in different perspectives, goals, and interests, and their involvement in defining what they want to accomplish with the technology is crucial to any community development initiative. Disparate voices also form intertwining elements in sustainable communities and these mutually affecting "parts" create a "whole" community that is greater than the sum of its "parts". However, collaboration and consensus-building are difficult, even when emphasis is laid on learning, ongoing adjustment, and transparency to minimize conflict among stakeholders.

In this scenario, the LIS professions can play an important role in community development via the use of ICT. LIS professionals can act as facilitators to establish collaborative partnerships between local stakeholders such as community networks, educational institutions, government and non-government organizations, public and academic libraries, informational centres, and local citizen-based groups and informal social networks. Their role as intermediaries shifts from what San Francisco's librarian Carl Fleishauer calls "building collections" to "making connections".

At the Prairienet Community Network, a nationally recognized computer-based community information network started in 1993 to serve the twin-cities of Urbana-Champaign and the surrounding East-Central Illinois region, strategies involved cross-disciplinary collaborations in support of efforts to promote community development. For instance, a community development initiative undertaken some years ago involved building a collection of Web resources for small business information exchange. The project entailed building collaborative partnerships between different agencies to develop culturally relevant online resources via participation and feedback from members of the Community Collaboration for Economic Development (CCED). The author was hired as a research assistant to work with the Director of the Network and other CCED members to develop and implement action research strategies.

The strategies included the training of low-income individuals; incorporating feedback from CCED members especially towards evaluation of existing information resources; analysis of business information needs of potential users; development of a collection of web resources to meet those needs; and understanding the social dynamics between CCED and disfranchised members in the community. Such strategies led to making an appropriate "fit" between the provision of small business information services and local expectations of disadvantaged community members.

TELECOMMUNICATIONS ACT HIGHLIGHTS

The Telecommunications Act of 1996 still requires broadcasters and cable companies to continue to observe the "public interest, convenience, and necessity" rule. As Krasnow, Longley, and Terry observe, the FCC' s powers to regulate are limited, at times, because of the fact that regulatory decisions must be based on the "public interest" standard. The public interest standard is mentioned and maintained throughout the Telecommunications Act. As specific regulations are presented, there is some discussion regarding how well it was embraced by all parties involved in the process of creating the legislation.

BROADCAST OWNERSHIP

The primary issues that the House, Senate, and the president had trouble resolving included particulars relating to broadcast ownership. Both the Senate and the House wanted television national audience caps regarding broadcast ownership changed from 25 per cent to 35 per cent. Further, both the House and Senate wanted the ownership caps for radio to be eliminated completely. After negotiations, it was determined that station ownership could not exceed 35 per cent of the nation's TV homes. For radio, the national ownership limits were eliminated while the local ownership limits were relaxed. The 1996 Act repealed the duopoly rule for radio station ownership, stipulating that in a market with forty-five or more stations an owner may operate eight stations, in a market with thirty to forty-four stations an owner may operate seven stations, in a market with fifteen to twenty-nine stations an owner may operate six stations, and in a market with fourteen or fewer stations an owner may operate five stations.

The Republicans pushed for even fewer regulations in this area, but eventually accepted the suggestions of the Democrats. This caused some anger among those in the Republican party because of the perception that the Republicans allowed the Democrats to gain the upper hand with this issue and several others.

OPEN VIDEO SYSTEMS

Before the Telecommunications Act, there existed a "cross-ownership" restriction that prevented telephone companies from offering cable service in the same areas where they were offering telephone service. The cross-ownership restriction provided cable companies protection from the large, established telephone companies. The 1996 Act lifted the cross-ownership restriction in an effort "to stimulate local competition in the multi-channel video market."

The Act allows telephone companies to provide video services in one of four ways:

- As an over-the-air provider;
- As a common carrier;
- As a cable television operator;
- As an open video service.

The open video service is a newly created hybrid service that allows telephone companies to offer video services and act as both a cable system and common carrier simultaneously. The 1996 Act requires that if demand is greater than existing available space, the telephone company cannot control more than one third of its system's capacity. These open video systems are not franchised locally. Local authorities, however, are allowed a portion of the open video system's revenues, which is similar to franchise fees that cable operators are required to pay to municipalities. Also, traditional cable systems may opt to offer video services via an open video system and thereby avoid many regulations that normally apply to cable systems and to avoid all of the regulations that apply to common carriers. Open video systems are required to provide channels to local non-commercial and commercial broadcasters.

Healey states that open video system operators must abide by cable regulations that do the following:

- Require the operator to pay for any commercially broadcast programmes that it carried voluntarily;
- Bar the duplication of certain network, sports, and syndicated programmes;
- Regulate contracts to transmit programmes known as carriage agreements;
- Bar the billing of programming that customers had not requested but had not canceled either;

- Bar programme distribution arrangements that prevent competition;
- Protect customer's privacy;
- Bar employment discrimination.

Unlike the regulatory issues discussed thus far, other issues required several months of negotiations. Before agreements were reached, the Senate and House of Represen-tatives agreed upon several things rather early in the process:

- Broadcast licensing;
- Advanced television and spectrum flexibility;
- Direct broadcast satellite;
- Must-carry rules;
- V-chip and TV programme ratings;
- Cable deregulation;
- Signal scrambling for indecent programming;
- Cable right of refusal of public and leased-access programming;
- Closed captioning; and
- FCC funding.

BROADCAST LICENSING

The agreement reached regarding broadcast licensing extended the license terms for television and radio to eight years. The previously amended 1934 Act allowed for television licenses to be renewed every five years and radio every seven years. The 1996 Act streamlines the license renewal process by automatically renewing broadcasters' licenses if:

- The station has served the public interest standard;
- If there have been no serious violations by the licensee of the rules and regulations of FCC;
- If there have been no other violations by the licensee that might constitute a pattern of abuse.

Competing applications are reviewed only if a license is not renewed. The 1996 Act also requires broadcasters to maintain a "summary" in their public files of all complaints they receive from viewers pertaining to violent programming.

ADVANCED TELEVISION SERVICES AND SPECTRUM FLEXIBILITY

The Telecommunications Act of 1996 allows the FCC to assign licenses for advanced television services, and the licenses are limited to existing television stations. Advanced television service is defined as digital broadcasts. If the broadcaster receives a second channel, then one of the two eventually must be returned to the U.S. government. The public interest requirement continues to apply to the second channel if one is assigned to the broadcaster.

Critics suggest that broadcasters are getting a "sweet" deal by having the new digital frequencies automatically assigned to them rather than having to purchase the rights to use the new frequencies. Former senator Bob Dole believed the provision was a multibillion dollar give-away.

Andrews stated, "Government officials estimate the licenses would be worth anywhere from $11 billion to $70 billion, if the Government auctioned them in the way it is doing for licenses to operate new wireless phone services."

DIRECT BROADCAST SATELLITE (DBS)

Complete control of "direct-to-home satellite services" is granted to the FCC under the Telecommunications Act of 1996. This prevents local communities, including homeowners associations, from prohibiting direct broadcast satellite dishes. The must-carry rule was established in April 1965 and requires all cable companies to carry the signal of local stations within a sixty-mile radius of the system. The must-carry rule is maintained in the new telecommunications bill. The Telecommunications Act requires the FCC to act upon must-carry complaints within a 120 days of the filing date.

Additionally, the Act stipulates that markets are to be defined by commercial publications that delineate television markets based on viewing patterns (or Nielsen's Designated Market Area map) when considering the must-carry issue.

RESTRICTIONS ON OBSCENITY, INDECENCY, AND VIOLENCE

The 1996 Act established the fines for transmitting obscene, lewd, lascivious, filthy, or indecent material with intent to annoy, abuse, threaten, or harass another person at $250,000 for individuals and $500,000 for corporations. This includes broadcasting media, cable systems, and computer networks. Section 501 of the Telecommunications Act of 1996 is cited as the "Communications Decency Act of 1996."

Immediately after the Communications Decency Act was passed, there was a challenge as to whether it was constitutional. There were several lawsuits filed, and in mid-1996 at least two federal courts prevented its enforcement. In June of 1997, the Supreme Court, in a 7-to-2 decision, ruled that Internet communication indeed was protected by the First Amendment.

In Reno v. American Civil Liberties Union, the court stated that the Internet deserved the same protection as, media such as books, magazines, or newspapers. Thus, the Supreme Court essentially invalidated Title V of the Telecommunications Act. The Supreme Court dismissed the government's argument that if children were not prevented from accessing indecent material over the Internet then the Internet would not grow to be an important and pervasive media outlet.

The government's rational was that the general public would not access the Internet because of the risk that children might be exposed to indecent material. The Supreme Court rejected this argument stating that it was unpersuasive.

V-CHIP AND TV PROGRAMME RATINGS

The Telecommunications Act requires television sets to be sold with a V-chip, or violence chip, which allows for the "ability to block programming based on an electronically encoded rating." The entertainment industry was required to develop a ratings system for "violence, sex and other indecent materials and to agree voluntarily to broadcast signals containing such ratings."

The bill requires the FCC to develop a ratings system if the industry fails to meet that requirement. The FCC was charged with the duty of overseeing the development of standards for blocking technologies.As a result of such findings, the Act states that there is a "compelling governmental interest" in providing parents the means to block such influences.

CABLE DEREGULATION

The 1996 Act deregulates cable rates for the expanded basic tier which usually includes such networks as MTV, Lifetime, ESPN, and Cable News Network. The cable companies are allowed to increase prices on the expanded basic tier within three years of the telecommunication bill's enactment (or on March 31, 1999). The bill requires that equipment rates continue to be regulated. Further, the Act allows for the complete deregulation of small cable companies, defined as including 50,000 or fewer subscribers. The Act allows for cable systems to be free from rate regulation if "a telephone company offers cable service by any means that is comparable to the competing cable system."

SET-TOP BOXES

With the 1996 Telecommunications Act, consumers now are able to purchase their own set-top boxes in retail stores. Cable companies are allowed to continue providing set-top boxes, but they no longer may subsidize the boxes by subscription fees. Discussion over this issue caused the "first major impasse" on the telecommunications bill.

Cable companies opposed the sale of set-top boxes in retail stores, asserting that it would "freeze the current technology in place." The new rules regarding set-top boxes were designed to prevent theft of cable services.

The rules expire in a market where:

- There are competing multichannel video providers,
- There are competing sources of set-top boxes,
- Where the rules stifle competition and do not promote the public interest standard.

SIGNAL SCRAMBLING FOR INDECENT PROGRAMMING

The bill requires cable operators to scramble any audio or video of programming that subscribers deem "unsuitable" for children. This service must be provided at no extra cost to the subscriber.

CABLE RIGHT OF REFUSAL OF PUBLIC AND LEASED-ACCESS PROGRAMMING

Under the new bill, cable companies can refuse to broadcast programmes that contain "obscenity, nudity, or indecency."

CLOSED CAPTIONING

The Federal Communications Commission was required to look into the possibility of making closed captioning a requirement for video programming. The Telecommunications Act of 1996 stipulated that the FCC can waive the requirement for certain classes of programmes if closed captioning is economically burdensome.

FCC FUNDING

Finally, the bill authorizes appropriations needed by the FCC to carry out the provisions of the 1996 Act. Quello' s comment could not have been more foreshadowing. Others held similar opinions regarding the future of telecommuni-cations regulation.

Approximately a year after Quello's remark, both the Senate and the House of Representatives introduced different versions of a bill that essentially would do exactly what Quello suggested, that is, modernize the regulatory framework under which the entire telecommunications sector operates.

Simply put, modernization was needed because when the Communications Act of 1934 was enacted, telephone, telegraph, and radio defined the field. Today, "television, cable, cellular, and satellite only scratch the surface of modern digital telecommunications." Hence, a new piece of legislation was needed to accommodate technological advances.

The Telecommunications Act of 1996 serves as that modernized regulatory framework for the telecommunications industry that Quello suggested is needed to help in the proliferation of new media. The 1996 legislation essentially creates "one marketplace for telecommunications services " Technological developments will transform the multimedia world as we know it today.

The Telecommunications Act of 1996 attempts to regulate media as a whole rather than as individual entities. Chong suggested this approach was needed for there to be a healthy and prosperous development of multimedia technology in the United States. To illustrate how just one aspect of the telecommunications bill attempts to converge the electronic media, examine the overlapping markets of the telephone and cable companies. The cable companies will be allowed to offer telephone services and the telephone companies will be allowed to offer cable services.

Fundamentally, the 1996 Act takes a deregulatory approach and relies on the marketplace as a control over electronic media policies and procedures. The telecommuni-cation legislation diminishes barriers that have prevented widespread competition and work towards the convergence of all media.

Because of the belief that competition is good, the Act allows for competition between and among different telecommunication outlets. As one could expect, new competition is not welcomed by the entire electronic media industry. For example, the industry opposed the cable-telco cross-ownership rules. Only time will allow observers of the telecommunications industry to determine the new legislation's effectiveness. The Telecommunications Act has created an ironic juxtaposition. Technology and programming were specific areas that the new legislation attempts to deregulate, or regulate in certain circumstances (*e.g.*, violent programming).

The foundation of the legislation is built upon deregulatory theory. Head, *et al.* Suggest that there are many motives fueling efforts to deregulate, such as a need to discard outdated rules, simplify complex rules, ensure that rules actually can achieve their intended objective, and lighten administrative roles. Additionally, they suggest that deregulation also originates from ideological motives stemming from the belief that the government should play a limited role in the everyday lives of Americans. This approach relies on the marketplace to regulate industries.

Yet the marketplace approach of regulating industries does not always work effectively. On one hand, the Telecommunications Act of 1996 essentially promotes the convergence of technology by disassembling the cross-ownership restriction and by establishing specific regulations regarding the promotion of direct broadcast satellite, set-top boxes, closed captioning, and cable deregulation.

On the other hand, it attempts to regulate programming through must-carry rules, v-chip technology, signal scrambling for indecent programming, and cable right of refusal of public and leased-access programming. Meyerson suggests that if "these new combinations do not compete with one another, then the Act may have only permitted the creation of large, deregulated monopolists (or oligopolists)." Monopolies were just what the Clinton administration wanted to prevent.

Finally, another juxtaposition includes the requirement that programme ratings be implemented. The industry was required to create a ratings system that would be content-based and would alert parents about programming they might want to prevent their children from viewing by way of the new v-chip. Initially, the industry created ratings that were age-based. Critics argued that the age-based system would not provide enough information to make a decision.

The industry argued that content-based ratings would be confusing and that advertisers might not want advertise during programming that had a perceived negative rating. Eventually, the industry adopted a content-based ratings system. Overall, it will require time to determine the effectiveness of the Telecommunications Act of 1996.

TECHNOLOGY AND THE PUBLIC MARKET-PLACE

Technology has radically altered the roles of major players in the television world. Networks are steadily feeling the pressures brought about by cable and satellite access, with a number of alternative paths being opened for national distribution of programming, their former oligopoly.

At the same time, the replacement of film with videotape and ever smaller instruments for live on-the-spot coverage have made the production of local news much more attractive for affiliate stations and independents, lowering the need for 'clearance' of network offerings further.

These same technologies of accessible and affordable production have added new encouragement to local stations to produce shows of such calibre that they can be sold to or otherwise shared with other outlets.

However, just as the networks are less necessary to local stations, so too are local stations less necessary to the local television market. The technology that has helped local broadcast stations has also enabled out-of-market 'superstations' to beam in on many lucrative markets all over the country.

Low-power television stations and other methods of expanding the available spectrum have been added to the multiple channels available through cable, whose share of market has catapulted in recent years. San Francisco, for instance, has gone from five to twenty-two television outlets in the eighties.

All of these factors are added to the burgeoning home use of VCRs, not only for rented videocassettes but for time-shifted viewing and commercial zapping of broadcast fare. The net result of all this technological innovation is to radically reduce the market share of each outlet and to even more seriously undercut the revenue base of advertiser-supported television media, whose rates are not only based on raw numbers but increasingly on demographically targeted market segments.

A further pressure on broadcast stations, at a time when revenue is being squeezed, is a demand from ownership for ever higher return on investment. This obsession for maximum profits in the immediate term is a broader disease of the entire corporate American economy, fueled by crushing debt service created by leveraged buy-outs. Although the effect on networks, all three of whom are now part of far larger corporate conglomerates with a great demand for cash flow, has been widely noted, the effect on individual stations, whether independent, affiliated with networks, or part of chains, is enormous. Despite increasing deregulation, stations remain the most highly regulated node in the many-stranded television web. They not only are the primary responsible agents for programming liability, they also are under pressure to serve the local community by both the terms of the license and the public interest tradition from the original Communications Act-an obligation not shared by other programme producers and distributors.

Enlightened management has over the years seen the obligation of local service as the advantage of local identification, the characteristic which a station can use as a classic 'unique selling point' against all those other competitors (except for other local stations, of course).

This is achieved in practice by building on traditional avenues of community involvement, adapted to broadcasting realities. It should be noted that 'identity' for any medium that exists in time, rather than space, takes the form of 'continuity'. Although the local station obviously has an address on a real street in a real town, it is presented to its market on screens everywhere, along with other entities from New York, London, Tokyo, even outer space.

Thus the repetitive display over time of the station logo, the network mark, the series 'billboard', is the fundamental tool of establishing identity, just as scheduling is the fundamental programming tool for reaching specific audiences. Since the enormous appetite of a 168-hour broadcast week requires that most production be imported from the tape factories that have replaced the film factory of Hollywood, the only window the local station has to establish its continuity is the local news window.

Its news presenters are the electronic equivalent of a magazine cover or a newspaper masthead and its coverage of local news is the way the station is 'present' locally. As a result, most stations have early evening news programmes that are often at least two hours long and late news from thirty minutes to one hour. More stations are inaugurating hour-length audience participation shows in early morning and late afternoon, to which some even provide van or bus service. In addition, regularly scheduled or 'special' programmes, usually on weekends or in fringe times, are focused on specific local issues.

What sort of content characterizes these local programmes, whatever the format? In 1983, the Television Information Office, as research arm of the television wing of the National Association of Broadcasters, conducted a survey on precisely this and allied questions. The sample was large and representative, 257 stations from every region, including Alaska and Hawaii, 111 of them from 47 of the top fifty markets and 60 from 37 of the second fifty.

Local news can be divided into three parts: hard, soft and feature. Hard news concentrates on spontaneous events, like floods and fires and as such cannot be part of a planning process. Most news is, in fact, soft: planned occasions of interest to the community.

The TIO Survey found sports was at the top of the list, followed by ethnic festivals, local government affairs, neighbourhood and church activities, awards,

Chamber of Commerce meetings, school matters and cleanup drives. The performing arts and any occasion that raises funds for charity, like the Special Olympics, form the second tier. Minority activities such as local celebrations of Martin Luther King Day came last. About 10 per cent of such coverage was in the form of specials, in addition to regular local news programming.

Feature news treatment consisted of discussions, specialist-interviews and often exhortation, about crime, drug abuse, good health practices, family conflict, education, sexual problems, employment, the environment and consumer complaints. Since these topics are perennial, they are recycled regularly, sometimes in the form of a short series, or a monthly 'drive' that orchestrates various formats, from specials to short announcements to news segments.

Although many of these topics raise heated controversy, such as abortion or nuclear hazards, the overwhelming tendency is to preserve an atmosphere of upbeat optimism. If hard news is bad news, then local public affairs features tend to be good news, or at least comforting information.

Controversy can be addressed in editorials, which are usually one- or two-minute talking heads, the head often that of the station manager or the public affairs director, if there is one. Another NAB survey, with a sample of 422 stations, found that less than one-third bother to editorialize and that of these less than 3 per cent will actually endorse a candidate in a contested election.

So, although the occasional station, like KPIX-TV in San Francisco, may occasionally take an unpopular position it believes in, most stations play it safe for fear of alienating viewers or of triggering equal-time rebuttals from sources that will surely alienate viewers, for whose loyalty all this localism is expended.

Boosting the status quo cannot be left to on-air activities. General managers, like executives of any business that depends on public acceptance, spend a great deal of time attending civic affairs, visiting schools, speaking at ceremonies. The better stations make sure that their on-air talent, which is the key to news and public affairs ratings, is visible in the flesh for public affairs and local charities. Stations themselves sponsor dinners for the elderly, music concerts, park and zoo days for families, fund-raising ball games with their own employees participating. Weather reporters are increasingly fitting a central casting type of the all-purpose warm community person, visiting schools and hospitals with some sort of science or health presentation.

Since all of these strategies, on- and off-air, are often common within the same market, the competition for ratings among local stations revolves around two intangibles: the personalities of the talent and the perception of the station as 'the' local station. Hiring charismatic talent is still much of a mystical operation, with successful producers referring to ineffable visceral cues as the determining factor.

Scarcely open to rational discussion, the star factor is thus underemphasized in studies of programming strategy. The other factor-competitive edge in local identification of the station as a whole-admits to some logical planning. The key to this planning is a special form of one of the oldest methods of organizing a variety of forces against a variety of obstacles in order to focus on one objective: the campaign.

Flowing from a creative transformation of an alleged weakness into a strength, the public or community service campaign manages to mobilize all the strategies local stations have mustered to meet their obligations to owners, advertisers, viewers, government and, of course, the local community in one policy gesture. It seems almost too good to be true.

MODERN COMMUNICATION TECHNOLOGIES

As the name itself implies, new communication technologies are those which are of more recent origin. Interactivity is their distinguishing feature. For the purpose of this unit, new communication technologies can also be understood as those which are capable of a much higher degree of interactivity than that offered by the traditional communication technologies. Writing, printing and electronic media like radio and television ax examples of traditional technologies which are essentially one-way in nature. Therefore, their interactive capabilities are very limited. Besides, this limited interactivity occurs after considerable delay. For example, a newspaper which depends on the traditional technology for print can be said to be interactive to the extent that it publishes readers' letters in its 'letters to the editor' column. Similarly, a radio station too is interactive in that it broadcasts programmes which carry responses to audience queries. We can, therefore, say that interactivity is at best a marginal property of traditional communication media. In the new communication technologies, on the other hand, interactivity is the main property. The use of computers in one form or the other, as an integral part of their system, is what enables them to be interactive. In the following sections, we will take up for study some of the main technologies under this category.

Computer Networks: The idea of interlinking and communicating with the aid of computers was as old as the mainframe computers of the 1970s. Owing to their prohibitive price, the mainframes came to be owned only by mega-establishments like governments, big business houses, universities etc. Individuals could not afford them for personal use. At the same time, the high cost of the mainframes required their owners to find ways and means to maximize their utilization in order to make them cost effective. The networking of computers, it was found, allowed simultaneous access to a single mainframe by any number of users. Naturally, this development suited owners and users alike. Computer networks thus emerged as a kind of public utility to help users communicate with a central computing facility such as a database, and retrieve information too. In the decades that followed, computer technology advanced by leaps and bounds. This resulted in the invention of much smaller computers that displayed greater capabilities at just a fraction of the price. At present the use of computer networks for various specialized and general purposes has become quite common, even in the less developed parts of the world. In our own country, computer networks are widely used by public sector organizations, big business houses, government department etc., for their day-to-day transactions. Indian Airlines, Indian Railways and a few state undertakings own computer networks dedicated to managing their operations. Such real-time flow of information enables planners and other decision makers at the headquarters to decide on appropriate policies, taking into consideration the latest statistics. In the absence of such computer networking in the past, it is said that vital decisions at the national level had to be taken with the help of data which were at least a decade old! Apart from helping administrators, NICNET is also said to be regularly used for other application like exchange of expert medical advice by specialists to doctors working in remote areas. On a global scale, INERNET is the largest computer network which permeated almost all parts of the world. Composed of thousands of interconnected networks initially in the united states, INTERNET can offer you an immense range of information services such as electronic mail file transfer, databases and multi-media INTERNET also provides connectivity to mobile receivers through a wireless broadcasting service operating on satellite links. Computer networks have several advantages over interpersonal communication. Asynchronocity that is the flexibility inherent in the system to enable information exchange without the need for the sender and the recipient to be present simultaneously, is one such advantage. However, it also suffers from various drawbacks like the lack of a human touch. Communication engineers constantly endeavour to improve the so-called 'user friendliness' of the system concerned by approximating it to interpersonal interaction.

Teleconferencing: Teleconferencing is a mean by which individuals or groups located at different places can exchange data, speech, visual materials like graphs or diagrams, or moving pictures of themselves and any other relevant information. Teleconferencing is made possible by the integration of computers and communication in such a manner as to form a holistic system which can work in real-time. Depending on the particular application, scope and complexity involved, Teleconferencing can be classified under the following types:

- *Computer conferencing*: in the case, only computer data can be exchanged among multiple locations. Real time interaction among the location is possible, but only the extent of computer data. The physical linkages among the several computers can be in the form of telephone wires or though wireless means as in the case of microwave or satellite.
- *Audio conferencing*: In this participant can actually talk to one another as if in a face to face situation facilities are provided for any one

location to talk any other or all of them simultaneously. In addition, audio teleconferences also enable exchange of computer data on the same physical link (telephone cables or wireless). Audio teleconferencing enables real time exchange of information without losing the human touch.

- *Audio Graphic conferencing*: This is a more advanced form of audio teleconferencing in which, in addition to audio and computer data, still graphics like drawing, maps etc, can also be exchanged. Further refinements in technology enable even slow scan video pictures to be exchanged as a part of the audio teleconferencing system. The same pairs of telephone wires would suffice to carry all the above 'Bandwidth Compression' techniques which are technically known as ISDN (integrated data network services).
- *Video conferencing*: This is the highest form of teleconferencing in which a two-way exchange of moving pictures is possible without any restriction, in addition to audio and data. The telecommunication links required for such conferencing system prove to be very costly because of the fact that moving pictures need very wide bandwidths. Hence, a lower version of video teleconferencing which is called 'one-way video and two-way audio is gaining currency. In the latter case, the main location (typically the headquarters of an organization) will have facilities for sending audio as well as video which are received by all the remote locations. But the remote locations will have facilities for sending only audio, and not video. In other words, while the remote locations can receive both—pictures and voices—they will be able to respond only through voice. Teleconferencing of this kind has been widely experimented with by many organizations in India using satellite links.

Already, Teleconferencing has been an accepted form of technology in advanced countries, especially for business communications. It is only a matter of time before this technology becomes popular in countries such as ours, because the necessary infrastructure like telephone links and satellite are already available. Teleconferencing is gaining popularity due to the minimal physical travel demanded of its participants. The time-saving involved in this process is also a significant factor. The experience of advanced countries has been that, apart from economizing on time and travel, teleconferencing also help in improving corporate efficiency and participatory management.

Teletext: Teletext is a form of broadcast technology by means of which several 'pages' of textual information (say, latest weather reports, stock exchange figures, airline train reservations etc.) Can be transmitted on an already existing television channel. The teletext information is encoded in the so called 'vertical blanking interval' of the television screen which is invisible in the normal course of television viewing. However, when activated by a teletext 'decoder' at the receiving end, the television screen starts displaying the-teletext information in lieu of the normal TV programme. Facilities exist in teletext to enable viewers to choose a particular page of teletext containing relevant information which serves their needs, and recall that particular page. Thus, a businessman wanting to know the latest trend in the stock exchange can press his decoder for the particular page containing stock market news, and get the display on' his TV screen instantly.

He will be able to view that page as long as he wishes, or he can turn over to some other page or revert back to the normal TV programme as per his wish. TV stations equipped with a teletext service, normally update the information at regular intervals, say every half an hour, for the benefit of the viewers. About 300 teletext pages (a page means one TV frame containing information) can be accommodated per TV channel and a collection of these pages goes by the name of 'teletext magazine'. The pages of a teletext magazine can incorporate illustrations like graphs, bar charts etc., in addition to simple text. The Delhi Station of Doordarshan provides a teletext service on the second channel; access to it is possible with the help of a decoder. The magazine contains specific pages earmarked for national and international news, travel information, sports, local announcements, weather reports etc. A few main pages of the magazine are also put out in the 'picture mode' *i.e.,* on the main channel itself for the benefit of use not equipped with decoders. It is possible to extend this service to other Doordarshan stations for the benefit of viewers all over the country: Teletext is a simple technology which can be used to advantage for public communication. The advantages inherent in broadcast media such as instant and widespread teach, to an unlimited clientele, are applicable to teletext as well. Different countries have teletext services which conform to different technical standards, and a universal code of transmission is yet to be invented. Its essential simplicity, instantaneous dissemination of messages and ease of updating information make it a worthwhile technology with myriad applications.

Radio Text: Better known by the term 'Radio data systems' (RDS), Radio text is a technology similar to Teletext but with the important difference that it works in conjunction with FM Radio (frequency Modulation) while Teletext works on television. While conventional radio broadcasts on medium wave and shortwave bands have the advantage of larger service areas for a given radio station, the severe congestion of radio stations in these bands in recent years has forced the use of higher frequency bands for radio transmission. Use of these higher frequency bands as in the case of the FM Radio, however, would mean restricting the reach of a radio station essentially to line of sight range which is about 30 km radius. FM stations are ideal as local radio stations, as they can offer programmes of local community interest, high fidelity music, local news etc., to the public. Radio text is to be seen as a value-added service on FM Radio. This technology essentially consists of transmitting data and other textual material piggyback on the FM carrier so that the listeners/viewers who are equipped with a radiotext 'decoder' can extract this signal from an ongoing FM transmission and watch the same on a computer screen which forms a part of the radiotext receiving system. Facilities are available in a decoder to select either the radiotext or the normal FM transmission at will. In addition, the listeners or viewers, as in the case of teletext, will be able to select the particular page of information of their interest and hold on to it for any length of time. Audio signals of speech quality (*i.e.,* of restricted bandwidth) can also form part of a radiotext signal. This would mean that institutions like Open Universities can transmit their audio lessons or radiotext, while simultaneously transmitting portions of their print material. Experiments of thin kind are already underway with the joint 'collaboration of All India Radio and Yashwantreo Chavan Maharashtra State Open University, Nasik. An important deterrent for widespread use of Radiotext of such applications, however, is that the receiving system works out to be several times costlier than the FM Radio set itself. Moreover, FM Radio is still in its infancy in our country and the availability of FM radio sets is rather rare. Under the circumstances, the widespread use of Radiotext in our country will be unlikely in the near future.

Videotext: Videotex (please note the absence of 't' at the end of the word) is another form of interactive communication technology which is in wide usage in several advanced countries. While the teletext operates on television and radio text on FM radio, Videotext works with the help of the public telephone network. The home computer, telephone connection and the domestic TV set/ computer screen form integral components of a Videotext system. Customers provided with Videotext facilities can make use of it for such varied applications as electronic shopping, access to databases, tele-banking, or exchanging messages with friends. As Videotext is essentially interactive it has much more to offer than teletext or radio text in terms of selective information exchange and retrieval. However, a well developed and reliable telephone network is essential for operating a Videotext service. For this reason, as of now, Videotext services are popular only in advanced countries. With gradual improvements taking place by way of digital telephone exchanges and replacement of conventional telephone wires with optical fibres, the reliability as well as capacity of telephone systems everywhere are bound to increase in due course. Value-added services like the Videotext too are expected to gain in popularity alongside such developments.

Interactive Cable Distribution Systems: Dissemination of television programmes via cable to a community of households started in the 50s. To begin with advantages of cable distribution was seen as improving the reception conditions of television in isolated mountainous-regions. Later on, TV signals received via satellite were put out on cable distribution systems, thus offering many more TV channels for the viewers. With this, the popularity and spread of cable distribution systems grew dramatically. Concurrently with the distribution of satellite channels, facilities like 'pay TV' in which individual viewers have the choice of receiving programmes of their preference at a price, have also been introduced. In other words, the cable systems have been endowed with interactive properties. Advancements in digital technology and fibre optics have resulted in further improved versions of cable distribution. For example, viewers in the advanced countries can now make use of the cable for receiving programmes of their choice at the press of a button. The selected programme is then down-loaded by the cable company onto the viewer's terminal as a compressed 'digital packet' in a matter of seconds. The programme is then held in the electronic memory of the receiving terminal which can be viewed straightaway or some time at leisure. The asynchronocity of interactive cable distribution systems is a unique advantage in the gamut of new communication technologies.

Communication Satellites: Transnational television, *i.e.,* transmission of television programmes from one country to, another, became a reality with the development of Communication Satellites. These satellites are stationed in an orbit above the earth's equator at a height of about 36,000 km. called the geo-stationary orbit. All satellites parked in the geostationary orbit have a period of rotation equal to 24 hours and hence, appear stationary to an observer on the earth. Besides, the great distance of the orbit also offers the advantage of the satellite to 'see' as much as one-third of the earth's surface thus enabling it to cover such a vast area. Communication Satellites are owned by various individual nations as well as collectively by groups of nations to cater for several applications like broadcasting, television and telecommunications. INTELSAT (International Telecommunications Satellite Consortium) is an international body consisting of more than 90 member countries of which India is one. The satellites commissioned by INTELSAT cater to, the collective needs of the member countries as per a mutually agreed tariff structure.

Ground terminals (these are known as earth stations) for receiving/sending signals from/to the satellites are located in several places in the member countries. In India, two such earth stations have been established for the INTELSAT network—one near Pune and the other near Dehradun. Most of the international telecommunications traffic and exchange with other countries of live coverage of events takes place via the INTELSAT network. India is credited with taking several major initiatives in the field of satellite communications. The famous SITE experiment (Satellite Instructional Television Experiment) during 1975-76, in which about 2400 remote villages in the country were served by television programmes via satellite, is a case in point. The experiment has proved the efficacy of satellite communications as a cost effective means for countrywide dissemination of educational and developmental TV programmes. Gradually, our country has developed its own satellite system, INSAT (Indian National Satellite System). INSAT is a multi-purpose satellite service catering to telecommunications, radio and TV transmission and weather forecasting. The second generation of INSAT satellites which are currently in operation, have a larger number of transporters which can be used for further expansion of satellite communications. In particular, regional telecasting can be extended in all language zones and new services like teleconferencing introduced.

Mushrooming of satellite-based transnational television in recent years is a cause for concern as well as hope. The sudden spurt in the availability of satellite channels all over the country from across our borders would mean a potential threat to our own national broadcast media. The virtual absence of any legal mechanisms to check or control these transmissions of extenlal origin can jeopardize our own priorities in the communication sector and divert the attention of the populace away from important information on developmental activities. On the other hand, the competitive presence of external channels call motivate the local broadcasters to become more professional and quality conscious.

Direct Broadcast Satellites (DBS) are specially designed for broadcast applications so that the signals transmitted from them can be directly received by home receivers equipped with a small dish antenna (typically half a meter diameter) and an interfacing unit. Use of such satellites obviates the need for land based retransmitting stations (called LPTs). DBS is in extensive use in Europe, the USA and Japan.

As mentioned earlier, the application areas to which multi purpose satellites like the INSAT can be put to use are many and varied. Satellite communications have in fact become so common that we take then for granted. Whenever you dial a long distance telephone call, say from India to the USA, your voice and that of the person you have called travel via some satellite route or the other, most probably via the INTELSAT network. You may notice in such cases, a very small but clearly discernible delay of a fraction of a second in receiving the response of the other person. A similar delay will be felt by the person at the other end while receiving your voice. This is because of the extraordinarily long journey of thousands of kilometres which the voice signals have to traverse on the satellite route. Of course, such delays are common not only to telephone conversations but also all other traffic taking place through satellite communications.

Many national newspapers which are published simultaneously from multiple locations take advantage of satellite communication for instant transmission of their pages from one publishing centre to another. For example The Hindu has arrangements for publishing its Delhi edition by transmitting pages from Madras to Delhi through INSAT.

COMPARISON OF NEW COMMUNICATION TECHNOLOGIES

In the foregoing sections, we have surveyed the salient features of some of the new communication technologies individually. It is to be noted, however, that real-life situations often employ the simultaneous use of more than one technology in a given situation. For example, the STAR TV programmes that you receive on your home TV set, reach you by means of satellite communications up to the point of your cable operator's terminal, and from then on, via cable. Similarly, a long distance telephone call may get connected via microwave or a submarine cable for part of the route and via satellite for the rest of its journey. Such combinations, however, usually do not affect the technical quality of the communication in question. So, the users for the most part remain unaware of the details of the technology mix involved. Nevertheless, every technology has its distinct attributes, advantages and disadvantages, because of which an optimal technology selection is possible for any given application. Some of these have already been discussed in the concerned sections earlier; what follows is a relative assessment of the various technologies with regard to communication parameters like interactivity, asynchronocity and demassification.

Interactivity: While interactivity is a property in which the new communication technologies, as a rule, excel over the traditional ones, some of them are evidently much more interactive than others. Teleconferencing and video teleconferencing can be cited as the most interactive while, teletext or radiotext can be placed at the other end of the interactivity scale. Even in the traditional communication media, the ordinary telephone is a very good interactive device. The strength of the new technologies in this regard, is that their interactivity is much more extensive and is not necessarily limited to just two individuals as in the case of the telephone.

Asynchronocity: The term asynchronocity refers to that property of the medium whereby the simultaneous presence of all the participants in a communication exercise is not compulsory. For example, in a computer network, facilities like "store and forward" enables the message to be retrieved at a convenient time other than the one at which the message has actually been sent. Thus, while real time exchange of communications is possible through such a technology, it offers the added flexibility of asynchronocity. The degree of asynchronocity varies from one technology to the other. It can be said to be the highest where only computers are required to interact without live human intervention, as in the case of Electronic Mail, or computer data are only kind of teleconferencing. It is least in a two-way video teleconferencing.

Demassification: Traditional media like press, radio or television are instances of 'one-to-many' kind of communications. Therefore, they are unsuitable where the communication needs are more individualized. Demassification refers to the extent to which a given technology can lend itself to such individualized communication. The normal telephone system is an ideal example of a technology endowed with a high degree of demassification. New communication technologies in general possesses this characteristic while at the same time enabling communication among large groups or individuals dispersed over large areas. In other words, the new communication technologies are the reverse of the traditional technologies. Teleconferencing or computer communication is high in their demassification while teletext is at the lower end of the demassification ladder.

SOCIAL ISSUES

As we have noted earlier, the new communication technologies have not yet penetrated sufficiently in Third World countries like ours. Therefore, we will not be able to determine their likely impact on our society with any degree of certainty. What we can conjecture in this regard is by studying the experience of developed countries like the USA which have been using these technologies over a considerable period and by extrapolating the impact of some of the present technologies like television. Noted communications scholar, Everett Rogers, says that the new communication technologies have a marked social impact in the following respects, especially during their adaptability stages.

- As newer technologies are relatively costlier and knowledge-intensive, they will be adopted only by the higher echelons of society at first, who can really afford them. Thus, ironically, communication gaps would widen among several sections of society because of the new communication technologies. This phenomenon is, of course, not unique for the new technologies. When television was introduced, a similar thing has happened as only the rich could embrace this medium in the beginning. As the ownership of TV sets gradually increased, the initial imbalances to have become less pronounced. A similar situation is expected in the case of the new technologies. Despite initial imbalances, however, overall information flow in the society is bound to go up.
- What happens by way of information imbalance within a society is also true of situations among countries at large. Advanced countries which are already information-rich tend to become richer, thereby widening the information gap between countries. This may lead to an unfavourable situation for the Third World countries which are already at the receiving end of the technological supremacy of the First World.
- Information overload is likely to happen, which in turn poses problems of coping with selective retrieval of required information, from heaps of randomly accumulated information. Here again, the new technologies themselves are likely to come to our rescue, as for example special computer software which may enable users to obtain such selective display of information as is relevant to them.

- Unemployment may abound in certain sectors as the new technologies would eliminate or render surplus certain traditional jobs and occupations. Some new jobs and new occupations may be created in their place, but not in numbers sufficient enough to compensate the loss of traditional jobs. Displacement of jobs may be felt more acutely during the introductory phase of the new technologies, than when the technologies in question get integrated fully into society.
- The universal presence of computers and easy access to them via networks is likely to raise problems concerning privacy and security of communications. Use of special passwords and the like are of course an obvious protection, but they too have their limitations. Clever use of special software may also enable computer miscreants/hackers to break the secret passwords and get at the classified information straight away.
- Greater use of the new technologies may enable the organizations concerned to become more decentralized in their decision making and other functions. Here again, an exact opposite may be possible as the new technologies permit much tighter monitoring on the movements and performances of subordinate staff thereby bringing about a 'Big-Brother' kind of centralized control. Much depends on the way the managements want to use the new technologies.
- It is feared the gender-inequality will increase. Though unfounded, the apprehension is prevalent that boys rather than girls will adapt themselves faster and more easily to things like computer programming, due to their supposedly inherent superiority in mathematical skills. This is of course a debatable point. However, in the initial stages of adoption of the new technologies, social pressures may be generated bemuse of gender inequalities.

From the above discussion, you may be inclined to think, that since these new technologies have certain undesirable effects on society, they might as well be avoided entirely. Such thinking, however, would be too short sighted and technophobic to be true. The history of technology is replete with instances of social. Instability and resistance upon introduction of major technological innovations. Eventually, however, as the society adapted itself to these new innovations and assimilated their full impact, the initial resistances were found to have melted away. Not only were those, the new technologies themselves found to be instrumental in finding solutions to the very problems what they had generated in the first place. In case any particular technology was found unable to conform to the above pattern, sociological forces would automatically tend to relegate such a technology into oblivion. The case of the new communication technologies that we have discussed in this unit, can be no exception to this overall trend.

7

Media for Civilization Values in Communication

INDIVIDUAL MEDIA CHARACTERISTICS

The four major mass media and direct mail have unique qualities, strengths, and weaknesses. We will examine them here and discuss research findings about each.

TELEVISION

Of all the media available to the business communicator to reach large, undifferentiated audiences, none is so potentially powerful as television. With its capacity for instant transmission from any point on the globe and its combination of sight and sound that engage two senses simultaneously, television dominates American media diets.Journalism professor and television critic David Littlejohn suggests that television may be the most potent of all the media, playing a dominant role in the media repertoire.

Television is the most thoroughly attended to, most pervasive, and probably most influential means of propagating ideas in the country today. It can be instantaneous in its reach, intimate generally in its reception. It can exercise the most extraordinary sensory and emotional appeal. You can find authorities who believe that it molds minds, fixes modes of perception, and determines what is thought of as desirable and even real for hundreds of millions of people.

The large amounts of exposure time given the medium have prompted concern over how society may be affected. Dr. George Gerbner and his staff at the University of Pennsylvania have demonstrated, in their Cultural Indicators Project, that viewers often form their impressions about society based on life as portrayed on television.

In his work, Gerbner attempts to plot a profile of social events as depicted on television against viewers' perceptions of these events as reality. For instance, in his research involving television's portrayal of violence, Gerbner has attempted to learn if those who spend more time watching television (which contains a good measure of violence) are more likely than others to perceive the real world as a violent place. Essentially, his findings conclude that such a relationship does exist. Gerbner and others have found that television

- Displays common patterns repeated in endless episodes, which provide a paradigm for learning
- Teaches, even though people attend the medium for entertainment, to pass time, and other reasons unrelated to educational fuctions

Cultivates within audiences a sense of reality commensu-rate with the way it depicts life

This conception of television's power has been well studied in the communication literature. Some have called television the "window to the world" because many people look there to learn about life and the world.

They believe what they see—not only in news programmes but in scripted programmes as well—that television accurately portrays characteristics of the real world. In 1982 the National Institute of Mental Health (NIMH) released an exhaustive study that examined thousands of reports, papers, and books assessing the effects of television. Observations of the NIMH advisory board summarized more than ten years of research. Among their conclusions were the following:

The research findings of the past decade have reaffirmed the powerful influence of television on the viewers. Almost all the evidence testifies to television's role as a formidable educator whose effects are both pervasive and cumulative. Television can no longer be considered as a casual part of daily life, as an electronic toy. Research findings have long since destroyed the illusion that television is merely innocuous entertainment. While the learning it provides is mainly incidental rather than direct and formal, it is a significant part of the total acculturation process.... Television viewing is so entrenched in American daily life that it can only be regarded as a major socializing influence almost comparable to the family, the schools, the church, and other socializing institutions.

No doubt television is influential, in part because of its great popularity. For Americans, television has become a friend, an educator, an entertainer, and more. Eric Sevareid has called television the "national hearth." A concise account of several important features of television is taken from conclusions of the U.S. government international trade project discussed earlier:

Television is immensely popular and among the variety of reasons for its popularity, people watch television because other people watch television, and to keep in social tempo, people listen to the beat of television.

There is solid evidence that television can foster credibility of a source and establish importance in a subject. Television can create awareness of an issue and impart information to the viewing audience. Furthermore, television serves an agenda setting function which works to elevate the salience of an issue in the public eye. It has been proposed that viewers expect all important issues to be displayed on television and if an issue is not found on television it cannot be very important. People have come to accept that any issue worth public attention will be found on television.

The strengths of television have important implications for business communicators, not only for information transmission but for persuasion and company image building. In the upcoming section, we will discuss several essential functions of television that contribute to a communication campaign.

First, let us restate the basic design of targeted communication. Recall that targeting is the selection of elements in a communication programme that meet the specific needs of narrow, homogeneous subgroups within a population. During the last few years, as advances in technology (namely, cable, satellite signal reception, VCRs) have provided a greater variety of viewing options, television has become more adaptable for reaching specialized audiences. Even with conventional network-affiliated stations, one can narrow audiences by selecting particular time periods.

For example, consider weekday afternoons when there are large female audiences, or particular programmes such as "Golden Girls" that attract older audiences. With the new television outlets, however, one can identify demographic groups not only by time and specific programmes but by station. Teenagers are attracted to music television channels, sports enthusiasts to all-sports networks, and people interested in current events to twenty-four-hour news formats.

Television audiences are breaking away from the large audience blocks that once clustered around generalviewing programming and are re-forming in narrower groups around specific interest material. As these expanded outlets diffuse further into the population, the targeting capacity of televison will become increasingly more valuable to the public communicator.

Whether we are considering television as a traditional mass audience medium or as a focused targeted medium, its characteristic communication power remains unaltered. Receivers will continue to increase their patronage of the medium. They will continue to be affected by what they see. And they will continue to ascribe the elements of trustworthiness and salience to what they observe on the screen. Differences, of course, will be found in the size of audiences, which we expect will become smaller, and in the composition of audiences, which are bound to become more differentiated but more alike within themselves. So, despite these inevitable changes, the business communicator can use television as a powerful tool to reach a variety of audiences.

The mass media, as we have said, impart a sense of trust in a message. Communicators who use the media can expect to enjoy an elevation of trust in their messages because of the media vehicle. Television is particularly well qualified to build not just trust in a message but also credibility for the company behind the message. We have described how three essential components constitute credibility, or the quality of perceived confidence and believability: trustworthiness, expertise, and charisma. The communicator can use these components to influence an audience. How customers view a company along these three dimensions may determine whether or not they wish to do business with that company. If they view a company as honest and caring for customers, as experienced and knowledgeable in its field, and as exciting and dynamic in its business practices, they will be more likely to have confidence in that company. While development of such an image involves many factors, not the least of which is actually possessing such characteristics, the business must be able to project these qualities to customers. Television, with its parallel bandwidths of sight and sound, can be particularly helpful in such a task.

Trustworthiness

People identify with people they see on television. They come to believe that they know these people. Television newscasters are better known and rated as more trustworthy than newspaper writers and editors. This may be so because people associate a face and a voice with the name of television personalities but cannot with newspaper professionals. People are more likely to trust someone they think they know than someone they view as an abstraction—a disembodied name. Perhaps they believe someone looking directly at the audience (into the camera) is more likely to be honest than someone who records his or her thoughts out of view. We like to meet people face to face, and television makes this possible.

Political candidates have been instructed to use television for this purpose. They are told: Talk into the camera, contact voters directly, let them see your face, hear your voice, feel your concern as you express your interest in them and seek their interest in you. A large number of political television commercials today are designed to fortify the trustworthiness of a candidate. They show the candidate and even the candidate's spouse and children to make viewers feel they know this person. Almost all political consultants agree that television is the principal medium for developing a sense of familiarity and trust among voters.

Examples of trust building through television are not limited to politics. Many businesses rely on the medium for the same purpose. Consider the Tylenol scare of 198

- Following the serious erosion of trust in its product after several deaths attributed to tainted Tylenol capsules Johnson and Johnson faced the formidable task of recovering its reputation. Specifically, the company had to rebuild public trust in its capacity to deliver safe, effective pharmaceutical products. As a major part of its public communication campaign, the company developed a series of

> television commercials stressing the trustworthiness of Tylenol. It used the word "trust" throughout its scripts and linked use of the product with physicians, nurses, and hospitals in which the public places great trust. Although the company used other media in the campaign, it credits television with playing a major role in restoring public trust.

Television may not deserve its reputation for trust, however, because it can mislead viewers and it may at times be used by people with less than noble intentions. Nonetheless, it has the capacity to instill a sense of reliability in the images it projects. Businesses with image problems or undesirable trustworthiness ratings should consider using television in a mass or targeted audience format to bring about a change.

Expertise

While television is by no means uniquely capable of conveying the expertise of a business, the dramatic nature of its presentation and illustrative powers enables this medium to be most effective in getting across this quality. The demonstration of a product or service in action may convey better than writing how well it works, how much the company knows about its field, and how capable that company is of delivering the goods. Seeing is believing. A company may tell someone about its expertise in the print media or on radio, but on television it can show the audience evidence of its claims.

Take, for example, the overnight delivery services that wish to demonstrate their ability to move a package across the country in a matter of hours. Television provides evidence of expertise by showing their elaborate procedures, equipment, and trained personnel. Viewers see a package leave New York and arrive hours later in Los Angeles. These commercials are effective because they show scenes that cannot be described as dramatically in print media or radio. From such commercials, audiences learn about a company's expertise by seeing it in action.

Several years ago, American automotive companies discovered that large numbers of U.S. consumers believed foreign automobile manufacturers had a higher level of engineering and production expertise than did domestic companies. As a result, many people felt foreign cars were better and, despite higher costs, were buying them over American cars. As part of an elaborate marketing scheme to draw back American customers, Detroit manufacturers stressed in many of their television commercials the expertise of their engineering and production staffs.

They showed complex computer designs developed by their expert engineers. They brought cameras into the production line and showed trained workers checking the quality of cars about to leave the factory. Television did more than describe the expertise of these companies; it showed how this expertise was applied to the product. In this case where expertise had such an obvious visual component, television was a wise and natural choice. American automotive companies have made some gains with U.S. markets.

For many products and services, television may not be the best medium in which to cultivate perceptions of the company's expertise. Its general audiences may be inappropriate for a product with limited appeal. Furthermore, in instances where this expertise is not easily demonstrated visually or where such credentials are cumbersome to handle in a thirty-second commercial, other media may be more appropriate. But in circumstances where these restrictions are not applicable and where the product has sufficiently wide appeal to merit this medium, television can be most effective.

Charisma

The projection of charisma or dynamism, the final component in our consideration of source credibility, may be important to many companies. Perceptions of dynamism suggest a strength and resourcefulness of a company willing to do what is necessary to develop a product worthy of purchase.

Never ignore consumer perceptions on such matters. A flat, colorless image does not build confidence and does not inspire interest in a company or its products. When research reveals low charisma ratings, a company may wish to bolster its image among target audiences.

It may enhance its image as powerful, up and coming, exciting, and at the cutting edge in order to demonstrate power in the marketplace. Television excels at showing activity and movement. It also can demonstrate a rich voice, show off a lively personality, and convey emotion. Television has been a natural platform for contemporary religious leaders, not just by projecting their charisma, but often by amplifying it beyond real life proportions.

The current microcomputer market offers an excellent example of an environment in which companies are eager to be seen as exciting and dynamic. They want to be recognized as big, powerful, innovative, and at the forefront of technological development.

Nearly all of the leading manufacturers have been promoting this image. Among the most successful are those using television. An IBM personal computer advertisement may offer the best example of television use.

The spot involves the now-familiar Charlie Chaplin character who bungles his operation of a roller skate factory by using old accounting, inventory, and production techniques. In his factory, people crash into each other, run out of necessary parts, and never can reach manufacturing quotas. The business is on the brink of collapse. Determined to make a change, Charlie installs an IBM computer and quickly learns how he can reduce his problems, increase production, and run a more efficient operation. This fast-paced spot demonstrates that the computer can correct problems and bring success. It shows the chaos of the precomputer days and the calm of the postcomputer days. It is difficult to imagine how IBM could have achieved the same effect so concisely with any other medium.

Cost

Expenses for communicating through any medium are derived from production of the message and buying the time or space in which that message is disseminated. There is great variance in television costs for both of these features according to market size, station popularity, and sophistication of media usage. Larger markets, and so larger audiences, are more costly. Airing of a thirty-second commercial in a small market may cost no more than one hundred dollars, whereas that same commercial in a major urban area may cost many thousands of dollars. Clearly, all cost considerations must take into account population considerations of the market.

When we buy media time, we buy access to audiences. The larger the audiences, the higher the costs of air time. Market size is one determining factor of audience size. Station popularity is another. Some stations draw larger audiences than others because of programming popularity, promotional efforts, and signal strength. Nearly all stations subscribe to ratings services and know the size of their audiences since these statistics serve as a principal factor in determination of rate schedules. Salespeople for television stations are eager to share and "interpret" these data with prospective clients. Be careful about claims and descriptions of audience size.

We have seen cases where each of three stations "proves" it is leading in a single market. Be sure you understand the parameters stations are using to assert their leadership position. If you are interested in reaching the largest possible general composition audience, look at the total audience percentage for comparable time slots across stations. If you are interested in audiences with specific demographic traits, be sure each of the stations provides statistics on these audiences for comparable time periods.

Production costs for television commercials vary widely. At the low-cost end, a television station can send out a camera crew with a minicam to tape a thirty-second message delivered by a spokesperson for the company. The station will then add music and graphics and put the final product on cassette.

The advertiser can also provide the station with a finished commercial that has been developed by a professional production company. Production costs for such spots are nearly always more expensive, ranging from a few thousand to tens of thousands of dollars or more for each spot. Cost factors include talent, location and setting, graphic features, format (film or tape), research, and other equipment and staff for the production. While most businesses would not need network-quality commercials, it is interesting to note that production of some national commercials has cost several hundred thousand dollars each. If a business plans to use a professional production company, it is best to work through an advertising agency.

Television advertising costs are also determined by the time of day during which a commercial is aired. As we have said, the size of an audience is a major determinant of costs, and clearly audience size varies throughout the day. There are larger audiences during prime time than there are at 2 a.m. Consequently, commercials aired during these periods are priced accordingly; prime-time rates, obviously, are more costly than night-owl rates.

Beyond audience size, we should also consider audience composition. Prime-time audiences are bigger, but they may not necessarily be better than those in another portion of the day when people with specific characteristics make up the audience. Nielsen statistics reveal soap operas attract female audiences and Sunday afternoon sporting events draw males. Children watch television on Saturday mornings and older people watch Saturday evenings. If we are selling soap powder, beer, breakfast cereal, or retirement communities, we may get more for our money by selecting times other than prime time. For businesses selling products that have broad public appeal, prime time may be attractive, even though it may cost more than other times of day.

When considering the use of television for a public campaign, shop carefully. Buy into markets, stations, and time slots that deliver only the audiences you need. Television is a costly medium, and audience overkill can waste money and quickly erode a media budget. Also, pay for production that delivers only the quality you need to get your message and image across to your audience. Production costs can devour a budget. A high-cost, slick spot is of little value if there are no remaining funds with which to air it.

Television Summary

Television is a vastly popular medium with an influence on its viewers that is now becoming even more apparent. Television not only reaches nearly every household in America (97 per cent saturation), but also occupies more than four hours of people's lives every day. It commands the viewer's respect and imparts credibility to those who appear on the medium. Television increases the perception of truthfulness and sincerity of its subjects, and it raises in the public mind a belief that subjects discussed on it are important. Television is particularly successful at inspiring trust because it can show the faces and air the voices of those who appear there. It instills in its audiences a sense of familiarity with the communicator in a way not possible with any other medium. This medium comes as close as any to the human interactions people have every day.

With its graphic presentations, television can show expertise in action. In other media a business must describe how the skill and knowledge of its employees bring about a better product or service. On television, proof of the expertise can be shown in the service or product. People believe what they see, and television shows them the evidence.

As a dynamic medium, using rapid shifts and changes in pictures and sound, television offers a natural forum for the portrayal of a company's charisma. If a company needs to project an image of excitement and dynamism, television is an obvious choice. The current climate of change, however, makes television use a tricky venture. The increasing numbers of available channel options have been accompanied by a reduction in strength of the network-affiliated stations. With the added targeting possibilities offered by segmented audiences comes a complexity heretofore unseen in use of the medium. Despite these added dimensions that must be considered, television, properly used in conjunction with other media, can make a powerful and decisive impact on a business communication campaign.

Radio

Radio stands as a versatile, targeted mass medium because of its production flexibility and audience focus. Despite considerable changes in the basic structure of the medium during the last forty years, it remains extremely popular for business communicators. For our purposes, several features of radio stand out.

First, the number of radio stations continues to grow every year, providing a greater number of audience outlets and ever more refined and narrow audiences. Radio accommodates the targeting needs of communicators. In addition, costs of using radio stand at a considerable advantage. Compared to television, radio production costs are low, and so are the costs of airing a commercial. These features allow flexibility in the creation of a wide variety of ads and in frequent repetition—the number of times a commercial may be aired. Unlike the development of television commercials, which often require a good deal of production time, radio advertisements can be produced quickly, allowing the business communicator to announce timely messages with little delay.

Before we examine these advantages further, let us review the development of radio. Its history reveals that it has become a targeting medium through which the communicator may reach specialized audiences. As our recount of this history will demonstrate, this once-mass audience medium has adopted a targeted audience format not as a preference, but as a matter of survival.

As the first broadcast medium, radio was without a precedent to suggest its utility for owners or audiences. The earliest public use of radio was to broadcast music, if only to a limited number of listeners. Newspapers were among the early owners of radio, and they used the medium as a public relations tool to sell more papers, not as a communications medium with its own special utility.

Even early business communicators such as General Electric and AT&T, which purchased radio stations in order to advertise their products, failed to recognize the broader commercial uses of the medium. They devoted their air time to the promotion of their own products and did not recognize that money could be made selling portions of this time to other businesses. In 1922, however, the AT&T-owned New York radio station WEAF found that radio, like newspapers, could be a profit-making enterprise. The word was out, and entrepreneurs around the country began buying radio stations, audiences began buying receivers, and commercial radio began its rapid diffusion into the American media repertoire.

In the years that followed, radio provided mass appeal programming formats that attracted large, heterogeneous audiences. Elaborate big-band performances were broadcast live to national audiences. Live drama and comedy shows such as "The Green Hornet," "The Lone Ranger," "Fibber McGee and Molly," "The Shadow," and "Inner Sanctum Mysteries" delighted large, faithful audiences from all demographic backgrounds. Families gathered around the radio to hear the next installment of serials that captured people's attention and imaginations.

Advertisers, too, enjoyed this new medium through which they could reach large customer audiences. Radio provided a wide demographic and geographic mix of people to businesses wishing to promote their products or services to undifferentiated audience groups.

Unlike today, when advertisers buy thirty- and sixty-second spots on a radio programme, in the early days national advertisers would underwrite and become identified with entire programmes. Lipton Tea was known as the sponsor of the "Arthur Godfrey's Talent Scouts" and Chase and Sanborn Coffee was well recognized as the sponsor of "The Edgar Bergen and Charlie McCarthy Show." Early radio had big productions, big sponsors, and big audiences. The late 1920s to the late 1940s was truly the Golden Age of Radio.

Then, about as abruptly as it had begun, the dominance of radio came to an end. Televison arrived and quickly became the favourite of American audiences. At the time, some analysts believed television was a gimmick of which audiences would soon tire. They predicted people would return to radio when the novelty of television wore off. Of course, this has never happened. Popular radio personalities shifted with their audiences to television, where they soon stole the limelight from radio. If talent and audiences went to radio, could advertisers be far behind? A final blow to the old radio formats came when the financial base eroded, leaving little opportunity to stage the great shows that once sustained the medium. Although radio never regained the prominence it once had enjoyed as the prevailing national medium, it did not fade away, but, adapted instead to a new role and gathered audiences around its new format.

Paradoxically, even as radio stations reeled from the arrival of television, the number of radio stations increased and the number of radio-equipped households continued to grow. With television as the principal broad appeal medium, radio was compelled to carve for itself special interest audiences. Recognizing that large homogeneous audiences could never be recovered, radio stations selected formats to attract portions of those audiences. Audiences were divided naturally and sorted according to their interests in rock and roll, country and western, classical, and other music formats that appeal to particular listener groups.

Compared with television expenses, costs for such operations were reasonable, involving minimal outlays for equipment, and talent and a small business staff. The music, which served then and serves now as the mainstay of radio entertainment, was generally provided free by record companies seeking promotion for their latest hits. Income for these streamlined operations usually came from local small businesses seeking access to limited portions of the population. Since costs were low, so, too, were charges for air time, and this enabled even small companies, heretofore unable to afford radio advertising, to buy time. What initially appeared to be an untenable position for radio turned out to be a positive stage in media evolution for station owners, audiences, and advertisers as well.

Commercial development of efficient transistors enabled manufacturers to build radio sets that were rugged and energy efficient. These portable, or transistor, radios, as they were once called, allowed people to take receivers wherever they went. This meant greater audience patronage, and radio grew still further. Now, nearly forty years later, this dynamic medium is still changing to fit audience needs as it continues to add new stations and new formats.

Largely because radio audiences are well defined and grouped into convenient interest and demographic groups, this medium offers a valuable channel for business communicators. With demographic information on audiences readily available from a variety of sources, the communicator can select which stations will reach specific audiences within the general population. Messages can be developed with direct appeal to those audiences.

They have potentially greater impact and generate more pronounced effects. Many businesses, for instance, use several approaches to promote the same product to different audiences, highlighting features of greatest appeal to each group. A convenience store, for example, may promote its line of ice cream, soda, and chips to youth audiences on rock-and-roll stations, its beer and tobacco products on a country-and-western format station, and its fast food and convenient hours on easy-listening music stations often played in offices and shops. In addition, radio may vary the format and delivery of the spots to match the format of each station, thereby creating a special appeal through content and form to each audience.

While audience targeting stands as a major consideration for business communicators, radio offers a variety of other valuable features. For similar markets, radio is less expensive than television. It requires less lead time for message production and so allows messages to be more spontaneous. Because it offers only sound, it makes available a wide variety of creative possibilities. We will examine each of these features in more depth.

Cost

For both production and the purchase of air time, radio can be a bargain. Radio production operations are simple, involving only a few components. In order to produce a radio spot, one must have a studio with a microphone, a mixing board, and a tape recorder or two. Also required are a script, an announcer, and a sound engineer who records the voice and blends it with any sound effects.

Not much more is needed. Because radio production is simpler than television production, it is also less expensive. Costs can be trimmed further by limiting sophisticated production requirements (such as complicated sound effects) and by arranging to purchase spots in quantity—they are cheaper by the dozen. In fact, many radio stations allow clients to avoid production costs entirely by providing only a script to the announcer or disk jockey who "performs" the commercial live.

The second expense of radio is the purchase of air time. Here, too, in comparable markets the costs of radio are considerably lower than those of television. We know of one station—admittedly in a small market—that will sell you thirty seconds during peak hours for just two dollars! As we saw with television stations, in larger markets, radio charges more. Nonetheless, radio time is relatively inexpensive.

Several elements apply to the purchase of radio time. First, like the telephone company that charges different rates at different hours, radio stations charge different rates throughout the broadcasting day, depending on the size of an audience. The largest audiences for most radio stations are in the morning, known as "morning drives," and the "evening drives". Usually, the midnight to 6 a.m. slot is the least expensive, and midday hours are priced between the drive hours and the night-owl hours. Depending on the desired audience and budget considerations, the business communicator may select either the blocks of time acceptable for airing of the message or the specific times when the message is to run. In most cases the more specific you become, the more it will cost.

There is one remaining option: the least specific of all purchase schemes, known as "run of station." Here the client arranges to have a specified number of spots run during the course of a week or a month, but does not stipulate the times when they are to be carried. Placement of the ads is left up to the radio station. This is the least expensive of all arrangements because the radio station can place the spots during the night-owl period or insert them where other advertisers have canceled. In most cases, though, to make this option more attractive, radio stations will agree to include some of the more popular time slots in the total mix. In order to see exactly when the spots were aired, the communicator can, upon request, inspect a copy of the air log.

Whatever approach is used, the low costs of radio usually allow for repetition of a message. That is why radio is often called a "high-frequency medium." It is unrealistic to expect that exposure to a single message in any medium will influence an intended audience. In most cases, communicators rely on repeated exposure. Owing to its low costs, radio is a particularly attractive medium. While cost alone should not dictate the way a medium is used in a communication campaign, it certainly must be taken into account for even well-funded operations. Given that radio offers reasonable rates for production (which permits development of a variety of messages) and time (allowing message repetition), this medium always merits consideration in a communication programme.

Response Time

Although any of the media can react quickly to allow the communicator to get out a message in short order, radio is particularly well adapted to this purpose. Businesses occasionally need to reach people without advanced notice. For instance, they may need to announce a change in hours, solicit sales help, promote sale of an overstocked perishable item, or announce the end of a strike and the beginning of shift work. In such cases with short turnaround times in production (or simply script preparation), radio can air a message within an hour of receiving the information. One of the authors has worked at radio stations that had agreements with regular clients to run such "emergency" spots whenever necessary. The typical music formats of most stations allow such an approach without disrupting the usual format.

Creative Possibilities

An interesting radio commercial, developed for the Radio Bureau of Advertising by Stan Frieberg, demonstrates the remarkably creative possibilities of the medium. The spot describes a sundae being made in Lake Michigan. An announcer provides play-by-play comment, and a number of sound effects set the tone. First, the listeners hear chocolate sauce filling the giant pit left behind after the draining of the lake. Next they hear a mountain of whipped cream sliding onto the chocolate; then the heavy engines of a Royal Canadian Air Force bomber dropping a ten-ton maraschino cherry onto the thick whipped cream. Finally they hear the roar of ten thousand screaming extras who, we are told, have witnessed this incredible scene. Frieberg concludes: Would anyone like to try the same thing on television? Television, because it provides both sight and sound, is a compelling medium, but radio can be even more powerful. Radio provides the sound, and listeners create the visual features of the message. All hear the same announcer's voice but envision differing pictures of his or her appearance. Cues in vocal quality, delivery, perhaps laugh trigger thoughts about appearance—height, dress, age. Our imaginations are powerful, and radio stimulates the imagination.

A programme particularly good at this in the old days of radio was called "Inner Sanctum Mysteries." Each episode began with the sound of groaning hinges as a large, old door slowly opened. Regular listeners of the programme say it was a frightful sound. These same listeners, though, who watched "Inner Sanctum" when it was televised found the door not nearly as frightening as they had imagined. With radio, listeners projected all their personal fears into their image of the door. On television the image was a door that frightened someone else. It was no longer the listener's private fantasy; it was a public sight.

We agree with many advocates of radio that, by enlisting the listener's imagination, the business communicator can tap a particularly powerful persuasive tool. The sound of a product may be more compelling than its picture. A description of an event may create a stronger and more lasting image than features shown. Radio offers creative possibilities beyond cost considerations. It makes available effects that either cannot be accomplished through other media or cannot be accomplished as well. These features of radio, along with its targeting potentials, relatively low production and time costs, and flexibility, make it a business communication staple.

NEWSPAPERS

The rapid rise to prominence of broadcast media during the last two decades has concerned many communicators about the viability of newspapers as an advertising medium. These fears are not entirely ill founded. Considerable evidence suggests that television and radio have stolen the thunder from newspapers. For fast-breaking news accounts, print can do little to compete with the immediacy of the airwaves—the broadcast media can cover live stories instantly from almost any location. Even the old newspaper extra editions, once the popular way of announcing breaking stories, have faded from American journalism. Today, people learn first about major news stories from broadcast media, and most continue to follow the story largely through television. Roper polls reveal that since the mid-1960s the majority reports they receive most of their news information from television not newspapers. Compounding this observation, Roper has found that television is generally viewed to be more believable than newspapers for the majority of Americans.

On the surface the prognosis for newspapers does not appear good; however, a strange paradox in the statistics of newspaper subscription and usage patterns reveals this medium remains vastly popular. American audiences continue to buy 60 million copies every day. Moreover, newspapers outstrip the combined revenues of radio and television, receiving approximately 30 per cent of total advertising expenditures. Although before television newspapers received forty-five cents of every advertising dollar, the present percentage has stabilized in recent years.

Despite broadcast competition for advertising dollars, talent, and public attention, newspapers have filled a communication need for vast audiences. Journalism professor and former manager of the Louisiana Press Association Ronald Hicks, who has worked with and studied newspapers for many years, finds value in the newspaper as an important contemporary information medium. Hicks highlights some of the reasons for newspapers' continued success:

One of the most significant characteristics of newspapers is their flexibility. Their messages can be given varied typographic treatment and displayed in colour and in illustration; pages can be added as necessary; there is flexibility in terms of page size and format. Newspaper content "holds still": it has a degree of permanence which permits readers to absorb information at their own time and convenience. Complex issues can be developed to any necessary degree, yet there is a timeliness to newspapers because of the speed with which they can be put together and distributed. Their portability and low cost make for ease of reaching mass audiences.

For millions of American adults, the day begins and ends with a newspaper and a cup of coffee. Newspapers have become an accepted part of daily life.

According to Leo Bogart, executive vice president and general manager of the Newspaper Advertising Bureau, considerable changes are afoot in the appearance and content of American newspapers. These changes, he argues, are largely a result of new technology, a growing concern for reader interests, and serious competitive pressures prevailing in the media business. First, Bogart's research has shown an increase in the ratio of feature material to hard news stories. Newspapers today are carrying more light, entertainment-oriented stories and fewer pure news stories than they have in the past.

They also have increased the balance of local stories to world and national news, emphasizing neighbourhood and regional events more than global issues. Perhaps newspapers are conceding these larger stories to television and focusing their resources on matters that are not well adapted to the larger formats of television. Finally, Bogart reports a reduction in the number of regular, special interest columns and features. He speculates that newspapers may be increasing the staff-written content or providing special interest sections that vary content from edition to edition rather than retaining identifiable, labeled features on a routine basis.

Several observations about newspapers may be made. Most clearly, newspapers have been affected by the popularity of television. This is reflected in the Roper statistics demonstrating a rebuff of newspapers for certain kinds of news and a greater credence by the audience in the veracity of television over newspaper versions of a story. Despite all this, newspapers remain popular, although audience uses of newspapers are changing as is newspaper content, in part to reflect readers' needs. Perhaps gradual remolding of newspapers over the years has enabled them to find a comfortable place in American media diets. Newspapers do not attempt to compete with television; they serve yet another information function. They provide entertainment in the form of features, advice columns, comics, and games such as crossword puzzles. They provide news about local government, people, and events that are not adequately covered by television, and they offer local angles on larger stories.

Finally, they provide an important service for consumers by carrying information about available products and services. Nearly 65 per cent of the typical newspaper is devoted to advertising. When polled, the majority of newspaper readers claimed to pay attention to this material. This is good news for business communicators because it implies that while newspapers may be viewed less as a principal news source, they remain important as an advertising medium. From our viewpoint, newspapers offer several features that make them particularly valuable: They have a relative permanence that renders them suitable for audience members whose schedules require flexibility. The physical and tangible characteristics of newspapers (which grant them permanence) extend the use of the medium to other than just information..

They are furthermore adapted to the presentation of complex information because they permit more studied exposure and they offer a wide assortment of formats to convey detailed and complicated information. Newspapers are both a general audience and a targeted audience medium. With careful selection and use, newspapers can be a real bargain for business communicators. We will examine these points more closely.

Permanence

The permanence of newspapers permits readers to absorb the material presented at a time and pace convenient for them. In contrast to audiences of the broadcast media, newspaper audiences dictate when they will deal with the information and how much time they will spend on it. If they are attracted to an advertisement, they have the luxury of studying it and rereading it. This has obvious implications for communicators who deal with more complex or detailed matters. This permanence, of course, is a result of the physical properties of the medium. Unlike ephemeral broadcast signals, newspapers can be touched and folded and cut with scissors. In fact, polls show the large majority of households routinely cuts coupons from newspapers or newspaper supplements for redemption in local stores and for mail-away rebates. Coupons are a successful marketing technique, drawing customers into an advertisement and into stores. Their use in newspapers has remained popular over the years.

Complex Treatment

The permanence of newspapers allows readers to move through a story or an advertisement at their own pace, spending more time to understand the information fully. Even though the broadcast media have been shown to convey complex information successfully, print can do a more thorough job with many audiences. Not only by providing readers the opportunity to study detailed information, but also by expanding the communication formats to convey this information, newspapers are an excellent medium for difficult and detailed subjects. They can present more complex artwork such as charts and graphs, a task for which television is ill suited. They can present lists, schedules, road maps, flowcharts to help explain processes, and tables of numbers, prices, times, and scores. They can make lengthy descriptions more manageable and compress a great deal of information into a small space. Readers can clip, store, and share much information that cannot be adapted readily to the broadcast media.

Audience Appeal

As members of a newspaper audience, you are identified by the sections you read. Some portions of the paper—the general news sections—attract a large heterogeneous mix of readers. These audiences rep. resent a blend of demographic and interest groups that match the broad profile of the general population. Special interest sections of the paper draw smaller but more homogeneous audiences. The sports section, for instance, draws larger male than female audiences. Business sections draw people in higher income brackets, investors, local entrepreneurs, and others interested in such matters. Food and home sections still attract large female audiences. The newspaper is both a general audience and a targeted audience medium.

The targeting possibilities of newspapers are of particular interest for specialized communication. Note the kinds of advertisements found in each of the three special sections mentioned above. In the sports section, most newspapers run ads for automobile products, home building supplies, outdoor equipment, and other products that often interest men. Even though women may also purchase these items, businesses base their placement decisions on market research information that shows men are the most likely consumers of such products. Efficient business communicators, of course, strive to focus on audiences that promise the greatest possible potential.

It would be interesting to examine the possibilities of using newspapers to expand a market, say, for home building supplies, to a non-traditional audience, say, women. Through research, a building supplies retailer identifies certain features of this business that are of particular concern to female consumers. For the purposes of this example, suppose it were discovered that many women were reluctant to shop at these male bastions because they were not familiar with the jargon and felt intimidated by sales personnel. Instead, many shopped for such items in department stores or through mailorder catalogs where they felt less threatened. In such a case, a home building supplies outlet might hire female sales personnel to make the environment less threatening. They might train all their clerks to be more sensitive to people unfamiliar with industry terminology and in other ways attempt to improve the environment. With such changes in place, the retailer might then target female audiences with special information about these new services. Quarter-page ads in the food and home section aimed at women and based on the theme "We speak your language" could go a long way towards bringing in new business. The newspaper is ideally suited for such a targeted communication strategy.

Cost

For newspapers, as for any medium, when audience size increases, so, too, do advertising costs. For purposes of specialized communications, though, there is more to consider than just audience size—audience composition must also enter the decision. In towns with more than a single newspaper, examine the patronage of each to determine if there is a concentration of target audience members among subscribers of one paper. Often, clear distinctions exist among audience characteristics of several papers. There are no savings in paying for an advertisement that misses the target group.

Production fees also factor into newspaper advertising costs. A company can provide either a camera-ready advertisement or for an additional expense allow the newspaper graphics department to prepare the ad. Unless one has graphic arts skills and equipment, at some point there will be a charge for advertisement production. Generally, newspaper production departments charge the same as, or less than, freelance graphics companies. Elaborate art, photographs, colour, and a great deal of typesetting all contribute to higher production costs. Photographs and colour printing also elevate the cost. Finally, for cost consideration in newspapers as in other media, there are quantity advertising discounts. Salespeople can usually arrange considerable savings for advertisements run several times per week over a long term. Advertisers can also mix the size and placement of ads over time and retain lower unit costs.

Despite the attention given to a shift from newspapers to television among American audiences, recognize that while people may be obtaining much of their world and national news from television, their loyalty to newspapers remains strong for local items, entertainment features, and advertising. Sales are strong, the number of available newspapers is growing, and all signs suggest the medium will continue to be strong for the foreseeable future. For the business communicator, newspapers provide some permanence and tangibility and a forum to present more complex information than is possible with the broadcast media. Newspapers can work nicely in a targeting strategy and can fit into a modest advertising budget.

MAGAZINES

Just as television has revolutionized the communication roles of radio and newspapers during the last forty years, it has stimulated a major modification of magazines too. Such broad appeal magazines as Look and Life, which required large national audiences to support their production costs and attract a big advertising base, have given way to targeted format magazines whose audiences are bound by specific interests.

More than ten thousand magazine titles are available across the country today, catering to even the smallest special interest group. One magazine publisher extends the challenge to "find me a list of names and I'll create a magazine for it!" This new role of magazines is explained here from a historical perspective:

The rise of special-interest magazines and the related decline of general interest magazines has been the most significant development in publishing since the end of WWII. Television has hastened the growth of special-interest magazines by making people aware of all that there is to be aware of. The age of the Renaissance man is over. There is just too much to know for [someone] to be satisfied with claiming a little knowledge in many areas. The time is past when a magazine can succeed by only scraping lightly on every possible surface.

From the business communicator's viewpoint, magazines have three characteristics that set them apart from other media. First, the most attractive feature is the targetability of magazines. Of all the public media available, magazines permit the greatest degree of targeting.

Next, remember that people choose the magazines they read, so magazine readers are interested in the subject they have chosen—there is even a good chance they will find the advertisements interesting! Research demonstrates that magazines usually are reviewed more than one time by a reader and that the pass-along audience extends the reach of each copy. Finally, as a print medium, magazines can accommodate complex information.

Because of their specialized printing methods, unlike newspapers, they also offer extremely high-quality reproductions. Such quality may be an important considera-tion for some communicators. Each of these advantages of magazines will be discussed in turn.

Targeting Potential

If you have ever examined the titles of magazines lined up at a newsstand (even an outstanding newsstand can stock only a fraction of the titles in publication), you may have begun to appreciate the level of audience specification available. For instance, there are dozens of computer magazines, each written with a different focus on computer issues. They are variously targeted to IBM users, Apple users, people who wish to apply computers to personal use, or those who use computers in a business setting.

There are software and hardware magazines and magazines for used equipment. For sports fans there are general audience sports magazines and titles dealing specifically with football, wrestling, weightlifting, and even more specific titles covering pro or college football, Olympic or commercial wrestling; and the list goes on.

In addition to magazines sold at newsstands are those available only through subscription and thousands of others with restricted subscription lists, such as corporate house organs, association journals, technical magazines, and college journals. As the list of available magazines grows, the characteristics of attending audiences become more refined. The direction for magazines has been the continued focusing and narrowing of audiences, resulting in homogeneous groups represented by a specific set of identifying characteristics. By purchasing a magazine, people identify with others who share an interest in the same topic.

The proliferation of special interest magazines can be an extraordinary benefit to the business communicator wishing to seek out and contact special audiences. Not only have magazine readers already been identified with a particular area of interest, but they also have expressed a level of commitment to that interest. They have spent the time, energy, and money necessary to acquire the magazine. Through their purchase, they have affirmed an interest in the product or service the company wishes to promote. Magazine audiences are self-selected and become active participants in the communication event. Television audiences, by contrast, often view ads and spot announcements as extraneous events, and many become passive and some even hostile participants in the process.

Imagine yourself as a manufacturer of precision altimeters for small aircraft. Where would you turn to promote this esoteric product? You could use prime-time television because even owners of small aircraft watch evening television, but consider the enormous waste of such a decision. You would be paying large sums to reach a barely measurable portion of the audience.

You could save a great deal of money and become more specific and no doubt more persuasive with your message if you were to advertise in a publication such as *Flying* magazine. Aircraft owners and pilots, people who read Flying, are already interested in new gadgets and equipment for airplanes. It is also more likely they could afford such a purchase. Using this approach, you have an audience that is self-selected and already interested in the subject and that understands the technical features. They will require minimal tutoring. Overall, these readers are better customer prospects because of need, resources, and motivation.

Consider another example, this time for an audio equipment retail chain whose products have wider appeal. You must consider, therefore, a broader, more expansive audience. Throughout this book we have argued for the logic of subdividing larger audiences into separate groups for special treatment. The total effects of such an approach will exceed the alternative one-size-fits- all mass audience strategy. Customer research will probably reveal a natural division within such a clientele.

To illustrate, let us assume there are three major high-volume subgroups of audio equipment buyers: teenagers, unmarried young professionals, and upper-income, middle-aged men. Suppose, furthermore, our research indicates the following: The teenage group is interested in portable sound equipment capable of great volume if not greatquality reproduction. Young professionals want not only high-quality sound, but equipment that has impressive appearance with digital read-out diplays, lights, and control switches. The middle-aged male buyers want high-quality equipment and are willing to invest a good deal of money for prestigious, upper-end items. With this information and no doubt a good deal more revealed by our research, we may find magazines an excellent vehicle for reaching the three audiences. We may use magazines such as *Teenage* and *Rock Star* to promote the lower-end, high-volume equipment to teen audiences. Cosmopolitan, Playboy, and *GQ: Gentlemen's Quarterly* may provide a natural channel to the young professional buyers (again depending on our research findings). *Newsweek*, *Audio Magazine*, and *Stereo Review* may give access to the middle-aged male audio aficionados.

Throughout this targeting process, we rely heavily on research for direction. Research provides the basis on which to make decisions about how to subdivide the general audience, how to reach each audience group with persuasive messages, and how to select the media that will yield the greatest audience impact. Because magazines are so well adapted to targeted communication strategies, they provide an excellent example for the use of research. Without detailed information on client audiences, there would be little basis, other than hunch, for making decisions about audience clusters. Specifically, how does one break the audience into subgroups? On age? Income? Education? Previous purchases?

Ideological commitment? Or on some combination of these or other variables not immediately apparent? To use magazines to their fullest potential, the communicator must pinpoint target audience groups and identify their preferred magazine channels. Research can further be used to identify the appeal with the greatest potential to inform or persuade group members. Magazines offer an efficient means of targeting audience subgroups, but decisions about their use (or, for that matter, the use of any targeted media) are best made with the guidance of thorough audience research.

Inherent Interest

Except perhaps at the dentist's office where we thumb nervously through any magazine available, we choose our magazines because they interest us. We find some appeal in the subject matter of a magazine, or we would not have spent money on it. This feature of magazine audiences, known as "receptivity," makes them particularly attractive to advertisers. Here potential customers have a natural interest in a product genre, and rather than viewing the message as an irritating interruption, which is often the case with broadcast media, studies have shown many magazines readers buy the publication specifically to read the advertisements. What an accommodating arrangement! Although we may wish to use various design and other techniques to maximize readership of our ads, we do not face a major hurdle of resistance encountered in some of the other media.

Take, for instance, *Organic Gardening*, a national magazine sold mainly by subscription, which focuses on techniques of home fruit and vegetable production without the use of chemical fertilizers or pesticides. Subscribers to this magazine have an interest in gardening in general and more particularly in a special form of gardening. Most of these readers probably have their own gardens, see value in the organic approach, and are interested in the equipment and other facilities necessary for the hobby. Consequently, companies who deal in compost bins, tillers, mail order nursery products, irrigation systems, and other such products and services find a receptive audience through this specialized magazine. People view the advertisements not as an interruption but as a service and a desirable feature of the publication.

Audience Exposure

Several other attractive magazine features have appeal for the business communicator. According to the MPA, readers go through a magazine an average of 1.7 times, thus providing multiple exposure to advertisements and a greater opportunity for message effects. Work cited by the MPA (1985) finds a second exposure to a magazine advertisement boosts brand familiarity, recall, and belief in ad claims. It also increases willingness to buy the brand and to maintain a level of recall. Clearly, the second reading is beneficial for message impact, and according to MPA statistics, magazines get that second chance with the majority of readers.

Not only is a magazine read more than one time by a reader, but it is read by 3.6 people, effectively expanding the overall reach of each copy. Moreover, since each of these readers uses the magazine alone, advertisers are able to communicate information more effectively without the distractions inherent to group settings. Each copy of a magazine reaches a number of people, one at a time.

MASS MEDIA

The mass media are diversified media technologies that are planned to reach a big audience by mass communication. Broadcast media (also recognized as electronic media) transmit their information electronically and comprise television, radio, film, movies, CDs, DVDs, and other devices such as cameras and video consoles. Alternatively, print media use a physical substance as a means of sending their information, such as a newspaper, magazines, comics, books, brochures, newsletters, leaflets, and pamphlets. The organizations that manage these technologies, such as television stations or publishing companies, are also recognized as the mass media. Internet media is able to achieve mass media status in its own right, due to the several mass media services it gives, such as e-mail, web sites, Internet, and television. For this cause, several mass media outlets have an attendance on the web, by such things as having TV ads that link to a web site, or having games in their sites to entice gamers to visit their web site. In this method, they can utilize the easy accessibility that the Internet has, and the outreach that Internet affords, as information can easily be broadcast to several dissimilar regions of the world simultaneously and cost-efficiently. Outdoor media is a form of mass media that comprises billboards, signs, placards placed inside and outside of commercial structures and objects like shops and buses, flying billboards (signs in tow of airplanes), blimps, and skywriting. Public speaking and event organizing can also be measured as shapes of mass media.

Issues with Definition: In the late 20th Century, mass media could be classified into eight mass media industries: books, newspapers, magazines, recordings, radio, movies, television, and the internet. With the explosion of digital communication technology in the late 20th and early 21st centuries, the question of what shapes of media should be classified as "mass media" has become more prominent. For instance, it is controversial whether to contain cell phones, video games, and computer games (such as MMORPGs) in the definition. In the 2000s, a classification described the "seven mass media" became popular. In order of introduction, they are:

1. Print (books, pamphlets, newspapers, magazines, etc.) from the late 15th century,
2. Recordings (gramophone records, magnetic tapes, cassettes, cartridges, CDs, DVDs) from the late 19th century,
3. Cinema from in relation to the 1900,
4. Radio from in relation to the 1910,
5. Television from in relation to the 1950,
6. Internet from in relation to the 1990,
7. Mobile phones from in relation to the 2000.

Each mass media has its own content kinds, its own creative artists and technicians, and its own business models. For instance, the Internet comprises web sites, blogs, pod casts, and several other technologies built on top of the common sharing network. The sixth and seventh media, internet and mobile, are often described collectively as digital media; and the fourth and fifth, radio and TV, as broadcast media. Some argue that video games have urbanized into a separate mass form of media. While a telephone is a two method communication device, mass media refers to medium which can communicate a message to a big group, often simultaneously. Though, contemporary cell phones are no longer a single use device. Mainly cell phones are equipped with internet access and capable of connecting to the web which itself a mass medium. A question arises of whether this creates cell phones a mass medium or basically a device used to access a mass medium (the internet). There is currently a system where marketers and advertisers are able to tap into satellites, and broadcast commercials and advertisements directly to cell phones, unsolicited by the phone's user. This transmission of mass advertising to millions of people is a form of mass communication.

Video games may also be evolving into a mass medium. Video games convey the similar messages and ideologies to all their users. Users sometimes share the experience with each other by playing online. Excluding the internet though, it is questionable whether players of video games are sharing a general experience when they play the game separately. It is possible to talk about in great detail the events of a video game with a friend you have never played with because the experience was identical to you both. The question is if this is then a form of mass communication.

Massively multiplayer online role-playing games (MMORPGs) such as Run escape give a general gaming experience to millions of users throughout the globe. It is arguable that the users are getting the similar message, *i.e.*, the game is mass communicating the similar messages to the several players.

Features: Five features of mass communication have been recognized by Cambridge University's John Thompson:

- "[C]omprises both technological and institutional methods of manufacture and sharing" This is apparent throughout the history of the media, from print to the Internet, each appropriate for commercial utility.
- Involves the "commodification of symbolic shapes", as the manufacture of materials relies on its skill to manufacture and sell big quantities of the work. Presently as radio stations rely on its time sold to advertisements, newspapers rely for the similar reasons on its space.
- "[S]eparate contexts flanked by the manufacture and reception of information"
- Its "reach to those 'distant removed' in time and space, in comparison to the producers".
- "[I]nformation sharing" - a "one to several" form of communication, whereby products are mass produced and disseminated to a great quantity of audiences.

Mass vs. Mainstream: "Mass media" is sometimes used as a synonym for "mainstream media", which is distinguished from alternative media by the content and point of view. Alternative media are also "mass media" outlets in the sense of by technology capable of reaching several people, even if the audience is often smaller than the mainstream. In general usage, the term "mass" denotes not that a given number of individuals receives the products, but rather that the products are accessible in principle to a plurality of recipients.

Mass vs. Local: Mass media is distinguished from local media by the notion that whilst the former aims to reach a extremely big market such as the whole population of a country, the latter broadcasts to a much smaller population and area, and usually focuses on local news rather than global events. A third kind of media, speciality media, gives for specific demographics, such as speciality channels on TV (sports channels, porn channels, etc.). These definitions are not set in stone, and it is possible for a media outlet to be promoted in status from a local media outlet to a global media outlet. Some local media, which takes an interest in state or provincial news, can rise to prominence due to their investigative journalism, and to the local region's preference of updates in national politics rather than local news. The Guardian, formerly recognized as the Manchester Guardian is an instance of one such media outlet. Once a local daily newspaper, The Guardian is currently a nationally respected paper.

SHAPES OF MASS MEDIA

Broadcast: Television and radio programmes are distributed through radio broadcasting in excess of frequency bands that are highly regulated by the Federal Communications Commission. Such regulation comprises determination of the width of the bands, range, licensing, kinds of receivers and transmitters used, and acceptable content.

Cable programmes are often broadcast simultaneously with radio and television programmes, but have a more limited audience. By coding signals and having a cable converter box in houses, cable also enables subscription-based channels and pay-per-view services.

A broadcasting organisation may broadcast many programmes at the similar time, through many channels (frequencies), for instance BBC One and Two. On the other hand, two or more organisations may share a channel and each use it throughout a fixed part of the day. Digital radio and digital television may also transmit multiplexed programming, with many channels compressed into one ensemble.

When broadcasting is done via the Internet the term web casting is often used. In 2004 a new phenomenon occurred when a number of technologies combined to produce pod casting. Pod casting is an asynchronous broadcast/narrowcast medium, with one of the main proponents being Adam Curry and his associates the Pod show.

Film: 'Film' encompasses motion pictures as individual projects, as well as the field in common. The name comes from the photographic film (also described film stock), historically the primary medium for recording, and displaying motion pictures. Several other conditions exist—*motion pictures* (or presently *pictures* and "picture"), *the silver screen, photoplays, the cinema, picture shows, flicks*—and commonly *movies*.

Films are produced by recording people and objects with cameras, or by creating them by animation techniques and/or special effects. They comprise a series of individual frames, but when these images are shown rapidly in succession, the illusion of motion is given to the viewer. Flickering flanked by frames is not seen due to an effect recognized as persistence of vision—whereby the eye retains a visual image for a fraction of a second after the source has been removed. Also of relevance is what causes the perception of motion; a psychological effect recognized as beta movement.

Film is measured by several to be a significant art form; films entertain, educate, enlighten, and inspire audiences. Any film can become a worldwide attraction, especially with the addition of dubbing or subtitles that translate the film message. Films are also relics created by specific cultures, which reflect those cultures, and, in turn, affect them.

Video Games: A video game is a computer-controlled game where a video display such as a monitor or television is the primary feedback device. The term "computer game" also comprises games which display only text (and which can so theoretically be played on a teletypewriter) or which use other methods, such as sound or vibration, as their primary feedback device, but there are extremely few new games in these categories. There always necessity also be some sort of input device, usually in the form of button/joystick combinations (on arcade games), a keyboard and mouse/trackball combination (computer games), or a controller (console games), or a combination of any of the above. Also, more esoteric devices have been used for input. Usually there are rules and goals, but in more open-ended games the player may be free to do whatever they like within the confines of the virtual universe.

In general usage, a "computer game", or a "PC game" refers to a game that is played on a personal computer. "Console game" refers to one that is played on a device specifically intended for the use of such, while interfacing with an average television set. "Arcade game" refers to a game intended to be played in an establishment in which patrons pay to play on a per-use foundation. "Video game" (or "videogame") has evolved into a catchall phrase that encompasses the aforementioned beside with any game made for any other device, including, but not limited to, mobile phones, PDAs, advanced calculators, etc.

Audio Recording and Reproduction: Sound recording and reproduction is the electrical or mechanical re-creation and/or amplification of sound, often as music. This involves the use of audio equipment such as microphones, recording devices, and loudspeakers. From early beginnings with the invention of the phonograph by purely mechanical techniques, the field has advanced with the invention of electrical recording, the mass manufacture of the 78 record, the magnetic wire recorder followed by the tape recorder, the vinyl LP record. The invention of the compact cassette in the 1960s, followed by Sony's Walkman, gave a major boost to the mass sharing of music recordings, and the invention of digital recording and the compact disc in 1983 brought huge improvements in ruggedness and quality. The mainly recent growths have been in digital audio players.

An album is a collection of related audio recordings, released jointly to the public, usually commercially. The term record album originated from the information that 78 RPM Phonograph disc records were kept jointly in a book resembling a photo album. The first collection of records to be described an "album" was Tchaikovsky's *Nutcracker Suite*, release in April 1909 as a four-disc set by Odeon records. It retailed for 16 shillings—in relation to the £15 in contemporary currency.

A music video (also promo) is a short film or video that accompanies a complete piece of music, mainly commonly a song. Contemporary music videos were primarily made and used as a marketing device planned to promote the sale of music recordings. Although the origins of music videos go back much further, they came into their own in the 1980s, when Music Television's format was based on them. In the 1980s, the term "rock video" was often used to describe this form of entertainment, although the term has fallen into disuse.

Music videos can accommodate all styles of filmmaking, including animation, live action films, documentaries, and non-narrative, abstract film.

Internet: The Internet (also recognized basically as "the Net" or less precisely as "the Web") is a more interactive medium of mass media, and can be briefly described as "a network of networks". Specifically, it is the worldwide, publicly accessible network of interconnected computer networks that transmit data by packet switching by the average Internet Protocol (IP). It consists of millions of smaller domestic, academic, business, and governmental networks, which jointly carry several information and services, such as e-mail, online chat, file transfer, and the interlinked web pages and other documents of the World Wide Web.

Contrary to some general usage, the Internet and the World Wide Web are not synonymous: the Internet is the system of interconnected *computer networks*, connected by copper wires, fibre-optic cables, wireless connections, etc.; the Web is the contents, or the interconnected *documents*, connected by hyperlinks and URLs.

Towards the end of the 20th century, the advent of the World Wide Web marked the first era in which mainly individuals could have a means of exposure on a level comparable to that of mass media. Anyone with a web location has the potential to address a global audience, although serving to high stages of web traffic is still relatively expensive. It is possible that the rise of peer-to-peer technologies may have begun the procedure of creation the cost of bandwidth manageable. Although a vast amount of information, imagery, and commentary (*i.e.*, "content") has been made accessible, it is often hard to determine the authenticity and reliability of information contained in web pages (in several cases, self-published). The invention of the Internet has also allowed breaking news stories to reach approximately the globe within minutes. This rapid growth of instantaneous, decentralized communication is often deemed likely to change mass media and its connection to society.

"Cross-media" means the thought of distributing the similar message through dissimilar media channels. A similar thought is expressed in the news industry as "convergence". Several authors understand cross-media publishing to be the skill to publish in both print and on the web without manual conversion effort. A rising number of wireless devices with mutually incompatible data and screen formats create it even more hard to achieve the objective "make once, publish several".

The Internet is quickly becoming the centre of mass media. Everything is becoming accessible via the internet. Instead of picking up a newspaper, or watching the 10 o'clock news, people can log onto the internet to get the news they want, when they want it. For instance, several workers listen to the radio through the Internet while sitting at their desk.

Even the education system relies on the Internet. Teachers can get in touch with the whole class by sending one e-mail. They may have web pages where students can get another copy of the class outline or assignments. Some classes have class blogs in which students are required to post weekly, with students graded on their contributions.

Blogs (Web Logs): Blogging, too, has become a pervasive form of media. A blog is a web site, usually maintained by an individual, with regular entries of commentary, descriptions of events, or interactive media such as images or video. Entries are commonly displayed in reverse chronological order, with mainly recent posts shown on top. Several blogs give commentary or news on a scrupulous subject; others function as more personal online diaries. A typical blog combines text, images and other graphics, and links to other blogs, web pages, and related media. The skill for readers to leave comments in an interactive format is a significant part of several blogs. Mainly blogs are primarily textual, although some focus on art (art log), photographs (photo log), sketchblog, videos (vlog), music (MP3 blog), audio (pod casting) are part of a wider network of social media. Microblogging is another kind of blogging which consists of blogs with extremely short posts.

RSS Feeds: RSS is a format for syndicating news and the content of news-like sites, including major news sites like Wired, news-oriented society sites like Slashdot, and personal blogs. It is a family of Web feed formats used to publish regularly updated content such as blog entries, news headlines, and pod casts. An RSS document (which is described a "feed" or "web feed" or "channel") contains either a summary of content from an associated web location or the full text. RSS creates it possible for people to stay up with web sites in an automated manner that can be piped into special programmes or filtered displays.

Pod Cast: A pod cast is a series of digital-media files which are distributed in excess of the Internet by syndication feeds for playback on portable media players and computers. The term pod cast, like broadcast, can refer either to the series of content itself or to the method by which it is syndicated; the latter is also described pod casting. The host or author of a pod cast is often described a pod caster.

Mobile: Mobile phones were introduced in Japan in 1979 but became a mass media only in 1998 when the first downloadable ringing tones were introduced in Finland. Soon mainly shapes of media content were introduced on mobile phones, and today the total value of media consumed on mobile towers in excess of that of internet content, and was worth in excess of 31 billion dollars in 2007. The mobile media content comprises in excess of 8 billion dollars worth of mobile music (ringing tones, ring back tones, true tones, MP3 files, karaoke, music videos, music streaming services, etc.); in excess of 5 billion dollars worth of mobile gaming; and several news, entertainment and advertising services. In Japan mobile phone books are so popular that five of the ten best-selling printed books were originally released as mobile phone books.

Similar to the internet, mobile is also an interactive media, but has distant wider reach, with 3.3 billion mobile phone users at the end of 2007 to 1.3 billion internet users. Like e-mail on the internet, the top application on mobile is also a personal messaging service, but SMS text messaging is used by in excess of 2.4 billion people.

Practically all internet services and applications exist or have similar cousins on mobile, from search to multiplayer games to virtual worlds to blogs. Mobile has many unique benefits which several mobile media pundits claim create mobile a more powerful media than either TV or the internet, starting with mobile being permanently accepted and always linked. Mobile has the best audience accuracy and is the only mass media with a built-in payment channel accessible to every user without any credit cards or PayPal accounts or even an age limit. Mobile is often described the 7th Mass Medium and either the fourth screen (if counting cinema, TV and PC screens) or the third screen (counting only TV and PC).

Print Media

Book: A book is a collection of sheets of paper, parchment or other material with a piece of text written on them, bound jointly beside one edge within covers.

A book is also a literary work or a main division of such a work. A book produced in electronic format is recognized as an e-book.

Magazine: A magazine is a periodical publication containing a diversity of articles, usually financed by advertising and/or purchase by readers.

Magazines are typically published weekly, biweekly, monthly, bimonthly, or quarterly, with a date on the cover that is in advance of the date it is actually published. They are often printed in colour on coated paper, and are bound with a soft cover.

Magazines fall into two broad categories: consumer magazines and business magazines. In practice, magazines are a subset of periodicals, separate from those periodicals produced by scientific, artistic, academic or special interest publishers which are subscription-only, more expensive, narrowly limited in circulation, and often have little or no advertising.

Magazines can be classified as:

- Common interest magazines (*e.g.*, Frontline, India Today, The Week, The Sunday Times, etc.),
- Special interest magazines (women's, sports, business, scuba diving, etc.).

Newspaper: A newspaper is a publication containing news and information and advertising, usually printed on low-cost paper described newsprint. It may be common or special interest, mainly often published daily or weekly. The first printed newspaper was published in 1605, and the form has thrived even in the face of competition from technologies such as radio and television. Recent growths on the Internet are posing major threats to its business model, though. Paid circulation is declining in mainly countries, and advertising revenue, which creates up the bulk of a newspaper's income, is shifting from print to online; some commentators, nevertheless, point out that historically new media such as radio and television did not entirely supplant existing.

Outdoor Media: Outdoor media is a form of mass media which comprises billboards, signs, placards placed inside and outside of commercial structures/objects like shops/buses, flying billboards (signs in tow of airplanes), blimps, and skywriting. Several commercial advertisers use this form of mass media when advertising in sports stadiums. Tobacco and alcohol manufacturers used billboards and other outdoor media extensively. In a 1994 Chicago-based revise, Diana Hackbarth and her colleagues revealed how tobacco- and alcohol-based billboards were concentrated in poor neighbourhoods. In other urban centres, alcohol and tobacco billboards were much more concentrated in African-American neighbourhoods than in white neighbourhoods.

Purposes: Mass media encompasses much more than presently news, although it is sometimes misunderstood in this method. It can be used for several purposes:

- Advocacy, both for business and social concerns. This can contain advertising, marketing, propaganda, public dealings, and political communication.

- Entertainment, traditionally through performances of acting, music, sports, and TV shows beside with light reading; since the late 20th century also through video and computer games.
- Public service announcements and emergency alerts (that can be used as political device to communicate propaganda to the public).

CHANGES IN MEDIA USE

A population deeply involved with the mass media. The statistics demonstrate that media are not just pleasant additions to our lives. They are integral components of our existence. Hardly a moment goes by that we are not in contact with one of the broadcast or print media. Large numbers of homes, known as "constant television households," have the television on from the moment the first person awakes in the morning until the last person retires at night. Most homes have magazines, newspapers, and books lying around, always available to absorb an idle moment. And now that portable radios have become truly portable through miniaturization and lightweight headphones that deliver sound of superb quality, we can take our music wherever we go. We are truly people of the media age.

As technological innovations provide ever greater varieties of media and more flexibility in the ways we use these media, the complexity of usage patterns has also grown. We are moving away from times when the media joined people into common exposure tracks.

For instance, in the mid- 1950s when the three major television networks provided the primary source of programming, those watching prime-time television had to be viewing one of these three networks. Everyone watched essentially the same thing. This is not so today.

In a recent study by one of the authors, interviewers investigated the television-viewing habits of two hundred fifty teenagers in a medium-sized city and found that during any half-hour prime-time segment, they had been watching as many as twenty-five different programmes. They selected from network and cable channels as well as from movie, concert, and special interest tapes played on their VCRs. The medium that once brought us together as a population with shared experiences now divides us by the vast programme diversity it offers.

Apart from the sociological implications of this phenomenon, there are important practical considerations for business communicators who need to reach people wherever they are. In the "old days," it seemed easy. There was one-stop shopping. You could go to one newspaper or one television or radio station and cover the market; you could reach large portions of the population with a single communication. Diversification of media usage patterns has made media selection procedures considerably more complex; and if current trends continue as expected, these procedures will probably become yet more involved.

While such trends appear to create a good deal of trouble, they may actually provide a number of advantages. As audiences sort out and attend specific media, they become smaller and more homogeneous. This homogenization can serve the needs of business communicators who so often wish to focus their efforts on strong, prospective customers rather than waste resources on larger audiences, only a portion of which are of interest.

With the character of media changing so quickly, it is becoming increasingly more difficult to provide a convenient typology of the media based on audience characteristics. Traditionally, television has been considered a broad appeal, large-audience medium whose content and style interest massive audiences. Certainly, this remains the case today, although audience statistics suggest that with some exceptions the vast popularity of large programme blocks has been eroding. Nonetheless, for special programmes, television can still command immense audiences with an unmatched potential of reaching millions of people at a single moment.

One television network reported in the mid-1970s that a greater number of people viewed its presentation of "Hamlet" in a single evening than all the combined audiences of the play since Shakespeare wrote it more than four hundred years ago. What power! What potential!

In times of great crises or of great ceremony, people en masse turn from a variety of media to one of the three networks. We see these great audiences again joined in a common experience. On such occasions the strength of this medium and the power of truly mass communication become evident. In the last half of the 1980s, however, we see television in transition from its days as a large mass medium, offering broad appeal programming exclusively, to its next stage in this evolutionary process. Television, like magazines and radio, inevitably will become a targeted, narrow audience medium.

Targeted Media

As we examine techniques of communicating with specialized audiences, we are intrigued by the potential offered through targeted media. Certainly, under limited conditions, when business communicators wish to reach broad customer groups and have little concern for the makeup of those groups, they should consider using the medium that can deliver the largest possible numbers, even if that audience is a demographic grab bag. But when they need to reach a population subgroup or several subgroups with individually tailored messages, they should seek such audiences through targeted media. Targeting is the key to specialized campaigns. Targeting is the essence of audience-based communication. The receiver lies at the heart of the communication process. Throughout this book we demonstrate that each step begins with consideration of the intended recipients of a message. We have reworked the Berlo SMCR model to include the receiver not just as an endpoint of the process, but as an integral component in each step constituting the communication event. Portrayal of the source should be developed in light of receiver concerns and impressions. The message content and delivery require close analysis of receiver needs and interests. In our discussion of channel manipulation, we rely heavily on identifying characteristics of the receiver to design effective approaches.

As we turn to an examination of the media channels through which messages are disseminated, the receiver continues to play a key role. From the business communicator's viewpoint, the worth of the media lies almost entirely in the kinds of audiences they can deliver. Either they provide the kinds of receivers we are interested in reaching, or they do not. If they fail to supply desired audiences, we should not consider them. If they do offer desired audiences, several additional considerations must enter the decision process.

First, do they reach the entire intended audience or only a portion of it? If they reach only a portion, in what medium do we capture the missing segment? Do they reach not only our intended audience, but also large numbers of receivers of no concern to us? In this case we must decide if the additional audience members impose added cost. If we should decide the audience composition is acceptable, we must then ask if that medium provides the physical characteristics to distribute the message. For instance, if we need to show a picture or diagram, we must consider print or television. If we need to provide statistics and details, we may be restricted to print. If we wish a good deal of repetition, then radio should be examined. These and a variety of other considerations about physical properties come into play when we decide which medium or combination of media should be selected in a public communication campaign.

The Media Effect the Message

Remember that the media are not like those hollow pneumatic tubes that carry checks back and forth at a bank drive-up window. The media have characteristics of their own that are imparted to the message. They effect the message and alter the way audiences receive it. The media engender or reinforce certain perceptions of legitimacy and truth in a message. They contribute directly to the perceived importance of a message, thus elevating among audience members the salience of a topic.

Legitimacy and Truth

"I know it's true; I read it in the newspaper." "I saw it on the evening news; it must be so." Through years of exposure, people have grown to recognize that mass media in this country routinely present accurate and dependable information. Owing largely to such consistency, they expect the truth, and they trust information carried by the media. Commercial advertisers exploit this notion of truth. One late-night television advertiser, after making some remarkable claims about a product, proclaimed that "what I have told you must be true; they wouldn't let me lie on television."

We are not suggesting that audiences naively accept any line tossed out by the mass media. We are proposing, however, that the effect of honest, accurate, and well-documented information is augmented by its presentation in the media. Some researchers speculate that audiences perceive that the media have a purging effect.

They believe that a source might mislead one person but would not risk discovery of a flawed message presented to large public groups. In light of our previous example, others hypothesize that messages are accepted as true because audiences assume federal and state laws prohibit inaccurate advertising.

Whatever the explanation, there is good reason to believe that the truth and legitimacy elements exist and can work in favour of the communicator, particularly in the presentation of new and relatively unfamiliar subjects. When audiences have no prior information about a subject, a communicator can expect to enjoy some legitimacy by virtue of the media vehicle alone.

Salience

In addition to the legitimacy and truth factors, each of the media contributes, in varying degrees, to the salience (perceived relative prominence or importance) of a subject. People accept that of all world events, the mass media report only those most noteworthy.

Newspapers discuss the important events in a city council meeting, not the routine matters. They provide playby-play coverage for the most important sports teams in a league or local area. Evening network news programmes report only stories of the greatest national importance.

With years of media experience, people expect the media to sort among the universe of information, to identify and disseminate only the most significant messages. Children learn this early when they see the name of someone they know in print for the first time—that person must be important to be mentioned in the paper. Part of the acculturation process in this society includes an awareness that the mass media recognize the importance of certain people or issues. Our discussion of agenda setting examined the dynamics of this process.

Even media practitioners operate on this principle in seeking and identifying stories for their own news operations. Interviews beget interviews.

Could an item discussed on the six o'clock news go unnoticed by a city editor who may have missed it for the newspaper or initially chose not to cover it? News directors and editors are voracious consumers of competing media to see which stories their competition thought important.

A noteworthy review of the impact of media on this society came from the seminal work by Paul Lazarsfeld and Robert Merton. These Columbia University sociologists recognized the media convey information not only in the words and pictures they carry, but in a more subtle way simply by carrying information about a topic at all.

The mass media bestow prestige and enhance the authority of individuals and groups by legitimizing their status. Recognition by the press or radio or television testifies that one has arrived, that one is important enough to have been singled out from the large and anonymous masses, that one's behaviour and opinions are significant enough to require public notice.

Message salience is not confined to news items. Well-developed commercial and educational messages enjoy the same benefit. One study conducted in Michigan sought to measure the effects of a coordinated media campaign on public perceptions of a complex set of international trade issues. As expected, pretesting revealed that local audiences were initially unfamiliar with the topic, and among those who had some familiarity, most thought the international trade issue was unimportant. For six weeks following the pretest this research provided for a carefully programmed use of major media (radio, television, and newspapers) that reached more than 1 million people.

This campaign disseminated general mass media information along with targeted messages to specific population subgroups. Messages employed the same formats that might be used by any business communicator (thirty-second radio and television spots, partial-page newspaper ads) and did not involve more lengthy promotional techniques (talk shows, features, special news stories, etc.). Essentially, researchers designed the campaign to increase the public's knowledge about international trade features and policies and to elevate public perceptions of trade importance (salience).Postexposure studies confirmed the success of the communication campaign: First, when compared either with pretest results or with findings from a control group, scores on items measuring public understanding of international trade issues increased significantly. Of particular relevance here, the data indicated a marked increase in reviewers' perceptions of trade as an important national issue.

The media campaign increased salience of the topic and elevated it on the public agenda. When asked specifically in the posttest why international trade was important to the United States, many respondents suggested it was chiefly because of the media attention. They simply assumed it must be important or it would not have been discussed in the media.Various features of this research apply to business communication practices:

- Although the topic—international trade—did not concern a specific product or service, it did provide an acid test. It measured the media's capacity to relay information and increase the perceived importance of a not inherently interesting issue.

- With proper use of targeting techniques and by using the media alone, even an obscure, dull, and complex issue can be promoted on the public's agenda.
- If such an issue can be packaged for a general audience, then the media can accommodate similarly almost any concern. Any topic, no matter how esoteric or complex, can fit into the targeted, audience-based approach to public communication.

This study is important for our purposes because it relied on the same media tools available to the business communicator: spot radio and television messages and periodic newspaper ads. Based on pretest studies, it targeted various subgroups with specially designed messages sent through popular media. Researchers knew the individual concerns of these target audiences and knew the medium through which it could best reach them.

The media are all important in executing the strategy of targeted communication. Some media blanket the entire population; others deliver specific audiences for special treatment. For efficiency and effectiveness, communication strategies should focus on narrower groups through carefully selected media.

MASS MEDIA AND SOCIAL PROBLEMS

Mass media content, including news coverage, entertainment programming, and advertising, carries an abundance of information about social problems. Media are considered to be a primary source of the public's information about social problems and thus are influential in the public's perception and definition of social problems and the formation of attitudes about them. Agenda-setting studies have found correlations between news coverage of social problems and those regarded as critical issues by the public. In addition, third-person-effect studies have shown that people rely on media coverage, rather than their own experience, to assess the gravity of social problems.

Beginning with Lazarsfeld and Merton's predictions of a mass mediainduced "narcotizing dysfunction," a number of media observers have speculated that pervasive media coverage of social problems may lead to desensitization. Notes Downs, "the piteous sight of an oil-soaked seagull or a dead soldier pales after it has been viewed even a dozen times."

Issue lifecycle studies, while focusing on the rise and fall of public interest in an issue rather than on fluctuations in emotional responses towards victims, provide support for the idea that there is a limit to the effectiveness of message repetition about social problems.

Public attention eventually reaches a threshhold point, beyond which increases in communication about the issue fail to elicit increased interest in the issue. This decline in interest is attributed to message saturation, the flooding of multiple communication channels with redundant messages.

While most issue lifecycle theorists recognize the competition between issues for public attention, Hilgartner and Bosk suggest that social problems also compete for the "surplus compassion" they can muster for causes beyond people's immediate concerns, although they do not empirically investigate levels of compassion in the issue lifecycle. The saturation phenomenon found in these studies raises the issue of marginality, an economic model which suggests a threshhold point beyond which additional messages would have no effect. By contrast, the concept of compassion fatigue posed by the present study suggests a threshhold point at which saturation has negative, rather than neutral, effects.

Thus, when messages about a social problem reach the point of saturation, rather than simply having no impact on an audience, they may have a negative impact on the audience, which might be measured in subjects' affective, attitudinal, and behavioural responses to the issue.

The literature points to a parallel phenomenon associated with repetitive messages in advertising. Ray et al. suggest that an ad which initially arouses positive affect may actually create negative affect after many repeated viewings. Atkin notes that there is also a clutter of "similar-looking PSA's [which] may be creating a 'PSA glaze' wearout problem."

Characteristics of the mass media which would be expected to contribute to compassion fatigue include its ubiquity in everyday life and journalistic news values which influence portrayals of social problems.

PERVASIVENESS

Pervasiveness is considered tobe a defining characteristic of the American mass media and one of the reasons for its power.

The media's ubiquity is magnified by a proliferation of media channels and the "sameness" of content between media channels, particularly in news content. Maloney and Schonfeld describe a media "bandwagon effect" in which media follow each other's leads for programme content "to the point that it becomes impossible to turn on the news or open a paper without reading another account of the same bad news."

This pervasiveness may lead to a normalization of social problems, described in a newspaper editorial about violent crime: "Such events have come to seem normal to us, just another part of living in America" and are no longer able to shock.

NEWS VALUES AND PRACTICES

Communication research suggests that contemporary news values and practices have relevance for compassion fatigue. Four factors, in particular, emerge from the literature: an emphasis on the sensational, a preponderance of "bad news," failure to provide context for social problems, and the presentation of problems but not solutions.

The desire to attract media consumers has fueled a preference for conflict, violence, and crises over chronic - but perhaps more profound problems, and for social problems which are visually dramatic and consequential for a large number of people. Thus, the media tend to sensationalize social problems as crises of large and overwhelming proportions.

At the same time, opinion polls have consistently shown a public perception that there is too much bad news. People report more concern with the volume of bad news, rather than the bad news itself, which was found to simultaneously attract and repel.

The bad news syndrome is exacerbated by the tendency of the media to present problems but not their solutions, contributing to feelings of inefficacy among media consumers. News reports often fail to provide "mobilizing information" - suggestions for action and details such as phone numbers or addresses which are necessary for action, In addition, antiinstitutional themes - what Robinson terms "journalistic Naderism" - often present established institutions as inept or incapable of solving social problems.

The result of this failure to provide solutions is that the media overwhelm people by showing "an unending procession of events to which they are expected to react, but which they cannot themselves affect." Feelings of inefficacy may constrain information seeking and interpersonal communications. Americans' feelings of inefficacy were blamed by aid organizations for poor public giving in the aftermath of the 1994 Rwandan massacres.

Finally, the media often fail to provide context or in-depth coverage of social problems, presenting social problems through the coverage of events and not necessarily their meanings. The fact that most news media have no social issue beats and that social issues may not fit into conventional press beats often means that news content about social problems reflects preparation by journalists with a superficial knowledge of the problem.

Thus, the communication literature points to a number of potential antecedent variables which explain how the mass media might foster desensitization to social problems. There is a paucity of research, however, to explicate the relationship between mass media and affective responses to social problems.

The study reported here investigates the existence of a compassion fatigue phenomenon and its relationship to mass media. For the issues of AIDS, homelessness, violent crime, and child abuse, three key research questions are explored:

- RQ1: Does a mass-mediated compassion fatigue exist?
- RQ2: If it exists, what variables are predictors of compassion fatigue?
- RQ3: If it exists, what are its manifestations?

Issue Selection. Issues considered for inclusion in the study were those that (1) met the criteria for definition as social problems, and (2) had high top-of-mind awareness among a general population. First, preliminary research was conducted with two groups of undergraduate students (n=50), who were asked the open-ended question, "What would you say are the current issues of the day?" and a number of follow-up questions.

This technique elicited seventeen distinct issues which could be considered social problems. Next, these issues were compared to issues identified by Gallup Poll data which asked American's to name the "nation's most important problem." Six items which emerged from the pretests and the Gallup poll were intially considered, including the war in Bosnia and the environment, as well as AIDS, homelessness, child abuse, and violent crime.

Several iterations of survey instruments, incorporating from one to six issues, were developed and pre-tested via telephone, including one in which issues were self-generated by respondents and another which included a control issue with no readily identifiable group of victims to serve as objects of compassion.

These pretests indicated that four issues were optimal: more than four issues became too long for respondents; less than four did not allow for sufficient comparison between issues. The self-generated issues version was found to be unwieldy to administer. The issue of Bosnia was eliminated because it stood out as the only non-domestic issue.

The environment was eliminated because it was overly broad and the only issue in which the most obvious "victim" was not a human being. The final version of the survey, focusing on the four issues of AIDS, homelessness, violent crime, and child abuse, was selected as most feasible because it allowed for comparison of compassion levels between several highly recgonizable social problems, while keeping the time required for interviewing to approximately fifteen minutes.

The literature review and preliminary research with subjects suggested a number of variables that are likely to be associated with compassion fatigue. Survey items assessed each of these variables for each of the four issues studied. These variables included: interest in the issue, emotional arousal towards the issue, information seeking (or avoidance) of the issue, interpersonal communication about the problem, emotional and physical reactions to media reports about the problem, efficacy feelings associated with the problem, attitudes associated with the problem, and media consumption patterns.

The survey consisted of thirty-five five-point Likerttype scales and a series of six open-ended questions related to key manifestations of compassion fatigue. Scaled items included ten questions employing the customary "strongly agree" to "strongly disagree" format, as well as thirteen questions employing response alternatives based on other variables which were scaled on a 1 to 5 continuum, such as "hopeful" to "hopeless," "definitely would watch" to "definitely would not watch" and so on.

Two different versions of the survey, varying the ordering of questions, were used to avoid an order bias. Interview times ranged from eleven to twenty-two minutes, averaging approximately fifteen minutes. Quantitative data analysis procedures employing SPSS(x) were used to assess the research questions.

To determine the extent to which a general population may experience compassion fatigue, a telephone survey of randomly-selected residents of greater-metropolitan Atlanta, encompassing urban, suburban, and semirural locales, was conducted. A random digit generating software programme was used to ensure random selection of telephone numbers. Seven call attempts were made to each number at various times of the day and week. A message requesting participation in the survey was left on answering machines. Call attempts to 550 eligible, residential numbers resulted in 316 completed interviews, for a response rate of 57.4 per cent.

Does Compassion Fatigue Exist? Based on the survey item43 which most directly assessed self-reports of emotional arousal, a substantial proportion of respondents reported feelings of burnout for each of the issues studied. Forty per cent of respondents rated themselves as either burned out or approaching burnout (a response of 1 or 2 on a scale of 1 to 5) on the issue of violent crime.

Thirtyfive per cent reported feeling burned out on AIDS, and 33 per cent on homelessness. Even for the issue of child abuse, which consistently elicited the most compassionate responses, nearly 15 per cent of respondents said they were burned out or approaching burnout.

A reliability check of this survey item with two other items assessing emotional sensitivity yielded Cronbach's alpha scores ranging from.56 for the crime issue to.78 for the homeless issue, indicating that this is a satisfactory measure of emotional arousal. Responses to the open-ended questions (reported below under "manifestations") provide further evidence to support the existence of a compassion fatigue phenomenon, reflecting affective and behavioural responses consistent with desensitization and hyper-sensitization.

Who Is Burned Out? A comparison of means for this item indicates a pattern in which whites, males, and college graduates express greater fatigue with the social problems studied than others. For all four issues, white respondents reported more intense feelings of burnout than black respondents, with t-tests showing the difference to be significant for every issue.

Males reported significantly more intense feelings of burnout than females for the issues of child abuse, homelessness, and AIDS. College graduates reported significantly higher levels of burnout than those with a high school diploma or less for all issues but homelessness. Respondents with household incomes of $50,000 or more reported feeling the greatest burnout for every issue, although income was significant at a=.05 only for the issue of violent crime.

Age was not a significant factor in burnout differences. Media consumption was a significant variable in burnout only for the issue of violent crime. Here, heavy media users (24.7 per cent of respondents) those who reported watching television news five or more times in the past week and reading the newspaper five or more times in the past week - were found to report less burnout than light media users, who watched TV news and read the newspaper less than twice a week (7 per cent of respondents).

No significant differences in levels of burnout were found between those who were highly TV-dependent and those who were highly print-dependent.

THE ORIGINS OF A SYMBIOTIC RELATIONSHIP

The history of communication for development can begin at any point in history, for human beings have, throughout their existence, always communicated, and their cumulative communication activities must have contributed to the process of development. This is true whether or not the historical changes occurred before the term "development" was coined. For purposes of this paper, however, a time limit of the last four decades is considered sufficient. For some, conventional history began after the Second World War (Hornik, 1988), with an extraordinary political change, namely the movement to independence of more than half the world's nations, most of them in the Southern Hemisphere and most of them poor by all the criteria held dear by all nations of the North-small per capital incomes, poor and overstretched health systems, non-existent industrial plants (the assumed engine of modernisation) and populace devoid of "modern" skills. Hornik goes on to state that these countries' underdevelopment was also distinguishable because their social organisations, intellectual dynamism, and psychological openness were all obstacles to their attainment of the stage of development occupied by modern Western nations.

The single most prevalent explanation of the underdevelopment of these countries was that certain deficits existed among the peoples of these countries. Specifically, these countries were said to lack what Schramm termed the "basic dynamic" of economic development-the propensity to save and invest enough in their industrial plant to fuel a take-off to rapid growth.

Since these deficits-illiteracy, lack of skills, and modern attitudes-lay with individuals, they demanded development solutions that stressed more formal education, more training for adults and more information diffusion. The theory went that: Education might, provide Intellectual skills; it might teach new health and agricultural practices and encourage political mobilisation. However, implementing education in poor countries proved difficult. Conventional Western educational strategies for doing these tasks through face to face instruction foundered on the thin supply of teachers and trained field agents and inadequate budgets to support theirwork".

It is the encounter with these problems that led to the utilisation of the mass media which presented a huge potential for reaching huge audiences to whom desired knowledge and skills could be imparted, and hence through whom desired change could be achieved. Communication activity planners needed to transmit their ideas to extension agents who would in turn take them to farmers. Inherent in these linkages between development and communication is an assumed potency and ubiquitousness of the mass media, an assumption that has preoccupied communication researchers for nearly five decades now.

DIFFERENCES

Having described the historical and contextual origin of the ideology of development communication, an attempt is made here to explain what is meant by development communication as opposed to non-development communication, development support communication, and development journalism, all of which differ markedly in their definitions and applications. In offering definitions of these terms, it is appropriate to first define what is meant by the words 'communication', and 'development' and 'journalism' which are the generic concepts from which these terms are derived.

Communication has been defined as "the transfer of ideas of knowledge in ways that enable the recipient to understand, react to, and act upon the information received," (Oliveira, 1993). Mercado (1992) has similarly defined communication as "a process of sharing messages between a source and a receiver either directly or through a channel." Effective communication is predicated on four elements: a source who initiates the process; a message which contains information that the source is transmitting; a channel or medium which enables the transmission of the message; and a receiver who acknowledges receipt of the message.

Development on its part, has serious definitional problems. It has been defined as a conceptual framework for a number of individual, institutional, national and international changes (Mowlana and Wilson, 1990). Another definition holds that development is conceived as "six lanes of large motor cars streaming powerfully into and out of gleaming cities; neon lights flashing and juke boxes sounding, and skyscrappers rising, storey upon storey into the sky" (Haque, 199). Other scholars have even questioned whether the term development should continue to be used instead of others such as "progress", "transformation", '"beneficial change", "liberation" or even "revolution".

For our purpose, Mercado's definition of development as "a process of providing disadvantaged people the opportunities to realise and improve their knowledge, attitude, and skill to utilise, sustain, and improve their productivity of available resources within their environment in order to improve the quality of their life and the society where they belong," (Mercado, 1992) shall be adopted. Implied in this definition, is the fact that development is a type of "social change" intended to bring about both social and material advancement, including the area of human rights.

Journalism refers to the practice of gathering, packaging and disseminating news to a homogeneous audience. This term covers the work of all practitioners in mass communication in general, and the work of newspapermen, television and radio producers, continuity announcers, newscasters, cameramen and sound technicians. Having defined the generic concepts from which development support communication, development communication and non-development communication are derived, the following are definitions of these terms.

DEVELOPMENT COMMUNICATION

Development communication came to Africa as part of the policy guidance favoured for experimentation in the developing world by the West in the 1960s, barely ten years after its advent as part of the development lexicon in the early 1950s. In the manner in which it was used by its founders, Lerner, Pye and Schramm, development communication referred to technology-based communication networks which, regardless of message and content, tended to create, a suitable climate for development. It was supposed to "generate the psychic ambience within which economic and productive activity occurred". In this context, the role of development communication was conceived as being a facilitative one; the means to an end called "development." But the ideology later came to be seen as "the systematic utilisation of appropriate communication channels and techniques to increase people's participation in development and to inform, motivate and train rural populations, mainly at the grassroots levels." More recently, development communication has been redefined as the planned and systematic use of communication, through interpersonal and mass channels.

An elabouration has been made on this definition by Mercado (1992) who states that development communication is a subsystem of the larger system of communication, which deals with the planned use of communication resources to gain multisectoral support in attaining national development goals. It is distinguished by the fact that it is purposive and has clear, welldefined objectives such as to change people's attitudes, skills, or behaviour.

Its sources of information are usually people involved in national development efforts such as farmers, researchers, health and population professionals, development planners, and policy makers. The nature of its message is such that it is aimed at aiding the attainment of specific objectives, for instance, increasing food production, family planning, adult literacy, and other aspects of development. The message is normally presented following an interpretative style, and it is passed on to the audience through not only mass media channels, but oramedia, folkmedia, theatre, below-theline-communication, extension workers, teachers, and even door to door campaigns. Messages are directed to specific target audiences, in whom development communication practitioners want to achieve knowledge, understanding, changes in attitude, as well as knowledge and practice of new skills and practice.

Critics blame it for its emphasis on top-down, government-topeople communication, and argue that it has lost credibility over the years. Hence Okigbo (1985) queried if "development communication is dead".

NON-DEVELOPMENT COMMUNICATION

Non-development communication, can only be defined in relation to development communication, and in terms of what it does and does not do. Perhaps no other scholar has explained the two concepts better than Mercado. According to him, non-development communication can be differentiated from development communication by its nature, its sources of information, its message, the channel it uses, its audience and its intended effects (Mercado, 1992). With regard to its nature, non-development communication is non-purposive. It neither has any clearly defined objectives to accomplish in the audience nor is it planned. Rather, it is publicity-oriented. It has varied sources of information who are not directly involved in national development, including functionaries like policemen, soldiers, etc. Its message is heavy on entertainment and sensational news such as crimes, war, and crises. This message is presented objectively as fact, and is based on what the audience wants.

Non-development communication limits itself to the use of the mass media as the key channels of communication. A heterogeneous general public forms its audience, in whom non-development communication hopes to instil awareness. However, non-development communication has been influenced by development communication giving rise to such concepts as "development journalism", media "crusades" and "campaigns," all of which borrow their techniques from development communication.

DEVELOPMENT JOURNALISM

This term designates the journalistic activity of gathering news with a view to satisfying the needs of a country's population. The news thus relates to development, and is invariably positive in its disclosure. There are scholars like Aggarwala (1981) who tend to confuse the issue by saying that development news, the by-product of development journalism, is "not, and should not be, any different from regular news or investigative reporting." With this kind of education, one wonders why the term exists in the first place, and why it should crop up if its sole purpose is to be a synonym of everyday journalism.

The fact of the matter, however, is that development journalism does in fact exist separately from what is generally referred to as journalism. Sussman (1978) for instance sees it, albeit in a restricting sense, as the coverage of scientific and economic news and relating them to the development needs of the country.

Rampal (1984) offers a much more expansive and inclusive definition by asserting that development journalism includes activities like the use of the media in formal and non-formal educational purposes. Nearer home in Africa, development journalism tends to be seen as the aggregate responsibilities added onto the usual business of journalism when it comes to be practised in a developmental setting.

In the words of Africa's foremost voice on this issue, "In Africa, the mass media fulfil an educational role which they are not necessarily called upon to assume in the advanced countries. News about development is important in stimulating further development" (Ansah, 1990). A new dimension is brought into this whole issue of what development journalism means when Ansah emphasises the value of development news as being in its demonstrative effect: Development news is new schools, hospitals, bridges, roads, etc., especially if these achievements were made possible through collective, self-reliant local effort. More importantly, such reports should illustrate how the projects were accomplished, so that they can provide inspiration to other people (Ansah, 1990).

Some people argue that in the light of the young age of African nations which makes them prone to instability, positive news should be stressed and negative news, meaning news that might undermine national unity, should be downplayed or not reported at all. This argument has always rested on shaky ground, mainly because it assumes gullibility on the part of Africans, but it did at least retain a certain appeal during the one-party systems in Africa. However, with the adoption of political and economic liberalisation on the continent in the recent past, which has resulted in greater media pluralism and freedom, such prescriptions are no longer practical, their merit or otherwise notwithstanding. What these changes have brought with them in the media would appear to be more adversarial journalism as African journalists copy Western journalistic conventions. In the wake of this new style of journalism, development journalism has been the first casualty of these changes.

8

Information Society and Economics Development

As a designated field of enquiry, economic sociology is not much more than a century old, even though its intellectual roots are identifiable in older traditions of philosophical and social thought. During the past quarter-century it has experienced an explosive growth, and now stands as one of the most conspicuous and vital subfields of its parent discipline. In this introduction we first define the field and distinguish it from mainstream economics. Next we trace the classical tradition of economic sociology, as found in the works of Marx, Weber, Durkheim, Schumpeter, Polanyi, and Parsons- Smelser. Finally, we cite some more recent developments and topics of concern in economic sociology. Throughout our discussion in this stage we emphasize the importance of paying attention to economic interests and social relations.

THE DEFINITION OF ECONOMIC SOCIOLOGY

Economic sociology—to use a term that Weber and Durkheim introduced—can be defined simply as the sociological perspective applied to economic phenomena. A similar but more elaborate version is the application of the frames of reference, variables, and explanatory models of sociology to that complex of activities which is concerned with the production, distribution, exchange, and consumption of scarce goods and services. One way to make this definition more specific is to indicate the variables, models, and so on, that the economic sociologist employs. When Smelser first put forth that definition, he mentioned the sociological perspectives of personal interaction, groups, social structures, and social controls. Given recent developments, we would add that perspectives of social networks, gender, and cultural contexts have also become central in economic sociology. In addition, the international dimension of economic life has assumed greater salience among economic sociologists, at the same time as that dimension has come to penetrate the actual economies of the contemporary world.

MAINSTREAM ECONOMICS AND ECONOMIC SOCIOLOGY COMPARED

We now compare economic sociology and mainstream economics as a way of further elucidating the sociological perspective on the economy. This is a useful exercise only if qualified by the caution that both bodies of enquiry are much more complex than any brief comparison would suggest. Any general statement almost immediately yields an exception or qualification.

To illustrate the caution on each side of the comparison:

- In economics the classical and neo-classical traditions have enjoyed a certain dominance— hence the label mainstream—but the basic assumptions of those traditions have been modified and developed in many directions. In a classic statement, Knight stressed that neo-classical economics rested on the premises that actors have complete information and that information is free. Since that time economics has developed traditions of analysis based on assumptions of risk and uncertainty and information as a cost. In addition, numerous versions of economic rationality—for example, Simon's emphasis on "satisficing" and "bounded rationality"— have appeared. Still other variations on rational behaviour have been developed in behavioural economics, which incorporates many psychological assumptions at variance with the mainstream. Looking in the direction of sociology, some economics now incorporates "norms" and "institutions," though with meanings different from those found in the sociological tradition.
- Sociology lacks one dominant tradition. Various sociological approaches and schools differ from and compete with one another, and this circumstance has affected economic sociology. For example, Weber was skeptical about the notion of a social "system," whether applied to economy or society, while Parsons viewed society as a system and economy as one of its subsystems. Furthermore, even if all economic sociologists might accept the definition of economic sociology we have offered, they focus on different kinds of economic behaviour. Some do so following Arrow's hint that sociologists and economists ask different questions—about consumption, for example. Others, including what is called new economic sociology, argue that sociology should concentrate directly on core economic institutions and problems.

These caveats recorded, a comparison between the central features of mainstream economics and economic sociology will clarify the specific nature of the sociological perspective. The following differences are most salient.

THE CONCEPT OF THE ACTOR

To put the matter baldly, the analytic starting point of economics is the individual; the analytic starting points of economic sociology are typically groups, institutions, and society. In microeconomics, the individualistic approach finds its origins in early British utilitarianism and political economy. This orientation was elucidated systematically by the Austrian economist Carl Menger and given the label methodological individualism by Schumpeter. By contrast, in discussing the individual, the sociologist often focuses on the actor as a socially constructed entity, as "actor-in-interaction," or "actor-in-society." Often, moreover, sociologists take the group and the social-structural levels as phenomena sui generis, without reference to the individual actor. Methodological individualism need not be logically incompatible with a sociological approach. In his theoretical stage introductory to Economy and Society, Weber constructed his whole sociology on the basis of individual actions. But these actions are of interest to the sociologist only insofar as they are social actions or "take account of the behaviour of other individuals and thereby are oriented in their course".

This formulation underscores a second difference between microeconomics and economic sociology: the former generally assumes that actors are not connected to one another; the latter assumes that actors are linked with and influence one another. We argue that this difference has implications for how economies function.

THE CONCEPT OF ECONOMIC ACTION

In micoeconomics the actor is assumed to have a given and stable set of preferences and to choose that alternative line of action which maximizes utility. In economic theory, this way of acting constitutes economically rational action. Sociology, by contrast, encompasses several possible types of economic action. To illustrate from Weber again, economic action can be either rational, traditional, or affectual. Except for residual mention of "habits" and "rules of thumb," economists give no place to traditional economic action.

Another difference between microeconomics and economic sociology in this context concerns the scope of rational action. The economist traditionally identifies rational action with the efficient use of scarce resources. The sociologist's view is, once again, broader. Weber referred to the conventional maximization of utility, under conditions of scarcity, as formal rationality. In addition, however, he identified substantive rationality, which refers to allocation within the guidelines of other principles, such as communal loyalties or sacred values. A further difference lies in the fact that economists regard rationality as an assumption, whereas most sociologists regard it as a variable. For one thing, the actions of some individuals or groups may be more rational than others. Along the same lines, sociologists tend to regard rationality as a phenomenon to be explained, not assumed. Weber dedicated much of his economic sociology to specifying the social conditions under which formal rationality is possible, and Parsons argued that economic rationality was a system of norms—not a psychological universal— associated with specific developmental processes in the West. Another difference emerges in the status of meaning in economic action. Economists tend to regard the meaning of economic action as derivable from the relation between given tastes, on the one hand, and the prices and quantities of goods and services, on the other.

Weber's conceptualization has a different flavour: "the definition of economic action [in sociology] must... bring out the fact that all 'economic' processes and objects are characterized as such entirely by the meaning they have for human action". Meanings are historically constructed and must be investigated empirically, and are not simply to be derived from assumptions and external circumstances. Finally, sociologists tend to give a broader and more salient place to the dimension of power in economic action. Weber insisted that "[it] is essential to include the criterion of power of control and disposal in the sociological concept of economic action," adding that this applies especially in the capitalist economy.

By contrast, microeconomics has tended to regard economic action as an exchange among equals, and has thus had difficulty in incorporating the power dimension. In the tradition of perfect competition, no buyer or seller has the power to influence price or output. It is also true that economists have a tradition of analyzing imperfect competition—in which power to control prices and output is the core ingredient— and that the idea of "market power" is used in labour and industrial economics. Still, the economic conception of power is typically narrower than the sociologist's notion of economic power, which includes its exercise in societal, as well as market, contexts. In a study of the power of the U.S. banking system, for example, Mintz and Schwartz analyze how banks and industries interlock, how certain banks cluster into groups, and how banks sometimes intervene in corporations in order to enforce economic decisions. More generally, sociologists have analyzed and debated the issue of the political implications of wealth inequality and the extent to which corporate leaders constitute a "power elite" in the whole of society.

CONSTRAINTS ON ECONOMIC ACTION

In mainstream economics, actions are constrained by tastes and by the scarcity of resources, including technology. Once these are known, it is in principle possible to predict the actor's behaviour, since he or she will always try to maximize utility or profit. The active influence of other persons and groups, as well as the influence of institutional structures, is set to one side. Knight codified this in the following way: "Every member of society is to act as an individual only, in entire independence of all other persons". Sociologists take such influences directly into account in the analysis of economic action.

Other actors facilitate, deflect, and constrain individuals' action in the market. For example, a friendship between a buyer and a seller may prevent the buyer from deserting the seller just because an item is sold at a lower price elsewhere. Cultural meanings also affect choices that might otherwise be regarded as "rational." In the United States, for example, it is difficult to persuade people to buy cats and dogs for food, even though their meat is as nutritious and cheaper than other kinds.

Moreover, a person's position in the social structure conditions his or her economic choices and activity. Stinchcombe evoked the principle that structural constraints influence career decisions in ways that run counter to considerations of economic payoff. For example, for a person who grows up in a high-crime neighbourhood, the choice between making a career stealing and getting a job has often less to do with the comparative utility of these two alternatives than with the structure of peer groups and gangs in the neighbourhood.

THE ECONOMY IN RELATION TO SOCIETY

The main foci for the mainstream economist are economic exchange, the market, and the economy. To a large extent, the remainder of society lies beyond where the operative variables of economic change really matter. Economic assumptions typically presuppose stable societal parameters. For example, the long-standing assumption that economic analysis deals with peaceful and lawful transactions, not with force and fraud, involves important presuppositions about the legitimacy and the stability of the state and the legal system. In this way the societal parameters—which would surely affect the economic process if the political legal system were to disintegrate—are frozen by assumption, and thus are omitted from the analysis.

In recent times economists have turned to the analysis of why institutions arise and persist, especially in the new institutional economics and game theory. They have varied the effects of institutional arrangements in various logical experiments. Nevertheless, the contrast with economic sociology remains. When economists talk about institutions, norms, and the like, their vocabulary is identical to that of sociologists, but they often mean something quite different. It is still very common, for example, for economists to treat the economic arena as lacking norms and institutions. The latter only emerge when markets cannot be constructed or when traditional rational choice analysis fails. Economic sociology, on the other hand, has always regarded the economic process as an organic part of society.

As a consequence, economic sociology has usually concentrated on three main lines of enquiry:

- The sociological analysis of economic process;
- The analysis of the connections and interactions between the economy and the rest of society; and
- The study of changes in the institutional and cultural parameters that constitute the economy's societal context.

GOALS OF ANALYSIS

As social scientists, both economists and sociologists try to explain phenomena encompassed by their respective subject matters. Within this common interest, however, different emphases emerge. Economists tend to be critical of descriptions— they condemn traditional institutional economics as too descriptive and atheoretical. Instead they stress the importance of prediction. Sociologists, by contrast, offer fewer formal predictions, and often find sensitive and telling descriptions both interesting in themselves and essential for explanation.

As a result of these differences, sociologists often criticize economists for generating formal and abstract models and ignoring empirical data, and economists reproach sociologists for their "post factum sociological interpretations". Though these differences have become part of the professional cultures of economists and sociologists, it should be noted that the last 10 years have seen a new interest for model building and game theory among sociologists, and a new interest in culture and use of empirical material among economists. It is also possible that the fields of economics and economic sociology may one day agree on some methodological compromise, say along the lines of "analytic narratives".

MODELS EMPLOYED

The emphasis on prediction constitutes one reason why mainstream economists place such high value on expressing hypotheses and models in mathematical form. Though the advantages of this formal theorizing are readily apparent, economists themselves have at times complained that it tends to become an end in itself. In his presidential address to the American Economic Association in 1970, Wassily Leontief criticized his profession's "uncritical enthusiasm for mathematical formulation".

When economists do turn to empirical data, they tend to rely mainly on those generated for them by economic processes themselves. Sample surveys are occasionally used, especially in consumer economics and in labour economics; archival data are seldom consulted, except by economic historians; and ethnographic work is virtually non-existent. By contrast, sociologists rely heavily on a great variety of methods, including analyses of census data, independent survey analyses, participant observation and fieldwork, and the analysis of qualitative historical and comparative data.

INTELLECTUAL TRADITIONS

Sociologists not only rely on different intellectual traditions that overlap only slightly, but they also regard those traditions differently. Evidently influenced by the natural science model of systematic accumulation of knowledge, economists have shown less interest than sociologists in study and exegesis of their classics. Correspondingly, economics reveals a sharp distinction between current economic theory and the history of economic thought.

In sociology these two facets blend more closely. The classics are very much alive, and are often required reading in theory courses. Despite these differences, and despite the persisting gulf between the traditions of economics and economic sociology, some evidence of synthesis can be identified. Major figures such as Alfred Marshall, Vilfredo Pareto, and Talcott Parsons have attempted theoretical syntheses.

Certain other figures, notably Weber and Schumpeter, have excited interest among both economists and sociologists. In addition, economists and sociologists find it profitable to collaborate in specific problem areas such as poverty and labour markets. Later in the stage as suggested, reraise the issue of intellectual articulation among economists and sociologists.

THE ECONOMIC SOCIOLOGY OF CAPITALISM

Capitalism is the dominant economic system in today's world, and there appears to be no alternatives in sight. Socialism, its main competitor, has been weakened immeasurably by the collapse of the Soviet Union in the early 1990s. Where socialism still prevails, such as in the People's Republic of China, serious attempts are made to turn the whole economic system in a capitalist direction so that it will operate in a more efficient manner.

"It doesn't matter if the cat is white or black as long as it catches mice", to cite Deng Xiaping. While the superiority of capitalism as an economic system and growth machine has fascinated economists for centuries, this has not been the case with sociologists. For sociologists capitalism has mainly been of interest for its *social* effects – how it has led to class struggle, anomie, inequality and social problems in general. Capitalism as an economic system in its own right has been of much less interest. Some of this reaction has probably to do with the unfortunate division of labour that developed between economists and sociologists in the 19th century: economists studied the economy, and the sociologists society minus the economy.

In this respect, as in so many others, sociology has essentially been a "left-over science". This division of labour between economists and sociologists, however, has not gone unchallenged. In the 1980s sociologists, especially in the United States, turned their attention to the study of the economy itself, asking questions such as the following: Where do markets come from?

How is economic action embedded in social relations? What role do norms and trust play in the economy?. That this set of questions heralded something new soon became clear. A huge amount of research – known as "New Economic Sociology" – soon came into being. By the mid-1990s enough work had been done to put together a handbook in economic sociology, with stages on such topics as "business groups", "a rational choice perspective on economic sociology" and "networks and economic life". This trend has continued very strongly, and as of today economic sociology represents one of the strongholds of American sociology.

In all of these writings by sociologists on the economy, the emphasis has primarily been on middle-range phenomena; and little attempt has been made to analyze capitalism. Why this is the case is difficult to say. One answer might be that capitalism is taken for granted; and this would seem to be especially true for the business schools, where a number of economic sociologists are currently to be found. Another may be that new economic sociologists do not seem to have been very interested in politics – and the concept of capitalism is by tradition often associated with a critique of capitalism.

The contributions to the study of capitalism that one can find in Marxist sociology have, for example, not been much explored by contemporary economic sociologists. If we now turn to the economists, these used to stay away from analyses of capitalism as an economic system and instead focus on the workings of the price system and how this led to an efficient allocation of resources. The word "capitalism" was rarely used by economists during the 20th century till a few decades ago when they suddenly embraced it.

Since this time, however, the economists have made quick strides forward. As a result, the leading academic scholars on the subject of capitalism are no longer sociologists but economists – from Friedrich Hayek and Milton Friedman, who started the trend, to Douglass North, Oliver Williamson and others who have continued it. In this opening stage an effort will be made to present an agenda for a sociological study of capitalism.

There are two reasons why this type of study may be called *an economic sociology of capitalism*. First, the main emphasis is not on the social effects of capitalism, but on capitalism as an economic system in its own right – on the firms, the banks, the markets and the other economic institutions that make up the core of the economy. This is where the "economic" in "economic sociology" comes in. Second, while we already have several economic theories of capitalism, we do not have one which sufficiently takes the social dimension of the capitalist machinery into account - and this is where the "sociology" in economic sociology comes in.

A study of capitalism as an economic system should consist of two parts. First of all, studies of individual, middle-range phenomena need to be made. Indeed, this constitutes by far the most important task of an economic sociology of capitalism and cannot be replaced by macro level studies of capitalism. But while studies of capitalism itself should not predominate, they have their own distinct *raison d'être*. One of these is that this type of studies outline the basic connections between the different parts of the economy – how the whole economic process hangs together.

They also show, related to this, how the study of the various parts of the economy should be interrelated – something which has hitherto been missing in economic sociology, but which is very important for its attempt to develop a more systematic approach. In studying each individual part of the capitalist system it is also important to be clear what drives the system as a whole. Finally, as already Adam Smith was well aware of, there exists an overall logic to capitalism as an economic system, which the individual actors are not aware of. Through the logic of unintended consequences capitalism not only produces individual wealth but also social wealth.

A BASIC MODEL OF CAPITALISM

The reference to Adam Smith leads in a natural way to the next step in this argument, namely to the analytical point of departure for an economic sociology of capitalism. This consists of the proposition that *interests* drive the actions of the individuals, and that interests come together in a very specific way in capitalism.

The actors in society are driven by a variety of interests – political, economic, legal and so on. It is important to insist here on the plurality of interests since this makes the analysis realistic as well as flexible. Interests of the same type, as well as of different types, may reinforce each other, counterbalance each other, block each other, and so on. Interests, very importantly, is what supplies *the force* in the economic system – what makes millions of people get up in the morning and work all day.

Interests also explain why banks, financial markets and similar institutions are so powerful: they can mobilize and energize masses of people into action through their control over economic resources. At this point it should be noted that sociologists have often tended to ignore interests and focus exclusively on social relations and the impact that these may have. This exclusive emphasis on social relations can to some extent be explained as the professional myopia of the sociologist. It is matched, in the economic profession, by a similar overemphasis on the purely economic side of things – on economic interests and their effects, *minus* social relations as well as other types of interests. A hardhitting economic sociology would attempt to draw on the best of sociology and economics, and to *unite* interests and social relations in one and the same analysis.

Our definition of institutions can be used to exemplify this need for drawing on both interests and social relations in the analysis. Institutions are often defined in sociology – especially in the approach that has been developed at Stanford University - in exclusively social terms, that is, as rules, social constructions and so on. Everything, from this perspective, can be an institution, from a handshake and a dance to the state and the firm. The individuals with their interests is abstracted away, to make room for a visions of institutions as pure and empty structures which are imitated, duplicated and so on in a fairly effortless manner. In contrast to this approach, institutions will here be understood to mean durable lock-ins or amalgamations of interests *and* social relations. This view is currently being developed at Cornell University but has still some way to go. According to this perspective, the interests of individuals as well as of corporate actors need to be taken into account. A business firm, for example, does not exist unless you also take the capital of the firm into account; similarly a family does not exist unless you also take the emotional interests of its members plus the sexual interest between the male and female into account. There is not only a time dimension to institutions – they tend to last for some time - but a normative element as well: they tell you *how* interests should be realized in society, be it family interests, political interests, economic interests or some other type of interest.

Institutions are of crucial importance to the functioning of society, and a sign of this is that they are typically regulated in law. A basic model for capitalism will now be presented which draws on a mixture of sociology and economics. Our general point of departure is the conventional definition of economics as consisting of production, distribution and consumption.

To cite a wellknown textbook: "Economics is the study of how men and society end up *choosing*, with or without the use of money, to employ *scarce* productive resources which could have alternative uses, to produce various commodities and distribute them for consumption, now or in the future, among various people and groups in society". This definition describes the economy as a process: all economies start with production, continue with distribution, and end with consumption. Now, all economies can be organized in what amounts to two fundamentally different ways.

Weber expressed this fact with the help of his two categories of "householding" and "profitmaking" —you either produce for consumption or for profit. Marx alluded to the same phenomenon when he spoke of "use value" versus "exchange value". And so did Aristotle, with his famous distinction between "*oekonomia*" and "*chrematistica*". The key to the different ways of organizing the economy is to be found in the way that the economic product is *distributed* in the sense of being passed on in the economic process. As the reader will notice I am here departing from the way that the term distribution is often used in economics - as the division of what has been produced - and instead focus on the different social mechanisms through which what has been produced is being passed on. To show the fruitfulness of this approach, it is convenient to refer to Polanyi's three concepts of *redistribution*, *reciprocity* and *exchange*.

Following Polanyi, it is clear that one way of distributing or passing on what has been produced is through *redistribution*. The agent who does the redistribution is typically the state or some other political authority. The modern socialist state is an example of an economic system that is based on redistribution. Other examples can easily be found, for example, in Antiquity. What has been redistributed is then consumed.

Some part of what has been produced is always set aside for future production; and the size of this part is decided by the political authority. An economy which is primarily based on redistribution is capable of growth – but not of the dynamic type of growth that is characteristic of capitalism. The second way of distributing or passing on what has been produced, according to Polanyi, is through *reciprocity*. This means some equitable form of distribution, as is common in a family or in a kin based economy. Again, some part of what is being produced, is always set aside for future production. But, again, the result of this way of distributing what has been produced, is not going to lead to a dynamic economy. An economy which is based on reciprocity tends towards traditionalism and some form of equity.

Only the third way of distributing or passing on production – through *exchange* – can lead to a truly dynamic economic system, with an evergrowing economy. The reason for this is that this system is not exclusively driven by the eternal human interest in consumption but also by the powerful interest of *profit*. The latter activates people in a very different way from redistribution or reciprocity. And on the assumption that the profit is also reinvested in production, a dynamic economic system – *capitalism* – will come into being. What is unique about capitalism, as compared to economic systems based on redistribution and reciprocity, is that it alone operates on the profit motive. The two most important social mechanisms in capitalism are consequently exchange and the feedback of profit into production.

Complexity is added to the capitalist type of economy by the fact that it also contains several sectors based on reciprocity and redistribution. What can be called *the household economy* is, for example, based on a mixture of redistribution and reciprocity; and so is the sector with non-profit organizations. What can be called *the state economy*, which in modern society accounts for 30-50 per cent of GNP, is on the other hand dominated by redistribution. The rest of this stage is devoted to an attempt to spell out what it would mean for economic sociology to set this model of capitalism at its center. It is clear that this would have important consequences for what will be seen as the central task of economic. *Comment:* The economic process in any society can be defined as consisting of production, distribution and consumption. The distribution or passing on of what has been produced can be organized in fundamentally three ways; and which of these is chosen will have an enormous impact on the productivity of the economy. Following Polanyi, we may call these *redistribution*, *reciprocity*, and *exchange*.

Exchange characterizes the capitalist organization of the economy; and this type of economy derives its dynamic from the fact that the end goal of the economic process is not exclusively consumption, but also *profit.* The more that this profit is reinvested into production, the more dynamic the economy will be. The two key mechanisms in capitalism, in other words, are *organized exchange* and *the feedback loop of profit into production*. It is the use of these two, it should be stressed, that makes the organization of economic interests in the form of capitalism into such an effective machinery for transforming economic reality. Following this model, the modern capitalist economies can be said to consist of several sectors.

There is, first of all, *the corporate sector*, where exchange dominates. There is also *the non-profit sector*, which is based, among other things, on redistribution. The state accounts for a huge part of GNP and what can be called *the state economy* is primarily based on redistribution. *The household economy* is based on a mixture of redistribution and reciprocity. sociology – namely, to produce studies of *production*, *distribution*, *consumption* and *profit-making*. Added to this are the following three topics: the impact on the economic process by *law*, *politics* and *culture*. For all of these topics it is also imperative to investigate how they can *speed up*, *slow down* or *block* economic growth. Still, our model obviously remains highly simplistic and is in its current shape silent on a number of important economic phenomena, from savings to the dynamics of the business cycle. Its focus in this stage is on the macroeconomic level of the economic process. The reasoning, on which the model is based, however, may also be used to capture essential aspects of what happens in the economy on the micro- and meso level.

Finally, there exist a number of theories of capitalism in social science; and how these can add to the approach that is being presented in this stage will be explored in the next part. Special attention will be paid to the works of Marx, Weber, Schumpeter, Douglass North and advocates of the varieties of capitalism-approach. The stage ends with a discussion of some ways to bring more complexity to the model of capitalism which is advocated here.

THE SOCIOLOGY OF DISTRIBUTION

While the capitalist system consists of three basic processes which are all interdependent and shaped by the fact that they are parts of a dynamic system – production, distribution and consumption - one of these is especially important: *distribution*, in the form of exchange on the market. This represents the reason why it is preferable to start with distribution rather than with production, which otherwise comes first in the economic process. Once it has been decided to proceed in this manner, it immediately becomes clear that there exists an important precondition for exchange to take place in the first place, namely private property.

From a sociological perspective, Weber explains, property can be conceptualized as a specific form of a closed social relationship. More precisely, it represents a relationship that allows the actor to exclude other actors from the opportunity to use some item or some person. This right is also alienable and can be inherited. Property is typically legally protected, which means that if it is infringed upon, a staff will use coercion to restore it. This view of property is close to the economists' view of property as a collection of enforceable property rights. The main difference is that the element of social relations is given a much more prominent and visible form in the sociological view of property. That there nonetheless exists a basic compatibility between the economic and sociological view of property can be illustrated by the fact that during the last few years a number of sociological studies have appeared, which draw on the notion of property rights. What is crucial about private as opposed to collective property is that the former appeals directly to the individual, and in doing so it activates her in a manner that collective property is unable to do. Some might argue that people should in principle be as motivated by the prospect of acquiring and using collective property as they are by the prospect of acquiring and using private property.

The reason why this is rarely the case, however, has much to do with the free rider problem. It is also very easy for a few individuals to misuse or destroy collective property. Once private property exists, exchange becomes possible. The driving force in an exchange is always that both parties will be better off by trading with each other than by not doing so. Actor A may value her bike at \$50 and Actor B at \$70; and if an exchange takes place both will be better off – and social wealth will have increased by \$20. For an exchange to take place, it is not necessary that one party becomes better off while no-one is worse off. What rather is needed is that both parties become better off by X, without a third party being worse off by more than X, according to the so-called Kaldor-Hicks concept of efficiency.

This latter concept of efficiency is often used in economics because its demands are less stringent than those of Pareto optimality. The reason for referring to it here, however, is that it explains the nature of exchange much better than the idea of Pareto optimality, especially what drives the two parties to engage in an exchange in the first place. Sociologists and economists have developed different approaches to markets – to the role that these play in the economic process, to what is typically regulated in a market, and so on. To economists, markets are primarily processes for price formation, in which the price helps to allocate scarce resources in an efficient manner. By tradition, economists have neglected the institutional dimension of markets, such as rules for exchange, the enforcement machinery and so on. Sociologists, on the other hand, tend to emphasize the role of social relations and institutions in markets. Today's sociologists will typically analyze the networks which are created by interacting market actors. Weber noted that markets not only consist of repeated acts of exchange, but also of competition among the actors for who will be the one to sell and the one to buy. This idea of "competition for opportunities of exchange" is perfectly compatible with a networks approach, as Ronald Burt has shown in his theory of structural autonomy.

Given the fact that economists and sociologists each hold half of the truth, so to speak, when it comes to markets, it seems natural that they should try to coordinate their efforts. Economists need to better understand the role of the social relations in the market, and sociologists need to better understand how prices are formed and what effect these have on the economy. Prices drive many economic changes in capitalism, as Douglass North has made clear – but they do so via a social structure in which interests are embedded, and where quite a bit else is going on as well. An economic sociology of markets should also study what changes in the exchange mechanism make the capitalist wheel spin faster as well as what slows it down and makes it grind to a halt.

According to the theory of transaction costs, lower costs for market deals is a sign of a more efficient exchange mechanism. This is true indeed, among other reasons since this means that the profit will be larger and that more can be reinvested in production. Lower transaction costs in this context, however, are typically accomplished through changes in social relations and in social mechanisms – and this is where the sociologist can be of help. Take, for example, the clause of *bona fide* or the fact that if the buyer is in good faith it does not matter if the seller did not propery acquire the goods in question. *Bona fide* naturally lowers the transaction costs - but is also a fact of such social complexity that the sociologist, rather than the economist, is best equipped to study it. The same is true for many other forms of trust in economic life. But economic sociology is not only interested in what makes the wheels of capitalism accelerate; there is the equally challenging question of what makes them slow down or grind to a halt. Again, Weber's work can be used for illustrations.

If bureaucrats in a firm gain power at the expense of the entrepreneur, for example, profit-making will be slowed down since bureaucrats by nature are alien to the idea of profit-making. One important reason for this, Weber says, has to do with the fact that people on a fixed income often find it dishonorable to be swayed exclusively by economic considerations. Similarly, if individual firms and capitalists are not stopped in their attempts to create monopolies, capitalism may wither away because there will be no competition to keep it alive.

Recent scandals in corporate America have also shown how dishonest and false accounting can slow down economic growth and prevent new investments. All in all, the market represents *the* central institution in capitalism. To this should immediately be added that this is only true on condition that most of the production passes through the market. In the great majority of societies throughout history, markets have indeed played a role, but usually a marginal one. It is only since the late 19th century, in countries such as England and the

United States, that the great bulk of production – food, clothes and so on – has been produced in the form of commodities which are exchanged in the market.

By 1790, for example, 80 per cent of all clothing in the United States was made in the home, while a century later 90 per cent was made outside the home. When most of production passes through the market, it can be added, the competition for exchange that Weber speaks about as characteristic of the market will also dominate what happens in the economy *outside* of the market. That is, instead of just bringing a few surplus items to the market, as peasants often did in the Middle Ages, the producers in a modern capitalist economy must start the competition long before they enter the market. When one speaks of a market economy, in other words, what is meant is an economy where the market is not only used for exchange; it also dominates production. Before leaving the topic of distribution, something also needs to be said about *money* since this is the place in the economic process where money enters into the picture; it is indeed the medium of exchange par excellence. The historical step from barter to exchange with money extended the number of goods that could be exchanged against each other enormously.

Money, more generally, also helps the process exchange to proceed smoothly and lowers the cost of exchange. Many other financial innovations – such as the bill of exchange, certificates of deposit and so on – have similarly helped to lower transition costs and developed in close touch with markets. While money, like any other economic phenomena, has a cultural dimension, it is its place within the overall economic process that is of most interest to economic sociology. In economies based on reciprocity, money often plays a subordinate role since other values than "the cash nexus" decide who should get what. In economies based on redistribution, money is often in use, as recent examples of state socialism are a reminder of.

Political interests, however, dominate the operations of money in this type of societies, and socialist states have usually failed in their attempts to simulate effective market prices. In capitalism, in contrast, money and markets are protected through the existence of "credible commitments" from the political rulers, that is, by assurances of the rulers that they will not intervene in the normal workings of the market. Money, in brief, is allowed to operate "freely" and can therefore help the market to operate more smoothly and cheaply. Money also plays an important role in the capitalist process in the form of capital, that is, as profit generated through exchange. Money and markets, in brief, belong together.

THE SOCIOLOGY OF PRODUCTION

The next major area within the economic sociology of capitalism is that of *production*. No society can live without production, and all production involves social coordination – a sociological element. Nonetheless, an economic sociology of production may want to start from the following wellknown economic premise: that production consists of combinations of some or all of the traditional factors of production. The sociologist may want to add that all of these factors of production have their distinct sociological profiles - before they enter into production as well as once they interact in the firm. In relation to the basic model of capitalism, the factors of production can be conceptualized as inputs into production. It should also be emphasized that it is not the organizational form itself that is the sole determinant of productivity. It represents a common error among organization theorists, for example, to think that organizations are what matters the most – just as Marxists think that labour is the key to all production, engineers that technology is the cause of all economic growth, and so on. All of these factors contribute to productivity, individually as well as in combination. This is also where entrepreneurship in its classical Schumpeterian sense comes in. Entrepreneurship is defined by Schumpeter as a new combination for profit making, of already existing factors of production. An innovation may consist of a new commodity or some novel way of lowering the price – and it will result in high profit for the entrepreneur, soon to be followed by competition, overinvestment and lower profit. This way, according to Schumpeter, a business cycle is set off and played out in the economy.

FACTOR OF PRODUCTION NO.1: LABOUR

When factors of production were discussed in the 19th century, land was usually assigned a prominent place. In today's capitalism, however, land is of much less importance, and the average person is not dependent on working the land for her livelihood. Land as a factor of production will therefore be passed over in this stage, and I shall proceed directly to labour, which has retained its importance for the process of production. Labour as a modern factor of production typically passes through two stages.

There is the first stage which takes place *before* labour enters into production, and this is followed by the stage once labour is inside the corporation. Two institutions which are central to labour, before it enters into production, are the home and the school. In the home children learn values, discipline and how to interact. They also get to live in a household economy and become influenced by its values.

In school, labour is taught various skills, some of which are of value in production, from reading, writing and elementary mathematics in school to engineering, computer programming and nuclear physics at the university. According to a well-known strand of sociological theory, when labour is distributed via the market it tends to form into large and loose groups of people with similar economic interests. When there is no market, or the market is being controlled, say, by a profession, labour instead tends to form into small and cohesive groups centered around honour and consumption. Whatever the exact relationship is between class and status, on the one hand, and labour, on the other, it is imperative for economic sociology to attempt to theorize the link between the economic process, on the one hand, and the formation of groups in society, on the other.

This is where economic sociology needs to connect with stratification theory – and perhaps also where stratification theory can get some inspiration from economic sociology. In modern capitalist society labour tends to form into three broad categories: workers, professionals and managers. Sociology is by tradition skillful in tracing the structure of groups as well as the mentalities of their members, while economists often tend to use a non-differentiated concept of labour and emphasize the crucial role played by the productivity of the worker. Again, it would appear that both sociology and economics can benefit from the insights of the other science. To what extent can labour, before it enters into the process of production, add to, slow down or block the wheels of capitalism? What happens in the home as well as in the school, in terms of creation of values and skills, is clearly of great relevance for an answer to this question, and it will also feed into the formation of status groups and/or classes.

Status groups, Weber argues, are inherently anti-capitalist since they set honour and other non-economic values before profit-making. Status groups are antagonistic to the market since the market disregards the values that its members hold dear. The more that labour feels the impact of the market, on the other hand, the more individual actors will accepts its logic: the need for efficiency, profit-making and constant reinvestment.

Factor of Production No. 2: Capital

Economists pay by tradition much attention to the role of capital in the process of production; while sociologists, if they study capital at all, tend to analyze its role outside of production, in the form of so-called wealth. Again, the two approaches may want to draw on each other's insights in order to get a full picture of what is going on. To this can be added that the groups in society who control the economic resources have different attitudes to wealth - how it should be acquired, what it can be used for, and so on. Aristocrats, for example, have traditionally had contempt for merchants and so have warriors.

There is also the fact that some groups of merchants take larger risks than others; and this will have an important impact on the generation of wealth and capital. Merchants furthermore deal in different types of goods, as exemplified by the historical appearance of *the businessman* – a term that was first used in the U.S. in the 1830s to denote a new type of merchant, who not only traded in goods but also in land and whatever could result in a profit. This type of phenomena can be explored with the help of sociology. Control over capital is often delegated by the owner to some other actor, and this creates a well-known problem for the owner. A flexible type of analysis that economists use to handle this type of situation is agency theory, which is based on the idea that the owner has a different interest than the one to whom she assigns some specific task.

This means that something has to be done about this divergence of interest. One solution is direct observation of the agent, another to give the agent an incentive to act in the interest of the owner. The former is less easy to carry out when it comes to managers, as opposed to workers; there is also the further problem of "who will monitor the monitor". Agency theory can enrich economic sociology by adding to its analyses of capital, especially when it comes to the question of how the owner can maintain control over her capital, once a manager is in place.

According to Harrison White, for example, the advantage with using agency theory is that "it is intensely social in its mechanisms, since it gets one person to do something for another vis-à-vis a third person but only with heavy reliance on the lay of the social landscape". James Coleman has a similarly positive view of the sociological potential of agency theory, as is evidenced by the following quote from *Foundations of Social Theory*: "once a transaction has been made, in which the principal satisfies interests of the agent in return for the agent's using his actions to pursue the principal's interests, a social system has been created". A corporation can acquire capital in a variety of ways – from banks, venture capitalists, the capital market, and so on.

Each of these institutions have their own distinct social structure and history which sociology can help to analyze. Pension funds and other mutual funds which have become key players in the modern capital market, are often managed by single individuals; and very little is currently known about these. Agency theory, in combination with economic sociology, represents one way of approaching this type of issues. The way that capital is brought to production will obviously affect the generation of economic value. Risk taking is a crucial factor at this point of the process, and closely related to the profit level. But risk taking is also directly affected by social relations, as the historical emergence of venture capital in the United States a few decades ago illustrates.

What characterizes venture capitalists is an intimate knowledge of the business in which they invest, often in combination with some form of control over the firm that is being targeted. Together, these two measures make risk taking more manageable – and thereby also increase the chance to make a high profit. Again, this is a topic where economic sociology can be of assiatnce.

Factor of Production No. 3: Technology

Technology is of crucial importance to the capitalist process, primarily because it helps to increase productivity. Exactly how this is done, however, is something that neither economists nor sociologists understand very well. The concept of productivity is in need of much elucidation. Economists realize the great importance of technology in this context, but have difficulty in theorizing it. A sign of this is the discussion about the role of computers in the economic growth in the United States in the 1990s.

"You can see the computer age everywhere but in the productivity statistics", to quote a famous line by Robert Solow. Another difficulty with the economists' view of technology is that they often see technology as the one and only reason for growth in productivity. While innovations in technology may well be *the* major reason for growth in productivity in modern capitalism, it is by no means the only one. Social organization, in particular, also affects productivity, a fact that industrial sociology made clear many decades ago. Sociologists differ from economists in that they rarely note that technology is of great importance to productivity as well as for the generation of profits.

Sociologists of science of the old school view science primarily as a public good, which may once have been true but is less so today. Modern sociologists of science, on the other hand, argue that science and technology essentially are to be understood as forms of social construction, which may well be true - but is of limited relevance to an understanding of the role of science and technology in the economic process. From historians of technology we know that economically relevant technology for a long time emerged in a slow, evolutionary manner – as evidenced by the history of boat, the ax, the plow, and so on. At the time of the Industrial Revolution, and even more so during the second half of the 19th century, however, a historical meeting took place between capitalism and science.

This alliance has continued till today and has become ever more important to the dynamic growth of capitalism. It has often been pointed out that social organization can accelerate or impede the emergence of new technology, which in its turn will affect the economy. In his study of religions in India, for example, Weber notes that the caste system blocked innovations by forbidding changes in the tools of the artisans. Since the penalty for a change of this type was religious, Weber's example also illustrates how a religious interest can be used to block an economic interest.

In today's society, to use a more contemporary example, we are witnessing an important change in the property rights to science, which has helped to speed up production. While science until recently was seen as a common good, ways are now increasingly found to turn it into a private good. The forces that have caused this change are obvious enough. A new pharmaceutical drug can, for example, be worth billions of dollars in profit. It currently also costs around 800 million dollars to develop a new drug.

Factor of Production No.4: Organization (Marshall)

Alfred Marshall sensed the limits to the economics of his days and argued, in *Principles of Economics*, that not only land, labour and capital should be considered factors of production but also "organization". By organization Marshall meant a number of phenomena, including the individual firm as well as a dynamic collection of firms in the same geographical area, which he termed "industrial district". The insight that organization is crucial to profit-making is also at the heart of what is known as organizational economics, which draws on a mixture of agency theory, game theory, transaction cost analysis, and law and economics – but not on sociology. Also sociologists have developed a series of conceptual tools that can be used to analyze the way that the factors of production come together in the profit-making firm.

Sociologists, however, are to a certain extent held back from making the contribution they should be able to make by their fixation on the stance of organization theory that the central unit of analysis is the generic organization and not the corporation. Research on firms is typically translated into knowledge about organizations in general.

The following facts about the modern firm are typically ignored in organization theory, especially as it can be found among sociologists:

- That the firm has its own institutional history;
- That the firm is treated differently from other organizations in laws and regulations; and
- That firms in modern society control more economic resources than any other type of organization, except for the state.

Regardless of this critique, it is clear that several of the tools that have been developed in organization theory can be of considerable help in analyzing corporations; and to some extent they have already been used for this purpose.

This, for example, is true for population ecology as well as for resource dependency. Networks also represents a helpful tool in tracing the relations between corporations that emerge as a result of their attempts to make a profit. There is furthermore the insight that work groups can develop norms that go counter to the goals of the corporation, so-called opposition norms.

It is obvious that the way a corporation is organized will speed up, slow down or block profit-making. What was once thought to represent the ideal design for a firm – the huge, bureaucratically organized firm with much of the knowledge concentrated at the top —is today much criticized. It is indeed true that new technologies as well as new ways of appealing to the interests of the employees can replace monitoring with interest alignment, and that this has led to changes in the old type of corporation. The point, however, is not to create a decentralized or a less formal corporation per se, as organization theorists are prone to argue, but to do what it takes to make a profit.

THE SOCIOLOGY OF CONSUMPTION

Consumption, to cite *The Wealth of Nations*, represents the end product of production: "consumption is the sole end and purpose of all production". From the viewpoint of the model of capitalism that has been presented in this stage, however, things are not that simple. For one thing, how the end result of production is divided between consumption and profit is of crucial importance. The more profit that is taken out by the owners and fed back into production, the faster the wheels of capitalism will spin.

There is also the fact that consumption will affect the productivity of labour. We can imagine a line that goes from consumption to production, via labour as a factor of production. Adequate food and some amount of leisure, leading to healthy minds and healthy bodies, are examples of this. Education that is paid by private means would be another. But even if consumption may have an indirect effect on production, its main contribution to capitalism is obviously that it takes place in the first place.

Given that human beings have to satisfy their material needs, this may sound like a triviality. And so it is - except that consumption always has to increase in capitalism, in contrast to economies based on a redistribution or reciprocity. If this does not happen, profit will stagnate and capitalism will loose its vitality.

This means that efforts always have to be made, as part of the process of *production*, to encourage consumption as much as possible. In modern capitalist society whole settings in the form of shopping centers and the like have been created, precisely for this purpose. These have aptly been called "means of consumption". Consumption can be speeded up, slowed down or blocked through the impact of various forces - and thereby affect the capitalist machinery. The United States, for example, has always been a commercial society, with a population with a strong desire for democratic "comfort", as opposed to aristocratic "luxury"; and this clearly greases the wheels of capitalism.

After September 11 – to use another example from the United States – shopping was nearly proclaimed a patriotic duty so that the economy would not slump. Examples also exist of societies which have tried to block consumption. One famous example is Florence in the 15th century, when the city was ruled by Savonarola who staged the famous "bonfires of vanities" – that is, public burnings of expensive dresses, sensual paintings, and the like which were judged to detract from a pious life.

THE CURRENT REVIVAL OF ECONOMIC SOCIOLOGY

Despite the efforts of Parsons and Smelser in the mid-1950s and the 1960s to revive economic sociology, it attracted little attention, and by the 1970s the field was somewhat stagnant. A number of works inspired in one way or another by the Marxist tradition—and its general revival in the late 1960s and the early 1970s—made their appearance in this period. Among these were Marxist analyses themselves, dependency theory world systems theory and neo-Marxist analyses of the workplace. In the early 1980s, a few studies suggested a new stirring of interest. And with the publication in 1985 of a theoretical thesis by Mark Granovetter—"Economic Action and Social Structure: The Problem of Embeddedness"— the new ideas came into focus. The same year Granovetter spoke of "new economic sociology"— yielding a tangible name. Why economic sociology, after decades of neglect, suddenly would come alive again in the mid-1980s is not clear. Several factors may have played a role, inside and outside sociology.

By the early 1980s, with the coming to power of Reagan and Thatcher, a new neo-liberal ideology had become popular, which set the economy—and the economists— at the very center of things. By the mid- 1980s economists had also started to redraw the traditional boundary separating economics and sociology, and to make forays into areas that sociologists by tradition saw as their own territory. It is also during this period that Gary Becker, Oliver Williamson, and others came to the attention of sociologists.

Likewise, sociologists began to reciprocate by taking on economic topics. To some extent this version of what happened resembles Granovetter's version in 1985. He associated "old economic sociology" with the economy and society perspective of Parsons, Smelser, and Wilbert E. Moore, and with industrial sociology— two approaches, he said, that had been full of life in the 1960s but then "suddenly died out". Parsons's attempt to negotiate a truce between economics and sociology had also been replaced by a more militant tone.

According to Granovetter, new economic sociology "attacks neo-classical arguments in fundamental ways," and it wants to take on key economic topics, rather than focus on peripheral ones. Since the mid-1980s new economic sociology has carved out a position for itself in U.S. sociology. It is well represented at a number of universities. Courses are routinely offered in sociology departments.

A part in the American Sociological Association has been formed. A number of high-quality monographs have been produced, such as The Transformation of Corporate Control by Neil Fligstein, Structural Holes by Ronald Burt, and The Social Meaning of Money by Viviana Zelizer. These three works draw on the insights of organization theory, networks theory, and cultural sociology, respectively. The subfield has also seen the appearance of several anthologies, readers, a huge handbook, a textbook, and a general introduction to the field.

GRANOVETTER ON EMBEDDEDNESS

While several attempts have been made to present general theories and paradigms in new economic sociology, the perspective that continues to command most conspicuous attention is Granovetter's theory of embeddedness. Since the mid- 1980s Granovetter has added to his argument and refined it in various writings that are related to his two major projects since the mid-1980s: a general theoretical work in economic sociology entitled Society and Economy:

The Social Construction of Economic Institutions, and a study of the emergence of the electrical utility industry in the United States.

The most important place in Granovetter's work where embeddedness is discussed is his 1985 article, which operated as a catalyst in the emergence of new economic sociology and which is probably the most cited article in economic sociology since the 1980s. His own definition of embeddedness is quite general and states that economic actions are "embedded in concrete, ongoing systems of social relations". Networks are central to this concept of embeddedness. An important distinction needs also to be drawn, according to Granovetter, between an actor's immediate connections and the more distant ones— what Granovetter elsewhere calls "relational embeddedness" and "structural embeddedness".

The most important addition to the 1985 article has been connecting the concept of embeddedness to a theory of institutions. Drawing on Berger and Luckmann Granovetter argues that institutions are "congealed networks". Interaction between people acquires, after some time, an objective quality that makes people take it for granted. Economic institutions are characterized by "the mobilization of resources for collective action". Granovetter's argument on embeddedness has been widely discussed and sometimes criticized.

An attempt to elaborate it can be found in the work of Brian Uzzi, who argues that a firm can be "underembedded" as well as "overembedded," and that a firm is most successful when it balances between arm's-length market ties and more solid links. Several other critics have pointed out that Granovetter omits consideration of many aspects of economic action, including a link to the macroeconomic level, culture, and politics. Zukin and DiMaggio suggest that to remedy this lacuna, one should not only talk of "structural embeddedness," but also of "political," "cultural," and "cognitive embeddedness."

CONTRIBUTIONS USING STRUCTURAL SOCIOLOGY AND NETWORKS

Structural sociology has played a crucial role in promoting and adding to network analysis in sociology, including economic socioloy. This approach is centered around the proposition that the relations of persons and positions are crucial to the social process. Its practitioners often use a mathematical approach, focus on social mechanisms, and avoid regression analysis and similar quantitative methods.

Its most prominent scholars are Harrison White and his students, such as Mark Granovetter, Scott Boorman, and Michael Schwartz. White's work in economic sociology has concerned networks, vacancy chains, and markets. He begins his analysis from people's physical dependence on their surroundings but notes that interests are soon embedded in social relations. Network studies have been at the center of the new economic sociology. Many studies have been made of the links between corporations and, more generally, within so-called industrial districts. Burt analyzes competition by drawing on Simmel's idea that you are in a good position if you can play out two competitors against one another. Brian Uzzi's study of embeddedness from 1997 also makes use of networks, as does Granovetter's thesis on business groups. A multitude of other fine studies could be mentioned. One criticism of the network approach is that it has ignored the role in economic life of politics and culture.

CONTRIBUTIONS USING ORGANIZATION THEORY

New economic sociology has been very successful in using organization theory to explore a number of important topics, such as the structure of firms and the links between corporations and their environments. One fine example is Nicole Woolsey Biggart's Charismatic Capitalism, which deals with a very special type of organization: direct selling organizations, such as Tupperware and Mary Kay Cosmetics. Three theoretical approaches in organization theory have been especially important for the development of new economic sociology: resource dependency, population ecology, and new institutionalism.

Resource dependency, as its name suggests, rests on the postulate that organizations are dependent on their environments to survive. An example of this approach is work by Burt, who suggests that three important factors that affect profits are the number of suppliers, competitors, and customers. The more "structural autonomy" a firm has, the higher its profits; that is, a firm with many suppliers, few competitors, and many customers will be in a position to buy cheaply and sell expensively. In population ecology the main driving force of organizations is survival. It has been shown that the diffusion of an organizational form typically passes through several distinct stages: a very slow beginning, then explosive growth, and finally a slow settling down. Individual studies of this process in various industries, such as railroads, banks, and telephone companies, fill a void in economic sociology. New institutionalism is strongly influenced by the ideas of John Meyer and is centered around what may be called cultural and cognitive aspects of organizations.

Meyer argues that organizations seem much more rational than they actually are, and that specific models for organizing activities may be applied widely—including to circumstances they do not fit. It has been argued that the strength of new institutionalism is its exploration of "factors that make actors unlikely to recognize or to act on their interests" and its focus on "circumstances that cause actors who do recognize and try to act on their interests to be unable to do so". The possibility of uniting a more traditional interest analysis with new institutionalism is exemplified by Fligstein's study of the large corporation in the United States. Fligstein notes that the multidivisional form of organization spread for mimetic reasons—but also because this organizational form made it easier for firms to take advantage of new technology and the emerging national market.

CONTRIBUTIONS USING CULTURAL SOCIOLOGY

A group of economic sociologists is committed to a cultural approach, and a substantial number also refer to symbols, meaning structures, and the like in their studies of the economy. Cultural economic sociology owes much to the work of its two most prominent representatives, Viviana Zelizer and Paul DiMaggio. In a programmatic statement Zelizer criticized contemporary economic sociology for its tendency to reduce everything to social relations and networks—"social structural absolutism".

She also rejected the alternative of reducing everything in the economy to culture. The goal should be to take economic and cultural factors into account. DiMaggio has been similarly skeptical of a full-scale cultural analysis of the economy, but argues that it should include a "'cultural' component"—but not more. According to DiMaggio, culture can be either "constitutive," referring to categories, scripts, and conceptions of agency, or "regulative," referring to norms, values, and routines. Viviana Zelizer's work on culture occupies a central position.

Her first major work was a study of life insurance in the United States, with special emphasis on the clash between sacred values and economic values. Over time the economic emphasis came to dominate. Later Zelizer published Pricing the Priceless Child, which describes a similar movement, but this time in reverse. Children, who in the nineteenth century had had an economic value, would in the twentieth century increasingly be seen in emotional terms and regarded as "priceless." In her most recent major study, Zelizer argues that money does not constitute a neutral, non-social substance, but appears in a variety of culturally influenced shapes.

CONTRIBUTIONS BUILDING A HISTORICAL AND COMPARATIVE TRADITION

A number of comparative and historical studies, bringing Max Weber's monumental works to mind, have been an ingredient of recent economic sociology. To this list should be added Bruce Carruthers's study of finance in seventeenth- and eighteenth-century England, and several attempts by economic sociologists to challenge Alfred Chandler's account of the rise of the large industrial corporation in the United States. Carruthers is interested in showing that not only do economic interests influence politics, but also the opposite: "political interests influence economic action".

Using primary material on the trade in shares in the East India Company in the early 1700s, he establishes that political ambitions clearly influenced the choices of buyers and sellers. The critique of Chandler has similarly emphasized the state's role in the emergence of the large industrial corporation. Chandler's key idea—that recent advances in technology had made it necessary around the turn of the last century to reorganize the large corporation as a multidivisional unit—has also been criticized. Explicitly comparative studies are fewer in number. One notable work is Forging Industrial Policy: The United States, Britain, and France in the Railway Age by Frank Dobbin. The author argues that industrial policy in these three countries between 1825 and 1900 differed on important points.

In the case of the United States, local self-rule and a weak federal state meant that railway regulation translated into antimonopoly policy and attempts to safeguard private initiatives. The tradition of a centralized state in France inspired strong interference from the authorities in the planning and running of the railroads. And the tradition of safeguarding elite individuals in Britain helped to bring about an industrial policy that shielded the small, entrepreneurial firm.

THE CONTRIBUTION BY JAMES COLEMAN AND INTEREST-BASED SOCIOLOGY

The most radical attempt during the last few decades to develop a sociological interest analysis is that of James Coleman. His efforts were initiated in the early 1960s and found final expression in Foundations of Social Theory. Coleman's intention was to use interest as the foundation for all of sociology, and initially he paid little attention to economic sociology. However, that in the same year Granovetter's thesis on embeddedness appeared, Coleman published a brief article in which he developed the parallel argument that economists have failed to introduce social relations into their analysis. The key theoretical stage in Foundations of Social Theory is entitled "Actors, Resources, Interest, and Control"; it attempts to reconceptualize interest theory and to make it sociological.

Coleman's point of departure is that it is not sufficient to speak of actors and their interests; "resources" and "control" must be considered. Coleman argues that if an actor has something of interest to another, the two will interact and thereby create a social system. In Coleman's terminology, if actor A has control over a resource that is of interest to actor B, they will interact. Foundations, as well as other works by Coleman, contains a number of analyses of much relevance to economic sociology. Three subjects of particular importance are trust, social capital, and the modern corporation. Trust is conceptualized by Coleman in a manner very different from Simmel.

While the latter emphasized trust as unthinking belief, Coleman characterizes trust as a conscious bet: you calculate what you can win and lose by trusting someone. Social capital is any social relation that can be of help to an individual in realizing an interest. "The function identified by the concept 'social capital' is the value of those aspects of social structure to actors, as resources that can be used by the actors to realize their interests". A firm represents, for example, a form of social capital—even if social capital is usually the unintended result of some action, undertaken for a different purpose. Finally, Coleman emphasizes that once people have created a firm to realize their interests, the firm can develop interests of its own. To Coleman, the firm is basically a social invention, and agency theory is particularly useful for analyzing it.

BOURDIEU AND OTHER EUROPEAN CONTRIBUTIONS TO ECONOMIC SOCIOLOGY

New economic sociology is primarily a U.S. phenomenon and has only recently begun to spread to Europe. Many of the major European sociologists have, however, written on the economy as part of their general concern with society. This is not only true of Raymond Aron, Michel Crozier, and Ralf Dahrendorf, but also of major sociologists with notable contemporary influence, such as Niklas Luhmann, Jürgen Habermas, and Pierre Bourdieu. Luhmann, for example, has written a number of thesiss on the economy, which, however, have been somewhat neglected in the current debate.

His consistent thesis is that "economic sociology can only develop if its approach is overhauled and it sets out... from the concept of the economy as a subsystem of society". Habermas has written much less on the economy than Luhmann and has not shown any interest in economic sociology. Nonetheless, his general thesis that in modern society the lifeworld of the individual has been uncoupled from the system world, including the economic subsystem, has been much discussed. Of the major European sociologists Pierre Bourdieu has shown the most interest in the economy, from his studies of Algeria in the 1950s to a recent work on the housing market in Les structures sociales de l'économie. Bourdieu has also devoted issues of his journal Actes de la recherche en sciences sociales to economic topics, such as "social capital", "the social construction of the economy" and "the economy and the economists".

Most importantly, however, he has developed an important theoretical alternative to the model of embeddedness and its offshoots, namely the idea of the economy as a field, with all that this implies. Bourdieu's foremost empirical study of interest to economic sociology—Travail et travailleurs en Algérie—can be described as a rich ethnographic study. Some of its strength comes from the author's juxtaposition of the traditionalistic worldview of the Algerian peasants with the capitalist worldview of modern people. While the peasant in Algeria has an intensely emotional and nearly mystical relationship to the land, this is not the case in a society dominated by wage labour and capital.

Work is not directly related to productivity in Algeria; one tries to keep busy all the time. Institutions such as money and credit are seen in a different light. Money and exchange are seen as inferior to barter; and credit—which, as opposed to assets, is tied to the person—is resorted to only in rare circumstances such as personal distress. In Algeria commercial ventures are preferred to industrial ones, since the risk involved is much smaller. In economic sociology Bourdieu has also developed a general approach; an application of his general sociology, which is centered around the concepts of the field, habitus, and different types of capital.

In 1997 he published an article entitled "The Economic Field," which was revised and given the new title of "Principles of an Economic Anthropology" a few years later. Since Bourdieu is very critical of Granovetter's approach—for ignoring the structural dimension embodied in the notion of the field—one may well be justified in speaking about two different approaches in contemporary economic sociology: that of embeddedness and that of fields. According to Bourdieu, the economy can be conceptualized as a field, that is, as a structure of actual and potential relations. Each field has its own logic and its own social structure. The structure of a field can also be understood in terms of its distribution of capital.

Besides financial capital, three other forms of capital are especially important: social, cultural, and symbolic. Social capital is one's connections of relevance to economic affairs; cultural capital comes from one's education and family background; and symbolic capital has to do with various items with a cognitive basis, such as goodwill and brand loyalty. The individual actors in the economic field bring with them their "economic habitus", which relates their future actions to their past experience. Homo economicus, Bourdieu says, is "a kind of anthropological monster".

Bourdieu's economic actor does not act in a rational way but in a reasonable way. In addition to the three concepts of field, capital, and habitus important in Bourdieu's general sociology, there exists a fourth concept that is equally important but often ignored: interest, or that which drives the actor to participate in a field. "Interest is to 'be there,' to participate, to admit that the game is worth playing and that the stakes that are created in and through this fact are worth pursuing; it is to recognize the game and to recognize its stakes". The opposite of interest is indifference.

Each field has its own interest, even if it masquerades as disinterestedness. Bourdieu criticizes the economists' version of interest as ahistorical—"far from being an anthropological invariant, interest is a historical arbitrary". The economists are also wrong in thinking that "economic interest" drives everything; "anthropology and comparative history show that the properly social magic of institutions can constitute just about anything as an interest". The error of assuming that the laws of the economic field are applicable to all other fields in society Bourdieu terms "economism". Bourdieu's analysis has been discussed in only limited ways in contemporary economic sociology.

Distinction, for example, has much to say on preference formation and also contains a new approach to consumption. Bourdieu's emphasis on economic suffering and his attempt to tie it to the problematic of theodicy is also of much interest. So is his related effort to discuss the normative aspect of economic sociology, for example, in his recent little book on "the tyranny of capital". It would, however, be incorrect to give the impression that Bourdieu is the only economic sociologist of interest in contemporary France. Luc Boltanski and Laurent Thévenot's work on the different ways that an action can be justified or legitimized is of potential relevance to economic sociology.

Their ideas about the way that people legitimize their actions by referring to different "worlds" of justification are hard to summarize, and one example will have to suffice. A person who works for a firm may justify his behaviour by referring either to efficiency or to loyalty—with very different results. Boltanski has also criticized the network approach as ideological and procapitalistic. In speaking of networks, it must also be mentioned that Michel Callon has added to network theory by arguing that not only individuals and organizations, but also objects, can be actors.

A machine, for example, can determine what kinds of actions a machine operator has to perform and also how she is connected to other people in the process of production. According to another important argument of Callon, economic theory often fits reality so well because it has helped to create this reality in the first place. Outside of the United States, France has become something of a center for innovative economic sociology, and to the work just mentioned one should also add the studies of Frédéric Lebaron on French economists, Emmanuel Lazeaga on work in a law firm, and Philippe Steiner on different types of economic knowledge. There is considerable research in economic sociology in other European countries as well. Sociology of money and finance has, for example, several skillful practitioners in England and Spain. An innovative study of inheritance has just been published in Germany, where the sociology of finance is also very strong. Industrial districts are being studied in Italy.

9

Development of Economic Policies in New Millennium

INTRODUCTION

Ever since India gained its independence nearly 40 years ago, the state has intervened strongly in some sectors of the country's economy. It has taken and kept the lead in setting priorities, formulating and implementing policies, and determining the direction and pace of change in industry, foreign trade, finance, transport and energy infrastructure where it has worked hand in hand with private Indian capital, allowing it a prominent role. But two of the largest sectors—agriculture and internal trade—together constituting the major part of the Indian economy, have been allowed to remain outside state control, with intervention limited to providing irrigation, fertilizers, and other inputs into agriculture at highly subsidized prices; buying wheat and rice at high support prices to build buffer stocks; and selling foodstuffs at relatively moderate prices in government shops in urban areas.

The partnership of the public and private sectors in controlling and running some parts of India's so-called mixed economy, has been more or less stable, continuous, and consistent over the last four decades, making due allowance for the usual quarrels that all such "marriages' have. What has made this possible is the fact that in India, so far, no one social class has emerged as dominant over all the others. Rather, several dominant social classes are evenly matched, obliging them to share political power and work out arrangements for dividing the economic surplus. This partnership of dominant classes consists of the rich farmers, the middle peasantry, the industrial and financial capitalists, the middle and top layers of the state bureaucracy (including the officers in the armed forces), the middle and large traders, and the unionized, relatively well-paid white- and blue-collar workers of very large enterprises and the transport and energy infrastructure.

This dominating collection of social and economic forces represents the interests of the middle and upper classes, both rural and urban, as well as of the so-called labour aristocracy of high-wage organized workers—a conglomeration of about 150 million people forming the top 20 per cent of the total population. These groups have formed the support base of not only the Congress Party, which has ruled India at the centre and in most of the 22 states of the federal union for more than 35 years, but also of several other non-Communist parties which have been in government for brief periods at the centre and in some states. In this sense of sharing power at the centre and in the states, through the Congress and other political parties, this collection acts as a loose de facto coalition. There are three major reasons why the political parties are beholden to this collection of dominating classes: first, the rich and middle farmers control the rural votes, thus deciding the outcome of general elections (75 per cent of India's population is still rural); second, the industrial and financial capitalists, along with the traders, finance the parties; third, the white-collar workers and the high-wage organized blue-collar workers, if antagonized, can halt the state machinery and modern infrastructure, as well as make the towns and cities ungovernable.

In this ruling coalition, the state has played the role of orchestrator, mediator, and arbitrator, thus ensuring for itself the dominant position. This arrangement has conferred on the state, and especially on the top echelons of the bureaucracy, a status of semi-autonomy within the state structure as a whole. Given this evolution, it is not surprising that the state and in particular the top state bureaucracy has internalized the conviction and propagated the message that it is the patriotic guardian of the national interest, standing specific sectarian and class conflicts and pursuing the goal of transforming India into a prosperous and strong nation-state and a great power. The main strategy chosen by the state in moving towards its goals took shape in the closing stages of the first Five Year Plan (FYP) in the mid-1950s and was put into operation during the second FYP period, 1955/56-1959/60.

The strategy underwent two fundamental revisions, in the mid-1960s and again in the mid-1980s, in response to severe crises. The post-independence history of India can therefore be divided into the three periods 1950-1965, 1966-1984, and 1985 onwards. The first encompasses the first three FYPs; the second begins with the suspension of planning during the three years 1966-68 (euphemistically called the "Annual Plan' periods) followed by the revival of planning on a much reduced basis in the fourth, fifth, and sixth FYPs; and the third period dates from the start of the seventh FYP.

"To plan is to choose,' said Julius Nyerere once. This self-evident truth has been sublimely ignored by the authors of the plan documents. The plans they have produced on paper envision the realization of numerous desirable objectives, all of which have been accorded priority. Constraints have been wished away. Between the all-encompassing rhetoric of the plan documents and the actual economic goals and economic strategies of the implemented parts of the plan there is a vast gap. The reason for the rhetoric is clear: since the proclaimed ideology of the state is that it is the promoter of the national interest and the welfare of all parts of the population, it is necessary to show that there is something for everybody in the Plan, that nobody has been forgotten.

In what follows, as suggested, try to identify and discuss the actual economic goals and strategies, ignoring the rhetorical trimmings. It is most important to recognize one fact of great significance right away: the related goals of substantial employment generation and substantial poverty reduction, although stressed in all Plan documents, have in reality been relegated to the bottom of the list. In relation to the needs of these two goals, the commitment of resources has been puny, the strategies weak, the impact of the programmes marginal. The state claims that there has been a noticeable reduction in proverty, but that is hotly contested by many analysts. But even if these claims are judged to be marginally true, any reduction in poverty has come about not because of, but irrespective of, the state's intervention.

OVERRIDING ECONOMIC GOAL DURING THE FIRST PERIOD (1950-1965)

The overriding economic goal during the first period (1950-1965) was self-sustaining growth in industry, transport, and energy. The major constraint was diagnosed to be the lack of adequate capital stock and technological skills. It was argued that if physical and human capital were rapidly created, the result would be dynamic growth in the three sectors.

This meant giving the highest priority to:

- Importing and producing of capital goods required for the manufacture of not only intermediate and consumer goods but also other capital goods, *i.e.*, machines for making machines, including equipment for the production and distribution of electricity and for the railways and other means of transport;
- The rapid expansion of higher education in science and technology. In addition, priority was given to the manufacture of iron and steel, cement, fertilizers, and heavy chemicals.

This strategy of going all out for the domestic manufacture of capital goods and some key intermediate goods, often termed the "heavy industry strategy,' was worked out for the Indian context by Mahalanobis and his team at the Indian Statistical Institute in Calcutta. To get it started, priority was given to the import of machinery and technological knowledge.

The investments required were huge. Foreign capital, however, was highly skeptical and reluctant to take part in this venture, which in the early 1950s was quite a novel and bold idea for a third world country. Even the biggest among the private capitalists in India were too small at that time to risk taking part in this individually, and the state discouraged the formation of cartels since it wanted to keep overall control of this strategic sector. Hence, partly by default of foreign and domestic private capital, and partly by ideology and design, the Indian state planned, financed, built, and controlled most of the capital-goods and large chunks of the intermediate-goods industries. The central and dominant position it thus acquired in Indian industry has continued into the mid-1980s. On the other hand, all consumer-goods manufacturing, including consumer durables and motor vehicles, as well as substantial parts of intermediate-goods production, was left to private Indian capital.

Access to domestic markets by both state and private industry was ensured by a ban on the import of goods that could be locally manufactured, by stringent import quotas, and in some cases by very high import duties. The import of technological knowledge and managerial expertise through royalty and lump-sum payments was permitted for limited periods, generally long enough to internalize the knowledge. The principal instrument of control for enforcing the strategy of industrialization through import substitution was not tariffs, but import bans and the granting of import licenses and industrial-production licenses on a highly selective basis.

The general criterion for granting import licenses was that the imported goods should be essential for the production of other already licensed goods for which there was as yet no domestic productive capacity. Similarly, criteria were set up for licensing increased productive capacity and starting new production. The authority to grant licenses was invested in the central bureaucracy in New Delhi.

In the ensuing scramble for scarce licenses, the really big fish in the private sector won out over their smaller rivals, because of superior ability to offer generous kickbacks and commissions to powerful politicians and bureaucrats and generous contributions to the funds of the ruling political party. As is already well known and well publicized, one of the results of this aptly named "Licence-Raj' was infiltration of corruption into the interstices of public administration and the political establishment. The other major plank of the economic strategy of the first period was public investment in huge dam-building projects for irrigation and the generation of hydroelectricity in a few selected parts of the country, which in the event accrued to the benefit of the rich and middle farmers and industrial entrepreneurs in those few chosen states. Economic and social programmes for ameliorating poverty have been in existence since the late 1950s but at a very low level relative to the allocations and efforts put into the "modern' sector.

The policy instruments included expenditures on food to be exchanged for work, other rural community development projects, and easier credits and loans to small peasants and artisans. As can be inferred from the foregoing, during the first period, agricultural development was given low priority: its contribution to the Net Domestic Product (NDP) grew at an annual rate of 2.4

per cent in contrast to manufacturing industry, transport, and electricity, which grew respectively at 7, 7, and 13 per cent, at constant 1960 prices.

At the end of the first period (1950-65), the state had succeeded in its major objective of establishing the base for a self-sustaining and fast growing integrated industrial sector, with good forward and backward interindustrial linkages among capital goods, intermediate goods, and consumer goods. Self-reliant industrialization had taken off. But in all the other objectives proclaimed of the first three FYPs, in particular agricultural development, employment generation, and poverty reduction, the state had failed dismally.

START OF THE SECOND PERIOD (1966-84)

The start of the second period (1966-84) was marked by several grave crises. The war with China in 1965 and the widespread famine in 1966 and 1967 (triggered off but not entirely caused by the droughts of 1965 and 1966) diverted resources to more expenditure on defence and to imports of foodstuffs. Meanwhile, the costly imports of machinery and equipment to lay the base for industrialization in the first period had eaten deeply into the foreign-exchange reserve. Western governments suspended credits in 1966, and under pressure from the IMF and the World Bank, the rupee was devalued to give a boost to exports. But neither the expected large increases in foreign aid nor the spurt in exports materialized. The food and foreign exchange crises thus forced the state to change its earlier economic goals and strategies. Planning was effectively suspended from 1966 to 1968. Investment in industry, transport, and energy was cut back sharply and concentrated instead on pursuing the goals of food self-sufficiency and export promotion.

On the food front, the strategy chosen was to invest in the new technology of high-yielding varieties (HYV) of staple foodgrains in a few states—wheat in the Punjab, Haryana, and Western Uttar Pradesh; rice in the deltas of the Godavari river in Andhra Pradesh and the Kaveri river in Tamil Nadu. With irrigation assured in these areas, farmers were offered the HYV package of seeds, fertilizers, and pesticides at highly subsidized prices. And electricity, which was already being generated in these states from earlier hydroelectric projects, was also supplied at cheap rates to pump water up from tube-wells. Credit was made available on easy terms, and the state offered to buy the farmers' produce at good support prices. Those who were able to invest in this new technology, including farm mechanization, were the large and middle farmers.

The size of their landholdings and the credit facilities available to them on the basis of their assets made the new technology a viable strategy. The results were dramatic: wheat production jumped from 11 million tons in 1960/61 to 23.8 million in 1970/71; rice from 34.6 to 42.2 million tons in the same period. As we go deeper into the second period, we notice the so-called Green

Revolution spreading to only a few more districts in a small number of states, *e.g.*, Jammu and Kashmir, Gujarat, Karnataka, Maharashtra, and West Bengal. However, seen in an all-India perspective, the production of both wheat and rice has registered remarkable increases since the introduction of HYVs in the late 1960s: by 1984/85 total wheat production was 44.2 million tons and rice 58.6 million tons, nearly a quadrupling and doubling respectively over two decades. But for other food crops the increases on a total national basis have been extremely modest, being nearly at a standstill for legumes and very low for oilseeds. One reason for this is, of course, that HYV technology has not yet been developed for the other major Indian crops. The public food grain stock held by the state for distribution through "fair price' shops, through food-for-work and other related programmes, and for emergency distribution in times of crop failure due to droughts and floods, reached 29.2 million tons in June 1985 (the highest so far), declined somewhat to 24 million by early January 1986, but is expected to climb to about 30 million by the end of 1986.

This is the best news on the food front in the sense that the state now has enough food stocks to distribute at relatively modest prices through "fair price' shops, thus keeping staple food prices down, and for distribution in case of national emergencies. The dependence on foreign imports of food grains seems to be definitely over. However, this can by no means be interpreted as having reached food "self-sufficiency,' as domestic and foreign publicists for the Indian state are claiming. The reality is different as the following facts reveal. The food distributed through "fair price' shops reaches only the urban population and is equally available to the richest and the poorest urban families at the same price, which of course means yet another increase in the purchasing power of the urban middle and upper classes at the expense of the poor. Further, some 300 million, out of a total rural population of about 560 million (in 1985), are net buyers of food grain.

These are the poorest of the poor, comprising landless laborers and marginal and small peasants, below the so-called "absolute poverty line,' which is defined by the World Bank as "that income level below which a minimal nutritionally adequate diet plus essential non-food requirements is not affordable.' The purchasing power of those below this "absolute poverty income level' (at present estimated to be about 1,400 rupees per capita per year in the rural areas, less than a tenth of a middle-class income) has seriously declined over the last few decades. The reason is that the price of coarse grains on which the poorest spend the bulk of their income has steadily increased. The theoretical net availability per capita per day of cereals remained the same, about 415 grams during the second period, while that of legumes has actually declined by a factor of one third from 60 grams in 1965 to 40 grams in 1985!

This protein availability in 1985 was about half of the 75 gram minimum world standard protein intake set up by the FAO. If to all this is added that 20 per cent of the net theoretical availability is held unsold in the state's public stock of foodgrains, it follows that the actual purchases by the poorest 300 million is bound to be well below the theoretical net availability. The stark dimensions of the malnutrition of 40 per cent of India's population thus stand clearly revealed.

What the huge unsold and unsaleable stock of foodgrains of about 24 million tons in 1986 means is that the poorest 40 per cent do not have the cash income to buy food in sufficient quantities. This "food mountain,' acquired at high subsidized support prices from middle and rich farmers in a few states, is imposing a very heavy financial burden on the state, which is of course being passed on to the poor (some 80 per cent of the total population) in the form of indirect taxes.

Irrigation, fertilizers, pesticides, farm mechanization, and good storage facilities for grain are the essential technological ingredients in the high-yielding-variety (HYV) strategy of the Green Revolution. The essential economic ingredients are credit facilities and good support prices for the farmers. The unequal availability of these technological and economic ingredients has produced a sharp worsening of existing disparities between states and between different classes of farmers within the states.

Irrigation-rich states where middle-level farmers constitute the bulk of the cultivators, like the Punjab, Haryana, and Uttar Pradesh, showed annual rates of growth in cereal production of 4.3 to 7.2 per cent, against an all-India average of 2.8 per cent during the period under consideration (1967-1985).Most of the Green Revolution has happened in these three states. Irrigation-poor states with small and marginal peasants and landless labourers making up the rural majority, like Bihar, Orissa, and Madhya Pradesh, have recorded very poor cereals growth rates of between 1 and 1.7 per cent. Broadly speaking, not more than half a dozen of India's 22 states (excluding the 9 union territories) have benefited so far from the HYV strategy, and within them the benefits have gone in the main to middle and large farmers.

A fundamental change in agrarian structures took place in this period, consolidating itself by the mid-1970s. It was brought about by abolition of the absentee landlord system and partial implementation of "land-to-the-tiller' demand. Very large landowners were obliged by the land reform law to sell land area above a certain ceiling to their tenants. Further, any amount of alnd, however small, not cultivated by the owner or his family members also had to be sold to the peasant household which cultivated it.

This gave rise to the emergence of a middle land-owning peasantry from the former tenant-cultivating part, comprising about 10 per cent of the rural population, which became very influential economically, socially, and politically. The pre-independence "patron-client' relationship between the very large landowners and the rest of the village population began to give way in some parts of the country to a class dominance by the middle peasantry which took the lead in local, regional, and even national affairs, organizing effective "farmers' agitation,' coopting a wide range of the rural population in support of improved material incentives like highly subsidized irrigation, electricity, and fertilizers, higher prices for state purchase of grains, cancellation of earlier loans, etc. The middle peasantry, together with the rich large farmers, now constitutes the dominant classes in rural India.

For the rest, however, the so-called land reform is a total sham. Of the massive amount of legislation on paper, the one thing of any significance to be implemented was the expropriation of absentee landlords, whose lands became the property of their former middle and large tenant farmers. Landless labourers and marginal and small peasants got virtually nothing out of it. Over the last four decades less than 0.6 per cent of the total cultivated area has actually been distributed among the landless. The single most important feature of Indian economic policy has been, and continues to be, not to collect direct taxes from farmers, irrespective of the size of their landholdings, other assets, and cash incomes. It is staggering that this sector of the economy which produces more than one third of the total net domestic product pays no direct tax. As though that in itself was not enough, from the mid-1960s onward the terms of internal trade began to move against industry and in favour of agriculture. This is the enormous price the state and the other members of the dominant coalition have had to pay to keep the semi-feudal landlords, the rich farmers, and the middle peasants happy, for they wield immense political power through their control of the rural population.

Turning now to the other major economic goal of the second period, *i.e.*, export promotion, one notes that the strategy of devaluation of the rupee in 1966, coupled with a temporary suspension of export subsidies, failed to bring the expected results. Moreover, there was no net increase in the inflow of aid. Instead net aid fell by over 40 per cent in real terms. Without the hoped-for large increases in foreign aid, the state soon found it necessary to reinstate export subsidies.

The combined effect of all this was that there was no dramatic increase in export earnings, or significant change in the structure of exports in favour of modern manufactures. In the period 1968-80 exports grew at an annual rate of 5.5 per cent, but fell sharply to 1.8 per cent between 1981 and 1985 at current prices, which means that the real absolute value of exports has been falling over the last five years. As for the composition of exports, primary agricultural and mineral products, and traditional manufactures like tea, iron ore, jute, textiles, leather manufactures, gems and jewelry, etc., account for 85 per cent, the remaining 15 per cent being made up of modern manufactures like capital goods, chemicals, and clothing. The fact that in 1985 the export revenue from gems and jewelry was nearly twice that from chemicals speaks volumes for the weakness of India's exports of manufactures compared to the exports of the other industrially advanced third-world countries. On the other hand, it is no surprise that among the exports of modern manufactures, the relative newcomer, capital goods, has taken the lead, beating textiles and chemicals to the second and third places respectively. Indian manufacturers discovered that there was some demand for relatively "non-sophisticated' and "non-up-to-date' metal products, machine tools, and machinery in a few industrializing South East Asian and oil-rich West Asian and North African countries.

Examples of such goods are non-numerically-controlled, non-computerized lathes, and 1950s vintage machinery in the cement and sugar and glass industries. Indians were able to make a modest entry into these markets with the excess production that the capital goods strategy had promoted but which could not be absorbed by a stagnating domestic industry. Low wages and government export subsidies helped a good deal in the price competition against other countries' exporters. Indian government export promotion bodies also provide market-information service, warehousing facilities, and other infrastructural support to exporters of manufactured goods. Another factor that has contributed to the relatively better performance of the capital goods sector in the export field within the Indian context (absolutely insignificant though this still is in the context of the world export trade in capital goods) is that there are some very big Indian firms in this sector with the minimum of financial, organizational, and managerial resources essential for entering the export market.

The reduction in investment in public-sector industry by the state at the start of the second period had a negative effect on the whole industrial sector, which suffered from both recession and structural retrogression up to the mid-1970s. But as investment rose again, industry pulled itself out of this recession, showing substantial real growth rates of around 10 per cent per annum during the fifth FYP period (1974-79). However, it failed to maintain this momentum during the sixth FYP period (1980-85), dropping to an annual rate of 5 per cent. From the end of the fourth FYP period (1969-1974), *i.e.*, from the mid-1970s, the emphasis on state ownership of Indian industry began a gradual decline. The claims of the private sector for a greater share became more insistent, as it sensed that the government was becoming more sympathetic to its arguments. Large-scale private industry demanded and obtained state subsidies and tax relief. Step by step, it became easier to import the latest in Western technology, signalling a retreat from the earlier ambition for indigenous development of the latest technology.

ONSET OF THE THIRD PERIOD: 1985 ONWARDS

By the onset of the third period, four things of fundamental significance had been achieved and consolidated in India: self-reliance in food production and food supply, self-reliance in modern industry, one of the highest savings rates (22 per cent of GDP) in the third world, and a good foreign exchange reserve of about $6 billion, 15 per cent of which came from remittances of Indians working abroad, especially in the Middle East.

Side by side with this "comfort-giving' picture of plenty, stands the reality of the poverty of 80 per cent (600 million) of the total population (750 million), of whom at least 40 per cent (300 million) are the poorest of the poor, in World Bank terminology "the absolute poor' who cannot afford a "minimal nutritionally adequate diet plus essential non-food requirement.' It is against this background that as suggested, attempt an analysis of the sectoral objectives and allocations in the seventh FYP (1985-90). The accompanying table presents a comparison of the allocations in the fifth, sixth, and seventh FYPs.

Although the transition from the second to the third period is not sudden, the departures are radical enough to signal the beginning of another era. Partly this shift is attributable to the change in the political leadership at the centre following the assassination of Mrs. Indira Gandhi. In theory, the main purpose of Indian planning is to allocate money to the development of various sectors of the economy. The Five Year Development Plans which are drawn up by the Planning Commission in New Delhi, are thus indicative financial plans. They are not the detailed material balance plans of the Soviet and East European type, governing the division and flow of raw material and other physical resources as well as labour and skills among the various economic and social sectors.

The Planning Commission estimates the financial resources, both in domestic and foreign convertible currencies, that would be required for achieving the development targets set in a five-year-plan period, for both the state-owned sector and the private sector. It proposes certain total volumes and sectoral allocations of development investment and development expenditure in the state-owned sector. In addition, it forecasts how the private sector, following the lead of the public sector, will make its own investments. The Prime Minister is the chairman of the Planning Commission.

The Indian Union consists of 22 states and 9 so-called union territories. While the latter are directly administered by the central government in New Delhi, the former have their own state governments and state legislatures. The states make their own state-level five-year development plans within the overall framework and targets set by the central five-year plan, and on the basis of the financial resources they expect to receive from the central government in New Delhi, as well as the resources they expect to raise themselves. Like the central plan, the state-level plans are in essence financial.

The states of the Indian Union are supposed to be able to influence the drafting of the central five-year plan not only through direct consultations between state and central officials and planners, but in particular also through the National Development Council, consisting of the Chief Ministers of all the states, which has the right to scrutinize the central plan and make changes in it. Here too, the Prime Minister of the central government of India acts as the chairman.

The central plan has to be approved by the national parliament in New Delhi, before it can be implemented by the central and state governments. The state-level plans have to be approved by both the state legislatures and the central parliament. Thus, the central national parliament sitting in New Delhi is the final authority whose approval of the plan is mandatory. But that is only a formal facade. The real decisions about how to allocate resources and which parts of the plans to implement are made by a relatively small group of people in control of the coalition of the political, social, and economic interests outlined earlier.

The central planning commission was relatively autonomous and influential during the Nehru era (1950-1964). Its rapid decline began with the assumption of supreme political power by Indira Gandhi. Today it is no more than a service department of the central government, drafting plans to order by the powers that be. And the national parliament, with its huge Rajiv Gandhi Congress Party majority, has been reduced to a rubber-stamp body.

While it is the task of the five-year plan to propose the allocation of financial resources to meet development targets in the state-owned sector and recommend and forecast corresponding investments in the private sector, it is the responsibility of the annual central-government budget to find those resources. The expenditure part of the annual budget thus has two sides: the yearly development spending that the plan requires, the so-called plan outlay, and the yearly non-developmental spending for the day-to-day running of the state and the general economy and society, the so-called non-plan outlay. The budget announces how much revenue in domestic and foreign convertible currencies the central government expects to take in during a year, how this money will be divided into plan and non-plan outlays, and how the deficit between expected revenue and intended expenditure will be financed.

The budget determines what taxes will be levied on whom, how much and from whom the government will borrow, and how much more money will be printed. Like the plan, the budget too has to be approved by parliament. While the plan is a shopping-list of desirable and desired "goodies,' it is the annual budget that really determines which ones will in fact be bought. It is the budget that makes sure that the political and economic interests of the ruling coalition are taken care of. Like state-level plans, the state governments also have their own annual budgets, but there are subservient to the all-powerful central government budget. For the first time in 35 years of planning, public-sector gross investment will be lower than private sector gross investment. On comparing the fifth, sixth, and seventh Plans, one sees that this declining public investment will continue the trend of the last ten years of reducing the share of public investment in industry and increasing it in the energy, transport, and communications sectors. The private sector is thus clearly expected and invited to take the leading role in the industrial sector, which the state is now preparing to relinquish.

However, the seventh FYP is reassuring the private sector that the state will not only continue its traditional role as a supplier of cheap energy and infrastructural services, but will also improve those services in quantity and quality. The single largest allocation (30.4 per cent) of the Plan goes to energy; and almost all of this to modern forms— electric power (19 per cent), petroleum (7 per cent), coal (4 per cent)—used by modern industry, modern transport, and upper—and middle-class households; for the "other' forms of energy, which are presumably meant for the bulk of the population living in the rural areas, there is only 0.3 per cent.

The allocation for "rural development' is 5 per cent. Its purpose is, among other things, reduction of poverty and unemployment in the rural areas, through such programmes as the "Integrated Rural Development Programme (IRDP),' The "Rural Landless Employment Guarantee Programme (RLEGP),' etc. It is marginally less than the 5.5 per cent allocated in the sixth Plan. Considering that 40 per cent of the population is below the "poverty line,' the allocation of an insignificant 5 per cent of the Plan outlay towards their welfare expresses eloquently the very low priority, even in theory let alone in practice, that the state assigns to the poor.

And this impression is strengthened if one takes account of the miniscule 1.5 per cent allocated to "village and small scale industries,' a category which is supposed to absorb a substantial part of the massive numbers of the unemployed and underemployed in the rural areas. Although the transition from the second to the third period is not sudden, and the characteristics that define the third period have been maturing in the womb of the second, still the departures are radical enough to signal the start of another era.

They are:

- Aceleration of the entry of private capital into the public-sector domain, in particular the industrial sector;
- Rtreat of the state from the "commanding heights' of the economy;
- Te fiscal crisis of the state brought about by the contradictions of a "mixed' economy and the contradictions within the dominant coalition;
- Icreasing dependence of the state on internal and external borrowings and the replacement of the strategy of "self-reliant-import-substitution' by the strategy of "luxury-consumption-led-growth' in the industrial sector.1

The real absolute value of public-sector investment in industry in the seventh Plan is less than in the sixth Plan. For the first time in 25 years of planning, there will be no new public-sector projects in industry; the 197 billion rupees (about $16 billion at the 1986 exchange rate) allocated in the seventh Plan is barely enough to service the ongoing public-sector industries whose aging equipment needs modernizing.

The central government budgets of 1985/86 and 1986/87 amply confirm the above patterns and trends.2 The 1985/86 budget caused a great stir and was rapturously welcomed by the private sector and the upper and middle classes for making the following proposals:

- Substantial cuts in individual and corporate income tax.
- Abolition of capital gains tax, wealth tax, and death duties on inherited estates.
- Imports of capital goods and project packages (*i.e.*, embodied and disembodied technologies) are to be further liberalized by adding 200 additional items from the capital-goods sector to the Open General License list.
- The entry of private capital into some industrial sectors formerly reserved for the public sector is to be allowed, such as in the electronics and telecommunication equipment fields.
- Industrial branches formerly barred to foreign capital are to be opened up for foreign investment, even on a foreign-majority share-ownership basis.
- "Whitewashing' of "black' money (*i.e.*, tax-evasion money) by allowing it to resurface into the visible economy without fear of penal action, as long as tax is paid on the resurfaced money at the new low rates ("black' money is variously estimated to equal between 30 and 50 per cent of the total annual GDP3).

Cuts in personal income and corporate taxes and attractive terms offered to both domestic and foreign private investors are meant to liven up the demand for and supply of luxury consumer durables (automobiles, consumer electronics, household electrical appliances, etc.), in the hope that the industrial sector will again show high growth rates.

The cuts in direct income tax are of no benefit to the poor 80 per cent of the population who pay no income tax. But the poor do pay indirect taxes on the purchases of food and a few other essential commodities which absorb 75 to 85 per cent of their income. Indirect taxes are the source of the great bulk (80 per cent) of the country's tax revenue, and they have been increasing. Between 1975-76 and 1984-85 when direct taxes as a proportion of GDP decreased, indirect taxes increased from 11.7 to 14.0 per cent. Thus, the poor will, as usual, pay for the increased luxury consumption of the middle and upper classes, and the increased profits of the private corporate sector.

The 1986/87 budget did not generate the same euphoria among the private sector and the upper and middle classes, who were highly disappointed that there were no further tax cuts, indirect allowances, or hidden subsidies. Rather, the private sector was worried by the fact that the finance minister was backtracking to a certain extent on the liberalization of imports; this partial retreat was due to the fact that within one year imports had jumped by 20 per cent without any noticeable increase in exports, punching a sizable hole in the foreign-exchange reserves. In other respects, however, the 1986/87 budget continued the main trends initiated by the 1985/86 budget.

A deepening fiscal crisis of the state and increased deficits necessitating borrowing from internal and external sources are the hallmarks of the beginning of the third period. They are intimately linked to one another, and they will profoundly affect the economy and society of India in the coming years.

Let us begin by stressing that by the mid-1980s, the Indian economy was showing the following striking features:

- Icreases in wheat and rice production and the piling up of huge public food stocks had continued steadily for a number of years.
- Bth the industrial sector and the economy in general had settled down to a respectable growth rate of about 5 per cent per annum.
- Te gross domestic savings were very high relative to GDP (22 per cent).
- Freign exchange reserves continued at the $6-billion level.
- Te untaxed money ("black' money) circulating in the non-agricultural sector alone was between a third and a half of GDP.

Therefore, there in no resource crisis now, nor is one looming on the horizon as far the general economy is concerned. However, there happens to be a crisis in the resources available to the state for investing in the public sector. As the seventh Plan Document freely admits, there is a serious resource crunch in the public sector, *i.e.*, there is a fiscal crisis of the state. The reasons for the paradox of the above-mentioned apparent "strengths' in the economy co-existing with a fiscal crisis are not hard to locate.

The non-developmental expenditure of the state has been rapidly increasing such as on defence (17 per cent); on interest payments on borrowings (17 per cent); on subsidies (9 per cent); to farmers, private industrialists, and urban consumers; on public administration (9 per cent); and on inflated prices of goods and services bought by the state. The revenues of the state have not kept pace with these accelerating expenditures.

No direct taxes are being collected from the farmers, *i.e.*, the biggest productive sector in the economy is not taxed. Further, the minute proportion of the population which is obliged to pay direct tax (most of them being in the middle- and high-income brackets of urban wage-workers and salaried employees) has had that tax reduced. A variety of direct taxes (on profits, capital accumulation, etc.) paid by private enterprises have also been cut. And the public-sector enterprises are suffering heavy losses.

The middle- and upper-class households, constituting less than 20 per cent of the total population, contribute an overwhelmingly large proportion to the total gross domestic savings in the visible economy; their share of savings has remained roughly constant at between 70 and 75 per cent from 1950 to 1985. The public sector's contribution to savings has also remained steady at about 17 to 18 per cent during the same period. But the share of the private corporate sector has declined from 9 to 7.7 per cent.

During the period 1980-85 the annual average revenue deficit was 9.1 per cent of expenditure. It nearly doubled to 17.7 per cent in 1985-86 and to 18.7 per cent in 1986-87. There is no new factor in the economy that can realistically be expected to increase the average annual growth rate of exports from the meagre 4 per cent of 1984/85. In fact, the U.S. dollar value of exports fell in 1985/86 as compared to 1984/85. The so-called "export-oriented-growth-strategy' of the Indian official policy pronouncements is mere wishful thinking, not least because of the import-protectionist measures of the developed countries of the West. The current levels of export subsidies have not induced the expected dynamism among India's exporters, and there is no way the Indian state can increase these subsidies to much more substantial levels, given its fiscal crisis. The public sector has been the locomotive that has pulled along the Indian economy over the last three decades. The ongoing and proposed new reductions in public-sector investment will slow down that locomotive. The private sector is incapable of providing the extra pull expected of it, at least in the short and medium term. Although the growth rate may go up a few percentage points in the next few years due to increased luxury consumption of the middle and upper classes, it will register a downward trend in the medium and long term if the present reductions in public-sector investment continue.

The proximate cause for this reduction is the fiscal crisis of the state, which in turn will become worse as the economy slows down, starting a downward vicious spiral. The fundamental underlying cause is not the fiscal crisis of the state as such but the refusal by the state to extract the required surplus from the resource-rich sectors of society, which also happen to be partners in the ruling coalition of dominant classes.This refusal is the real explanation for the apparent paradox of the coexistence of a very high rate of domestic savings with slow rates of growth in the economy. The state borrows heavily from, and pays high interest to, the household-sector savers, in order mainly to finance its non-developmental, non-productive branches, *e.g.*, defence spending and interest payments which together make up as much as 80 per cent of the total tax revenue, or one third of total budget expenditure!

ECONOMIC PLANNING IN INDIA

The non-economic aspects of India's economic development in the recent past and the future. Since independence was attained in 1947 India has made significant economic progress. A three-year moving average of the national income over the last decade shows that the real national income has increased at an average annual rate of about 3 per cent. Productive capacity in the Indian economy has increased through increasing investment and the rate of economic performance has been quickened. There is little doubt that the Indian economy is moving away from dead centre and cannot be characterized as "stagnant," a term which could have been applied to it with some justification during the earlier decades.

It is, however, clear that this rate of growth is small relative to the rate of population increase, which has been estimated to be 1.5 per cent per annum. The rate of increase of per capita income, therefore, comes to 1.5 per cent per annum. If the rate of increase of population accelerates in the future, as some experts forecast on very good grounds, the present rate of increase of national income will be found to be completely inadequate and India will have to run faster and faster even to keep herself at the same level of per capita income.

Could India have done better than she has during this period? If so, why did she not? And if we know why, can she be made to perform better in the future and by what means? These are big questions, and no student of Indian problems can be expected to have all the correct answers. We are here trying to indicate in a tentative way some of the answers to these questions.

There is considerable evidence, both official and non-official, from Indian and foreign observers, to indicate that the development effort in India during the last decade has been characterized by much inefficiency and waste; that the available economic resources have not been as productively used under the given conditions as they could have been. And when one begins to consider and analyse this, he soon comes up with the fact that the causes lie deep in the whole Indian cultural and social setup and that it involves the whole problem of the social efficiency of the Indian society. But this is to anticipate. Let me first substantiate the opening gambit that the Indian development effort during the fifties was inefficient.

Perhaps we can begin by noting the observations of the latest Indian delegation to China, which visited that country early in 1959 to study the Chinese achievements in the conservation and maximum utilization of water, including rain water. What the delegation found most impressive, it is reported, was the type of organization employed for achieving the remarkable results in this field rather than the use of any new techniques which were being used in China and which were not known or used in India.

This is an important observation because in India' irrigation is not a new problem, and a failure in this respect cannot be explained away by pleading lack of know-how or inexperience. Yet the failure in this field is glaring and extensive. At the end of the First Five Year Plan the irrigation potential created by major irrigation works was 559,000 acres in Bihar and 465,000 acres in West

Bengal, of which only 265,000 and 223,000 acres respectively were actually irrigated, thus leaving about half of the potential unutilized. In many of the irrigated areas water is available for more than one crop per year. Yet a recent survey showed that only about 12 per cent of the land under irrigation has more than one irrigated crop per year.

This failure of organizational effort is by no means unique or solitary. Many others can be easily met with in India today. Take the programme of Community Development Projects launched in 1952 with the express purpose "to set free the creative energies of the people so that they may build up through their own effort and through their own institutions a richer and improving social life." The recent appraisals, both official and non-official, of the achievements of this programme have indicated that this objective has not been reached; that there has been more concentration on welfare aspects than on productivity aspects; that the programme has settled down to a dead administrative routine so as to smother the growth of local leadership and initiative. It is again very largely an organizational failure.

This list of failures need not be added to except to note that the same kind of failure is evident, in more or less degree, in regard to land reforms, population control, education, social legislation, etc. The failures are too widespread and blatant to be explained away by such factors as inexperience or expediency. We should try to probe deeper, if we can.

An interesting aspect of the situation is that there is consciousness in the country regarding these failures. In the examples here given the appraisals and observations of responsible Indians have been principally cited. Many Indian leaders have drawn attention to them from time to time, have deplored them, and have emphasized the need for their speedy removal. If one mentions these failures in India today, there would be no reluctance to admit them. There would also be almost unanimous agreement regarding the desirability of removing their causes. But this candor will not be in evidence as soon as one goes on to discuss the reasons underlying them. A common view would be that these defects and failures are not abiding but passing and that they require only like remedies. A variation of the argument would be to take a historical view and attribute them to the long period of foreign rule in India. Self-rule, given time, will almost automatically cure them. No wonder there is complete apathy or reluctance to undertake a deeper appraisal of the situation.

The causes of the present *malaise* in Indian society lie deeper and cannot be explained by the superficial arguments. Our reflections on this theme were sparked a few years ago when we began to assess the success of economic planning in independent India. We have since been struck again and again by the repetition of similar mistakes in government policy with similar consequences. The failure to learn from experience was everywhere patent in the economic sphere. For some time we attributed this to the political element that dominates everything in India today. Politicians are notoriously shortsighted, and we thought that this was the main reason for repeated failures in the economic sphere. But later we realised that the same kind of failure was also evident in the political sphere in India, and in many other spheres also. We was forced to the cease that the causes were more pervading and deeply embedded in the whole society than we had suspected.

An analysis of these causes, however, is not easy. First,our own limitations as a social scientist are overwhelming. Secondly, it involves introspection, a difficult art to practice anywhere. Being a part of the Indian society and having been born and brought up in it, we are not sure of our ability to look at it from outside from a critical angle. we decided, however, to make the effort, perhaps in a foolhardy way, because we thought somebody must begin to do this sometime, and if we are wrong at least it would provoke abler minds to attempt the task sadly neglected so far. We have to examine for this purpose the social efficiency of the Indian society as a whole in relation to economic and social development. *But as Davis observes*: in the matter of societal efficiency we have a concept but little else. In practice it is hedged about by the preconceptions and institutions of a going society; in social science it is handicapped by the unreality of ignoring these practical limitations and by the lack of an adequate set of measuring devices. The concept says: Given a certain quantum of natural resources and human population, there exist numerous ways of bringing the two together for the production of goods and services, some of these ways being more effective than others. But it does not tell us how to measure effectiveness with respect to the non-economic parts of the social system. We can make use of such makeshift indices as exist, but in the last analysis we are thrown back on speculation and general theory.

Davis goes on to warn: "Depending on verbal description and intuitive judgement, one tends to see causal relationships *in principle* and then to assume erroneously that they exist in fact. The case of India is particularly difficult because of the country's extreme cultural diversity." The analysis that we are attempting here is of course subject to all these limitations and should be understood as such.

One must, we think, begin by analyzing the basic ways and *mores* of the traditional Indian or Hindu society, note the changes that have taken place in them in modern times under British rule, and then try to see if these in principle and in fact give some clues to the analysis of the complex problem.

Max Weber's analysis of the sociology of Hinduism is perhaps the best point of departure for this purpose from many points of view. Weber found that in religion, cultural values, personality, motivation, and social structure come together, and he discussed Hinduism from that point of view. In summarizing his analysis, we quote the able summary given by Dr. Bellah: Weber finds the notion of *dharma*, religiously prescribed obligation, to be the core of Hinduism, especially in its deep inner connection with the idea of *karma*, the endless chain of causation working itself out in successive rebirths. The orthodox view is that whatever position one finds oneself in, in this life and one's obligation is to fulfill the *dharma* of one's position so that one will improve one's chances in the next incarnation. The intellectuals, revolting against this notion, always sought escape from the wheel of rebirth through some sort of individualistic salvation. Weber shows how these conceptions hindered cultural rationalisation beyond a certain point.

On the one hand they contributed to the development of special technologies appropriate to the *dharma* of each profession — from construction technique to logic as the technology of proof and disproof to the technology of eroticism — but at the same time they hindered the development of levels of generalisation above the technological because of the fragmentation involved in the notion of occupational *dharma*. On the other hand, the intellectuals were so completely preoccupied with the problem of salvation that all philosophy was made subservient to this end. With respect to the social structure, it is the *dharma* concept as integrated with the idea of caste, which is the key to the situation.

In spite of the remarkable achievements of certain castes, there is always a limit imposed by the traditionalistic definition of the caste *dharma* itself. Further, the division of society into innumerable watertight compartments, while engendering a very stable integration of sorts allows a minimum of flexibility and especially limits the generalisation of political power making the society an easy prey to foreign conquest. The major religious movements which reject this mode of social organisation either fall back into it in the form of a new caste, or, as in the case of Buddhism, remain an individualistic and socially negative group existing symbolically in relation to traditional society and unable to generate any really different mode of social organization.

In terms of personality, the *dharma* idea results in the fragmentation of response directed to the external demands of ritual obligation on the one hand, or a passive withdrawal into mysticism on the other. There is no basis of inner unification of personality for action in response to the command of a transcendental God. The Indian alternatives tend to be action without unification and unification without action. Theoretically, nobody would disagree that this kind of socioreligious framework is not very suitable to modern economic development. But many have denied its relevance to the day-to-day life of the people as actually lived in India in the past and the present. Some have stressed the tradition of practical values in India which, it is said, is evident throughout her history. Others have insisted there exists an ethic in Indian life which can "sanction" the materialistic values of an industrial society.

Whether the main beliefs and ideals embodied in Hinduism shape and influence the actual *mores* of Hindu society today is a question that can be answered on the basis of such reliable and well- tested information as may be available on this point. So far as we know, the available information is not very ample; nevertheless what is available is, in our opinion, significant.

O'Malley has discussed such information in his *Popular Hinduism, the Religion of the Masses*. He cites the work of Miriam Young, in 1931 in the Punjab, who after a three-year study concluded that *karma* was a practical philosophy colouring the villager's whole outlook on life. He also refers to Crooke's study in the same region in 1897, which takes an opposite stand. O'Malley also refers to several enquiries bearing on this carried out in different regions in India at the 1891 and 1901 censuses. He refers to these discussions and to his own extensive experiences in India and arrives at the following, we think, balanced judgement:

Materialistic, however, as the villagers may be in their relations to the outside world and in the conduct of their everyday life, there can be no question that their general trend of thought is strongly devotional and that religion is deeply ingrained in thought and feeling and is a very real thing to them. One impelling force is undoubtedly the desire to accumulate merit in the expectation of a higher or better life in the next existence, and of eventually obtaining release from the burden of individual existence, though it is doubtful how far the attainment of such a distant goal as the latter is actually a motive idea among the masses.... Another factor is the absence of a nationalistic spirit and lack of scientific knowledge. Two recent studies using modern anthropological and psychoanalytical methods broadly confirm the importance and influence of the Hindu belief systems in the day-to-day life of the people.

These recent studies focus on the cumulative effect of attitudes towards each other, towards the social order, and towards the supernatural on the formation of adult personality. W. S. Taylor, who worked and lived in Madhya Pradesh, concluded that Orthodox Hinduism is able to create a basic personality pattern in which personal initiative is replaced by the sense of conformity, in which responsibility is exercised without personal authority, in which security is associated with the sense of dependence and self-respect with a sense of helplessness, and in which opportunities for frustration and acute anxiety are minimized. It is a basic personality whose integration and stability are primarily a function of the cultural system to which it belongs and are not organized around any system of personal choices.

G. Morris Carstairs, who intensively studied a village in Rajastan, confirmed generally Taylor's findings and tried to take the analysis further in psychoanalytic terms. These two recent studies in fact go deeper than the two cited before, because they delve into the personality formation process which governs the conduct of individuals throughout life, and both of them show the great influence of the basic values embodied in Hindu culture. They also show how the institutions of joint family and caste play a dominant role in this set up. We submit that an analysis accepting this, at least as a hypothesis, is likely to be more fruitful than one which loses itself either in arguing away its significance or rejecting it altogether. We proceed by accepting the hypothesis that the institutional structure and functioning of Hindu society was and continues to be inimical to the development of a community. This together with its *mores* gives rise to a widely common personality pattern devoid of personal initiative, purposefulness, involvement, etc. To attribute all the evils resulting in social inefficiency in India today to British rule is surely to ignore realities. The basic framework of Hindu society was complete and in full operation before the British and also before the Mohammedan conquest of India.

The lack of social and political cohesion in the Indian society made it, as Weber notes, an easy prey to foreign conquest. So far as the basic attitudes, personality patterns, motivations, etc. are concerned, they were independent of the British and the Mohammedan rulers. It is, of course, true that they were influenced by foreign rule. So far as the Mohammedan rule is concerned, the Mohammedans seemed to have been themselves influenced by Hindu social institutions, as witness the development of castes among Mohammedans in India. So far as British rule is concerned, it is possible to note more specifically what it did to Hindu society.

This is neither the occasion nor the place to dilate at length on the whole theme of British impact on India. We shall confine myself here to the influence of British rule on the caste structure, the pivotal structural parameter of the Hindu social system. Under the British many things happened to weaken as well as to strengthen the caste system but on balance the latter outweighed the former. The British, in contradistinction to their predecessors, progressively refused to perform certain social functions, perhaps the most important of which were those connected with the regulation of a caste society involving the functioning and relative status of castes.

The pre-British rulers, including the Muslims, by performing these functions helped maintain, even in a caste society, a degree of social integration. Thereby the process of continuous adjustment and wider integration was always at work. This process of over-all social regulation and integration could no longer be maintained when the British refused to perform these functions; as a result the social structure lost its adaptability and integration. In the preBritish days caste loyalty was tempered by the sense of loyalty to the Hindu society as a whole which was maintained by the secular authority. The loyalty to one's own caste increased under the British as occasions and opportunities for emphasizing or exhibiting the over-all sense of Hindu loyalties decreased. It is in this manner that the institution of caste became more rigid than before in the period of British rule.

Under the British also economic and social dividing lines in society became parallel, which they were not before. J. S. Furnivall has observed that the impact of the West on India has been less violent than, for instance, on Burma, because of the caste system in India which afforded considerable protection to the social system in India. It is true that it prevented social disintegration, so characteristic of other societies, but it also left the Indian society loose and weak and hampered its transformation into a modern social and industrial community.

British rule also brought to India new ideas from the West -bureaucracy, the judiciary, and an effective system of laws. It also gave rise to nationalism. As suggested, try to assess their effects, briefly in the reverse order. The development of nationalism in India was sparked by British rule and, though it began as a movement allied with social reformism, it gradually lost this aspect and became more and more a purely political movement. Only the negative aspects of nationalism developed in India, *i.e.*, its aim were the negative one of driving away the foreign ruler, but the positive aspects of nationalism did not appear. In 1947 India acquired nationhood but has not been able to develop as yet sufficient unity and emotional integration for the effective functioning of a modern society.

The judiciary and the law system developed by the British brought about far-reaching changes in the concepts of private property. Together with the bureaucracy, they smothered village self-rule and helped to bring about a malfunctioning of the social system. The bureaucracy developed by the British effectively killed whatever little self-rule there was and furthered the demise of most vestiges of initiative. Perhaps the bureaucracy as an impersonal machine, with its impersonal character, its hierarchical order, its prescriptions of definite action in definite contexts, etc., was well suited to the general social structure of caste society. We suspect that this is one of the reasons the bureaucracy developed so well in India as compared to other underdeveloped countries and still continues to flourish. It finds a social background that is very favourable to the growth of its formal structure, though not necessarily to its working efficiency.

With British rule came English education, and this opened up the whole world of Western knowledge to educated Indians. This knowledge was and has been absorbed more at the theoretical than at the practical level. The intellectual tradition in India, which is mainly the Brahmin tradition, has that characteristic. It is singularly free from restrictions or inhibitions regarding intellectual speculation. In India there has rarely been a persecution for holding certain opinions, even heretical opinions.

This was partly because, though intellectual speculation was free, the translation of any new ideas into practice was hidebound by the prevailing ethics and modes of behaviour. The Brahmins themselves had laid down the rule that though many things might be rationally obvious and good, they should not be brought into practice if they were not in tune with the traditional behaviour pattern and against popular folkways. Such a tradition would naturally be much more ready to absorb ideas on the philosophical plane than in actual life. Today, therefore, the intellectual climate in India appears to be much more pronouncedly Western than in Japan or China.

Taking everything into account, it would be fair to say that British rule did introduce some bad kinks into the old social structure and its functioning, but it cannot be held responsible for all the evils. It would be perhaps better to say that the Indian social structure responded to the British impact in a way in which some of the bad characteristics were scored deeper while some of the good characteristics could not develop much further than they perhaps would have done in the absence of British rule. But the basic cultural and institutional patterns have very largely remained unchanged. As a result, in India today we find in the people a widespread lack of personal initiative, involvement, and purposefulness in life, a tendency towards empty ritual, general apathy, casteism, communalism, indifference, and absence of a feeling of participation in national endeavor. This has often been noted and deplored by Indians themselves with reference to the two plans of economic development undertaken by the Government of India in recent years. It represents a position of confusion and social ambivalence not conducive to social or economic efficiency.

A critical and historical examination of the Hindu social organization brings out the fact that Hinduism is not a religion in the Western sense of the word. It is really a social system, a method of organizing society. In its earlier stages it proved a powerful instrument of absorbing diverse kinds of peoples and tribes into the Hindu fold without disturbing their individual rituals and practices. It is conceivable that if this process had gone on, perhaps caste rigidity would not have developed and the social and occupational mobility would have been maintained so as to weld all the Hindu people into an integrated community.

This grand process, however, did not go on but stagnated. The Hindu society today is an unfinished social experiment that has rigidified the social institutions into a mold. In understanding this it is necessary to realise that the doctrines of *karma, dharma*, etc. in their philosophic context would not have mattered much had they not had in Hindu society their social institutional counterparts in terms of the caste system and the joint family. Weber has referred to the developments in China and Japan, where this did not happen to the same extent as in India.

As a matter of historical fact, the growth and development of nationalism should have accomplished many of the things that are needed for the rejuvenation of Hindu society. But the growth of nationalism in India has not done this. The Hindu social institutions have subdivided the social organism in such a way as to make the units (caste and family) smaller and smaller and unrelated to the general society. *"Thus it denies the entire theory of community and bases the organization of Hindu life on the opposite principle of disintegration and division."* Nationalism in India has not been able to reverse this process. In fact, it bent the nationalist movement in its own direction rather than the other way round. Nationalism struck flame on foreign rule. The first generation of the English educated Indians was completely bowled over by Western culture as brought to India by the British.

The effective suppression of the Mutiny in 1858 impressed on them the superiority of the British. Fired by the ideas imbibed through English literature they came to the view that the old Indian ways had to be remodelled on Western lines. They came to regard British connexion with India as a providential dispensation for the good of India. They visualized political and social development to go hand in hand and believed that social reform was of basic importance even for political advancement. The Brâhma Samâj in Bengal and the Prârthana Samâj in Bombay (founded in 1865) which bore the stamp of Christian ideas were manifestations of this tendency in the social and religious field. The Indian National Congress was founded in 1885.

The next generation that came of age around the 1880's developed a more virile strain of nationalism. It was backward-looking and appealed to India's past glory. The ideology of resurgent Hinduism as put forth by Vivekananda, provided the social and religious basis for this school of nationalists. While acknowledging the benefits of British rule, this school refused to recognise it as a providential dispensation. It further maintained that these benefits will be nullified if they were not followed by home rule which was their logical culmination. The demand for self rule cannot be satisfied by good rule by a foreign bureaucracy. Political advancement was primary to all social reform. The latter will automatically follow political independence and therefore the national movement must not dissipate its strength in fighting for social reform but must concentrate on the struggle for liberation from the British yoke. For that, all means, whether constitutional or otherwise, should be used. This stand was more nationalistic than that of their predecessors. If the first generation suffered from an inferiority complex with regard to the West this generation was overcompensating for it. The neglect of social reform further underlined their backward looking orientation and made them line up with socially reactionary elements. It inevitably took a Hindu colour and ensured in time the development of a separate Muslim nationalism as a reaction. The Muslim League was founded in 1906. The more direct type of action in the struggle for independence assumed the form of the Swadeshi movement, which included the use of Indian goods and the boycott of British and foreign goods. This suited the newly rising class of industrialists and brought them into the fold of the national movement.

Gandhian orientation of the nationalist movement in the 'twenties of this century was pronouncedly Hindu, anti-intellectual and more backward-looking than that of the generation that had gone before. It condemned Western science and technique and advocated revival of cottage industries, village uplift, etc. It gave to some of the religious terms of Hinduism, like *satyâgraha*, *ahiEsa*, *cwaraj*, etc., a political meaning, and political doctrines were clothed in spiritual terms. Its intellectual content was very much inferior but its emotional appeal was great as was evidenced by the various mass movements that were conducted under the leadership of the Indian National Congress in the period after 1914. It can perhaps be said that without a watering down of the severe intellectualism of the earlier movement, it could not have appealed to the masses. It also became progressively more political, and its already declining social content gradually dwindled into insignificance. It only came to the surface when political exigencies required it, as for example, in the case of the untouchables in the 1930's.

Nationalism in India has been oriented much more towards the negative goal of ending foreign rule and much less towards evolving the positive content of what was to be done after achieving that goal. This we have called the lack of positive aspects of nationalism. The social content of positive nationalism therefore remains to be developed in India, and that is the task facing the present national leadership. The immensity of the task of bringing about the necessary extent of social change in India can be gauged from the fact that it is nothing short of the whole problem of the remaking of a nation. History affords examples of such problems being solved by violent as well as peaceful methods, and perhaps the examples of the former kind are more numerous than those of the latter kind.

India has chosen the latter and, perhaps, the harder path of change, but possibly has not yet appreciated the wide ramifications of the problems and the all-sided and clear-sighted effort that is necessary for accomplishing the difficult task. Attention and effort have been focused primarily on economic development and change. The other fields have not received as much attention.

ECONOMICPOLICIES OF THE INDIAN STATE

Under the slogans and fanfares of "rapid economic growth,' "efficiency,' "modernazation,' and "export promotion,' the Indian state in collaboration with big Indian private capital, has launched its latest policies and strategies in a stream of specialist committee reports and policy documents, followed by the seventh Plan and the two budgets of 1985/86 and 1986/87. The state promised to lead India into the computerized-paradise of the twenty-first century on the tidal wave generated by this new economic strategy. We would like to offer a different interpretation of the aims and actions of the Indian state and Indian capital. Let us that Indian industry suffered a serious recession from 1965 to 1973, from which it recovered briefly during the fifth Plan period 1974-79, only to slide back again to slow growth rates during the sixth Plan period 1980-85.

The relative stagnation of Indian industry and large parts of the Indian economy over the last two decades, in comparison with, the rapid growth and dynamism of the East Asian industrialized economies, can be aptly summed up in the phrase "low-level equilibrium trap.' The proximate cause of the inability to get out of this trap is the fiscal crisis of the state, but the underlying explanation lies in the contradictions within the dominant coalition of the ruling classes. Deficit financing and increased indirect taxation are two of the main sources of financing the seventh Plan (1985-90).

The burdens of both of these are carried almost exclusively by the poor majority (80 per cent of the population) through price-inflation of their essential consumption goods and services. The state is using the bulk of the economic surplus squeezed out of the poor through indirect taxation and inflation, as well as its huge internal borrowings from the savings of the middle and upper classes, to finance its non-developmental and non-productive expenditure. So it has to cut back on productive investment in the public sector, which of course perpetuates the industrial and infrastructural crisis, leading to a vicious cycle of stagnant incomes and markets.

Since the state cannot break out of this crisis without mortally endangering its social support base in the dominant coalition, it sees its choice as necessarily restricted to two strategies:

- Luxury consumption-led growth,
- Export-led growth.

The first requires inducements on the supply side to private industry to produce more of the latest East Asian brands of consumer durables, and on the demand side to upper-middle and upper classes by freeing more of their incomes for purchases through cuts in direct taxes.

And Indian industrialists, even the biggest among them, will not take the road of export growth unless they are molly-coddled by the state through export subsidies, credits, and guarantees. Moreover it is essential for both strategies that a reliable and adequate supply of electricity, petroleum, and coal be available at subsidized prices as prime movers in industry, transport, and upper-income households (what good is an air conditioner or a refrigerator or a car, if electricity is cut most of the day and petrol consumes a quarter of the take-home pay?).

This is the context for lavishing 30 per cent of the seventh Plan's total outlay on the energy sector, the largest allocation to any one sector, almost all of it earmarked for modern forms of energy like electricity, petroleum, and coal, and almost nothing for traditional fuels used by the poor. Further, both strategies depend on the import of advanced technologies to produce and market the latest type of consumer durables, which only the transnational corporations can provide. The recently adopted industrial and technological policies make perfect sense against this background.

We know that the domestic costs of this ruling-class extravaganza will be borne by the poor in India. But, pray, who will bear the foreign exchange cost? That is nicely taken care of by foreign debt. India is highly creditworthy at present, with "only' $22 billion of foreign debt. The commercial banks, the official agencies, the World Bank, and the IMF are pressing India to go in for more. On present calculations, India's foreign debt will double by 1990 to $46 billion. Foreign creditors will be happy as long as India regularly services its debts, which after all today absorb "only' about 18 per cent of export income.

India's ruling coalition has launched the country on a journey which, unless cut short through internal political, economic, and social processes, will soon take India into the exclusive club of the largest debtors of the third would which now claims Argentina, Brazil, and Mexico as its leading members. The "laundering' of foreign loans and "aid' through India back to safe and lucrative repositories in the West and East Asia—so-called net capital flight—seems to be accelerating: it is estimated at $10 billion for the period 1976-85(5). The "Latin Americanization' of India may well be on its way in more senses than one.

Bibliography

Ashok Kumar Sahu: *Information Management in New Millennium : Opportunities and Challenges for Library Professionals*, Ess Ess Publication, Delhi, 2008.

B.A. Prakash and V.R. Prabhakaran Nair: *Kerala's Development Issues in the New Millennium*, Serials Publication, Delhi, 2008.

B.P. Mahesh Chandra Guru: *Grassroots Development Communication*, Sarup & Sons. Publication, Delhi, 2011.

B.S. Yadav, Anand Singh and F.A. Ahmad: *New Economic Policies and Employment Opportunities in India*, Shree Publication, Delhi, 2012.

Bipan Chandra: *The Rise and Growth of Economic Nationalism in India : Economic Policies of Indian National Leadership, 1880-1905*, Har-Anand Publication, Delhi, 2010.

C. Jayaraj and R.K. Dixit: *International Law in New Millennium*, Manak Publication, Delhi, 2006.

C.M. Chaudhary: *India's Economic Policies*, Sublime Publication, Delhi, 2008.

Debabrata Das Gupta, Sarthak Chowdhury and Siddhartha Dev Mukhopadhyay: *Development Communication in Rural Sector*, Abhijeet Publication, Delhi, 2007.

J.V. Vilanilam: *Development Communication in Practice : India and the Millennium Development Goals*, Sage Publication, Delhi, 2009.

James Boyce and Madalene O. Donnel: *Peace and the Public Purse : Economic Policies for Postwar State Building*, Viva Books, Delhi, 2008.

K. Madhusudan: *Traditional Media and Development Communication*, Kanishka Publication, Delhi, 2006.

K.R. Gupta and Manoranjan Sharma: *Indian Economic Policies and Data*, Atlantic Publication, Delhi, 2010.

Krishan Sondhi: *Development Communication and Information Economics in the New Millennium*, B R Publication, Delhi, 2003.

M Maharajan: *Mahatma Gandhi and the New Millennium*, Discovery Publication, Delhi, 2001.

Madhurendra K Varma: *Nurturing Change Through Your Human Assets : Optimising Organisational Challenges in the New Millennium*, Response Books, Delhi, 2000.

Manoj Kumar Singh: *Mass Communication And Journalism : In New Millennium*, Saad Publications, Delhi, 2009.

Mridula Menon: *Development Communication and Media Debate*, Kanishka Publication, Delhi, 2004.

R.B. Jain and Anuj Jain: *Induced Development to Good Governance : Paradigm Shift in the Concept of Development Administration in the New Millennium*, Deep and Deep Publication, Delhi, 2011.

R.K. Panchal: *New Millennium and the Social Change*, Sumit Enterprises, Delhi, 2006.

Raj Kapila and Uma Kapila: *India's Banking and Financial Sector in the New Millennium (With 2 Compact Disks and Computer Disk) 2 Vols-Set*, Academic Foundation, Delhi, 2001.

Ramjee Singh: *Jainism in the New Millennium*, Commonwealth Publication, Delhi, 2010.

Subhesh Chand Sharma and Sweta Bakshi: *Development Communication and Journalism*, A.K. Publications, Delhi, 2009.

Suraj Singh: *Journalism in the New Millennium*, Centrum Press, Delhi, 2010.

Surjit S. Bhalla: *New Economic Policies for a New India*, Har-Anand for Indian Coun..., 2000.

Uma Narula: *Development Communication: Theory and Practice* , Har-anand Publications, Delhi, 2010.

V. Bijukumar: *Reinventing the Congress : Economic Policies and Strategies Since 1991*, Rawat Publication, Delhi, 2006.

V.K. Dubey, K.N. Pandey and Rajshekhar Pandey: *Development Communication : Applied to Journalism and Mass Communication, Extension Education and Communication, Rural Development and Management Studies*, International Book Distributors, Delhi, 2009.

V.S. Vyas: *India's Agrarian Structure, Economic Policies and Sustainable Development : Variations on a Theme*, Academic Foundation, Delhi, 2003.

Vaidehi Shriram Daptardar: *India: Economic Policies and Performance: 1947-48 to 2015-16*, New Century Publications, Delhi, 2015.

Vatsala Shukla: *India's Foreign Policy in the New Millennium : The Role of Power*, Atlantic Publication, Delhi, 2014.

Vibhuti Patel and Manisha Karne: *The Macro Economic Policies and the Millennium Development Goals*, Gyan Publication, Delhi, 2007.

Y. V. Reddy: *Economic Policies and India's Reform Agenda: New Thinking*, Orient BlackSwan, Delhi, 2013.

Index